Liquefied Natural Gas

Developing and Financing International Energy Projects

The titles published in this series are listed at the end of this volume.

International Energy and Resources Law and Policy Series

Liquefied Natural Gas

Developing and Financing International Energy Projects

Editor
Gerald B. Greenwald

KLUWER LAW INTERNATIONAL

THE HAGUE – LONDON – BOSTON

Published by
Kluwer Law International Ltd
Sterling House
66 Wilton Road
London SW1V 1DE
United Kingdom

Sold and distributed in
the USA and Canada by
Kluwer Law International
675 Massachusetts Avenue
Cambridge MA 02139
USA

Kluwer Law International incorporates
the publishing programmes of
Graham & Trotman Ltd,
Kluwer Law & Taxation Publishers
and Martinus Nijhoff Publishers

In all other countries, sold and distributed by
Kluwer Law International
PO Box 322
3300 AH Dordrecht
The Netherlands

ISBN 90-411-9664-1
Series ISBN 1-85333-796-X
© Kluwer Law International 1998
First published 1998

British Library Cataloguing in Publication Data
A catalogue record for this book is available from the British Library

Library of Congress Cataloging-in-Publication Data
Liquefied natural gas: developing and financing international energy
    projects / editor, Gerald B. Greenwald.
        p.   cm.—(International energy and resources law and policy
    series)
    Includes index.
    ISBN 9041196641
    1. Liquefied natural gas industry.   2. Energy policy.
I. Greenwald, Gerald B.   II. Series.
HD9581.2.L572L57   1998
338.4′766573—dc21
                                                            98–29106
                                                                 CIP

Typeset in 11/12 pt Baskerville by EXPO Holdings Sdn Bhd, Petaling Jaya, Malaysia
Printed and bound in Great Britain by Antony Rowe Ltd

Table of Contents

**Chapter 2   LNG MARKETS: HISTORICAL DEVELOPMENT
                AND FUTURE TRENDS**
Robert J.E. Jones

Chapter 3   LNG PROJECT FEASIBILITY
Andrew R. Flower

Chapter 4   THE CHAIN OF LNG PROJECT CONTRACTS
Peter P. Miller

Chapter 5   THE LNG TRANSPORTATION LINK
Richard G. Eddy

Chapter 6 LNG PROJECT FINANCE: SHARING RISKS WITH PROJECT LENDERS
Gerald B. Greenwald

Chapter 7   LNG: THE STRATEGIC PLANNING ISSUES
Kimball C. Chen

Acknowledgements

This book had its inception in the suggestion of Dr Thomas Wälde, Director of the University of Dundee's Centre for Energy, Petroleum and Mineral Law and Policy, that a volume on liquefied natural gas be added to the Centre's *International Energy and Resources Law and Policy* series. With his encouragement, the editor selected authors to contribute chapters on assigned topics that were informed by their experience and insight in the LNG industry. Under the auspices of the Centre, the authors had the opportunity to present their preliminary work in September 1997 at a two-day seminar in St Andrews, Scotland which was generously sponsored by Ruhrgas A.G. Although the author of each chapter remains solely responsible for its content, this collaboration resulted in a co-authored book rather than a collection of related essays. The editor is grateful to his co-authors who overcame heavy work and travel schedules to create this volume.

List of Contributors

Kimball C. Chen is the Co-Chairman and Co-Chief Executive Officer of Energy Transportation Group, Inc. (ETG). ETG's activities focus on international energy infrastructure development, including LNG shipping, power plants, cryogenic fuel terminals and gas distribution systems. ETG LNG ships have carried approximately 18 per cent of all LNG moved in world trade. Mr. Chen and his family have owned or controlled major companies and industrial assets in the US, China and other countries for over 100 years. ETG is controlled by Mr. Chen and his family. His background includes the B.A. degree magna cum laude in 1973 from Harvard University, the M.B.A. degree in 1978 from Harvard Business School, banking experience in Boston and London, and development of several high technology companies. Mr. Chen's past and present outside activities include the Council on Foreign Relations, board service at Financial Services Corporation of New York (New York's economic development bank) and various Harvard University committees. He is also a frequent contributor, as author or speaker, at major LNG and gas conferences.

Richard G. Eddy has a B.S. degree in Naval Architecture and Marine Engineering from Webb Institute and an M.B.A. degree from New York University. He is employed by Osprey Maritime (Europe) Inc., the successor company to Gotaas-Larsen, primarily in developing new LNG transportation business. Mr. Eddy was Project Engineer during the 1950s on the world's first LNG carrier, 'Methane Pioneer', and has been active in the industry ever since. Prior to joining Gotaas-Larsen in 1989 he was Director of LNG for Malaysia International Shipping Corporation, where he was responsible for construction and operation of the LNG fleet. During the 1960s he was Project Engineer responsible for the design, construction and trials of the 'Bridgestone Maru', the world's first low temperature LPG carrier. Mr. Eddy is also a founding director and past President of the Society of International Gas Tanker and Terminal Operators (SIGTTO).

Andrew R. Flower is the Manager, LNG Business Development of BP Exploration. Mr. Flower has an MA in Mathematics from Oxford University and an MSc in Statistics from Birmingham University. Mr. Flower joined BP in 1969 and worked in Research, Corporate Planning and the European Region before joining BP Gas in 1979. During his 19 years in the LNG business he has participated in projects in Nigeria, Abu Dhabi, Qatar and Australia. He has had experience of projects at all stages of development from initial feasibility studies through to operation. He has been involved in all phases of the LNG chain from natural gas production to the marketing of LNG where he has led the negotiation of LNG Sales and Purchase Agreements with both European and Japanese buyers. In his current position Mr. Flower manages a team responsible for providing commercial support to BP's existing LNG schemes and for developing new opportunities.

Gerald B. Greenwald began providing commercial advisory services in 1994 as a consultant on LNG project development to corporate planners, project developers, suppliers and purchasers of LNG. For 25 years Mr. Greenwald practiced law in Washington, D.C. as a partner in large New York and Washington law firms and legal advisor to participants in LNG projects designed to serve markets in the United States, Europe and the Far Fast. As a maritime lawyer he was extensively involved in construction, finance and operation of LNG tankers. As an energy lawyer, he participated in the early development of LNG trades from Algeria to the United States and from Indonesia to Japan. As a commercial lawyer he was active in negotiation of LNG sales and purchase agreement, structuring contracts for LNG transporation and finance and in resolving contract disputes. In addition to LNG project experience, Mr. Greenwald formerly chaired the Oil and Gas Law Committee of the International Bar Association, and is currently an Honorary Associate of the University of Dundee's Centre for Energy, Petroleum and Mineral Law and Policy.

Robert J.E. Jones is Principal Consultant, Wood Mackenzie Global Consultants. Mr. Jones has been working in the energy sector since graduating in 1977 with a BSc in geology; he subsequently obtained an earth science Masters Degree. He worked initially for Phillips Petroleum before joining Norsk Hydro with whom he worked in Norway, Egypt and latterly as regional exploration and production manager for Asia, having responsibility for the company's assets and business development initiatives. In 1996, he joined Wood Mackenzie and is in charge of the company's

Asia-Pacific energy team. In this capacity, he is responsible for a variety of projects, consultancies and publications which Wood Mackenzie provides. His particular areas of interest include the dynamics of the energy sector, how market forces create change and opportunity for energy companies, and the role of hydrocarbons in the development of power in Asia.

Peter P. Miller was educated at Yale University (B.A., 1960) and at Stanford University School of Law (J.D., 1968), where he was a member of the Board of Editors of the *Stanford Law Review*. He was associated with Sullivan & Cromwell for six years commencing in 1968, serving for two years in that firm's Paris office, before joining Mobil Corporation's Office of General Counsel in 1974. Over more than 22 years Mr. Miller held various legal positions in Mobil's Exploration & Producing and Marketing & Refining Divisions, with postings in London, Stavanger and Jakarta as well as in the company's New York and Fairfax headquarters. Upon his retirement from Mobil in 1996, Mr. Miller founded Energy Law Consultants (International), LLC, which provides legal and other advisory services in respect of all aspects of the petroleum industry, including licensing, exploration, field development, construction, financing, marketing and transportation. Mr. Miller has specialised expertise in the field of LNG through his 19-year involvement in the Arun (Indonesia) and North Field (Qatar) project developments.

Table of Figures

List of Abbreviations

AB	able-bodied seaman
ADB	Asian Development Bank
ADNOC	Abu Dhabi National Oil Co.
ADP	annual delivery programme
AFE	authorisation for expenditure
AGIP	Azienda Ganerale Italiana Petroli (Petroleum corporation affiliate of ENI)
APCI	Air Products and Chemicals Inc.
bbl	barrel
bcf/d	billion cubic feet per day
bcm	billion cubic metres
BIS	Bank for International Settlements
BLNG	Brunei LNG Ltd
BNPP	Bataan Nuclear Power Plant
BOT	build/own/transfer
BSP	Brunei Shell Petroleum
BST	Brunei Shell Tankers
Btu	British thermal unit
CCGT	combined-cycle gas turbine
CIF	cost, insurance and freight
CNOOC	China National Offshore Oil Corporation
COFACE	Compagnie Française D'Assurance Pour Le Commerce Exterieur (French export credit agency)
COMECON	Council for Mutual Economic Aid
CPC	China Petroleum Corp.
CTMS	custody transfer measuring system
DA	development agreement

DCQ	daily contract quantity
DEPA	Public Gas Corporation of Greece
DES	delivered ex-ship
DFA	development and fiscal agreement
DPSA	development and production-sharing agreement
DSCR	debt service cover ratio
EBRD	European Bank for Reconstruction and Development
ECA	export credit agency
ECGD	(UK) Export Credit Guarantee Department
EDC	Export Development Corporation (Canadian export credit agency)
ENEL	Ente Nazionale Energia Electtrica (Italian electric power company)
ENI	Ente Nazionale Idrocarburi (Italian hydrocarbons corporation)
EPC	engineering, procurement and construction
EPCC	engineering, procurement, construction and commissioning
ESD	emergency shutdown
ETG	Energy Transport Group
FEED	front end engineering and design
FOB	free on board
GAIL	Gas Authority of India Ltd
GdF	Gaz de France
GDP	gross domestic product
GGCL	Gujarat Gas Co. Ltd
GIP	gas in place
GMDSS	Global Maritime Distress Safety System
GT	Gaz Transport
GW	gigawatt
HERMES	Hermes Kreditversicherungs AG (German export credit agency)
HFO	heavy fuel oil
HOA	heads of agreement
hp	horsepower
ICC	International Chamber of Commerce
IFC	International Finance Corporation (of the World Bank Group)
IGC	Gas Tanker Code
IGCC	integrated gasification combined cycle
IMCO	International Maritime Consultancy Organisation
IMF	International Monetary Fund
IMO	International Maritime Organisation
IPP	independent power producer

IRR	internal rate of return
ISM	International Safety Management
JDA	joint development area
JDB	Japan Development Bank
JEXIM	Export-Import Bank of Japan
JILCO	Japan Indonesia LNG Co.
JNOC	Japan National Oil Co.
JVA	joint venture agreement
KEPCO	Korea Electric Power Corporation
KESC	Karachi Electrical Supply Corp.
KGC	Korea Gas Corporation
LDC	lesser developed country
LH scale	left-hand scale
LIBOR	London Inter-Bank Offered Rate
LLCR	loan life cover ratio
LOI	letter of intent
LPG	liquefied petroleum gas
MCR	mixed component refrigerant
MDB	multilateral development banks
MIGA	Multilateral Investment Guarantee Agency (of the World Bank Group)
MIMI	Mitsui & Co./Mitsubishi Corp. joint venture company
MITI	Ministry of International Trade and Industry (Japan)
mmBtu	million British thermal units
mmcm	million cubic metres
MMMMS	Marathon, Mitsui, McDermott, Mitsubishi, Shell group
mmscfd	million standard cubic feet per day
MOTIE	Ministry of Trade, Industry and Energy (Korea)
MOU	memorandum of understanding
mt	million tonnes
mtpa	million tonnes per annum
MW	megawatt
NATO	North Atlantic Treaty Organization
NPV	net present value
OA	operating agreement
OECD	Organisation for Economic Cooperation and Development
OECF	Overseas Economic Cooperation Fund
OIL	Oil India Ltd
O&M	operating and maintenance
ONGC	Oil and Natural Gas Corp.
OPEC	Organization of Petroleum Exporting Countries

OPIC	Overseas Private Investment Corporation
P&I	protection and indemnity
PLCR	project life cover ratio
PPA	power purchase agreement
PSC	production-sharing contract
PTF	project task force
PTT	Petroleum Authority of Thailand
PWR	pressurised water reactor
QGPC	Qatar General Petroleum Corporation
RasGas	Ras Laffan Liquefied Natural Gas Company Limited
RH scale	right-hand scale
SACE	Sezione Speciale per l'Assicurazione del Credito all'Esportazione (Italian export credit agency)
SEC	Securities and Exchange Commission
SFC	Standard Financing Conditions
shp	shaft horsepower
SIGTTO	Society of International Gas Tanker and Terminal Operators
SIPM	Shell International Petroleum Maatschappij
SMUT	spirit of mutual understanding and trust
SNAM	SNAM S.p.A. (Natural gas corporation affiliate of ENI)
Sodeco	Sakhalin Oil and Gas Development Co.
SOLAS	International Convention for the Safety of Life at Sea
SOR	statement of requirements
SPA	sale and purchase agreement
SPC	State Planning Commission
STCW	Standards for Training, Certification and Watchkeeping
TAGS	Trans-Alaska Gas System
tcf	trillion cubic feet
TEPCO	Tokyo Electric Power Co., Inc.
tpa	tonnes per annum
TWh	trillion Watt-hours
UNCITRAL	United Nations Commission on International Trade Law
USExIm	Export-Import Bank of the US
WAPET	Western Australian Petroleum Pty Ltd
WTO	World Trade Organization

Introduction

It is a truism that 'liquefied natural gas projects are complex'. The truism is woven from various strands of complexity. An LNG project is a unified series of separate 'projects within a project' and this is one strand. Another strand is the operation of a market with unique characteristics of demand for large quantities of natural gas delivered over many years and a single supply created to fill that demand. A third strand marks the multiplicity of contracts, i.e. the negotiation of acceptable bargains by diverse parties. Finally, there is a strand for time: long lead times, long-term contracts and long-delayed paybacks.

'Projects' are separate complex activities each of which has its own characteristics and mode of accomplishment. A natural gas field is exploited by developing sustained large daily gas production over 20 or more years. Oil companies have the skills and experience to develop this project within an LNG project, but the magnitude of field development can be daunting and the terms of engagement with the host state can be a challenge. Design and construction of a liquefaction plant is another project. Again, designers, process engineers, contractors and subcontractors have the necessary skills and experience. But this project within an LNG project makes impressive demands: billions of dollars of expenditure, thousands mobilised into a labour force and a construction period that can stretch over half a decade as two or three successive production trains are built.

The liquefaction plant is of no commercial value without supporting marine infrastructure such as sea walls, jetties, docks, berths, loading apparatus and cryogenic piping that are another project within an LNG project, requiring special skills and experience. Port development, consisting of the breakwater, anchorage, channel, turning-basin, navigation lights and channel markers, must also be put into place to accommodate the LNG ships, a distinct project often within the responsibility of a sovereign rather than the LNG project sponsors. The shipping component of an LNG project is again a free-standing project to produce a sufficient number of LNG ships to service the particular LNG trade by utilising marine engineering, design and procurement available from only a fraction of the world's shipyards. The end-use of the LNG as natural gas fuel creates another project within a project. For the electric power company purchasers of LNG it is necessary to build or expand facilities for electric power generation and nearby LNG receiving terminals; for the gas company purchasers, new or expanded trunk pipelines and receiving terminals will be built.

These projects within a project give meaning to the lines in the second section of Chapter 1 that read:

> None of these dependent factors is unique to the LNG industry, but in no other industry are all of them seen as essential for a successful project development.

There is also the complexity of the LNG market to be considered. The markets with which most of us are familiar operate spontaneously and almost invisibly to achieve short-term transactions through mechanisms such as stock exchanges and organised commodities markets. Futures markets extend the time-frame of transactions for up to a year. Hedging transactions extend time-frames further, but now the need for direct negotiation between the parties begins to appear. When LNG projects are contemplated, natural gas delivery periods of from 20 to 30 years are the rule. This is plainly a market of a different kind: a market laden with uncertainties for both buyers and sellers of LNG.

Another complexity is the plethora of contractual agreements that must be in place before an LNG project can deliver its first cargo. Each contract is a kind of 'project' requiring the resolution of competing and conflicting interests. Each contract must have cognisance of its relation to other contracts, preceding and to follow, so that the contractual series flows unimpeded to LNG project completion.

Time adds complexity because the planning and execution of the LNG project requires acts that impose very long time horizons, notably the LNG sale and purchase agreement, the project sponsors' investment decision and the lenders' extension of credit. The LNG trade has its own structure. The stakes for entry are high. The players have their own motivations which will resolve themselves into a strategic plan to participate in the LNG industry.

These are the strands that are untangled and analysed between the covers of this book. The co-authors have spent most of their professional careers in the international gas business. Collectively, they have contributed to the development or operation of LNG projects in Abu Dhabi, Australia, Indonesia, Malaysia and Qatar. Their goal is to explain the complexities of LNG project development as they elucidate the principles and practices by which LNG projects have achieved success.

Chapter 1

LNG Themes and Variations

Gerald B. Greenwald

1.1 NATURAL GAS INTO LNG

The LNG industry is founded on the physical principles that underlie the change of state from a gas into a liquid. Boyle's Law teaches us that pressure or temperature reduction or a combination of both can be applied to achieve this transformation of physical state. Natural gas consists mainly of methane, a hydrocarbon vapour whose chemical symbol is C_1H_4. The simplicity of methane's molecular structure means that the transformation from gas to liquid requires either tremendous pressure or extreme cooling (or a combination of both). The LNG industry chose to forego the application of pressure, recognising that the accidental quick release of that pressure would be explosive. By choosing a process of cooling that operates at atmospheric pressure, the industry was compelled to liquefy methane gas by applying extreme temperature reduction until the gas reached its boiling point of minus 158 degrees centigrade.

Origins of LNG production can be found in the cryogenic processing of air liquefaction during the 1920s. The first production of LNG recovered helium gas from natural gas. The helium was used in the 1930s by the US Army to lift military balloons, and the LNG was returned to natural gas for pipeline use. In 1939 Hope Natural Gas Co. built an LNG plant to liquefy natural gas and store it for later use as natural gas in Consolidated Natural Gas's pipeline system. Metallurgy science produced metals that would not become brittle at extremely low temperatures, a development that was aided

1

by the US Space Program's construction of fuel tanks to hold liquid gases used for propulsion of rockets. Although these historical references are to developments in the United States, similar cryogenic activities were being pursued in Europe. By 1954 there were active studies in Norway, France, the United Kingdom and the United States for ship designs to transport LNG. Continental Oil Co. and Union Stockyards joined to convert a dry cargo vessel into an LNG carrier. The resulting *Methane Pioneer* transported a cargo of LNG from Louisiana to the UK's Canvey Island in 1959.

The compaction of methane gas into liquefied methane yields a volume reduction of 600 to one. This supercold liquid can be contained in insulated tanks built of special steel or aluminium. The insulated tanks can be installed in ocean-going ships. Thus was LNG commerce opened to distant markets. In 1960 the first base-load liquefaction plant was built at Arzew, Algeria to process natural gas from the giant Hassi R'Mel field. Regular exports of Algerian LNG began to reach British Gas at Canvey Island in 1964 and Gaz de France at Le Havre in 1965. The UK deliveries were made by two purpose-built LNG ships, the *Methane Progress* and the *Methane Princess*, each of 12,000 deadweight tons and carrying about 27,000 cubic metres of LNG. The French deliveries were made by the *Jules Verne*, slightly smaller at about 25,000 cubic metres in size. When the *Methane Princess* set sail from Arzew for Canvey Island on 7 October 1964, she carried the first LNG cargo shipped under a long-term commercial sales contract. By 1969, Marathon Oil and Philips Petroleum were liquefying natural gas on Alaska's Kenai Peninsula for shipment to Tokyo Electric Co. and Tokyo Gas Co. In 1976 and 1977 Brunei and Indonesia respectively became the first Asian suppliers of LNG. Twenty years later, LNG was trading to Europe, the United States and the Far East from North Africa, the United States (Alaska), the Middle East or Asia-Pacific.

The LNG itself is predominantly methane, with small portions of ethane, propane, butane and pentanes. The resulting liquid is chemically inert with respect to most substances and will not burn or explode. At ambient temperatures, the LNG boils away and leaves no residue. LNG that returns to natural gas is about half the density of air and therefore rises and disperses. If LNG is spilled on land, it could penetrate the soil, freezing moisture in the ground, and, until evaporated, its low temperature could injure plant or animal life. After LNG evaporates, however, the ground and animal and plant life it supports would usually return to its natural state. In the event that LNG reverts to its gaseous state, the flammable range of the methane is 5–15 per cent, which means that it must comprise between 5 and 15 per cent of a mixture with air in order to burn. Otherwise, the mixture is too 'lean' or too 'rich' and cannot sustain a flame. LNG density is about half the weight of water. If spilled in transit, it floats on the water's surface. As a marine cargo, LNG is regarded as hazardous because, if vapourised, the natural gas is flammable within its narrow limits, but LNG is regarded as less hazardous than many common petroleum products and chemicals that are transported in ordinary maritime commerce. A US Coast Guard study concluded that LNG vapour presents no health, environmental or reactive hazards, though natural gas can act as a simple asphyxiant. In other words, LNG is a relatively benign hydrocarbon product. Its gaseous state presents a degree of fire hazard that is well understood and has been well contained by practices of natural gas industries worldwide.

Notwithstanding these benign characteristics, the LNG industry is marked by a near-obsession with reliability and safety. Reliability, because its customers depend on LNG supply to ensure sufficient natural gas and electricity to meet their society's needs. Safety, because of the flammable range of natural gas and the huge up-front capital costs required for processing natural gas in LNG plants, transferring it from shore to ship, transporting LNG in ships and then transferring the LNG cargo from ship to shore. Perhaps the most compelling rationale for safety practice is the widespread recognition in the industry that an LNG accident anywhere may imperil the LNG industry everywhere and must be avoided for the sake of all parties concerned.

1.2   THE PROCESS OF PROJECT DEVELOPMENT

The overall subject of this book is process—the process of developing an international energy project for the production and marketing of liquefied natural gas. LNG projects are extremely complex and extremely expensive. There is a large combination of factors that must be knitted together into a seamless fabric in order to produce the LNG trade. None of these dependent factors is unique to the LNG industry, but in no other industry are all of them seen as essential for successful project development.

The number of variables in a nascent LNG project is very large. Organisational issues will turn on host government policies, feedgas ownership, ownership interests in sequential phases of the project activities, target markets for the project's production, and so forth. Sponsors will consider the relative merits of an unincorporated joint venture as compared to shareholdings in one or more project companies. Marketing objectives may require sharing of project ownership with potential buyers. Transportation services may be provided by the project as shipowner or operator, or by time charter of LNG ships from third parties or from project sponsors. The transportation obligations may fall on the project as seller on ex-ship delivery terms or on an FOB (free on board) buyer. Each of the authors draws upon his many years of experience in successful LNG projects to tell about how it was done in his experience. As each project proceeds through the development process described in this book to resolve the many variables, it will emerge with its own unique organisation, contract chain and distribution of LNG risks and rewards.

1.3   PROJECT DEVELOPMENT SCHEDULES

In the LNG industry it takes time to make a project, and time is another significant aspect of the process of LNG project development. All of the chapters convey this theme. Macro-studies of energy supply and demand locate potential markets for LNG that will emerge a decade or more in the future (Chapter 2). The feasibility study for an LNG project that begins when decision is taken to seek opportunities for commercialisation of a gas discovery continues until the final investment decision of project sponsors. This study will take years to complete (Chapter 3). The number of contracts necessary to implement a project is large and their negotiation is time-consuming (Chapter 4). Construction of a fleet of LNG ships to transport project sales over long distances will take more than three years to complete, and the shipyard orders will not be let until construction of all other components of the facilities chain have been placed under contract (Chapter 5). The acquisition of finance can also be time-consuming as projects access a variety of finance markets to obtain term sheets, negotiate detailed terms, achieve financial close and then meet lenders' conditions precedent to the project's drawdown of funds (Chapter 6). The entrepreneurial commitment to the business of LNG is a long-term one. Over time it entails strategic and tactical decisions at many stages of project development and implementation (Chapter 7).

The result is a project development schedule divided into discrete phases, each consuming years of activity. Project identification is a period for appraisal drilling, site investigation and preproject feasibility study. Specification development for the overall project, including upstream gas production, liquefaction plant and shipping requirements, overlaps and extends this first phase. Implementation begins with more rigorous feasibility study until reaching the financial investment decision that initiates tendering and contracting for project facilities. During this phase the marketing team must complete years of intensive activity to obtain the project's LNG sales and purchase agreements; the finance team must lay the groundwork in financial markets to raise funds to pay for the project. The construction period will take a minimum of three years, and longer when the project requires multiple liquefaction trains and a fleet of LNG ships. The first LNG cargo is likely to be delivered 10 years or more after the process began, with deliveries to continue for another two or more decades. The development time-frame can be considerably longer in the 'worst case', as witness the experience in Nigeria. The Conch Methane project sponsors began their LNG efforts in 1963, but were thwarted four years later by the discovery of North Sea natural gas. Competing Nigerian LNG initiatives began in 1973, were merged in 1977 and were then abandoned. Nigeria LNG Ltd began project development work in 1985, was relaunched in 1993 and committed to project construction in 1995 for startup in 1999. In all, it was a 30-year saga to develop the Nigerian LNG project.

LNG is indeed a demanding commitment to a line of business activity. Therein lie both the burdens and the benefits of the LNG trade. In a world of international commerce that offers transitory opportunity, changing tastes, market instability and momentous technical change, LNG tempts potential sponsors with the prospect of stable and reliable energy sales over the very long term.

1.4 LNG MARKETS

1.4.1 LNG Market Cycles

LNG projects are demand-driven; that is, the commitment of a buyer to purchase a substantial quantity of LNG for a long duration is essential to providing the economic support for project development. For this reason the pace of LNG project development has been cyclical. In periods of growing natural gas demand or growing demand for all fuels, the cycle will turn upwards with potential greenfield projects and expansions of existing projects vying to meet the demand. When rising energy prices lead to demand conservation or macro-economic forces limit economic growth or reduce energy demand, there is little, if any, stimulus to increase LNG supply. In all gas trades, whether delivered by pipeline or LNG ship, the farther to market, the greater the expense of providing supply. Alternative fuels, be they crude oil, oil products, liquefied petroleum gas, coal or pipeline gas, tend not to incur as high a unit transportation cost as that of LNG transported over long distances by expensive LNG ships. Worldwide energy trade has seen some anomaly in pricing LNG. Long-haul LNG does not seem to obtain a price in the market much in excess of short-haul LNG. Rather, LNG price has been set in close relationship to the prices of alternative fuels available in the market. Thus, another controlling factor in the cycle of LNG expansion is the relation between LNG market price and its delivered cost.

1.4.2 Regional Markets

Gas markets are highly segmented regionally. The state of these regional markets and the national markets which comprise the regions is the focus of Chapter 2. The first large gas market was the United States, as indigenous gas discoveries were exploited in the first half of the 20th century to build a comprehensive long-distance gas transmission pipeline system. LNG imports from Algeria were initiated during the 1970s but various factors, including the substantial pool of Canadian gas available for export to the United States by pipeline, limited the penetration of imported LNG in the US market.

The gasification of Europe was prompted by the Dutch discovery in 1959 of the Groningen field, lying within 250–300 miles of Germany and Belgium. Dutch exports extended beyond these two countries to France, Italy and Switzerland as a European transmission pipeline system was constructed. The former Soviet Union became a major pipeline exporter to Europe in the 1970s. By the end of that decade, Norwegian North Sea gas was flowing to Europe. In 1983, pipeline gas began flowing to Italy from Algeria via the Trans-Mediterranean Pipeline System. With this availability of pipeline supplies from diverse sources, Europe's appetite for LNG imports has been limited. Nevertheless, existing LNG trades to France, Belgium, Italy, Spain, Turkey, and soon to Greece, are instructive. Southern European countries, particularly Spain, Portugal, Italy, Greece and Turkey, are all viable markets for LNG exported from Algeria, Nigeria, Trinidad and perhaps the Middle East. There are strong tendencies which encourage LNG trade when there would seem to be more economical or proximate alternatives of pipeline natural gas. The logic of imported LNG is rooted in a blend of entrepreneurship, timing and, perhaps more significantly, the policy of both governments and energy importers to favour diversification of fuels and sources of supply.

The third major international market is in the Pacific Basin: Japan, Korea and Taiwan, each an LNG importer without access to supply alternatives from gas pipelines. Japan dominates worldwide LNG trading, growing steadily as an LNG importer since 1969. Future growth prospects in Japan are tempered by slower national growth rates and energy policy constraints which seem to limit imported LNG to about 20–25 per cent of Japanese fuel consumption for electric power generation.

New regional LNG markets are expected to emerge. China, recently turned from an oil exporter to an oil importer, is expected to initiate LNG imports early in the next century. South-East Asia, a major gas-producing region, may supplement indigenous gas with LNG imports, as has been considered by Thailand. India is actively pursuing activities to initiate LNG imports to regions on both its east and west coasts. The development of segmented regional LNG markets, with regional characteristics and regional pricing, is likely to continue.

1.4.3   Marketing the Project

Quantitative and qualitative forecasts of natural gas demand over the mid-term provide the macro-analysis that sets the stage for LNG project development. The goal of the project is to monetise natural gas reserves at the earliest time practicable. The forecasted time-frames in which substantial natural gas demand will take place in national markets is crucial for the project's first review of potential gas buyers. Forecasts such as those of Wood Mackenzie in Chapter 2 traverse LNG supply as well as demand. While news media routinely report ambitious LNG schemes, it is this macroanalysis which collects the potential supply data and correlates projected startup dates with gas demand. When a project marketing team enters a competitive supply market, it is compelled to direct its marketing efforts to multiple markets. The likelihood that its supply will be delivered to multiple markets in turn affects the planning for LNG production trains and transportation capacity. Project marketing requires analysis as well as salesmanship. The hard work of the marketing team begins with quantitative analysis, identifying the entities most likely to generate a concentrated portion of the demand that is forecast in the macro-study. During the first 30 years of the LNG trade this initial effort was a rather transparent task. Gas demand was controlled by established natural gas and electric utilities with secure regional or national franchises. The task can be far more complex now, as witness the profusion of Indian locations and entities that are vying to secure India's first imports of LNG. Study of project demand also requires qualitative analysis, evaluating competing fuels and their competitive effect in the targeted gas market.

Marketing LNG goes beyond the optimism expressed by potential buyers. To a greater extent than previously, greenfield LNG projects must be capable of generating their own quantitative and qualitative analysis of potential customers' mid-term demand. This can be a daunting process when infrastructure development in a targeted gas market must extend beyond the LNG receiving terminal to as yet unbuilt natural gas distribution pipelines, domestic petrochemical or industrial projects, power generation plants or electricity transmission lines. The objective, of course, is to secure an LNG sales and purchase agreement that supports returns on equity investment and survives the scrutiny of lenders, particularly project finance lenders who must share project risk (Chapter 6). It is conventional to state that LNG sellers take price risk through linkage to volatile oil prices, but that LNG buyers take quantity risk through the mechanism of the sale and purchase agreement's take-or-pay clause. However, no LNG producer or lender can rely upon receiving the estimated long-term revenue stream from an LNG buyer whose projected natural gas demand fails to materialise, is substantially delayed or significantly deteriorates.

1.4.4   Transparency

Sellers and buyers of commodities are usually separated by an intermediary impersonal marketplace or by direct negotiation across the table.

On the other hand, sellers and buyers of services can be expected to have ongoing direct access to each other in order to ensure that service providers and recipients achieve their expected benefits. The sale and purchase of LNG partakes of both the direct negotiation of the long-term sales and purchase agreement and the on-going joint activities necessary to achieve a successful long-term trade, the most visible of which is the cargo scheduling activities that produce the annual delivery programme, implemented by short-term delivery schedules. Often, however, additional mechanisms evolve that provide more contact between seller and buyer than usually prevails in the international sale of goods.

1.4.4.1   The Role of Japanese Trading Companies

In the early LNG trades to Japan, project sponsors enlisted one or more Japanese trading companies as shareholders in the project company to act as 'seller's helpers' in introducing their LNG supplies into the Japanese market. Mitsubishi partnered in both the Brunei and Malaysian projects, Mitsui participated in the Abu Dhabi project and Mitsubishi and Mitsui set up a joint company to take a one-sixth interest in the Australian North-West Shelf project. Initiation of the Indonesian LNG trade (in 1977) was assisted by Nissho Iwai's services as 'buyer's helper' to the six Japanese importers of LNG from Bontang and Arun. Mitsubishi, Mitsui and Itochu joined the Oman project, Mitsui and Marubeni hold shares in Qatargas, and Itochu and Nissho Iwai took stakes in the Ras Laffan project. Their roles are multiple. First and foremost, they provide a bridge between the project supplier and the Japanese market, bringing to the project international trading skills, market intelligence, cultural familiarity and long-time relations with Japanese electric and gas utilities. Moreover, the potential Japanese customers benefited from a 'bridge' that facilitated two-way communication and interpreted constraints in the Japanese market to foreign project sponsors. This bridging function provides a measure of transparency that facilitates market insight, strengthens project credibility and eases communication between LNG sellers and buyers over the long term.

1.4.4.2   Buyers as Project Investors

Recent developments have introduced the direct participation of LNG buyers in the project sponsor group. Korean entities were offered the opportunity of direct investment in both the Oman and Ras Laffan projects as reciprocation for Korea Gas's purchase of LNG quantities that underpin development of the two greenfield projects. Similarly, Repsol became an investor in the Trinidad project after its subsidiary, Enagas, purchased 40 per cent of the project's production. Cabot Corp., both an original sponsor of the Trinidad project and purchaser of 60 per cent of its production, also holds an equity stake in the project. There can be a variety of rationales for buyer shareholding in seller projects, such as investment return opportunity, LNG price hedge and access to a new line of business that may offer future commercial opportunities. Whatever the rationale, the effect is to promote transparency in the sales transactions as buyers scrutinise capital and operating costs and are privy to project operations from the other side of the table.

1.4.4.3   *The Indonesian Model*

The Indonesian state hydrocarbon company, Pertamina, was a pioneer in developing the LNG trade, signing its first sales contract in 1973. In the years since, Pertamina has become the largest LNG exporter in the Pacific with successive additions to liquefaction plants in Bontang and Arun. Pertamina is sole owner of its liquefaction plants, yet it has managed to provide its Japanese customers with a high level of transparency, in respect of both LNG production and transportation. As to liquefaction, the project is organised to include an LNG plant operating company with no equity stake in the plant itself. The operating company is a service provider to Pertamina. The operating company is owned not only by Pertamina but also by its production-sharing contractors and by Japan Indonesia LNG Company (JILCO) that has as its shareholders LNG buyers, Pertamina's Japanese lenders and Japanese trading companies. JILCO has board representation in the operating company and is therefore privy to production and operating data. This transparency was of vital importance in the wake of an industrial accident in the 1980s which destroyed a third of the production capacity in Pertamina's Bontang LNG plant. Japanese buyers, faced with reduced LNG deliveries for an indefinite period, could, through both Pertamina and JILCO, stay informed of efforts to restore production and resume normal delivery schedules.

   LNG transportation arrangements are another unique aspect of Pertamina's LNG sales to Japan. An independent transporter provides shipping services for ex-ship sales to Japan. The transportation cost incurred by Pertamina is passed through to LNG buyers as a component of the delivered price of LNG. As an adjunct to this cost pass-through arrangement, the Japanese buyers meet quarterly with Pertamina and its transporter to review marine costs and operations, making available to LNG buyers a level of transparency in LNG transportation services not found in any other ex-ship LNG trade to Japan.

1.5 LNG CHAINS

As the content of this book developed, the narrative became to a large extent a description of LNG chains. Each discrete activity in the continuum from natural gas well-head to natural gas burner tip creates value that can be rewarded in the marketplace. This continuum produces the LNG 'value chain'. Chapter 7 focuses on the entrepreneurial aspects of the LNG industry, seeking to identify the essential pieces that are encased in the LNG industry's kaleidoscope. The kaleidoscope is a useful analogy because the sum of the LNG industry's constituent parts is finite, but a variety of means exists to organise their combination. Chapters 3 and 6 discuss this variety. Chapter 3 describes the process by which LNG project sponsors evaluate project value in reaching their decision to develop an LNG project. Chapter 6 describes the process by which lenders assess the value to be realised from the project's performance. A second chain is the 'facilities chain', the sequencing of physical requirements needed to produce gas, clean and liquefy it, store LNG, load LNG into ships and transport it to receiving terminals which in turn begin a reverse transformation of LNG into natural gas that is ultimately consumed at the burner tip. The story of this functional LNG facilities chain is told in Chapters 3, 4 and 5. The third chain is the linked series of contracts and contractual relationships which must be put in place before an LNG project becomes a reality. The LNG sales and purchase agreement is the fundamental document in the 'contract chain', but the smooth interfacing of all of the project contracts is required for the project's success. The LNG contract chain is described in Chapters 4 and 6.

In describing these three significant chains in the commercialisation of natural gas as LNG, it is plain that the key topics in LNG project development will appear and reappear in more than one context. This is a strength of the book. Each activity, each facility, each contract should be seen from a variety of perspectives in order to convey its full import and its significance in the overall project development process. Animating this book is the belief that an understanding of the whole can inform the performance of those who have personal responsibility for only a small part in the development and implementation of an LNG project.

1.6 TECHNOLOGY, ECONOMY OF SCALE AND TRADE EXPANSION

There has been a continuous increase in size of both liquefaction facilities and LNG ships over the past 30 years. As a result, unit cost of LNG has declined, but this has been accompanied by rising investment in larger

LNG project facilities and dependence on expanding markets to absorb the greater capacities of a single train of LNG production. The capital cost estimates for LNG projects are now being challenged in a variety of ways as industry-wide efforts aim at capital cost reductions. Technical developments aim at capital cost reduction at all functions in the LNG chain:

(1) larger LNG train size to achieve greater scale economy;
(2) higher thermal efficiency in the liquefaction process;
(3) gas treatment process tailored to specific feedgas composition;
(4) larger compressors and gas turbine drivers for the refrigerant process;
(5) increased plant efficiency and availability;
(6) larger LNG storage tanks;
(7) larger LNG ships.

Yet interest is being shown in developing smaller LNG projects. The earliest LNG trade to Japan, from Alaska's Kenei Peninsula, was based on a small liquefaction plant of a single LNG train. Thereafter, multi-train plants of increasing size for each train were considered essential to both project economics and reliability of supply. The Trinidad LNG project, scheduled to begin production in the year 2000, countered this trend with a single-train plant. With a smaller project configuration, more undeveloped gas fields can serve as a source of supply for LNG. New technologies are being vetted, such as simpler liquefaction plants and floating liquefaction plants, to estimate small-scale project economics. Floating receiving terminals are promoted to reduce capital investment and make small-scale LNG imports practicable.

The LNG industry has entered a period of optimism and competition. Locations of both actual and potential supply and actual and potential demand are expanding. Qatar, Trinidad and Nigeria are the newest entrants to the LNG supply scene. Potential LNG supply sources in Yemen, Egypt, Alaska and Sakhalin are mentioned in the press. Turkey and Greece are the newest LNG importers. China, India, Portugal and Brazil are mentioned as potential LNG markets. All of these new sellers and buyers are unlikely to materialise in the next decade but, undoubtedly, some will. As more loading terminals and receiving terminals are built worldwide, opportunities increase for directing new supplies to multiple markets, for spot trades, and perhaps for more efficient utilisation of LNG ships that now spend half of their operating lives on ballast voyages. Altogether, it's a good time to assess the conditions and describe the process that underlie development of the LNG trade.

Chapter 2

LNG Markets: Historical Development and Future Trends

Robert J.E. Jones*

2.1 INTRODUCTION

In January 1997, the 137,500-cubic metre *Al Zubarah* docked at Chubu Electric's Kawagoe terminal in Japan with the first cargo of LNG from the Qatargas project. This delivery represented a new phase of growth in world LNG trade. After years of slow though steady growth in the LNG market, the industry has had a spurt of activity over the last two years, with rapid progress on new supply projects in Qatar, Oman, Trinidad and Nigeria. This has been coupled with the prospect of new markets being opened up in countries such as India, China and Thailand and in southern and eastern Europe. As a consequence, LNG, particularly in its core Asia-Pacific markets, will show the fastest demand growth of any fuel.

The LNG industry originated in Europe, but growth in this market has been slow, with strong competition coming from supplies of cheaper pipeline gas from Russia, Algeria, Norway and the Netherlands. The LNG market has instead become dominated by Japan, a country with no indigenous fossil fuels and a high dependence on imported oil, and which as a

* The author wishes to acknowledge the contributions, direct and indirect, made to this chapter by Wood Mackenzie's Asia-Pacific Energy team.

**Figure 2.1   Forecast rate of demand growth for fuels in the
Asia-Pacific region, 1995–2015**

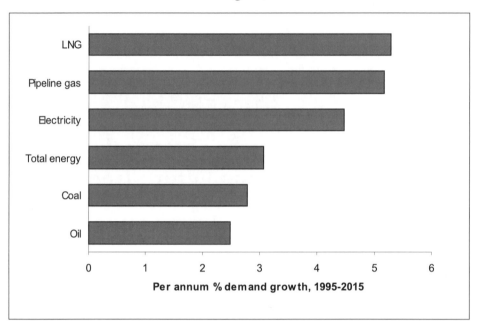

Source: Wood Mackenzie Asia-Pacific Energy Service

consequence of the 1973 oil crisis needed to diversify away from oil. LNG
provided an ideal solution, and Japan set a goal of achieving 25 per cent of
its electricity output being generated from gas. Japan has largely reached its
target for gas/LNG penetration and so the mantle has passed to South
Korea as the new dynamic player in the market, providing the world's fastest
growing LNG market and accounting for most of the incremental demand.
In a new development, supply projects in Oman and Qatar are proceeding
with most of their output destined for South Korea.

Faced with ever-increasing demand for electricity, the developing
countries of Asia, most notably India, China and Thailand, are turning to
gas because of its high efficiency, speed of installation, low cost and clean-
ness of use. Combined-cycle gas turbines (CCGTs) built by independent
power producers and fired on regasified LNG have become a key potential
solution for rapidly expanding electricity demand in Asia. New developments in the industry are also stimulating a new growth phase. Contracts
are becoming more flexible and innovative with, for example, Oman
accepting a gas sales agreement with South Korea wherein the LNG price
is indexed to that of oil, but with no minimum 'floor' price. This placed
pressure on the Qatar, Ras Laffan project to accept similar terms.

Cost-cutting is another measure that could make LNG more competitive in world fuel markets and will be an imperative for competing projects to penetrate new markets. Cost reductions may take place in all segments of the LNG value chain from upstream gas production through to lique-faction, transport and regasification. The liquefaction plant accounts for about 40 per cent of the capital expenditure on an LNG scheme, with transport representing around 30 per cent, and accordingly these are the most important areas for cost reduction. In LNG production, improve-ments are being made to the liquefaction process and average train sizes are increasing. Competition amongst constructors is also forcing costs down. In shipping, the largest LNG tankers offered by shipbuilders have now increased from 137,000- to 165,000-cubic metre capacity, and this figure is expected to increase further in future. Decreasing costs could make LNG more competitive in Europe. At present, Middle East LNG can only be sold to the Far East because of the significantly higher prices paid. New markets in southern and eastern Europe could also open up as demand for gas for power generation increases rapidly. With new LNG supplies expected in Europe from Nigeria and Trinidad, Europe may yet join Asia in the new rapid growth phase in the LNG market.

The new markets of India and China will present the gas industry with new challenges. These markets have been very isolated from western influence, are still dominated by state enterprises in the electricity sector, which will be the principal offtaker, and lack the regulatory and economic structure to facilitate other than high-risk investment. They represent a complete contrast to the traditional north-east Asian markets and will therefore present new challenges in developing LNG value chains.

The availability of gas as LNG feedstock is plentiful, whether on the North Slope of Alaska, in the Middle East or in the Asia-Pacific region. Consequently, there are many gas fields which could be developed for the LNG industry. Some gas fields are close to existing LNG infrastructure, and will enable existing facilities to increase production to maximum capacity, or to expand facilities with additional trains at Bontang in Indonesia, Sarawak in Malaysia or the North-West Shelf of Australia. Exploration efforts in other parts of the region have resulted in the discovery of new gas resources such as in eastern Indonesia (Irian Jaya), a long distance from gas markets and for which an LNG project is the most feasible commercial alternative. The viability of an LNG project will be discussed in detail elsewhere in this book, and it will show that viability boils down to economics; in this respect LNG price is pivotal and with virtually unlimited gas supply, a competitive queue for new sales and purchase agreements is bound to form. There are many market issues which will determine the pace at which projects, whether expan-sions or greenfield, can come onstream. These issues are addressed in this chapter, following an initial review of the historical development of LNG trade.

2.2   HISTORICAL DEVELOPMENT OF THE LNG TRADE

2.2.1   LNG Roots in Europe

On 12 October 1964, the world's first commercial cargo of LNG arrived at British Gas's Canvey Island terminal from Algeria. The following year France joined the UK in importing LNG from Algeria and these two counties remained Europe's only two consumers until 1970, when Spain started to take the fuel, and 1971, when Italy joined the trade. The development of LNG trade was then, and unexpectedly, confronted by the establishment of a domestic pipeline gas market with the first landing of North Sea gas from the West Sole field in 1967; the UK gained access to cheap supplies of pipeline natural gas with the result that LNG imports never took off in the country. Imports have rarely exceeded a level of 1 billion cubic metres (bcm) per year and significant trade stopped altogether in 1981. The receiving terminal at Canvey Island has now been decommissioned.

France, without the indigenous gas reserves of the UK, rapidly built up its imports of LNG during the 1970s and early 1980s. By 1983, France was importing nearly 9 bcm of LNG per annum, although imports have largely plateaued at this level since then, with electricity production being based predominantly on nuclear power. France now receives the majority of its gas via pipeline from Russia, Norway and the Netherlands.

Spain has gradually and consistently built up its LNG import levels to reach a volume of 7 bcm in 1995. Now, however, with the commissioning of the Mahgreb gas pipeline from Algeria, incremental supplies to the Iberian peninsula are likely to come from this source rather than in the form of LNG.

Italy, after early growth, has not taken significant quantities of LNG since 1980. The trade has largely ceased due to access to cheaper pipeline gas from Russia, the Netherlands and, most significantly, Algeria via the TransMed pipeline. Germany, the largest gas market in Europe, has made virtually no use of LNG and has relied on pipeline imports mostly from Russia, the Netherlands and Norway. Belgium joined the ranks of LNG importers in 1982 and, most recently, Turkey became an importer in 1994. Both, however, use considerably more pipeline gas.

A picture begins to emerge. In spite of the origins of the LNG industry in Europe and the region's historical importance to the industry, LNG has never found the major market in Europe that it later found in the Far East. The reason for this may be found in the availability of cheaper pipeline gas in Europe. With the western European border price of pipeline gas being around US\$2.50 per million British thermal units (mmBtu) in recent years, LNG, except that from Algeria (and Libya) has not been competitive. An extensive gas pipeline network, culminating with the inter-connector, has been built in Europe. The European pipe-line infrastructure was justifiable on the basis of gas volume and trans-portation distance being paid for by state companies or state funds. This has not generally been the case in Asia, with the result that LNG has been the only way in which gas has become available in the Far East.

Particularly for potential Middle East suppliers, delivered gas prices of around US$3.50 per mmBtu have been far more attractive than the US$2.50 per mmBtu benchmark available in Europe, and this explains why export from countries such as Qatar has only been feasible for supply to the Far East. The Eurogas scheme, a QGPC/SNAM/Hunt joint venture which had the aim of shipping Qatari LNG to the Italian state natural gas subsidiary (SNAM) and electricity utility (ENEL), foundered for this reason. In future, it is possible that cost reductions in the LNG industry may enable Middle Eastern LNG to become competitive in Europe, and this is one of the possible factors that could lead to the renaissance of the LNG industry in Europe which is discussed at the end of this chapter. Nonetheless, it is the Far East which dominates, and will continue to dominate, LNG market development.

The graph below shows how, after the origins of the LNG industry in Europe, the Far East has come to dominate the business with about four-fifths of total trade. Of this Far East trade, Japan is responsible for 82 per cent, South Korea 13 per cent and Taiwan 5 per cent.

Figure 2.2.1   LNG Trade in Europe and Asia

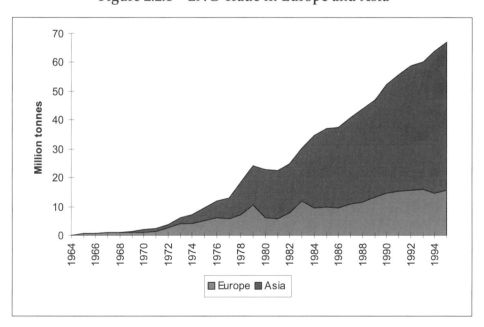

2.2.2   The Emergence of the Japanese LNG Trade

In 1970, Japan was dependent on oil for over 70 per cent of its primary energy supply and 60 per cent of its fuel requirement for power generation. When the 1973 oil crisis occurred, Japan was severely over-exposed to the vagaries of the oil price so the decision was taken to diversify the fuel mix by a large expansion in the amount of electricity generated from gas and nuclear sources. The aim was that gas, mostly in the form of imported LNG, would eventually account for 25 per cent of power output. The 1979 oil crisis further emphasised the need to reduce oil dependency. The first cargo of LNG had been imported into Japan from Kenai, Alaska in 1969 under a contract for a supply of 0.96 million tonnes per annum (mtpa). However, rapid build-up of supply did not occur until 1972, when the new liquefaction plant at Lumut, Brunei, started exporting to Japan. LNG sales from Brunei to Japan had reached over 7 mtpa by 1977, the year in which Abu Dhabi and Indonesia joined the ranks of the country's suppliers. Malaysia entered the trade in 1983 and Australia in 1989. Japan has successfully diversified its fuel supply and its fuel sources.

As can be seen from the chart below, Japan achieved a gas penetration into power generation of nearly 20 per cent by 1985. After this time, the percentage of gas in the power generation mix has largely plateaued, and Wood Mackenzie expects that the 25 per cent target will not be reached until around 2005. The implication is that LNG will no longer make rapid inroads into the energy mix in Japan, and increased consumption will be due to (relatively slow) overall growth, rather than displacement of other fuels, though the nuclear sector growth has been slowed by recent environmental crises.

One possible positive scenario in favour of further LNG penetration is that many nuclear reactors will reach the end of profitable life towards the end of the first decade of the new millennium; LNG could take market share as a result. Japan may, on the other hand, more seriously evaluate pipeline gas from Russia; an annual volume of at least 15 million tonnes (mt) would probably be required to achieve economic viability, and this would have some impact on LNG.

Japan's Ministry of International Trade and Industry (MITI) forecasts that LNG demand in Japan will rise to around 65 mt in 2010 from its 1995 level of 44 mt, a growth rate of only 2 per cent per year. The large majority of LNG in Japan is used for power generation and so it is the plans for the electricity sector, and the choice of fuel used to generate electricity, that drive the official forecasts of LNG consumption. In March 1996, MITI announced its 1996 Electricity Supply Plan which includes an estimate of electricity demand for the next 10 years and outline of facilities submitted to MITI by the nine regional electric power companies. This plan estimates an electricity demand of 1036 trillion watt-hours (TWh) in 2005, of which

Figure 2.2.2A   Japan—Electricity Generated from Gas

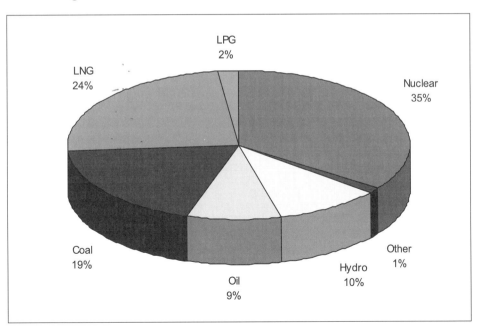

Source: Wood Mackenzie

Figure 2.2.2B   MITI Forecast for Power Generated 2005

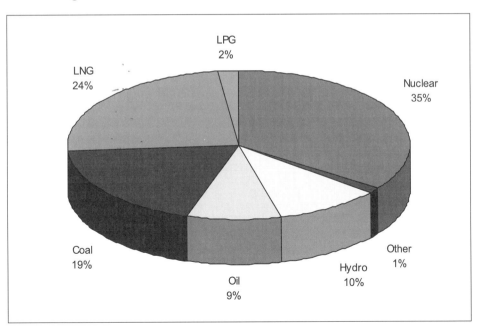

Figure 2.2.2C   Japan Gas Infrastructure

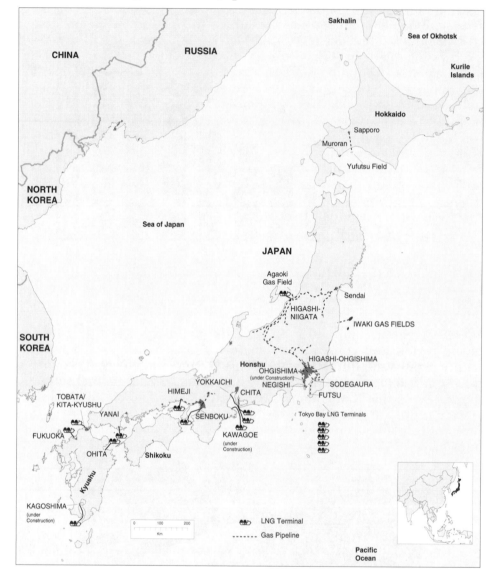

an electricity demand of 1036 trillion watt-hours (TWh) in 2005, of which 244 TWh will be generated from LNG.

It is reasonable to believe that MITI's forecasts for LNG consumption are underestimated because the forecasts for nuclear power generation are overestimated. MITI's policy is to encourage nuclear power for security of energy supply reasons and also to enable it to meet its ambitious targets on CO_2 emission reductions; however, its plans are being thwarted by growing public opposition to nuclear power. This was exacerbated in December 1995 by the accident, and subsequent attempted cover-up, of a leakage of three tonnes of liquid sodium coolant at the plutonium-based Monju experimental fast-breeder reactor. In March 1997, a leak at a nuclear fuel reprocessing plant at Tokai run by Power Reactor and Nuclear Fuel Development Corporation led to management having to make a door-to-door apology to residents in the area. Several municipalities in Japan have now passed by-laws requiring a referendum to be held before any nuclear plant can be constructed in their jurisdictions. Increasing public disquiet over nuclear power means that MITI is unlikely to meet its targets on nuclear electricity generation and this will mean that greater reliance will have to be made on coal and LNG. Wood Mackenzie calculates that if Japan is to meet its targets for power generation and is limited in the rate at which it can commission nuclear plant, it will need to import 60 to 65 mt of LNG in 2005, rising to between 70 and 80 mt in 2015.

2.2.3   New Market Leadership from South Korea and Taiwan

In 1995, Japan accounted for 80 per cent of LNG demand in the Asia-Pacific region and consequently drove regional trade. Japan is now a mature market and future growth is likely to come from overall economic growth, and tempered by efficiency gains, rather than from fuel substitution. Other Pacific Rim countries are continuing to grow at higher rates, providing the current dynamism in the industry. In particular it is the newly-industrialised countries of South Korea and Taiwan which are stimulating growth in LNG demand.

2.2.3.1   South Korea

South Korea contracted its first LNG from Indonesia in 1983, with deliveries starting from October 1986 to last a period of 20 years. The volume of gas currently traded under this contract is 2.3 mtpa, most of which is supplied from the Arun plant in Indonesia.

The first long-term LNG contract with Indonesia was followed by a second and a third. The second contract with Indonesia came into force in 1994 and will supply a further 2 mtpa until 2014; production will be shared between Arun and Bontang. The third LNG contract covers the period 1998–2007 and is for a volume of 1 mtpa. As well as the long-term contracts, the South Korean gas corporation (KGC) is also taking quantities of Indonesian gas on two medium-term contracts:

Figure 2.2.3.1A   South Korea's LNG Contracts with Indonesia

Contract	Period	Volume
First long-term	1986/2007	2.3 mt/year
Second long-term	1994/2014	2.0 mt/year
Third long-term	1998/2007	1.0 mt/year
First medium-term	1995/1999	6.08 mt total
Second medium-term	1996/1999	3.92 mt total

Malaysia is now also supplying South Korea with LNG. In early 1993, a contract was signed by KGC to import 2 mt of LNG for 20 years from 1995. This followed on from a short-term contract for a volume of 785,000 tpa running from 1992 to 1995.

Brunei is also likely to become a long-term supplier for South Korea. In February 1994, Brunei delivered a spot shipment of 56,000 tonnes to KGC. KGC then signed a contract to import 700,000 tonnes in both 1995 and 1996. South Korea also takes 'regular spot' from Brunei, at a rate of about 200,000–300,000 tpa, and the occasional cargo has also been taken from Australia.

South Korea signed a contract in July 1997 to take LNG from Qatar's Ras Laffan (Rasgas) project from 1999. A gas sales agreement has been signed between Ras Laffan and KGC for South Korea for the supply of 4.8 mtpa of LNG for 25 years from 1999. South Korea has negotiated to take 4.0 mtpa from Oman. Deliveries will start in the year 2000. The contract is interesting in that Oman have removed the 'floor' price from the pricing mechanism. This means that the Omanis will not be guaranteed a minimum price in the event of the price of the indexing fuel (oil) collapsing. Rasgas then followed suit.

By 1995, total imports of LNG to South Korea had risen to 7.09 mt, up from 5.87 mt in 1994. Demand is mostly shared between power generation and the residential and commercial sector; in 1995, 46 per cent of gas demand was for power generation, 48 per cent was for residential and commercial use and 6 per cent was for industrial use. The South Korean authorities expect a rapid future build-up of gas consumption, based on the country's relentlessly expanding power generation requirement. Increased demand will also come from the residential and commercial sectors as the government pursues its policy of replacing kerosene with city gas. Gas penetration in the industrial sector has remained low due to lack of availability and unfavourable pricing with respect to fuel oil, but with the deregulation of prices, gas demand in the sector is expected to grow rapidly, although from a low base.

The Ministry of Trade, Industry and Energy (MOTIE) estimates that LNG demand will rise to 23.3 mt by 2010. This is an aggressive target and any bottlenecks in infrastructure construction could jeopardise its achievement. South Korea has one existing LNG terminal at Pyongtaek, which was commissioned in 1986. Pyongtaek has now been expanded to take a maximum of 6.6 mtpa of LNG and will be further increased to 9 mtpa in 1998. The current configuration of seven 100,000-cubic metre storage tanks allows for a gas send-out rate of 55 million cubic metres (mmcm) per day.

A second LNG terminal has now been commissioned at Incheon with a regasification capacity of 3.3 mtpa, operational at the end of 1996, but with expansion to 5 mtpa planned by 1998. A third terminal, based on the expected growth in gas demand, is also proposed. It is thought that this will be situated on the south coast, possibly at Yosu. Terminal expansions will need to be co-ordinated, with construction of new transmission lines, city gas distribution systems and gas-fired power stations adding to the cost of infrastructure development. As an alternative to LNG, KGC is seriously considering a long-distance pipeline from Irkutsk to Seoul at a total cost of some US$10 billion, though LNG would seem to provide a more realistic solution to satisfying rising gas demand.

Based on Wood Mackenzie's demand model, imports of LNG to South Korea will have risen to around 16 mt by the year 2000, to 20 mt in 2010 and to 25 mt by 2015. This corresponds to an annual rate of increase of 6 per cent between 1996 and 2015. By 2010, the shares for each sector of the gas market will have remained roughly the same as at present, with power generation's share of gas consumption at 47 per cent, residential and commercial use on 43 per cent and industrial use having increased slightly to 10 per cent.

Figure 2.2.3.1B   Regasification Terminals in South Korea

Terminal	Capacity (mt/year)	Commissioning
Pyongtaek	6.6	1986–1995
Pyongtaek expansion	2.4	1998
Incheon	3.3	1996
Incheon expansion	1.7	1998

2.2.3.2   Taiwan

Government energy policy has been driven by a need to provide sufficient fuel for a rapidly expanding economy while also protecting the environment. Increasing public concern over the environmental impact of various

Figure 2.2.3.2A   South Korea Gas Infrastructure

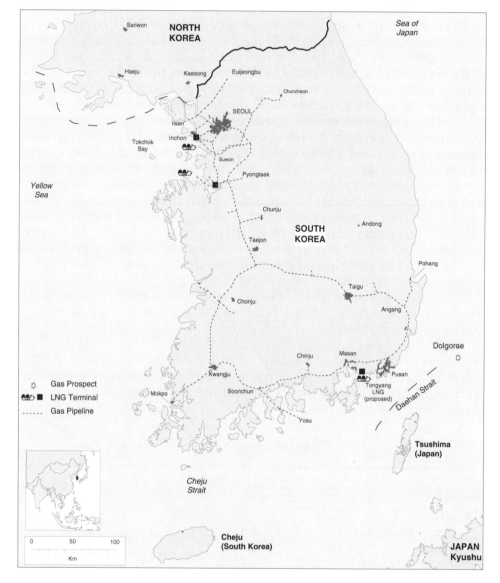

fuels in what is a densely populated area has caused the authorities to encourage a bias towards gas and away from coal and oil. Nuclear power has also met growing opposition, putting an even greater emphasis on gas. As a result of the increasing demand for gas and the low level of indigenous supplies, LNG imports began in April 1990.

The Taiwanese gas industry is based on an LNG terminal at Yung An, near Kaohsiung in the south of the island. The plant is operated by China

Figure 2.2.3.2B Taiwan Gas Infrastructure

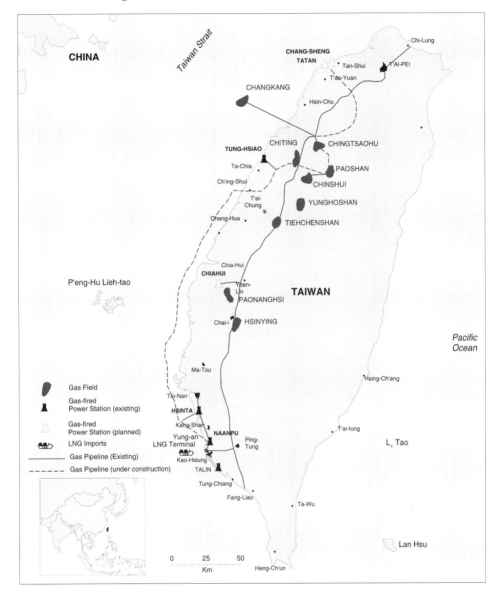

Petroleum Corporation (CPC) and cost around US$1.2 billion to construct. Originally built to handle 1.5 mtpa of LNG from Bontang in Indonesia, the plant imported around 2.8 mt in 1996 under an expanded 1.84 mtpa contract from Indonesia, supplemented by cargoes from Malaysia, with whom Taiwan has a contract for supplies building up to 2.25 mtpa in 1998. Taiwan is expected to contract an extra 2.5 mtpa from Indonesia.

Demand for LNG in Taiwan is being fuelled by rapid economic expansion in the country. Wood Mackenzie demand estimates are based on the assumption of annual GDP growth of around 6 per cent to the end of the century, but slowing to 5 per cent by 2005, 4 per cent by 2010 and reaching a trend rate of 3 per cent in 2015. Demand for LNG will predominantly come from power generation, and Taipower is planning for an electricity demand of 200 TWh in 2006. A fourth nuclear plant now seems certain to be built but increasing environmental opposition suggests that this will be the last to be commissioned before at least 2015. With the country aiming to limit oil imports, likely future generation policy will be based on gas and coal. The need to increase LNG imports rapidly to cater for increased power generation requirement will be constrained by the availability of infrastructure. The Yung An terminal is being expanded to handle 4.5 mtpa by 1997, with a further expansion to 7.5 mtpa being planned. By the year 2000, Taiwan will be able to import 7 mt of LNG, with a level of 12 mt being attained by 2010. After that, LNG demand growth will slow slightly, as coal gains share of the generation mix due to the availability of high-efficiency integrated gasification combined cycle (IGCC) technology. An LNG demand of 15 mt is forecast for 2015.

2.3   POTENTIAL NEW ASIAN MARKETS

Throughout Asia, rapid growth in energy demand, in particular for fuel for electricity generation, is acting as a stimulus for new LNG trade. Population giants India and China are now planning to import LNG, presenting new challenges for the business. Previously, LNG buyers have been large blue chip utilities in Europe, the US, Japan, South Korea and Taiwan who have bought large, stable quantities of LNG on long-term contracts. This has given secure, low-risk, markets to the suppliers and has given comfort to the bankers financing these multi-billion dollar capital projects. The new markets are very different. They are often cash-poor, have moderate credit ratings, have little existing gas infrastructure and have requirements for small, variable quantities of LNG. Under these conditions, project developers will need to be innovative in terms of contract structures, financing mechanisms and apportionment of risk. As the developing countries of Asia deregulate their electricity industries, much of the new power generation infrastructure will be built by independent power producers (IPPs) and these, in addition to the state utilities, are potentially a market for LNG. However, there are problems with LNG supply to IPPs, with the suppliers' need for a large stable gas offtake not matching the generators' needs for a smaller, variable gas supply. No LNG-fired IPPs have yet been built in Asia and until imaginative solutions are found to the mismatch of requirements between supplier and IPP, this market is likely to remain constrained.

The South-East Asian economic crisis in 1997 has exemplified some of the complexities which will confront the LNG industry in new markets where the ultimate offtakers in the value chain, state electricity companies, will be paid in local currency by the consumers. Because of the high costs of infrastructure, LNG importation will be very much the domain of the private sector (multinationals) which will require payment, even if involved in power generation, in US dollars. Issues including take-or-pay, government guarantees and revenue repatriation will be critical to the decision process and clearly introduce a new level of risk in these potential new Asian markets.

Nevertheless, in spite of the obstacles to be overcome in creating LNG markets in the developing Asian economies, new buyer countries will enter the market over the next 20 years, and in the sections below the potential newcomers are reviewed. For the LNG producers, new markets will be imperative. Achieving LNG sales and purchase agreements may be difficult but with several projects in competition the delivered price of LNG will be critical. Wood Mackenzie continually assesses LNG supply projects and categorises them according to their likely timing that they will come to market. The number of planned, probable and possible LNG projects is considerable, as the accompanying table indicates and can bring 47 mtpa to the market, while possible LNG projects are capable of further doubling that volume. The potential new markets are assessed in the following section.

2.3.1 Thailand

In August 1996, the Petroleum Authority of Thailand (PTT) signed a heads of agreement (HOA) with Oman to take supplies of LNG. The agreement required Oman to begin delivering 1 mtpa of LNG to PTT in 2001, rising to 1.7 mtpa in 2003 and 2.2 mtpa in 2004. The HOA was based on assumptions about the pace and volume of growth in the Thai economy, which had for the past 10 years been extremely rapid. Even with a moderate to high growth scenario, Wood Mackenzie forecast that Thailand would experience a gas supply 'bubble' in the early part of the next decade, with plentiful supplies of cheaper pipeline gas coming from Myanmar, the Malaysia–Thailand joint development area (JDA), new Gulf of Thailand fields and possibly even from Indonesia's giant Natuna D-alpha field. Thailand's strategic goal is to maintain a diversity of supply with the intention that this should create price competition. Accordingly, PTT's objective to import LNG from 2001 was for security of supply reasons, rather than because there would be any absolute need for it. In other words, LNG would be imported because PTT did not want to be exposed by a potential disruption of pipeline supplies from Myanmar or from the Gulf of Thailand.

The economic crisis in Thailand had a precipitous impact. A series of fiscal problems has beset the economy with a resultant dampening of

Figure 2.3A   Existing, Planned, Probable and Possible LNG Supply Projects

Existing LNG Projects

Country	Project	Current/Planned Capacity (MTPA)	Plant Operator	Gas Suppliers
Abu Dhabi	Das Island	5.3	Abu Dhabi Gas Liquefaction Co Ltd (ADGAS)	ADNOC
Australia	NW Shelf	7.5	Woodside Offshore Petroleum Ltd	Woodside Petroleum BP Chevron BHP Shell MIMI
Brunei	Lumut	6.2	Brunei LNG Ltd	Shell State of Brunei Elf Aquitaine Fletcher Challenge JASRA Pg Jaya Negara
Indonesia	Arun	11.5	PT Arun Natural Gas Liquefaction Co.	Mobil Gulf Indonesia Aceh Oil & Gas

Figure 2.3A *(cont'd)*

Country	Project	Current/Planned Capacity (MTPA)	Plant Operator	Gas Suppliers
Indonesia	Bontang	14.5	PT Badak Natural Gas Liquefaction Co.	VICO LASMO Union Texas CPC Universe Gas & Oil Total INPEX Unocal
Malaysia	MLNG	8.0	Malaysia LNG Company (MLNG)	Shell
	MLNG Dua	7.8	Malaysia LNG Company (MLNG)	Shell Petronas Carigali
Oman	Oman LNG	6.6	Oman LNG	Omani State Shell Total Partex

Figure 2.3A   *(cont'd)*

Country	Project	Current/Planned Capacity (MTPA)	Plant Operator	Gas Suppliers
Qatar	QatarGas	6.0	QatarGas	QGPC Mobil Total Marubeni Mitsui
	RasGas	5.0	RasGas	QGPC Mobil Itochu Nissho Iwai
USA (Alaska)	Kenai	1.3	Phillips/Marathon	Marathon Phillips Unocal Forcenergy
Total		79.7		

Figure 2.3B   Existing, Planned, Probable and Possible LNG Supply Projects Planned LNG Projects

Country	Project	Current/Planned Capacity (MTPA)	Plant Operator	Upstream Operators
Australia	NW Shelf Expansion	7.0	Woodside Offshore Petroleum Ltd	Woodside Petroleum
Indonesia	Bontang Expansion	3.5	PT Badak Natural Gas Liquefaction Co.	VICO Total Unocal
Malaysia	MLNG Tiga	6.8	MLNG	Occidental Nippon Oil Shell
Total		17.3		

Figure 2.3B *(cont'd)*

Probable LNG Projects

Country	Project	Current/Planned Capacity (MTPA)	Plant Operator	Upstream Operators
Australia	Gorgon/ Chrysaor/ Dionysus	7.5	WAPET/Chevron	WAPET Chevron
Canada	British Colombia -Kitimat	3.5	Phillips Petroleum Canada Ltd	Yet to be established
Indonesia	Tangguh	7.0	Pertamina-led Joint Venture	ARCO BG
Qatar	Enron Qatar	5.0	Qatar-Enron LNG Marketing Company	QEPC Enron
Yemen	YLNG-Balhaf	5.0	Total	Total Hunt
Zone of Co-operation	Bayu-Undan	2.0–3.0	BHP or Phillips	Phillips BHP
Total		30.0–31.0		

Possible LNG Projects

Figure 2.3B *(cont'd)*

Country	Project	Estimated Reserves (TCF)	Upstream Operator
Australia	Bonaparte Gulf	13	Woodside
	Scott Reef /	22	Woodside
	Brecknock		
Indonesia	Natuna D Alpha	46	Exxon
PNG	Highlands LNG	9	BP
USA	Alaska North Slope	31	ARCO
			BP
			Exxon
Russia	Sakhalin	15	Exxon
		14	MMMS
Total		150	

industrial output and consequent reduction in electricity demand growth. In combination with balance of payments considerations, the likelihood of importing LNG before 2010 now looks uncertain with other sources of gas finding markets first. Nonetheless, once the economy recovers, gas demand is likely to have risen to a level where there becomes an absolute requirement for the fuel, rather than just as a security of supply measure. Wood Mackenzie would expect that Thailand will need to import at least 5 mt by 2015, and possibly 7.5 mtpa.

Figure 2.3.1   Thailand Gas Infrastructure

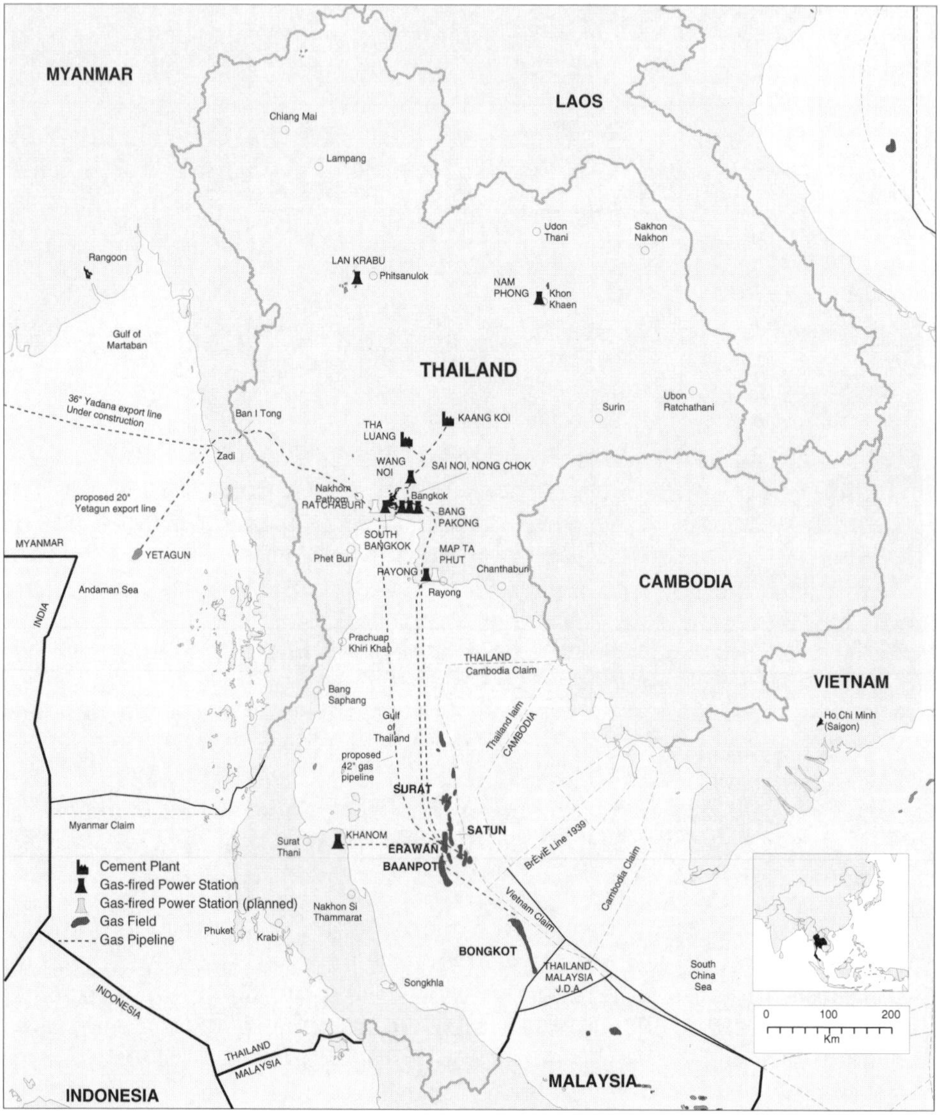

2.3.2   India

Gas penetration in India remains relatively low. A demand of 19 bcm in 1996 only represented 7 per cent of the country's total primary energy requirement. However, there is little doubt that the potential market for natural gas in India is vast. The study group set up by the Ministry of Petroleum and Natural Gas and convened by U. Sundararajan reported, in 1996, that potential gas demand in 2000–2001 could be 96 bcm (100 mtpa) amongst industrial and power generation users: five times the 1996 demand figure. There cannot possibly be the supply to satisfy this level of demand, but it gives an indication of the prospective growth in the market if it were not constrained by gas availability.

Given the future gas supply shortfall in India, many alternatives for importation have been proposed. Foremost amongst these was the Oman–India pipeline. However, the 20 bcm per annum pipeline scheme has now been abandoned although, of course, plans may be resurrected at some future date. The proposal eventually foundered because of the technical difficulties of laying a pipeline in 3500 metres of water, because of pricing difficulties and because it was always in competition with Oman LNG for gas reserves. Other pipeline proposals are complicated by geopolitical considerations. Proposals for pipelines from Iran or Turkmenistan to India will only proceed if tripartite agreements can be reached between Iran or Turkmenistan, Pakistan and India. Notwithstanding the threat of US sanctions, a tripartite agreement, though difficult to achieve, could be quite robust; the general trend of political liberalisation, not least in the subcontinent, undoubtedly adds political realism to the projects. Nonetheless, India is unlikely to rely on gas supplies which would transit one unstable country (Afghanistan) and another with whom tensions could escalate. Long-distance projects will equally depend on technical, commercial and financing considerations while India will, in any event, still wish to retain diverse sources of gas supply. Plans for a pipeline from Bangladesh to India have also been mooted, though there are several political, technical and commercial issues to be resolved, not least the establishment of a sufficiently large gas reserve in Bangladesh to justify export.

The problems associated with pipeline supply to India lead Wood Mackenzie to the view that most gas imports into the country up to 2015 will be in the form of LNG. It is planned that the first supplies of LNG will be to Enron's Dabhol power station. Following the cancellation of the original project, terms have now been renegotiated. The 740-megawatt (MW) phase I will now start around 1999 and will run on naphtha. Phase II, to start around 2001, will add a further 1710 MW of LNG-fired capacity and will also involve the conversion of phase I to LNG-firing. Several other foreign companies, in response to Indian initiatives, have indicated the intention to import LNG; foremost amongst these are Shell, British Gas and Total.

India's oil and gas majors are also planning to import LNG. India's three largest state oil and gas companies, Oil and Natural Gas Corp. (ONGC), Oil India Ltd (OIL) and the Gas Authority of India Ltd (GAIL), and Bharat Petroleum have formed a joint venture (Petronev LNG) to import LNG, a consortium which will be augmented by a foreign partner. Initially 5 mtpa of LNG would be imported into the two ports of Ennore, on the east coast, and Mangalore, on the west coast. Ennore is a particularly important site as it is being developed as a port to supply the city of Madras, with its 5.4 million population. LNG supply to the two ports of Ennore and Mangalore could eventually be raised to 10 mtpa. Seventeen foreign companies originally bid to become the joint venture partner, which was indicative of the need to develop a new market. Other LNG import alternatives have also been proposed. Oil refiner Hindustan Petroleum Corp Ltd has formed a partnership with Total of France to develop an LNG import terminal in southern India and an associated power plant. Enron, in addition to its Dabhol project, has submitted a proposal to the Indian prime minister to build 10 gigawatts (GW) of LNG-fired power plant in the country to be fuelled by about 10 mtpa of LNG. However, this is a massive amount of generating capacity, and it would seem more probable that India would want to tender this out, rather than give it all to one developer. Enron also has a memorandum of understanding (MOU) with Gujarat Gas Co. Ltd (GGCL) to supply 2.5 mtpa of LNG, although this was put in doubt following British Gas's purchase of a majority per cent stake in GGCL.

Wood Mackenzie expects that imports of LNG into India are likely to start soon after the turn of the century, assuming that Dabhol gets access to supplies. Other LNG import projects will soon follow, giving a total import of 4.2 mt in 2005. By 2015, imports will have risen to 13 mt and will constitute one-third of all gas supply in India.

2.3.3 China

Economic growth in China has averaged over 11 per cent per year in the last five years and it is reasonable to expect this phenomenal expansion to continue, although at a rate gradually declining to about half that by 2015. The growth in the Chinese economy will be particularly translated into increasing demand for electricity and this in turn will be the most important factor fostering demand for natural gas.

China's ninth five-year plan envisages an electricity output of 1500 TWh in the year 2000, although Wood Mackenzie is slightly more conservative at around 1400 TWh. No meaningful official forecasts for 2015 exist, but Wood Mackenzie predicts that electricity output will have risen to 2700 TWh by then. This demand will still be met overwhelmingly from coal, although there will be a large increase in the contribution from hydroelectric power after 2005 with the construction of the Three Gorges Dam

Figure 2.3.2   India Gas Infrastructure

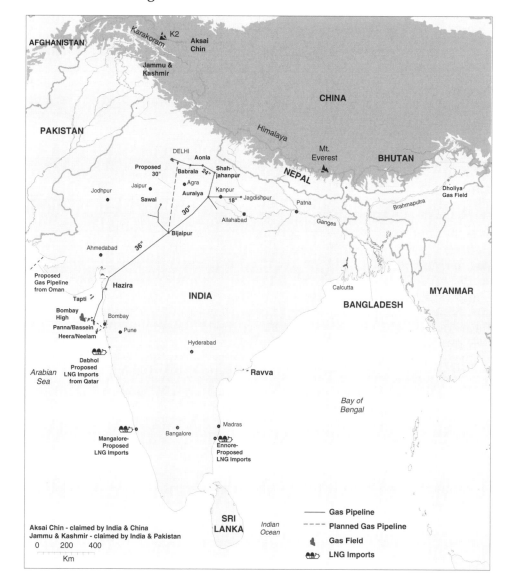

(whether it is built as one vast dam or as a cascade of smaller ones). Nuclear power will expand, while official policy is to phase out the use of oil for power generation. This leaves gas to be chosen for many new power generation projects in China. The attraction of gas is primarily because of the speed at which high-efficiency CCGT capacity can be added, but also because of the need to reduce emissions in China's highly polluted cities. Furthermore, China's coal is a long way from the fastest growing demand centres which are illustrated by the accompanying map and table.

Figure 2.3.3A   Regional 1995 GDP Estimates

	Population	GDP	GDP per capita	GDP Growth 1990–1994
North	102.4	58.60	572	11.0
N. East	122.5	71.32	582	8.5
East	298.5	191.29	641	13.6
S. Central	313.6	137.66	439	14.0
S. West	223.2	66.34	297	10.1
N. West	79.7	27.64	347	9.3
China	1,208	552.86	461	11.0

It is the southern and eastern provinces that are some of the most energy-deficient in China. In terms of gas, most of the current production is from the interior province of Sichuan and is also associated with oil production in the north-eastern provinces. This means that the booming states of the south-eastern seaboard represent a ready market for gas as soon as supplies can become available. The potential for long-distance gas pipelines to the eastern seaboard are very limited; LNG offers the only realistic alternative for transportation to those areas. The most likely constraint on gas availability will be the speed at which LNG reception terminals can be financed and constructed and, because of these factors, imports of LNG into south-east China are unlikely to be achieved until around 2005. Wood Mackenzie's demand model indicates that LNG imports could start soon after 2005 and would rise to 7.2 mt by 2010 and 12.3 mt by 2015. Such levels will require at least one terminal and possibly as many as four, each predominantly supplying power generation users in their hinterland although there would also be some industrial use and even supply to local distribution companies.

The most likely locations for terminals would be the four adjacent coastal provinces of Guangdong, Fujian, Zhejiang and Jiangsu (including Shanghai). Indeed, the China National Offshore Oil Corporation (CNOOC) has already conducted feasibility studies for sites in Guangdong. These proposed sites are shown in the following table, with the official forecasts for commissioning dates. Our view is that a first terminal is unlikely to become operational before 2005.

A study recently carried out by Shell has shown that imported LNG or imported coal are the only realistic options for the coastal provinces, and that electricity generated from LNG would be competitive with that generated from imported coal. A significant part of project costs would be the import duty on LNG, levied at 6 per cent, and VAT, levied at 13 per cent. A relaxation of these taxes would further improve the economics of

Figure 2.3.3B   GDP Per Capita by Province

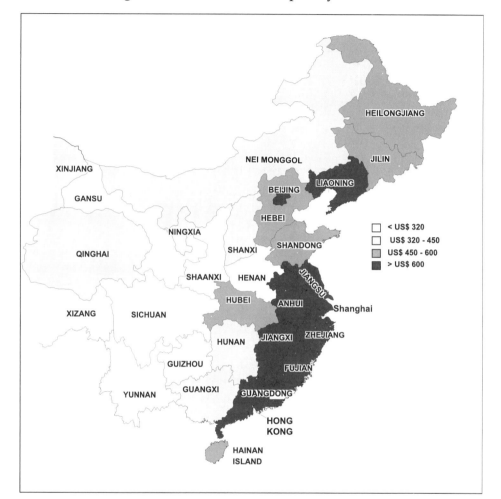

LNG-fired power generation. Shell envisage that one terminal would be constructed in the Pearl River Delta (i.e. the Hong Kong–Guangdong area) and one in the Yangtse Delta (Shanghai area). A third could possibly be built between these first two, on the Fujian coast.

2.3.4   Philippines

Developments are under way which could finally secure the exploitation of the Camago-Malampaya gasfield offshore Palawan Island, south of Luzon. The field is the largest in the country, with reserves estimated at 3.1 tcf of gas

Figure 2.3.3C   Chinese LNG Terminals

LNG Terminal	Operational date	Customers	Volume (mt/year)
Shenzhen (3 mt/year)	2001	Eastern power plant 2640 MW	1.7
		Qianwan power plant 1000 MW	0.65
		Conversion of existing gas turbines	0.4
		Industrial, res. and com.	0.25
Huizhou (2.7 mt/year)	2002	Bijia power plant 4000 MW	1.3
		Industrial, res. and com.	1.4
Zhanjiang (2 mt/year)	2002	Zhanjiang power plant 4000 MW	1.4
		Industrial, res. and com.	0.6

(Wood Mackenzie proven plus probable estimate), and is being developed by Shell and Occidental. Exploitation of the field has been stalled for some time because of difficulties related to simultaneous execution of a series of agreements along the full value chain. In order to achieve economic viability and initiate development, the contractors need to sell gas at a daily contract quantity (DCQ) rate of around 400 million cubic feet per day (mmcfd) for some 3000 MW of power facilities. The latest developments mean that the 3000-MW target finally looks like being reached, or even surpassed.

In January 1997, contracts for a 1200 MW build/operate/transfer (BOT) CCGT at Ilijan were awarded to South Korea Electric Power Corp. (KEPCO). This represented one of the largest 'intra-Asian' IPP awards, with KEPCO beating off rival bids from Alsons/ Tomen/Singapore Power, CEPA / Mitsubishi, Sithe /Marubeni, Siemens / PowerGen, and Enron. The plant will be KEPCO's largest investment outside South Korea and will earn it US$2.3 billion of revenue over the 20-year life of its power purchase agreement (PPA), beginning in 2002. A Caltex-operated group is also set to secure the contract for a 304- MW cogeneration power plant at its refinery at San Pascual. The project started life as an unsolicited proposal to the Philippines' National Power Corporation, which was then opened up for additional bids. Five other companies expressed interest in challenging the original San Pascual offer, but then could not secure Caltex's agreement to buy steam from anything other than its own original project. This left the field clear for exclusive negotiations between NPC and the San Pascual consortium. The plant is scheduled to be in operation by 2001, and may run on light oil for an interim period before Camago-Malampaya gas becomes available. The plant will sell power to NPC, as well as on-site power and steam to the Caltex refinery.

In a third development First Gas Holdings, a joint venture between British Gas and First Philippine Holdings, is to build a 990-MW CCGT at

Santa Rita. The operating and maintenance (O&M) contract for the plant has been awarded to Siemens. The station is due to commission in 1999 and plans to become a customer for Camago-Malampaya gas when this comes onstream in 2001–2002. In the interim, the plant will run on condensate, supplied under a long-term agreement signed with Enron. This will be converted into a back-up fuel contract when gas becomes available.

Another project has been proposed by a consortium consisting of Manila utility subsidiary Meralco Industrial Engineering Services (Miescor), Morrison Knudsen, Westinghouse and Mobil Corporation. The consortium has proposed the construction of a 420-MW CCGT plant at Cavite, to the south of Manila. The plant could use two Westinghouse 501F gas turbines given to the Philippines government by Westinghouse in settlement of the dispute over the Bataan nuclear station. Again, the station could run on gas from Camago-Malampaya, using liquid fuel as an interim substitute until gas is available.

Finally, conversion to gas-firing of the Bataan Nuclear Power Plant (BNPP) remains a possibility. This 620-MW pressurised water reactor (PWR) was completed by Westinghouse in 1986 but never operated, amid seismic safety fears, bribery allegations and a lawsuit (now settled) brought against Westinghouse by the Philippines government. Under the conversion proposals, a number of gas turbines would be added and the existing 620-MW steam plant would be used as the heat recovery boiler in combined cycle operation to give a new capacity of around 1500 MW. The station could run on Camago-Malampaya gas, supplied via pipeline extension from the landfall at Batangas to the Bataan peninsula.

Shell/Oxy have now signed GSAs with National Power Corporation and First Gas Holdings for the sale of gas at an estimated price in the region of US$4.00. Although LNG would be more expensive at a regasified cost of between US$4.30 and US$4.60 per mmBtu at Batangas, the number of planned power projects shows that there could be a market for LNG after pipeline gas supply from Malampaya-Camago has plateaued. Of course, when the new infrastructure is in place, further exploration will be encouraged, and if successful, this could delay the import of LNG.

2.3.5 Pakistan

Pakistan is expected to have a gas supply–demand gap early in the next century and the possibility of LNG imports has been raised. Indeed, Lasmo and National Power have carried out a feasibility study on behalf of the Pakistan government on the issue. However, Wood Mackenzie's view is that gas imports to Pakistan are more likely to be via pipeline. Three main sources of pipeline gas are under consideration, namely Turkmenistan, Qatar and Iran. Unocal are planning to deliver gas from Turkmenistan to

Pakistan. The gas will have to transit Afghanistan and, despite the efforts of US company Unocal, the viability of the route is dependent on cessation of the civil war and stabilisation of the country with an internationally recognised government. The Qatar proposal has also fallen dormant through lack of agreement on gas price and lack of potential investors. This leaves the Iran plan as the most likely to proceed. Relations between Iran and Pakistan are good and the threat of US sanctions is unlikely to be a deterrent to Islamabad. For technical, financial and political reasons, pipeline gas from Iran is the most probable source of gas imports to Pakistan and since economies of scale could be improved by an extension to India, LNG demand is not foreseen until at least 2015.

2.3.6 Singapore

Imported oil accounts for about 94 per cent of Singapore's total primary energy requirement, and with such an oil dependency, issues of security and diversity of energy supply are becoming more important in the island's energy planning process. Added to this are the environmental problems of burning large quantities of fuel oil for power generation. Because of these factors, Singapore is anxious to secure supplies of gas. At present, the country takes 150 mmcfd (1.5 bcm per annum) of gas from Malaysia's PGU II pipeline, but there appears to be little current prospect of this volume being increased. A letter of intent has recently been signed between Sembawang of Singapore and Indonesian state oil company Pertamina for the supply of 325 mmcfd of gas from the West Natuna Sea to be supplied from production-sharing contract (PSC) areas operated by Premier Oil, Conoco and Gulf Canada. LNG would be a further option and the Ministry of Trade and Industry recently commissioned a study examining the feasibility of an importation. The stumbling block, however, is that medium fuel oil for power generation can be bought from the local refinery market for around US$100 per tonne (US$2.40 per mmBtu) and LNG is unlikely to be competitive with this price, even though Singapore would probably pay a premium for diversity of supply and clean fuel. For these reasons, LNG is not built into the Wood Mackenzie demand forecast.

2.3.7 Summary

LNG supply to the emerging markets of the Asia-Pacific region presents major new challenges. Projects will be difficult to finance where the customer is cash-poor and without a triple A credit rating, as is the norm for traditional Japanese buyers. New trades to these countries will also be hampered by the lack of infrastructure, lack of experience in the LNG business and absence of clear regulatory frameworks. Notwithstanding, the economies of these countries are growing and the appetite for gas and other fuels is undeniable. In this environment, certain projects can be made to work; in particular, importation to Thailand, India and China will go ahead over the next 10 years. However, those proposed for the Philippines, Pakistan and Singapore are unlikely to proceed before 2015 because of competition from rival pipeline alternatives.

The table and chart below show how the entry of new countries will be responsible for the strong growth in the LNG market in the Asia-Pacific region, particularly after 2010:

Figure 2.3.7   Forecast Asia-Pacific LNG Demand (Million Tonnes)

	1995	*2000*	*2005*	*2010*	*2015*
Japan	43.6	50.0	57.0	65.0	70.0
South Korea	7.1	14.0	17.0	20.0	25.0
Taiwan	2.5	7.0	9.5	12.0	15.0
India	0.0	0.0	4.2	8.7	13.0
Thailand	0.0	0.0	0.0	1.9	7.5
China	0.0	0.0	0.0	7.2	12.3
Total	53.2	71.0	87.7	114.8	142.8

2.4   THE LNG SUPPLIERS

There are a number of countries now exporting LNG. These include Indonesia, Malaysia, Brunei, Australia, Abu Dhabi, Qatar, Oman and the US (Alaska). The supply of LNG from these countries is described in the following sections.

2.4.1   Indonesia

With 19 years' experience in the liquefied natural gas business, Indonesia has grown to become the world's largest supplier, with a 40 per cent market share. It currently dominates the Asia-Pacific LNG market, and in 1995 exported over 25 million tonnes (mt) to customers in Japan, South Korea and Taiwan.

The birth of the LNG business in Indonesia was brought about by the discovery of significant amounts of gas in both East Kalimantan and North

Sumatra in the early 1970s. Indonesia was fast to take action and in 1973 signed its first LNG supply contract with buyers in Japan, allowing the development of a two-train LNG facility at Bontang (East Kalimantan) and a three-train facility at the Arun field (North Sumatra). In 1977 the first deliveries were made from Bontang, followed by Arun in 1978. Since then, the Indonesian LNG business has grown in stature and now comprises six trains operating at Arun and six trains at Bontang. A further two trains are also planned for installation at Bontang by 1998 and the year 2000 respectively. The country has established long-term supply contracts with Japan, South Korea and Taiwan currently accounting for exports of over 25 million tonnes per annum (mtpa). Wood Mackenzie currently estimates that Indonesia's 2p (proven and possible) gas reserves (as of 1 January 1997) are around 110 trillion cubic feet (tcf) (including the 46-tcf Natuna gas field and 13-tcf Wiriagar Deep field). With around 23 tcf effectively committed under existing contracts it is believed that a further 10 tcf is available to the existing LNG facilities under new or extended contracts. In 1994, production of gas for LNG accounted for around 79 per cent of the total sales gas produced in Indonesia and generated US$1.5 billion of revenue for the country, around 25 per cent of the total for oil and gas.

Despite the prodigious growth of the LNG industry in Indonesia, some storm clouds may lie on the horizon. After 18 years of operation, the Arun LNG plant is facing a decline in output as a result of depleting reserves; a first in the LNG business. Despite extensive exploration in the surrounding areas in recent years, only small additions to reserves have been made and under the existing contracts it seems likely that trains will have to be shut down in the next 10 years. Elaborate suggestions for delivery of Natuna gas to replace Arun gas have been suggested, but the process of developing Natuna at all is to be lengthy. In light of this decline, the critical question now facing the Indonesia government is how to maintain its grip on its existing Asian markets. With the likelihood that Indonesia's existing long-term supply contracts will be extended as long as reserves are available, it is apparent that any shortfall in gas supply could result in the buyers going elsewhere—most likely to Australia. In the sections following, the current Indonesian LNG business and the question of how potential new projects could help fill the gap in supply to existing markets are evaluated.

2.4.1.1 Contracts

By any standards, the emergence of the LNG business in Indonesia was rapid. Following the gas discoveries of the early 1970s, the opportunity was seized and by 1973 the first long-term supply contract with Japan had been signed. This contract, for over 170 mt, was capable of justifying the massive capital investment involved in LNG plants at both Arun and Bontang. Within six years of the first discovery, Indonesia was exporting its first cargoes of LNG. In 1981, a second long-term contract with Japan was signed and as reserves grew the number of contracts increased, allowing the continued growth of the plants. In total, Indonesia currently holds contracts for over 670 mt of LNG to customers in Japan, South Korea and Taiwan. This equates to around 37 tcf of sales gas at the plant gate. To date, around 286 mt of LNG have been delivered from the Indonesian plants (147 mt from Arun and 139 from Bontang).

Due to the initially high production performance of the Arun field, the adjacent plant captured the lion's share of contracted volumes in the early years. However, as reserves have declined in Arun and exploration success in East Kalimantan has gone from strength to strength there has been a gradual switch in contract shares towards Bontang. It is for this reason that the Bontang plant now holds over 70 per cent of the total remaining contracted gas for LNG in Indonesia.

Despite the large amounts of LNG contracted gas in Indonesia, there are, without doubt, still significant reserves which remain available but as yet uncontracted (particularly around the Bontang plant). For the development of these reserves, Indonesia's ultimate strength lies in the markets it has already captured; existing buyers will undoubtedly favour the extension of existing contracts from a reliable and proven supplier over the establishment of new contracts with unfamiliar suppliers. From the chart below, it is apparent that despite the fact that currently contacted volumes are due to start to decline in 2003, the possibility of extensions to

Figure 2.4.1.1   Indonesia—Existing LNG contracts and possible extensions

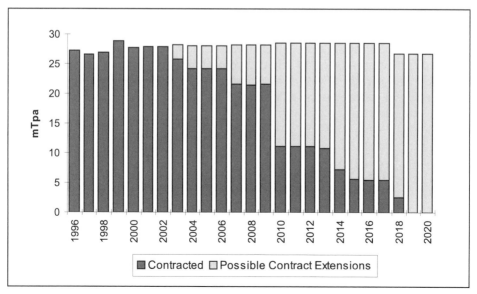

existing contracts could maintain a market for around 26–28 mtpa for many years to come. With LNG revenues currently making up over 5 per cent of Indonesia's total domestic revenues, the maintenance of this lucrative export business is of significant material value to the country and contractors.

The critical issue for Indonesia however is over its ability to bring new reserves to market in a timely manner, i.e. at the times when contract extensions are being considered by the buyers. If sufficient reserves are not available, then the buyers will have little choice but to go elsewhere (it is most likely that the next stop would be Australia due to its political stability and Japan's reluctance to become further reliant on Middle Eastern sources for its fossil fuels). In this event, new long-term contracts would probably be signed and the buyers could be lost to Indonesia for 20 years or longer. In recent years, however, oil and gas companies have been very successful in making material additions to Indonesia's gas reserves. If this can be continued, then the possibility of signing new contracts, allowing the development of additional facilities (either greenfield plants or extensions) cannot be discounted. With its relatively stable political environment and a long history of successful supply, Indonesia is positioned well against its competitors for the attainment of new markets.

2.4.1.2   Facilities

Currently Indonesia boasts the world's greatest concentration of LNG trains with 12 (and a further two planned) at two sites: Arun and Bontang. All the LNG facilities are owned by the state oil company, Pertamina, and are operated by companies headed by Pertamina and including the principal gas producers and LNG buyers. The plants operate on a non-profit basis and capital expenditure on new trains, port facilities, and other infrastructure is now exclusively debt-financed. Revenues generated from the LNG sale are first used to pay for the plant operating and debt-servicing costs before being distributed to Pertamina and the production-sharing contractors.

2.4.2   Malaysia

Malaysia's Bintulu LNG plant, located on the north coast of the island of Borneo, in the state of Sarawak, was commissioned in January 1983. The plant originally produced around 8.1 mtpa of LNG, exporting to customers largely in Japan, but increasingly to South Korea and Taiwan. A major expansion, MLNG Dua, involving the construction of three new trains, was completed recently, boosting capacity to around 16 mtpa, making Bintulu the largest single LNG site in the world. A second expansion project, MLNG Tiga, involving the construction of a further two trains by mid-2000, is expected to raise output further still to 22.8 mtpa.

2.4.2.1   MLNG

The MLNG plant is located at Bintulu, on the north coast of Sarawak. Construction commenced in 1979 and commercial operations started in January 1983. Since then, LNG deliveries have increased sharply. The five hundredth cargo from Bintulu was delivered in April 1989 and the one thousandth in May 1993. The plant has three identical trains, each of which had a nameplate capacity of around 2 mtpa of LNG. A debottle-necking programme completed in 1990 raised the plant's capacity from 6 to 8.1 mtpa (2.7 mtpa train). Each train is identical, featuring gas treatment (removal of impurities such as small quantities of acid gases), dehydration, mercury removal, stabilisation and liquefaction units. Currently, around 1254 mmcfd (418 mmcfd per train) is charged to the plant. The site also has four LNG storage tanks with a combined capacity of 252,000 cubic metres.

2.4.2.2   MLNG Dua

Encouraged by the success of the original LNG facility, Petronas decided to explore the possibility of expansion utilising the immense undeveloped gas reserves offshore. The MLNG Dua project was the outcome. Shell Internationale Petroleum Maatschappij (SIPM) was commissioned in early 1990 to prepare specifications for the project which was designed to cater for the Taiwanese and South Korean markets, besides Japan. In June 1993, a production-sharing contract was signed between Petronas Carigali and Sarawak Shell, covering a total of 11 fields, largely dedicated to MLNG Dua. A detailed engineering, procurement, construction and commissioning (EPCC) contract was awarded to a joint venture composed of JGC, MW Kellogg and Sime Engineering for three new LNG trains, an additional LNG storage tank, rundown lines, flare system and modifications to the existing utility distribution network. Petronas appointed a team from Foster Wheeler to manage the project.

The new plant has a design capacity of 7.8 mtpa (2.6 mt per train) and uses the same process as MLNG, but with enhancements gleaned from a decade of operations of the original facility as well as from other sites around the world. The most significant improvements include the powering of the main refrigeration compressors by gas turbine, and a hybrid cooling system, using a mixture of air and sea water, which will use only 25 per cent of the water required for the original plant. Construction has been staggered to match the build-up of gas production from the offshore fields, demand for LNG, deliveries of new tankers and deployment of construction resources. The first cargo from the first of the three trains left Bintulu for Taiwan in May 1995. The second train came onstream the following September, with the third at the end of the year.

Figure 2.4.2.2   Malaysia (Sabah and Sarawak) Gas Infrastructure

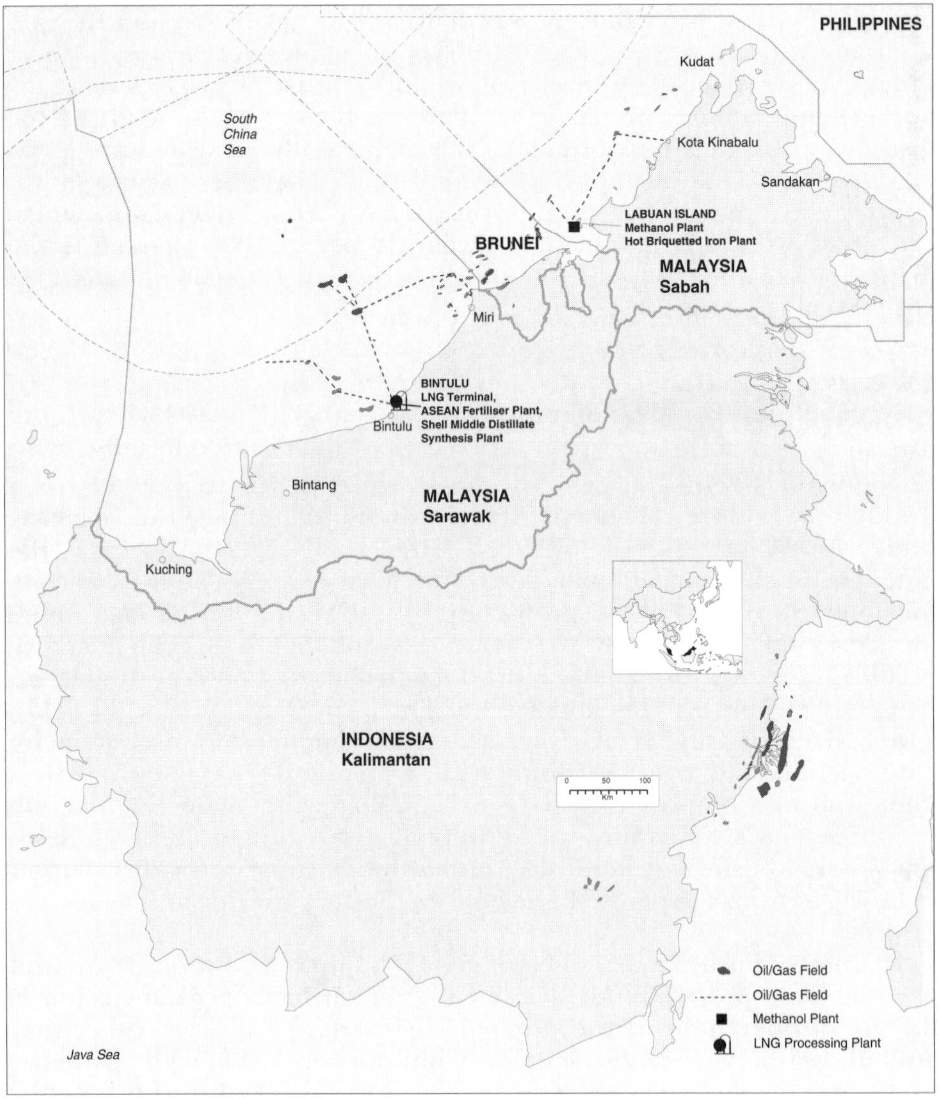

2.4.3   Australia

Australia joined the ranks of LNG exporters in 1989, and has in less than a decade become a key player in LNG markets, particularly with the discovery of large volumes of gas on the North-West Shelf and in the Timor Gap.

At the outset, North-West Shelf LNG was to be developed as part of a wider North-West Shelf gas development project, involving the upstream participants. The size of the LNG project was such that the existing participants decided to involve additional partners in order to reduce exposure and spread the risk. As a consequence, MIMI (a 50:50 joint venture between Mitsui & Co. and Mitsubishi Corporation) bought a one-sixth share of the LNG project. The new joint venture agreement was formally approved in the latter part of 1984 with the project being operated by Woodside, but also including BP, Chevron, Shell and BHP.

The LNG facilities are located near Karratha on the Burrup Peninsula and were developed in two stages; the first (two-train) stage was completed in 1989. The second stage, or train three, was completed in November 1992. The facilities can produce 7.5 mtpa, and the project has eight dedicated LNG tankers for use in delivery. The bulk of the LNG is sold to the Japanese market with cargoes having reached 130 per annum by 1997. Significantly, over-capacity in 1993 led to the first spot cargo of LNG to Spain, a precedent which has led to subsequent shipments elsewhere.

The NWS joint venture participants are proposing to expand the LNG supply through development of at least 14 tcf of undeveloped gas reserves. As of 1997 a formal MOU had yet to be signed and the procurement of additional sales volumes will ultimately depend upon three factors, namely the volume of certified, uncontracted reserves, Japanese or other Asian demand and competitive pricing given the variety of other potential supply projects.

2.4.4   Brunei

The Lumut LNG Plant commenced production in late 1972, the second-oldest LNG facilities in the Pacific Rim. Brunei Shell dominates the production of gas in Brunei from its SW Ampa, Fairley, Champion and Gannet fields. The gas is sold by BSP to Brunei LNG Ltd (BLNG), which is a Shell, Mitsubishi and Brunei State joint venture. The LNG is then sold to Brunei Coldgas Ltd (same ownership) who are responsible for LNG sales to customers in Japan, and more recently in South Korea. A fourth company, Brunei Shell Tankers (BST), transports the LNG to the end-users. The Lumut LNG Plant was commissioned in late 1972, and was at the time the largest LNG export project ever proposed. Agreement in principle for shipments of LNG to Japan was reached in 1968. Four trains were initially built, with a fifth added in 1975, each with a gas-processing capacity of 166 mmcfd (1.24 mtpa of LNG). The plant is of immense importance to Brunei, as annual revenues from the 6 mtpa LNG sales currently exceed those from oil exports. The Lumut complex also includes steam-generating plant, a power station with a capacity of 40 MW, two refrigeration make-up units, and a loading jetty built 4.5 km long due to the shallowness of the water inshore.

The first LNG contract was signed with three Japanese companies in June 1970 to supply a peak rate of 3.7 mtpa over a 20-year period; the principal buyer is Tokyo Electric. After an initial build-up period the contract allowed for 5.14 mtpa to be delivered for 17 years. Discussions to extend the original contract beyond 31 March 1993 began in February 1988. The main issue of contention, apart from the price, was the future of the ageing BST tanker fleet. The Japanese wanted replacement of some of the fleet with larger and more modern carriers, providing greater reliability and economies of scale. Brunei Coldgas maintained that with good maintenance programmes, the existing fleet could remain in service for several more years, and that the costs of replacement would have to be recovered through higher prices. Agreement was finally reached for a new 20-year contract with the existing buyers to begin on 1 April 1993. In addition to an increased price, it calls for a 7.8 per cent increase in shipments to 5.54 mtpa, which represents 14 per cent of total Japanese LNG consumption. It was also agreed that the existing tanker fleet would remain in service indefinitely, provided they are seaworthy, with the buyers being invited to attend the annual inspections.

The new 20-year contract to supply Japanese utilities, agreed in April 1993, allowed for a price increase in favour of Brunei Coldgas. The new price has not been disclosed, but it is understood that it was in the region of US$3.70 per mmBtu, based on a crude oil price at that time of US$20.00 per bbl. In June 1995, it is thought that the price was around US$3.40 per mmBtu. The new contract also allows for a regular review to keep the Brunei LNG price on a par with that of other LNG suppliers. Brunei Coldgas are also looking to secure markets for their LNG outside Japan. In June 1994, a sales contract was signed with KGC, for the delivery of 0.7 mtpa during 1995 and 1996, using the *Port Harcourt*, which had been chartered until end-1996.

Figure 2.4.4 Brunei Gas Infrastructure

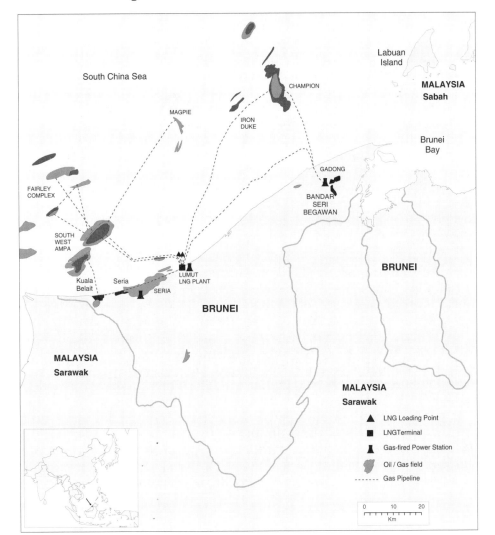

2.4.5 Abu Dhabi

LNG exports from Abu Dhabi's Das Island began in 1977. The operator is the Adgas consortium, comprising Abu Dhabi National Oil Co. (Adnoc) 51 per cent, BP 16.33 per cent, Total 8.17 per cent and Mitsui

15 per cent. The two-train plant had an original capacity of 2 mtpa, all of which was contracted to Tokyo Electric Power Co. (TEPCO) for a 20-year period, starting in 1977. However, following debottlenecking, in the years up to 1994, Tokyo Electric was taking something in the range of an additional 200,000–400,000 tpa from the plant. In 1994, a third train was inaugurated at Das Island. Based on taking additional gas from the new train, TEPCO contracted in October 1990 to increase its annual purchase of LNG to 4.7 mt for a 25-year period starting 1 April 1994. TEPCO is currently taking around 4.5 mtpa of LNG from Abu Dhabi. Because of flagging demand in Japan, Adgas was able to ship surplus production to Belgium, France and Spain. In 1995, Adgas produced 5.3 mt of LNG.

2.4.6   Alaska

Japan started importing LNG from Alaska in 1969. Marathon Oil and Phillips Petroleum contracted to sell 0.96 mtpa of LNG from Cook Inlet to Tokyo Gas and Tokyo Electric for 15 years. Subsequently, the contract was extended five years to 1989, and now an extra 15 years to 2004 with an option to extend to 2009. Present volumes are 1.23 mtpa; Tokyo Electric takes three-quarters of the gas. The gas price was originally fixed at US$0.52 per mmBtu, with periodic review. However, in the early 1980s, the price was linked to a basket of crudes, CIF Japan.

   Alaska has abundant gas reserves and several companies are seeking ways to commercialise them in order to stem the eventual tide of declining oil revenue. Foremost is the consortium of Arco, BP and Exxon which is investigating the possibility to deliver LNG competitively to Japan, even considering the extremely high costs of piping gas to Kenai for liquefaction.

2.4.7   Qatar

2.4.7.1   *Qatargas*

The Qatargas project is Qatar's first operational LNG scheme. First LNG was produced from train one in November 1996, followed by LNG from train two in December. The first shipment of LNG departed Ras Laffan port in late December and arrived at Chubu Electric's Kawagoe terminal

Figure 2.4.6 Alaska Gas Infrastructure

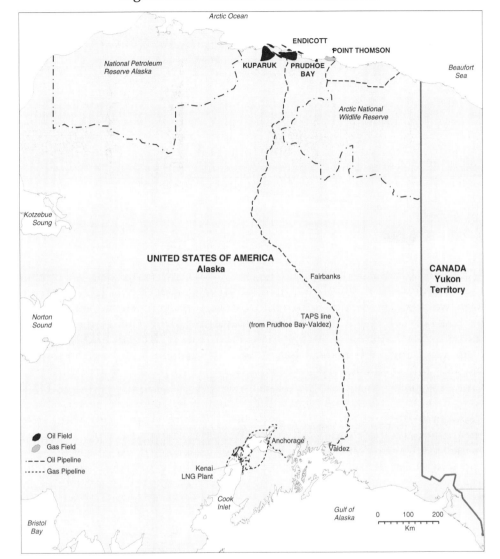

on 10 January 1997. Supplies will continue at a rate of 4 mtpa for a period of 25 years. A further 2 mtpa will be sold to seven other Japanese power and gas utilities for 25 years from mid-1998. This will give total annual shipments of 6 mtpa. Qatargas is 65 per cent owned by QGPC, 10 per cent each by Mobil and Total, and 7.5 per cent each by Japan's Marubeni and Mitsui.

2.4.7.2   Ras Laffan

Ras Laffan Liquefied Natural Gas Company, Limited (RasGas) is a 70:30 joint venture between Qatar General Petroleum Corporation (QGPC) and Mobil. On its first LNG shipment to Korea Gas Corporation (KGC), planned for July 1999, Ras Laffan will become Qatar's second LNG scheme. KGC has agreed to buy 4.8 mtpa of LNG from RasGas for 25 years beginning in 1999. Subsequent trains will be added if further gas sales agreements are forthcoming. Mobil is actively marketing this extra capacity, talking to potential buyers in Taiwan, India, Turkey and elsewhere. Enron meanwhile is pursuing its own Qatar LNG project to supply its 2.5 GW power project at Dahbol in India.

2.4.8   Oman

Oman, with gas reserves of around 10 tcf (300 bcm) but only small local markets, has long had the potential to become a gas exporter. The two most likely routes for export were considered to be via pipeline to India or in the form of LNG. However, while the India pipeline scheme has collapsed under its weight of technical and financial difficulties, the LNG project has moved forwards in leaps and bounds to become one of the fastest LNG schemes ever to be put together. Oman LNG is a joint venture of the government of Oman (51 per cent), Shell (30 per cent), Total (5.54 per cent), Mitsubishi (2.77 per cent), Mitsui (2.77 per cent), Itochu (0.92 per cent), Partex (2 per cent) and five South Korean companies (KGC, Samsung, Hyundai, Daewoo and Yukong) (5 per cent). The consortium has an agreement with KGC for the sale and purchase of 4.1 mtpa of LNG from the year 2000 until 2025. Osaka Gas of Japan has an MOU for 0.66 mtpa from the year 2000 over a 25-year period.

The Oman plant will initially consist of two trains, each of 3.3-mtpa capacity, giving a total capacity of 6.6 mtpa. If KGC takes 4.1 mtpa and Osaka Gas takes 0.66 mtpa, this still leaves scope for some further sales. The site also has the capability of taking up to three extra trains if demand grows.

2.5   POSSIBLE FUTURE SUPPLIERS

Gas reserves in the Middle East and Australasia have been steadily increasing to the extent that there are now several planned, probable and possible LNG projects which could supply Asian markets. These include

Indonesia, Malaysia and Australia, all of which could increase their market share, plus some new potential suppliers such as Papua New Guinea and Yemen. Details of the various schemes are summarised as follows:

Figure 2.5   Possible Future Suppliers

	Planned mt/yr	*Probable mt/yr*	*Possible TCF*
Australia	7.0	7.5	25
Indonesia	3.5	7.0	46
Malaysia	6.8		
Qatar		5.0	250
Oman			35
Yemen		5.0	
Zone of Co-operation		2.0–3.0	
Papua New Guinea			9
Russia			29
US (Alaska)			31
Iran			300
Total	17.3	27	725

2.5.1   Indonesia

In addition to the Arun and Bontang schemes, the possibility of new 'greenfield' projects in Indonesia cannot be ignored and recently two such potential projects have come to the fore in Natuna and Wiriagar.

2.5.1.1   *Natuna*

The Natuna field is a giant gas field situated in the Natuna Sea, with in-place reserves of up to 222 tcf, 71 per cent of which is CO_2. Currently held by a 50:26:24 Exxon/Mobil/Pertamina joint venture, the field was first discovered in December 1973, when Agip plugged and abandoned wildcat AL-1X as a gas discovery. The field itself is a dome-shaped structure approximately 25 km long by 15 km wide, with a potential productive area of approximately 320 km^2.

Although still only in the conceptual stage, it is planned that development of the field for LNG could be carried out on a phased basis, in line

with growth in markets and demand. Wood Mackenzie expects initial
sales gas production levels to be around 800 mmcfd, which will translate
to around 4.8 mtpa of LNG. However, eventually it is envisaged that the
field could produce up to 2.4 bcf/d of sales gas, which will be processed
into around 15 mtpa of LNG. Produced gas would be processed initially
offshore on treatment platforms each capable of processing up to
1.8 bcf/d, yielding around 400 mmcfd of sales gas. Treated sales
gas, which would then be composed of about 80 per cent methane,
18 per cent CO_2, 1 per cent N2 and small amounts of H_2S, would be compressed for export to Natuna Island via pipeline. Removed CO_2 would be
transported via pipeline to up to four satellite platforms, from where it
would be injected into the aquifer in the form of a super-critical fluid at
high pressure. A greenfield LNG plant is proposed for a site on the northern tip of Natuna Island. There the gas would be further treated to
remove remaining CO_2 and H_2S, prior to liquefaction. The plant at peak
production rate would require up to six trains of a comparable size to
those in operation at Bontang.

The joint venture partners estimate that the final total cost of the
development including offshore facilities, LNG plant and the infrastructure
required will be of the order of US$35–40 billion (money-of-the-day), two-
thirds of which will be spent on the offshore facilities. The project however

Figure 2.5.1.1   The Natuna and Wiriagar (Tangguh) Fields

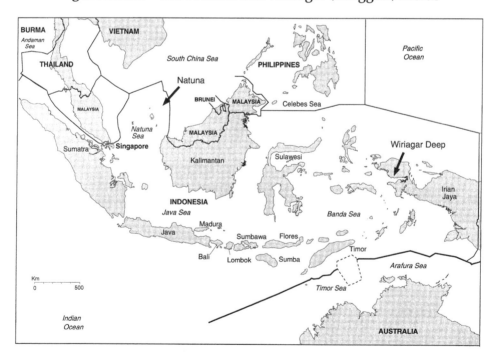

faces a number of serious hurdles, not least of which is the joint venture's ability to market a huge volume of LNG which would be significantly more costly than its competitors. In addition, the significant lead time between the start of construction and first LNG of around eight years adds significantly to the risks involved in such a mammoth project. In light of these problems, Wood Mackenzie believes that first deliveries of LNG from a project will be unlikely to take place before 2015. Most recently, the whole concept of Natuna as an LNG project has been put into doubt by alternative proposals to supply Natuna gas by pipeline to Thailand. It has even been mooted that Natuna gas could be taken on from Thailand to the Arun LNG plant in north Sumatra to compensate for declining gas production in the area.

2.5.1.2   *Wiriagar Deep (Tangguh)*

Located both on and offshore western Irian Jaya, the Wiriagar Deep gas field was discovered by an Arco-led joint venture in 1994. The field is understood to contain recoverable reserves of in excess of 15 tcf with a additional upside in surrounding areas, including British Gas's Muturi PSC. With the level of reserves confirmed, it is probable that the field will be developed for the export of gas as LNG. Since around one-third of the Wiriagar field is located onshore it is believed that the field development costs could be kept relatively low (at least for the start of the project) and thus the price required for the LNG would be competitive in the Asia-Pacific market.

It is currently believed that sufficient reserves are present for the Arco-led joint venture project, dubbed Tangguh, to build a two-train greenfield facility adjacent to the field with an output of around 5–6 mtpa. Assuming that the reserves can be proved up in the coming two years, then it is possible that the new plant could see its first exports in around 2003–2004.

With the decline of exports from the Arun LNG plant imminent, Indonesia is facing the uncertainty of whether it will be able to hold on to the significant Asian market it has worked so hard to build up. From the examination of existing contracts it is evident that currently contracted volumes are expected to decline sharply from around 2003. In order to secure the existing markets through contract extensions, it will be necessary to have sufficient reserves and plant capacity available. The chart below shows that with Bontang running at full capacity of around 20 mtpa from the year 2000 and the expected decline in contracted volumes (and possible closure of trains) at Arun in 2003, Indonesia will not be able to maintain its output at over 25 mtpa without additional reserves and new LNG facilities.

The chart below illustrates how the output from a two-train Tangguh facility at Arco's Wiriagar Deep discovery could avert a decline in Indonesia's overall supply capability by compensating for Arun and maintaining existing markets at around 26–27 mtpa until around 2015 (included are the currently uncontracted reserves from East Kalimantan which will likely sustain capacity output from Bontang until 2015). In the event of such a greenfield development, Pertamina could rely heavily on the extension of existing Indonesian contracts for the new plant and would not be forced out into the competitive market for new contracts.

The key factor for Tangguh, however, will be timing; if the plant is to start deliveries in 2003 ahead of competing greenfield projects, it will be necessary for Pertamina (and the suppliers) to take the reserves to market in the next year or two. Serious delays to this schedule could prove critical to the ability of Indonesia to keep a firm hold on its existing markets. In addition, the possible construction of a ninth train at Bontang cannot be ruled out. Such an extension could add an extra 2.5–3 mtpa to Indonesian output—a volume which could require additional contracts, assuming the Wiriagar project was to proceed. Although the potential input of LNG from Natuna is not shown due to the perceived problems of cost and the likelihood that first LNG would not occur until post-2015, it is evident that from a supply/markets basis, the Tangguh development is not a significant competitor to Natuna. Indeed, by maintaining contracted

Figure 2.5.1.2   Potential Sources of Supply for Contracted LNG

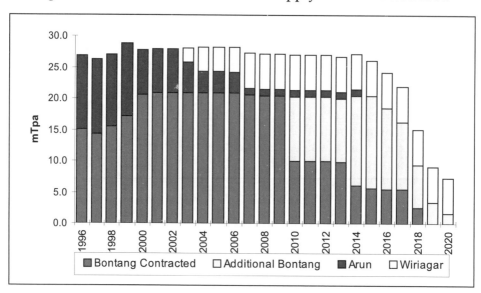

volumes at over 25 mtpa beyond 2010 the Tangguh development could actually be beneficial in the marketing of Natuna gas, i.e. a large portion of the gas could be sold into existing markets on the basis of contract extensions.

2.5.2 Malaysia

2.5.2.1 *MLNG Tiga*

In December 1995, Petronas, RD/Shell, Occidental and Nippon Oil announced the formation of a new joint venture to build two additional liquefaction trains adjacent to the existing facilities at Bintulu. The project will be supplied initially by Occidental's SK8 fields, Jintan, Serai, Saderi, Cili Padi and Selasih, from Nippon Oil's Helang field in SK10 and also, it is understood, from Sarawak Shell's Beryl field in the MLNG Dua PSC. Once production decline sets in by the end of the next decade, further Shell fields such as B11 and B12 and a number of Petronas-held discoveries will be developed to make up the shortfall.

Initial engineering studies are now underway for the offshore facilities, with the design of the onshore plant under study by RD/Shell subsidiary, SIOP. Two 3.4 mtpa trains will be built, with its situation close to the existing plant allowing the sharing of some facilities and the benefits of economies of scale. The plant is expected onstream in 2001, or within four years of buyers being signed up. The joint venture differs from the previous MLNG consortia in that the marketing of the gas will be carried out by the MLNG Tiga consortium rather than MLNG. It is hoped that memoranda of understanding will be in place by 1998, with the plant taking three to three and a half years to build under an engineering, procurement and construction (EPC) contract.

2.5.3 Qatar

2.5.3.1 *Enron*

Enron is proposing to construct a 5-mtpa LNG liquefaction plant in Qatar. The project would be a 65:35 joint venture, with QGPC holding the larger stake. Around 2.5 mtpa would go to Enron's Dabhol power plant situated in India's Maharashtra state. It is possible that the total output from the plant could go to India; Enron has an MOA with Gujarat Gas Co. for a supply of 2.5 mtpa from 2001. Enron originally wanted to sell half the output from the plant to Israel and Jordan and the company signed an MOU with Israel for the supply of at least 2 mtpa from 2001. However the agreement has now lapsed. Enron has now proposed building 10 GW of further CCGT stations in India, a capacity which would require about 10 mt of LNG. Some of this could now come from the company's Qatar scheme, although its planned capacity of 5 mt would be insufficient to supply all the proposed stations. There are still major doubts as to whether this project will proceed, especially with capacity still unsold at Mobil's rival Ras Laffan facility.

2.5.4   Australia

2.5.4.1   North-West Shelf Expansion

The North-West Shelf joint venture partners have submitted a proposal to their eight Japanese utility customers for the construction of two extra 3.4 mtpa trains, which would increase the overall capacity of the plant from 7.5 mtpa to 14.3 mtpa. The expansion could be online by 2003. There had been some doubt over whether there were sufficient reserves available to the partners for an expansion. However, the recent announcement of an intention to proceed with the new phase of the development suggests that the participants are now satisfied that there is sufficient gas available, as is also evidenced by a Japanese LOI. This is even without utilising the reserves in the Gorgon field, discussed below.

2.5.4.2   Gorgon

The Gorgon area comprises four gas/condensate fields with a massive combined recoverable reserve base. The Gorgon field was discovered by WAPET (Western Australia Petroleum Pty Ltd) in 1981, who also discovered the nearby Chrysaor field in 1994.

WAPET is a joint venture of Chevron, Texaco and Shell, each with two-seventh stakes, and Ampolex with a one-seventh stake. In June 1996, Mobil acquired Ampolex. Ampolex's stake in the WAPET consortium was the company's most important asset and Mobil had been anxious to participate in new LNG schemes to offset the decline at its highly lucrative Arun LNG plant in Indonesia. It is estimated that the Gorgon and Chrysaor fields contain approximately 25 tcf of gas in place (GIP).

Figure 2.5.4.2A   Location Map: Offshore North-West Australia

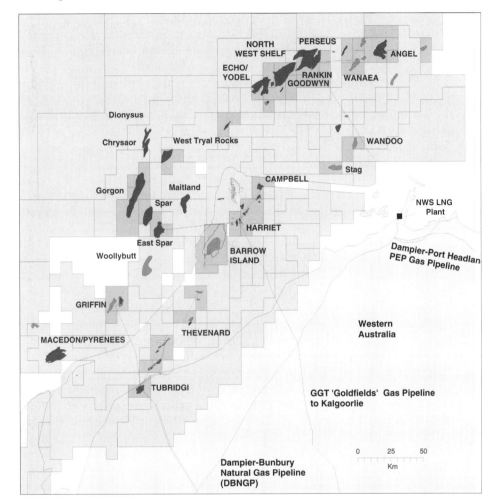

Over the years, a number of scoping studies have been performed to investigate the Gorgon area's development potential. LNG has always been the preferred option. However, the water depth, the high inerts content (mainly CO_2 and N_2) of the gas and stiff competition from other Pacific Rim projects (specifically the Woodside-operated North-West Shelf project) have reduced the viability of an export-based gas development.

Two development options have been identified for the Gorgon fields; a stand-alone development (involving the construction of a two-train green-field LNG plant with capacity of around 6.8 mtpa), or a joint development with the North-West Shelf joint venture (involving shared facilities and a partial merger of the joint venture groups). However, the announcement

Figure 2.5.4.2B   Gorgon Area—Estimated Recoverable Reserves

	GIP (TCF)	Dry sales gas (TCF)	Condensate (Mbbls)
Gorgon	7.0	4.7	20.0
North Gorgon	8.0	5.4	32.0
South Gorgon	3.5	2.3	10.0
Chrysaor	6.5	4.3	18.0
Total	25.0	16.7	80.0

by the North-West Shelf partners that they intend to add two extra trains to their facility without the inclusion of Gorgon reserves has put a serious question mark over the future of a Gorgon development. WAPET could still go it alone, but the economics are unlikely to be favourable, especially compared to those of the North-West Shelf expansion. Gorgon may eventually find its market, but it is unlikely to be until well into the next decade.

2.5.4.3   Other Australian Projects

Australia has several other large gas discoveries that have been proposed as potential LNG developments. These include the Scarborough field, the Scott Reef area, Petrel-Tern and Bayu-Undan which are discussed below. However, with the proposed expansion of the North-West Shelf facility, these projects are now all likely to be put back in time, so that there will be no significant developments until well into the next decade. As long as gas reserves continue to be turned up in the North-West Shelf area, increased capacity at Australia's one existing LNG plant will always be more competitive than expensive greenfield projects. Even after the addition of two new trains at the North- West Shelf, there is the possibility that new discoveries in the area could justify a fifth, and even further, trains.

Esso/BHP have outlined plans for a stand-alone LNG plant, to be fed by the estimated 8 tcf in the Scarborough field, 250 km off the West Australian coast. However, the Scarborough field, discovered as long ago as 1979, lies in 900 metres of water and would involve expensive new technology including sophisticated tension-leg platforms and associated floating production platforms.

The Scott Reef and Brecknock fields are two large, deepwater gas fields discovered by Woodside in the central Browse basin. Although the Scott Reef area contains estimated recoverable gas reserves of 22 tcf, the field is located 300 km from the nearest landfall, which is also in an environmentally sensitive area. Consequently, the development of the Scott Reef area is not anticipated until next century.

Petrel and Tern are two gas fields situated in the Bonaparte basin, around 250 km west of Darwin. However, with only around 3 tcf of estimated recoverable gas, more reserves will need to be proved up before an LNG project can be seriously countenanced. A minimum recoverable reserve base of between 4 and 5 tcf would be required to justify a medium-scale LNG project.

The 3.3–4.0 tcf Bayu-Undan discovery in area A of the Australia–Indonesia Zone of Cooperation straddles blocks held by BHP and Phillips. BHP has proposed developing Bayu–Undan as the world's first offshore LNG facility. Under the plan, the gas would be piped to a concrete gravity structure on 'Big Bank', a carbonate bank around 70 km west of the field (see map below). BHP is only one of a number of operators around the world who are examining the potential for offshore LNG. Recently, Mobil unveiled the design for a floating LNG barge. Phillips has proposed an alternative scheme for a Bayu–Undan LNG scheme. This would involve the construction of a 470 km pipeline to a 3.0 mtpa liquefaction plant near Darwin. The liquefaction process would use Phillips' own proprietary (cascade) technology, used in the Kenai facility in Alaska and recently licensed to the Atlantic LNG project in Trinidad.

In May 1997, Woodside and Shell preempted the decision on the Bayu–Undan LNG plant by proposing a combined Bonaparte Gulf and Zone of Cooperation LNG scheme. With an anticipated startup date of 2005, the planned 7.5 mtpa LNG facility in Darwin would be underpinned by gas reserves in Shell's Sunrise and Troubadour fields (reported to be 5 tcf), but would also need to call on additional reserves from the region to be able to fulfil long-term LNG contracts. Potential gas reserves that could be tied in to the scheme include Santos' Petrel–Tern fields in the Bonaparte Gulf (around 3.0 tcf) and the Bayu–Undan field.

2.5.5 Papua New Guinea

The Hides field is a large onshore wet gas field, located in the highlands region of Papua New Guinea (PNG) with ultimate reserves of around 5 tcf. Since gas demand in PNG is almost non-existent, the long-term development prospects for Hides hinge principally upon supplying a greenfield LNG project. The options for LNG development have been floated by the joint venture. The first envisages a gas pipeline following the route of the existing Kutubu oil pipeline to the south coast where a 200-kilometre subsea pipeline would then be required to transport the gas to Yule Island (100 km north-west of Port Moresby), the nearest possible site for an LNG plant. This route would allow the group to take advantage of existing infrastructure

Figure 2.5.4.3   The Bonaparte Gas Pool

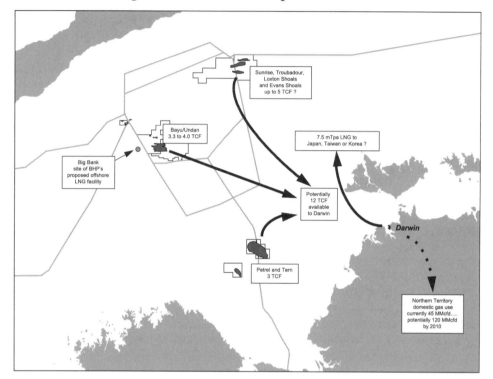

as well as encouraging the supply of gas to the local market. In addition, an LNG plant in the Gulf of Papua would favour development of the offshore Pasca and Pandora gas discoveries. The main disadvantage associated with this option is the distance of the project to LNG markets and the extra shipping time involved.

A second option involves a gas pipeline from Hides-Karius to Madang on the north coast, where sheltered deep water and proximity to Asian LNG markets would be an advantage. However, the pipeline would first have to tackle extremely rigorous topography and potential problems regarding the issue of landowners' rights.

An entirely Hides-based LNG project is doubtful; the additional gas which is being flared at other developments could boost the reserve base required for an LNG plant. However, prospects for an LNG scheme on PGN were put into further doubt when plans for an alternative pipeline to supply Queensland were mooted. In early 1996, Chevron, which has gas reserves in its onshore concession areas, announced that it had initiated investigations into the feasibility of a combined offshore/ central high-lands gas project which could include Hides gas. The project would involve the construction of a subsea and 990 km overland gas pipeline to take advantage of emerging markets in northern Queensland. Much depends on the go-ahead for a power plant and new mining developments in the northern Australian state, but first gas, at least from a Pandora development, could be early in the year 2000.

2.5.6   Alaska North Slope

Exxon, BP and Arco are joint owners of the Prudhoe Bay field on Alaska's north coast with its estimated gas cap of 26 tcf. The gas is currently being reinjected to maintain pressure for oil recovery, but at some stage gas sales could become viable. Two routes have been proposed for the pipeline which would be needed to take the gas to a suitable site for export. One route would be to pipe the gas west from Prudhoe Bay to a site on the Alaskan west coast. However, it is questionable whether such a location would be sufficiently ice-free. The second route would be south across Alaska via a 500-km Trans-Alaska Gas System (TAGS) to Valdez, which has been proposed by Yukon Pacific. The Alaska North Slope project would be a very expensive development because of the lengths of pipeline needed and because of the inhospitable conditions that will be encountered. The barrier for Alaskan LNG, like many other possible projects in the near term, is securing a buyer.

2.5.7   Yemen

After complicated and protracted tenders and negotiation, the Yemeni Ministry of Oil and Mineral Resources awarded a contract to Total to develop an LNG project. Hunt/Exxon/Yukong (the equity gas holders) took a share in the project. The share-holdings are now structured Hunt/Exxon/Yukong (38 per cent), Total (36 per cent) and the government of Yemen (26 per cent). The plan is to construct a 380-km pipeline from the Marib field to an LNG terminal at Balhaf on the Arabian Sea coast, which could be used to export around 5 mtpa of LNG to markets in Europe and Asia from as early as 2001; in addition YLNG has an MOU to supply Turkey.

Yemen LNG has the advantage that all reserves are onshore and in close proximity. Also, in contrast to Abu Dhabi and Qatar, the country is outside the Straits of Hormuz and is well-positioned for supply both to Europe and Asia. On the debit side, the project has no customers as yet and the political risk for Yemen must be considered high.

2.5.8   Sakhalin

Russia's Sakhalin Island has four projects known as Sakhalin I–IV. The Sakhalin I group comprises Exxon (30 per cent), Japan's Sakhalin Oil and Gas Development Co (Sodeco) (30 per cent) and Russia's Rosneft (17 per cent) and Sakhalinmorneftegaz (23 per cent). The consortium has reserves of around 15 tcf available to it, held in the Chaivo, Arkutun and Odoptu fields. Sakhalin II, the most advanced of the projects, is a joint venture of Marathon (37.5 per cent), Mitsui (25 per cent), Shell (25 per cent) and Mitsubishi (12.5 per cent), sometimes known as the MMMS group. Sakhalin II acreage contains the Lunskoye and Piltun Astokhsksoye fields and is thought to contain reserves of about 14 tcf. Sakhalin III and IV are still at the exploration phase.

Sakhalin's great strength is its proximity to the Japanese market. On the down side, however, the law on resource extraction is still confused in Russia, especially as relating to PSCs. Until this becomes clearer, foreign operators are likely to be reluctant to invest significant amounts of money. Another problem is the high cost of field development in the Sea of Okhotsk; the area is seismically active as well as being prone to shearing ice. Also, relations between Russia and Japan remain strained and this could limit the extent of Japanese investment in the area.

2.5.9   Middle East

Gas reserves in the Middle East, notably Saudi Arabia, Qatar and Iran, are sufficient readily to satisfy Asian LNG markets well beyond the lifetime of most Asian projects. In the event that Iran is 'welcomed' back into the international fold, South Pars alone has gas reserves of around 300 tcf which could be utilised in LNG projects.

2.6   ASIAN LNG: MATCHING SUPPLY AND DEMAND

2.6.1   Forecasting Supply and Demand

Matching LNG supply and demand is critical to the planning and decision-making processes for LNG projects. It is an imperative that investors are guaranteed payment for the LNG by the buyers. The buyers must therefore have a clear view of their own market. For the major buyers of North-East Asia this necessitates an ongoing forecasting effort by which estimates of industrial, residential and electricity generating demand are generated.

Energy forecasting methodology (and Wood Mackenzie's is typical) is built on historical relationships between gross domestic product (GDP):*per capita* and energy use in each of the following areas of the economy: electricity output, industry and non-energy use, transport and other sectors (including residential). Energy:(GDP: *per capita*) coefficients are calculated for each part of the economy, and the historical trends over time are inferred. Using forecasts of GDP and population growth, the trends are used to extrapolate future energy demand growth for each sector taking into account increasing efficiency of use over time. Demand projections are made for each fuel type.

Past trends as an indicator of future energy use can never be relied on exclusively. Consequently, a substantial range of qualitative information is used in the forecasting process, especially for Asia-Pacific countries where the current trend of economic re-structuring invalidates the use of trend analysis. Qualitative interpretation includes an analysis of market forces such as deregulation and liberalisation, as well as the physical pace at which infrastructure can be installed, the latter considerations being especially important in new markets in the emerging economies.

The two most critical factors are GDP growth and energy efficiency. The more mature the economy, the more efficient, so that the pace of economic growth alone (near- or long- term) in the traditional markets is not necessarily enough to create bigger LNG markets. Economies which require comparably large energy inputs per unit of GDP or *per capita* are regarded as intensive users of energy. Conversely, economies which require comparably small energy inputs per unit of GDP or *per capita* are regarded as extensive users of energy.

Overall energy demand growth for each sector of the economy can be forecast but the fuel mix within each sector is far more difficult to model. More qualitative factors impinge on the modelling process so historical trends in fuel mix can be utilised to a certain extent. The inevitable decline in the use of coal within the residential sector, and its replacement in the fuel mix by gas, is an evolutionary process which can be extrapolated into the future. Other parts of the economy are more difficult as fuel price forecasting, environmental legislation and macro-economics may be critical to the growth in demand for a particular fuel. The choice of fuel within each sector of each country's economy is a function of available infrastructure, combustion plant and price. Interfuel competition will act on all three parameters. To model interfuel competition in relation to price requires a highly developed econometric model which may not fully consider the role of infrastructure and combustion plant.

Ultimately, total electricity demand for each country must be forecast. Taking into account the fuel mix, the generation efficiencies of differing fuels and plant, it is possible to calculate the fuel inputs into electricity generation required to generate the electricity output. Clearly, technological gain and switching to more suitable fuels will, with all other things being equal, alter the total fuel inputs required for electricity generation. For each country, Wood Mackenzie has analysed the policy and infrastructure issues which will affect the development of the fuel mix in the electricity generation sector and have incorporated the information into a model as described.

For countries which produce oil or gas, indigenous energy production must be forecast in order to calculate import dependency ratios. Wood Mackenzie maintains a detailed analysis of producing oil and gas fields, but for longer-term modelling a view on ultimately discoverable resources must be considered. This is of particular importance for countries which might have limited potential resources and which, as a consequence, may, in the foreseeable future, turn from exporter to importer.

The final step in the forecasting process is to establish scenarios; these will normally be low-, medium- and high-side scenarios, and may be statistically simulated using key variables to derive a most likely outcome. Clearly, there will always be a range of demand numbers; these will only be indicative of a market. The acid test is getting the buyer to agree to a purchase agreement; only then does demand become a reality that will be matched by supply.

2.6.2　Asian Supply and Demand

The table and graph below show Wood Mackenzie's most likely forecast for LNG supply in the Asia-Pacific region up to 2015. This consists of contracted supply, planned extensions to existing projects (Malaysia

Figure 2.6.2A　Asia-Pacific LNG Supply (million tonnes)

	1995	2000	2005	2010	2015
Indonesia*	24.2	27.7	30	30	29
Malaysia	9.5	15.8	24.6	24.6	24.6
Australia	7.3	7.5	14.5	14.1	14.1
Brunei	5.7	6.2	6.0	6.0	6.0
Abu Dhabi	5.3	5.3	5.3	5.3	5.3
USA	1.2	1.3	1.2	1.2	1.2
Qatar	0	8.4	12.4	12.4	12.4
Oman	0	6.6	6.6	6.6	6.6
Total	53.2	78.8	101.6	99.6	98.6

* includes Tangguh

Figure 2.6.2A   Asia-Pacific LNG Supply

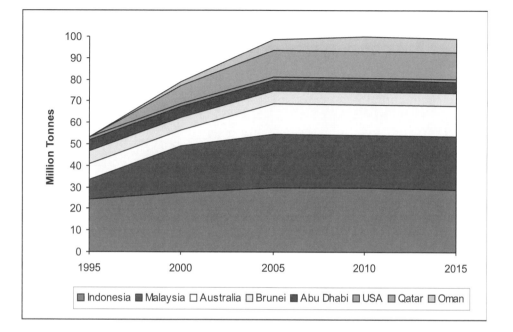

MLNG TIGA, Australia North-West Shelf) and new projects in Qatar (Qatargas and Ras Laffan) and Oman. It does not include other potential supply projects which would be competing for market positions.

The next graph shows a most likely scenario for LNG demand in Asia building from a level 53 mtpa in 1995 to 150 mtpa by 2015. The critical factor is when new markets will actually be able to take new supplies of LNG. Earlier sections indicated that India and China would be the next buyers, whilst Thailand would be unlikely to take LNG before the end of the next decade. Clearly, there are other scenarios, but what is clear is that for investors, timing is everything when the balance between supply and demand is so sensitive.

The following graph shows a high scenario forecast supply and demand match for LNG for the Asia-Pacific region. Forecast LNG supply is shown in the solid area and forecast regional demand in the stacked bars. Supply consists of existing contracts, excess production, project expansions and committed new projects. Of course, many existing contracts are likely to be extended and new projects will come onstream and so the supply/demand gap indicated is unlikely to exist to the extent shown, rather it is indicative of the timing of when new projects are likely to find market for their gas.

Figure 2.6.2B   Asian LNG Demand (high)

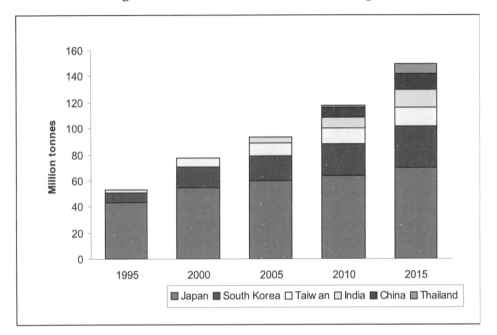

Some excess production could be replaced by new supply contracts which might be entered into in the interest of securing long-term supply.

Supply and demand in the short term are properly matched, however by the middle of the next decade LNG may be in over-capacity position, which would not be absorbed until the latter part of the decade. The graph indicates that supply and demand are largely in balance up to 2005, with existing projects, extensions, the two committed Qatar projects and Oman being sufficient to satisfy demand. Any unexpected deficit could be satisfied by surplus production. The implication of this is that there is little scope for a greenfield project up to around 2005.

Thereafter new projects would find markets rather more easily. After 2005, a gap appears in the market with a shortfall of around 20 mt by 2010, increasing to 50 mt in 2015. In this scenario, the window of opportunity for some of the greenfield projects described above will not be until post-2005.

A lower growth scenario, increasingly realistic in Asia's current energy markets would extend the period of over-capacity and thereby delay new projects. There is little doubt that LNG projects will be entering a new phase of competition with one another, rather than being used to displace oil or coal in the fuel mix. Competition between projects will be keen, with those able to offer the lowest gas prices likely to triumph.

Figure 2.6.2C   Asia-Pacific Supply–Demand Match

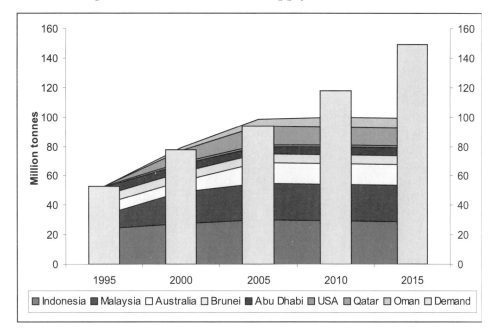

2.7   A NEW ERA OF LNG FOR EUROPE

A final point of interest is the emerging development of potential LNG markets in Europe. Already there are buyers showing interest in Middle East LNG, and one of Yemen LNG's competitive advantage is its relative proximity to Mediterranean markets.

In the traditional markets of Europe, LNG has struggled to be competitive against supplies of pipeline gas from countries such as Russia, Norway, Algeria and the Netherlands. However, there is now a growing interest in the emerging gas markets of southern and eastern Europe. These new markets, combined with new Atlantic basin liquefaction projects in Nigeria and, to a lesser extent, Trinidad, have created the prospect of a new expansionary phase for the European LNG market.

In southern Europe, Italy, Spain and Turkey are existing gas markets where rapid demand growth is expected, and these are being joined by the new gas markets of Portugal and Greece. In eastern Europe, gas penetration in the energy economy has historically been much higher than in southern Europe with an extensive pipeline network having being built up for importing Soviet gas during the Council for Mutual Economic Aid (COMECON) era. These eastern European countries are now anxious to diversify their sources of gas supply away from the former Soviet Union, and although import options remain geographically problematic, LNG could be part of this strategy.

One stimulus to the development of these new European markets has been the go-ahead of the Nigeria LNG project. LNG export from Nigeria has been talked about for around 30 years, but construction at the site has now finally started following gas sales agreements with ENEL (3 mtpa), Enagas (1.26 mtpa), Gaz de France (0.4 mtpa) and Botas (0.84 mtpa).

The project was, however, put into doubt when ENEL cancelled its contract at the end of 1996 following its inability to construct a reception terminal at Montalto di Castro on the western Italian coast. ENEL cited environmental opposition for its decision and Nigeria LNG is now seeking damages from ENEL. A solution to the problems has been reached with Gas de France and ENEL agreeing to swap with ENEL, such that Nigerian LNG is to be delivered to Montoir in France, while SNAM are to take gas from Russia and some Algerian LNG at La Spezia.

Spain has long-term LNG supply contracts with Algeria and Libya and has also bought spot cargoes from Abu Dhabi and Australia. From 1999, Enagas has contracted to take 1.2 mtpa of LNG from the liquefaction plant now under construction on Trinidad.

Turkey is one of the world's fastest-growing gas markets, and state gas company Botas has been very active negotiating supply agreements. The country is an existing importer of LNG from Algeria in addition to the gas sales agreement with Nigeria mentioned above, and has MOUs for LNG supply with Qatar, Yemen and even Egypt, where successful exploration in the Western Desert and Nile Delta has led Amoco to propose a liquefaction plant.

Portugal started to import gas from Algeria via the Mahgreb pipeline at the end of 1996. State gas company Transgas is also in talks with Nigeria LNG to take 0.5 bcm of the gas annually. The gas would probably be imported into Enagas' Huelva receiving facilities in Spain.

Also in 1996, Greece became the final member of the European Union to use natural gas when pipeline imports from Russia began to flow. In addition, an LNG terminal is being built at Revithoussa Island in the south of the country and the Public Gas Corporation of Greece (DEPA) has a gas sales agreement with Sonatrach of Algeria for the import of 0.6 mt of LNG from 1999.

These new LNG trades in Europe represent at present relatively small volumes. With the establishment of new infrastructure and the opening up of new markets, there is potential for major new growth. Of course, LNG will still be in competition with pipeline supplies, in particular from Algeria in southern Europe, but also from the North Sea, Russia and even eventually from the Middle East.

Chapter 3

LNG Project Feasibility

Andrew R. Flower

3.1 INTRODUCTION

The discovery of natural gas is only the first stage of a long process leading to an operational LNG project. As soon as it is established that sufficient reserves exist to support an LNG development, the potential project sponsors will want to establish whether development is technically and economically feasible. An assessment of LNG project feasibility will cover many of the same issues as a study of an oilfield development, with one major difference. The existence of a market for the natural gas will be a critical factor in determining whether economic development of the gas is possible and when it is likely to take place.

It is the markets for the natural gas which will determine whether LNG needs to be considered as one of the options to develop the gas reserves. For many natural gas discoveries there will be markets sufficiently close to allow the gas to be delivered to customers by pipeline. Indeed, some 96 per cent of the world's gas consumption is delivered to market in this way. Even in cases where pipelines are not a feasible option, LNG will not necessarily be the only alternative. Other options might include producing the gas, extracting condensate and then reinjecting the gas into the reservoir. The natural gas may also be injected into nearby oilfields to enhance oil recovery. Converting natural gas to liquid hydrocarbons such as diesel oil or other middle distillates is also emerging as a possible option for developing natural gas reserves. The technology was developed in the early part of this century and has been applied in a number of locations, mainly where lack of access to conventional oil markets meant the production of oil products from gas had strategic value. However, the capital costs are high and the process is relatively inefficient (only around 60 per cent of the natural gas is converted into liquids). As a result the process requires very low-cost gas supplies and, even then, in most potential applications, it is not yet economic against oil prices under US$20 per barrel. Considerable effort is being made by many companies to find ways of bringing the costs down to make the gas-to-liquids process competitive. If a breakthrough can be made in the costs, then gas-to-liquids conversion could be an attractive option for remote gas reserves. The liquids produced can be sold into oil markets, avoiding the need for long-term contracts which are required to underpin most LNG developments. They can also be transported in the same way as other oil products, which removes the need for specially built LNG ships. However, the gas-to-liquids process results in a product which will be sold into the oil market. It will not, therefore, have a direct impact on the markets for LNG.

The potential sponsors of the LNG project will normally carry out the assessment of project feasibility. However, it will be a key part of the process of providing other interested parties such as buyers, the host government and lenders with confidence that the proposed development is viable. Each of these parties will be prepared to support the project only if it is confident that any development is soundly based and will be capable of supplying LNG safely and reliably for the life of the project which will generally extend for 20 years or more. There will be many common features to be addressed in establishing an LNG project's feasibility wherever the natural gas discovery and the prospective markets are located. However, each project will have to face its own particular challenges to achieve technical and economic viability. It may, for example, be the size of the natural gas reserves and the producibility of the gas, the quality of the gas, finding a suitable location for the liquefaction plant, the distance from the market or the demand for LNG in the market. Individual feasibility assessments will be shaped by the major challenges faced by the particular development.

The assessment of project feasibility is an ongoing process which will develop as work on the project progresses. The project sponsors will probably want to carry out an initial study to decide whether LNG is a feasible option for the development of the natural gas reserves soon after they have been discovered. As the project becomes more closely defined, the uncertainty on capital and operating costs, markets, prices and volumes and other factors which impact on the feasibility will be reduced and this will be reflected by frequent updating of the feasibility assessment as more detailed data becomes available. Ultimately, a definitive project feasibility assessment is likely to be made to provide a basis on which the project sponsors can make the investment decision. This process can extend over a long period of time. Although it is theoretically possible to bring an LNG scheme onstream six to seven years after first discovery of the natural gas, time-frames have tended to be much longer. For example, the North Rankin natural gas field off the north-west coast of Australia was discovered in 1971 but the final decision to invest in an LNG scheme was not made until 1985, with first LNG production in 1989. The Nigerian LNG project was under consideration in various forms for nearly 30 years before the decision to invest was finally made.

A comprehensive feasibility assessment will cover the production of the natural gas, its liquefaction and transportation to the market. Potential markets for the gas will be identified and the outlook for prices will have to be considered. The impact of the host government on the project, including the fiscal regime and the environmental regulations, will also have to be addressed, as will the options for financing the project. Finally, the information on costs, production volumes, prices and taxes will have to be brought together in an economic model which will allow the prospective project sponsors to evaluate the economic viability of the planned investment. This chapter will focus on each of the main elements impacting on project feasibility. It will also look at some of the issues individual projects may have to face.

3.2   WHY LNG?

LNG is a relatively costly and inefficient method of moving natural gas to market. The gas has to be liquefied and transported in specially built ships to an LNG receiving terminal where it is turned back into its original, gaseous, form. This involves significant investment in facilities and the consumption of 10–15 per cent of the gas in its production, liquefaction, transportation and regasification. Pipelines employ simpler technology and involve a much smaller loss of gas (perhaps 2–3 per cent). As a result, a pipeline is generally the preferred method of transportation for natural gas. However, over long distances or where water too deep for pipelines has to be crossed, LNG is often the only technically and economically viable transportation option.

The effect of distance between the natural gas reserves and the market on the relative costs of pipelines and LNG projects is shown in Figure 3.2. The vertical axis of the graph represents the approximate cost per million British thermal units (mmBtu) of delivering gas over the distance shown on the hor-izontal axis. The cost of constructing a pipeline is largely a function of the length of pipe and the number of compressor stations installed on the line, so it is almost entirely dependent on the distance involved. An offshore pipeline is generally more expensive than one over the same distance onshore although, where the latter has to cross difficult terrain, environmentally sensitive areas or regions of high population density, costs can be similar or even higher than those for an offshore pipeline.

In the case of an LNG project, a significant proportion of the cost is in the construction and operation of the LNG plant. This cost is independent of the distance from the market. Shipping costs, although significant, especially when compared with those for moving oil, typically represent somewhere between 25 and 40 per cent of the total capital cost of an LNG scheme. As a result, the cost of moving LNG is less dependent on the distance between resource and market than for pipeline gas. As Figure 3.2 shows, for distances of less than around 2000 kilometres (1300 miles), offshore pipelines will generally be the lower-cost option, but in excess of that distance LNG will be more economic. Where an onshore pipeline is a viable option, it may be competitive with LNG up to a distance of 4000–5000 kilometres (2500–3300 miles). The cost estimates used in preparing Figure 3.2 can be no more than illustrative, since the actual costs for any development will be heavily dependent on its particular characteristics. Furthermore, the relative costs of pipelines and LNG may change as technology impacts on costs. As a result the crossover point between pipeline and LNG costs may well move over time. However, the overall message is that as distance between resource and market increases, LNG will tend to become an increasingly competitive option.

Cost may not be the only factor which has to be taken into account in deciding between an LNG and a pipeline development. The need to cross several international boundaries can increase the complexity of developing a pipeline project since the developers will have to deal with one or more

Figure 3.2   Gas & Oil Transportation Costs

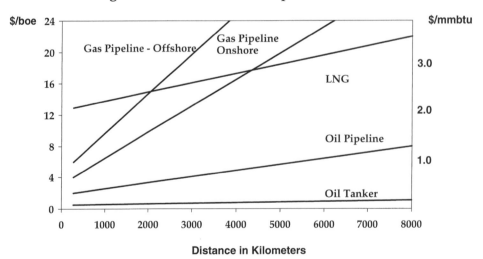

governments in addition to those of the host country and the buyer. LNG is generally transported across international waters so only the governments of the buyer and of the country in which the natural gas reserve is located are likely to be involved in the development. The other advantage that LNG enjoys over pipeline gas is the ability to deliver to two or more markets located some distance from each other. This can help facilitate the marketing of the natural gas since the bringing together of several buyers can achieve both the scale of demand and the build-up needed by the project. In contrast the economic viability of a long-distance pipeline may require that a large volume of natural gas be delivered to a single market. In a new market it may take some time and considerable investment to develop the size of market needed to justify the investment in the pipeline. Consequently, an LNG project may be the chosen method of developing a gas reserve even in cases where a pipeline development may be the lower-cost option.

Figure 3.2 also shows estimates of the cost of moving oil by pipeline and by ship. The costs are much lower than for natural gas. There is more energy per unit volume of oil than for gas and hence an oil pipeline can move more energy than a similar-sized gas pipeline. The cost of an oil tanker is much lower than an LNG ship making the cost of moving oil by ship only a small fraction of the cost of transporting LNG. The comparatively low cost of moving oil has meant that it has become an internationally traded commodity with, for example, only small variations in prices between markets. In contrast, the higher cost of moving gas has resulted in markets developing on a regional basis with different pricing regimes and, often, different contractual arrangements in each market.

3.3   THE LNG CHAIN

In assessing the feasibility of an LNG project each element of the chain which links the natural gas in the ground to the ultimate consumer of the natural gas has to be considered. This chain is shown in Figure 3.3. The main links are natural gas production, liquefaction, shipping, receiving terminal (including regasification), distribution of the regasified LNG and, finally, consumption of the gas. In the majority of the currently operational LNG schemes, the buyer takes delivery at its receiving terminal so gas production, liquefaction and shipping are the responsibility of the seller. This is an ex-ship or cost, insurance and freight (CIF) contract. The main difference between ex-ship and CIF is the point at which the buyer takes ownership of the LNG. In a CIF contract this is either as the LNG is loaded on to the vessel or on the voyage to the receiving terminal. Payment is made at the time that ownership transfers but the seller remains responsible for the transportation and insures the

Figure 3.3   LNG Chain

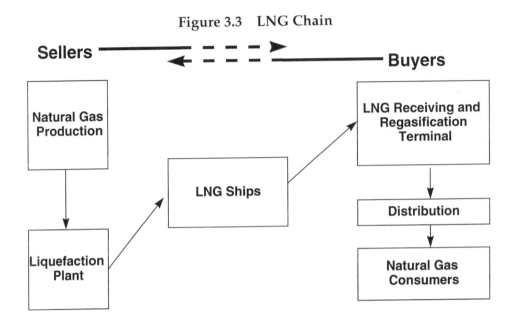

cargo on behalf of the buyer. In an ex-ship sale, ownership of the LNG transfers to the buyer as the LNG is unloaded and payment becomes due at that time. In the remainder of the operational projects, the buyer lifts the LNG from the liquefaction plant and is responsible for transporting the LNG to the receiving terminal. This is a free on board (FOB) contract. In these cases, it is the buyer who is responsible for the shipping, either owning the LNG ships or chartering them from a shipowner. The seller will be less interested in the economics of the shipping, but he will want to be sure that the buyers' plans for shipping will provide a safe and reliable offtake for the LNG.

All the LNG projects developed between 1964 and 1997 have had as their buyer (or buyers) financially sound companies. In Europe the buyers have been gas utilities, most of which are wholly or partly government-owned. In Japan, the buyers have been privately owned gas and electricity utilities, all of which are strong and reliable customers for an LNG project. The most recent entrants into the LNG market in Asia have been Korea and Taiwan. In both countries the buyers are companies in which the government is the major shareholder. In all these cases the buyer could be relied on to construct the facilities to receive, regasify and distribute the gas or, in the case of the electricity utilities in Japan, the power stations to consume the gas. As a result, the assessment of the feasibility of an LNG project only needed to consider gas production, liquefaction and shipping. The feasibility of the remainder of the chain was an issue for the buyer. The only issues downstream of the shipping phase that the seller needed to address in the feasibility study were the volumes the buyer would take during build-up and at plateau, the potential seasonal or other variations in offtake, the timing of the buyer's requirements and the expected price.

This may change as new markets for LNG are developed. In many countries, Independent Power Producers (IPPs) are expected to be the main customers for new supplies of natural gas. Such projects will provide a very different risk profile compared with traditional buyers. They will often be single-project companies without the balance sheet strength or the government support enjoyed by the gas or power utilities that have been the LNG buyers in the past. It may be necessary for the LNG seller to invest in the receiving terminal and the power plant in order to make the project viable. Even where this does not happen, the financing of the gas production, liquefaction plant and shipping is likely to be closely linked with the financing of the receiving terminal and the power plant. This means that the assessment of project feasibility may have to consider the entire LNG chain from gas production through to gas consumer.

3.3.1 Natural Gas Reserves

Each million tonnes of LNG delivered to a customer is equivalent to around 130 million stream cubic feet per day (mmscfd) of natural gas. Over 20 years this amounts to around 1 trillion cubic feet (tcf) of natural gas. Around 10–15 per cent of the gas is lost in the process of production, liquefaction and transportation of the LNG, so the daily rate of gas production necessary to deliver 1 million tonnes per annum (mtpa) to the customer is around 150 mmscfd. Over a 20-year life of an LNG sales contract this is equivalent to approximately 1.1 tcf of gas. The typical LNG project developed in the 1990s delivers around 7 mtpa to its customers, which means it needs a feed of over 1 billion cubic feet per day (bcf/d) of natural gas. LNG production has to be sustained at the plateau level for the life of the project so the gas reserves must be able to support production of over 1 bcf/d even in the twentieth contract year. The gas reserves needed to support an LNG project of this size have to be large—over 9 tcf when we take into account the gas which has to remain in the reservoir to allow production to be maintained throughout the life of the LNG sales contract. The gas production profile for a 7 mtpa LNG project is illustrated in Figure 3.3.1.

The need to ensure a regular and reliable supply of natural gas has meant that most LNG projects are based on non-associated natural gas (i.e. reserves found in fields where natural gas is the main hydrocarbon in the reservoir). Many oilfields have substantial volumes of natural gas associated with the oil but for these fields it will usually be the level of oil production which determines how much gas is produced. As a result, natural gas production is likely

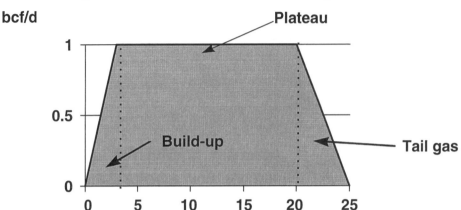

Figure 3.3.1   Gas Production for a 7 mtpa Scheme

**7mtpa for 20 years requires approx 7TCF
Tail gas and losses 2+TCF**

Total reserve requirement = 9+ TCF

to fluctuate with oil production. This will not generally be an acceptable basis
on which to develop an LNG project since the project owners will want to
operate the plant to maximise production in order to generate the revenues
needed to remunerate the capital investment. Furthermore, the buyers will
require a regular and reliable supply of LNG. The only major operational
LNG plant where associated gas provides a substantial proportion of the
feedgas is the ADGAS project in Abu Dhabi. Even here, additional natural
gas reservoirs have been developed to provide the back-up supply needed to
ensure LNG production is maintained at times when oil production is
reduced or halted.

Most of the operational LNG plants and those under construction in 1997
are located close to large gas reserves—much larger than the minimum
volume required to support a 20-year contract life. The LNG plant with the
smallest reserve base is located on the Kenai peninsula in southern Alaska.
This is a small LNG plant with a capacity of just over 1 mtpa. It was developed
in the very early days of the international LNG trade. Since then economies
of scale have resulted in the size of LNG plants increasing to a stage where
around 7 mtpa is typical of the capacity of projects being planned and built
in the latter part of the 1990s. However, the advantages of small-scale LNG
plants are once again being recognised and there is an increasing interest in
projects with a single LNG train producing of the order of 3 million tonnes
of LNG each year. Plants with even smaller capacity have also been studied.
As LNG markets diversify in the future, there are likely to be an increasing

number of buyers but each may have a smaller demand for LNG than some of the existing buyers. Smaller projects may be better sized for such customers and, hence, it may be easier to find buyers for the proposed production. The total investment for a small-scale project is considerably lower than for a world-scale project (say 7 mtpa capacity) which should make it easier to raise finance. Finally the smaller requirement for natural gas reserves to support small-scale projects means that they may provide an opportunity to develop smaller gas fields which are not currently considered economic.

The location of the reserves is important since the cost of piping the natural gas to a suitable location for the LNG plant (including access to deep water for the LNG ships) can be a significant cost for the project. The reserves may be onshore or offshore as shown in Figure 3.3.1A which lists each of the operational LNG projects and those under construction in 1997 together with the location of the gas fields which supply the LNG plant.

Figure 3.3.1A   LNG Projects—Location of Natural Gas Reserves

Status	Country	Plant	Location of Reserves
Existing	Algeria	Skikda	Onshore
		Arzew	Onshore
		Bethouia	Onshore
	Libya	Marsa el Brega	Onshore
	Alaska	Kenai	Offshore
	Brunei	Lumut	Offshore
	Abu Dhabi	Das Island	Offshore
	Indonesia	Arun	Onshore
		Bontang	On/Offshore
	Malaysia	Bintulu	Offshore
	Australia	Whitnell Bay	Offshore
	Qatar	Qatargas	Offshore
Under Construction	Qatar	Ras Laffan	Offshore
	Oman	Oman LNG	Onshore
	Nigeria	Bonny	Onshore
	Trinidad	Atlantic LNG	Offshore

3.3.2   Feedgas

Although nearly all LNG plants receive non-associated natural gas, the quality of the gas varies widely between projects. This can have a significant impact on the cost of both field development and the LNG plant which, in turn, will affect the economics of the overall project. The existence of condensate or other heavier hydrocarbons in the gas produced from the field can be of particular benefit. These products will be separated from the natural gas and sold in the oil market, providing an additional revenue stream which helps offset the cost of gas production. Condensates are an important additional revenue stream in projects such as Indonesia (Arun), Qatargas and the Australian North-West Shelf project. Liquid petroleum gases (LPG)—propane and butane—are also present in most natural gas fields. They are separated from the lighter gases, methane and ethane, before the feedgas enters the liquefaction process. Propane is used as a refrigerant gas for the initial cooling of the feedgas. In some projects, there are sufficient LPGs available to justify selling them separately from the LNG, thereby generating a further revenue stream. This happens, for example, in the Indonesian (Arun and Bontang), Abu Dhabi and Australian North-West Shelf projects.

In other projects, it is not economic to sell LPG separately since the volumes available are not large enough to remunerate the capital investment in facilities for its storage and loading. In these cases the LPGs remain with the methane and ethane in the LNG increasing the heat content (calorific value) of the LNG which adds to the income from each unit volume of LNG since payment is based on the heating value of the resulting gas vapour. Ethane, another hydrocarbon found in varying quantities in most natural gas reservoirs, is generally left in the LNG. However, it can be used as a feedstock for petrochemical manufacture so where there is a relatively high proportion of ethane in the feedgas its separation could provide a feedstock for an adjacent chemicals plant.

Impurities in the natural gas will increase costs since the liquefaction process needs a very clean feedgas in order to work effectively. All gas reserves contain contaminants such as water, carbon dioxide, hydrogen sulphide or trace elements such as mercury. Carbon dioxide, hydrogen sulphide or water would freeze out in the liquefaction process and stop the flow of gas while mercury would have a catastrophic corrosive effect on the aluminium which is used extensively in the process units. Contaminants have to be removed before the gas enters the liquefaction process which can add significantly to the capital cost of the project. The Natuna field in Indonesian waters north of the island of Borneo contains at least 40 tcf of methane and is relatively close to LNG markets in Japan, Korea and Taiwan. Unfortunately, it also contains around 200 tcf of carbon dioxide. The technical problems and the costs of separating out and disposing of the carbon dioxide has meant that the gas remains undeveloped over 20 years after it was first discovered. The design of the liquefaction process will have to take into account the composition of the feedgas. This can have a significant impact on the overall cost of the plant, especially where it has to process gas from two or more fields which may provide feedgases with very different compositions.

In some cases there may be local markets which can receive natural gas by pipeline, but are not large enough in themselves to consume more than a small proportion of the reserves in place. This can provide an opportunity for joint development of a domestic gas scheme and LNG exports. Such a domestic gas scheme can generate extra revenues to supplement income from the sale of LNG and, as a result, impact on the overall project economics. This has been the case with the Australian North-West Shelf project where natural gas has been piped some 1000 miles south to the Perth area for local use. A second example is the Arun LNG project in Indonesia where some of the gas produced from the Arun gas field is used domestically for fertiliser production.

The one common requirement for any LNG project is that the cost of the feedgas delivered to the LNG plant (after taking into account revenues from condensates, LPGs and gas sold for local use, if any) must be low enough to allow LNG to be delivered to the customer at a price which, after taking into account the buyers' storage and regasification costs, is competitive with other fuels in the market. The costs which a project can afford to incur in producing the natural gas and delivering it to the plant will depend on the cost of the LNG plant and the LNG ships. Thus, for example, a project located in the Middle East and supplying Japan will have relatively high shipping costs and will generally have to be supplied with lower-cost gas than a project located in South-East Asia, much closer to the market. Overall, it is likely that an LNG project will need to be supplied with natural gas which costs less than US$1/mmBtu to produce.

With a 7 mtpa LNG plant consuming of the order of 1 bcf/d of gas, the capital costs of the upstream facilities are likely to be high and will, in many cases, amount to over US$1 billion. This will be a key area where opportunities for cost optimisation have to be identified. It may be possible to develop low-cost fields first, bringing higher-cost facilities into operation later. It may also be possible to produce gas initially using the natural pressure of the reservoir with compression being installed later to maintain production as the reservoir pressure declines. In both these examples, the effect will be to defer capital expenditure, thereby improving the return on the overall project investment.

3.3.3 LNG Plant

The site for the liquefaction plant will generally be chosen as close as possible to the gas reserves to minimise the cost of piping the gas to the plant. The plant site also has to have close access to deep water. The largest

LNG ships in operation in the 1990s (with the capacity to carry 135,000 cubic metres of LNG) need around 14 metres' water depth to berth safely. It is possible to use a long jetty to access deep water—a 5-kilometre jetty was originally used at the Brunei LNG plant—but this will add to project costs. It is also necessary to select a location with sheltered berthing facilities and easy access for the LNG ships in order to minimise the risk of delays to the fleet. A further requirement of the plant site is good soil conditions to carry the weight of the process facilities and tanks. Any requirements for land reclamation or major piling to support the tanks and other equipment will add to the development costs.

Having chosen the site for the plant, one of the next key decisions for the project developers will be the capacity of the plant and number of LNG trains. An LNG train consists of the gas processing and liquefaction units required to treat and liquefy the gas. Most LNG plants consist of two or more LNG trains each of which can operate independently of the others. This means that in the event of problems on one train, or when a train is shut down for overhaul or maintenance, the others can remain in operation, thereby minimising the risk of total loss of production for both the LNG producer and the buyer. The Kenai plant in Alaska was the only LNG plant in operation in 1997 based on a single train. However, the plant in Trinidad, which is due to commence production around the year 2000, is planned to start life as a single-train unit. Many of the plants in operation have had extra trains added as they have been expanded to meet increased demand. The Bontang plant in Indonesia was originally constructed as a two-train plant. By 1997 it had six trains in operation, a seventh being commissioned and an eighth due to come onstream by the year 2000. A ninth train was also being considered for commissioning after that year.

Figure 3.3.3   Capacity of LNG Plants Supplying Asian Markets

LNG Plant	Original No of Trains	Original Nominal Capacity	No of Trains in 1997	Capacity in 1997
Kenai (Alaska)	1	1.1	1	1.3
Brunei	5	5.3	5	6.6
Abu Dhabi	2	2.1	3	5.5
Bontang (Indonesia)	2	3.2	6	15.6
Arun (Indonesia)	3	4.5	6	12.0
Malaysia (1 and 2)	3	6.0	6	15.9
Australia (N.W. Shelf)	3	6.0	3	7.5
Total	19	28.2	30	64.4

The size of LNG trains has increased over time as technology has improved. The early plants built in the 1960s and early 1970s used trains with capacities of around 1 mtpa but this increased to around 2–2.5 mtpa by the late 1980s when the Australian North- West Shelf project was commissioned. The Oman LNG project, which is due to come onstream in the year 2000, has LNG trains designed to produce around 3.4 mtpa of LNG. Designs now exist for train sizes of 4 mtpa or more. The decision on the size of the LNG plant will take into account a number of factors including the size of the gas reserves, the technology chosen for the liquefaction of the natural gas and the expected demand for the LNG. Figure 3.3.3 lists the design capacity of each of the operational LNG plants supplying the Asian market and their estimated 1997 production capacity. All the projects are producing more than their original design capacity and in some cases the increase is very large. In designing and constructing LNG trains owners and contractors have generally built in significant margins to minimise the risk of the project failing to meet its contractual obligations with the buyers. As operational experience is gained, confidence in the ability of the plant to produce above design capacity increases and the project is able to offer to sell the additional LNG on a long-term basis. Debottlenecking of the facilities can further add to the production capacity. For example, the Australian North-West Shelf plant is producing and selling some 25 per cent more LNG than the design capacity of the original three trains. In many LNG plants, major additions to capacity are achieved by building additional LNG trains. This is a cost-effective way of increasing capacity since advantage can be taken of existing infrastructure such as storage and loading facilities. As Figure 3.3.3 shows, both of the Indonesian LNG plants, the Abu Dhabi plant and the Malaysian plant have all had additional trains added. The most dramatic increase in capacity is at the Bontang plant in Indonesia where the number of trains has increased from two to six and the production capacity has increased nearly fivefold over the original design. As discussed above, further LNG trains are under construction and being planned at Bontang which will take its production capacity to over 20 mtpa by the turn of the century.

The process for the liquefaction of the feedgas is essentially the same as that used in domestic refrigerators, but on a massive scale. A refrigerant gas is compressed and released through a valve which reduces its temperature (the Joule Thompson effect). It is then used to cool the feedgas. The temperature of the feedgas is eventually reduced to minus 161 degrees centigrade (minus 253 degrees Fahrenheit) at which point methane, the main constituent of natural gas, liquefies. At this temperature all the other hydrocarbons in the natural gas will also be in liquid form. In the LNG process constituents of the natural gas (propane, ethane and methane) are used as refrigerants either individually or as a mixture. The earliest LNG plants (for example the Kenai project in Alaska) employed a cascade process developed by the Phillips Company where separate refrigerants (propane, ethylene and methane) are used in sequence to liquefy the feedgas. In this process, ethylene is used as a refrigerant since it is a product widely available on the open market and avoids the need to separate the ethane from the feedgas. In the case of the Kenai project, the natural gas supplied to the plant consists mainly of methane so both propane and ethylene refrigerants are brought into the plant from outside sources.

A simplified diagram of the cascade process is shown in Figure 3.3.3A. The first refrigerant circuit uses propane which, in addition to cooling the feedgas, also precools the ethylene and methane used in the second and third stages of the liquefaction process. The feedgas, which emerges from this initial cooling stage at a temperature of minus 35 degrees centigrade, is then passed through the second refrigerant, ethylene, which brings its temperature down to minus 105 degrees centigrade. The ethylene also cools the methane refrigerant used in the final stage of the process. The methane refrigerant brings the feedgas temperature down to minus 161 degrees centigrade and the resulting liquid (LNG) is pumped to the storage tanks to await loading on to an LNG ship. The cascade process employs plate fin heat exchangers which are also used in liquefaction technologies now being offered by other manufacturers.

Most of the LNG plants built in the 1970s, 1980s and 1990s employed technology developed by Air Products and Chemicals Inc. (APCI) which uses a mixed component refrigerant (MCR) made up of propane, ethane and methane. In more recent versions of this process, a propane circuit is

Figure 3.3.3A   Classic Cascade Process

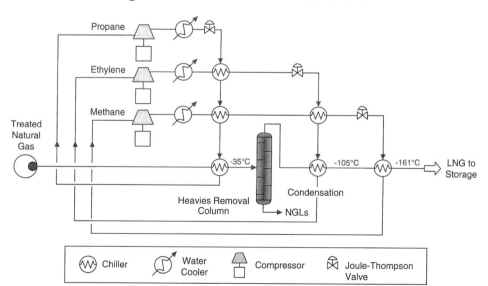

used as a precoolant for both the feedgas and the MCR which increases the overall efficiency of the process. A simplified diagram of the propane-precooled mixed refrigerant process is shown in Figure 3.3.3B. The propane precooling circuit reduces the temperature of the feedgas to minus 35 degrees centigrade. The feedgas is then passed through spirally wound tubes in the main heat exchanger where its temperature is reduced to minus 161 degrees centigrade by the MCR refrigerant. In both the cascade and the APCI processes the final removal of the heavy hydro-carbons (LPGs and condensates) is made after the precooling of the feedgas by the propane refrigerant. Although the APCI technology has been dominant in the last 25 years, advanced versions of the cascade technology were developed during the mid-1990s and a modern version of the Phillips process, first used in the Kenai project in Alaska in the 1960s, has been chosen by Trinidad LNG project. Other suppliers are also developing their own liquefaction processes. This means that there are now alternative types of heat exchanger available to companies planning a new LNG project. Each of the processes has its own advantages and disadvantages, but the project developer now has the opportunity to choose the process best suited to its particular requirements.

The compressors are important pieces of equipment in the LNG plant whatever the technology. In the early LNG plants, the compressors were steam-driven but more recent plants have used industrial gas turbines as the compressor drivers. This has reduced capital costs since the need for steam-generating facilities and water treatment plants for the boiler water

Figure 3.3.3B   Propane Precooled Mixed Refrigerant Process

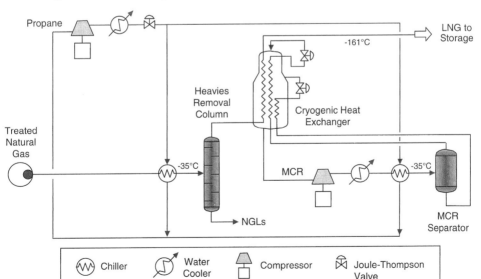

feed has been eliminated. One of the contributors to the increase in train capacity has been the use of ever-larger gas turbines.

In most LNG plants sea water is used as a coolant. This requires facilities to handle large volumes of water drawn from some distance offshore and from as great a depth as practicable to ensure that the temperature of the inlet water is as low as possible to increase the efficiency of the cooling process. The Australian North-West Shelf plant is unique in relying entirely on air cooling. The Kenai plant in Alaska uses air cooling in the initial stages of the liquefaction process and freshwater cooling for the final, methane, refrigerant circuit.

3.3.4 Storage and Loading

After the gas has been processed into a liquid it is transferred to the storage tanks to await loading into the LNG ships. The tanks are generally constructed of nickel steel (i.e. steel containing 9 per cent nickel) to withstand the extremely low temperatures of the LNG. The tanks are insulated to maintain the liquid at minus 161 degrees centigrade. Some of the stored LNG boils off and the resulting vapour is used as fuel gas for the plant. There are three main designs of LNG storage tank: single containment, double containment and full containment (Figure 3.3.4). A single containment tank has a nickel steel wall and roof. A second carbon steel wall surrounds the tank and holds the insulation. This second wall is

Figure 3.3.4   LNG Storage Tank Design

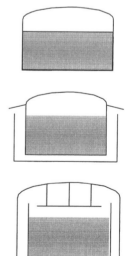

- Single containment

   – Inner shell contains liquid and vapour

- Double containment

   – Inner shell contains liquid and vapour

   – Outer shell contains liquid only

- Full containment

   – Inner shell contains liquid only

   – Outer shell contains liquid and vapour

not designed to hold the LNG so, in the event of a failure of the inner tank, the LNG could leak out. The tank is normally surrounded by a bund (low wall) which would contain any spilled LNG. Facilities to spray foam and water on to the LNG will also generally be installed to ensure that the risk of ignition of the vapour from any spilled LNG is minimised. A double containment tank has an inner nickel steel wall and roof. A second outer concrete wall surrounds the tank and is designed to contain the LNG in the event of the inner wall failing. Vapour would vent to the atmosphere in these circumstances but foam and water spray would be used to protect against any risk of an ignition. Finally, a full containment tank has an inner tank, with nickel steel walls and an aluminium floating roof, which contains the liquid LNG. It is surrounded by a second concrete outer tank which can contain both the liquid LNG and the vapour.

The full containment tank provides maximum integrity against failure and, hence, the tanks can be placed much closer together than for single containment tanks. However, the costs are significantly higher so it may be an expensive option especially if there is adequate land area available for the tank farm. Single containment tanks require a greater distance between tanks, but the cost of each tank is lower. Whatever the choice of tank design, sufficient safeguards are put in place to ensure that the risk of an LNG spill is an absolute minimum. Many of the tanks in the early LNG plants were single containment. Following some problems with cryogenic tanks (in LPG rather than LNG storage), there was a move towards full containment tanks. The most recent LNG projects to come onstream (Malaysia, Australia North-West Shelf and Qatargas) have all used full containment tanks. The storage tanks represent a significant part of the total cost of the LNG plant—as much as 20 per cent or more. In addition to choosing the design of the storage tanks, the project developers will have to make decisions on the total volume of the storage capacity and the number of tanks to be built.

The total volume of storage is determined taking into account the need to provide sufficient capacity to minimise the risk of delay to the LNG ships, balanced against avoiding unnecessary additional capital costs of extra storage capacity. The optimum volume of storage required is usually evaluated using a sophisticated simulation programme which models the operation of the LNG plant and the shipping fleet, taking into account the probabilities of the plant shutting down and the ships being delayed by weather or other factors. The main factor determining the storage needs is usually the size of the LNG ships. Most operational plants have the capacity to store at least two shiploads of LNG. Thus a project using 135,000-cubic metre ships would require about 250,000–300,000 cubic metres of storage. This is generally achieved with three to five tanks each with a capacity of between 60,000 and 80,000 cubic metres. Larger tanks with a capacity of up to 200,000 cubic metres have been designed and are currently being developed for use at receiving terminals where buyers often have to hold strategic stocks of LNG to deal with possible interruptions to supply and fluctuations in demand. Operators of liquefaction plants generally prefer to use several smaller tanks to increase flexibility and to minimise any disruptions in the event of a tank being out of commission.

3.3.5   LNG Plant Design and Construction

In most LNG projects it is the LNG plant which has a longer time-frame for design and construction than any other part of the chain. It is also likely to be the major item of capital investment for the project developers. Therefore, the LNG plant will be critical in determining both the overall project development schedule and the total project cost. However, work on the LNG plant has to be co-ordinated closely with the planning and development of natural gas production, the design and construction of the LNG ships, the financing of the project and the marketing of the LNG.

The main stages in the design and construction of an LNG plant are; conceptual engineering, front end engineering design (FEED) and, finally, the detailed engineering and construction of the plant itself. As the work moves through each of these stages the design of the plant becomes more closely defined, the equipment needs are identified and the confidence in the estimated cost increases. Conceptual engineering involves turning the initial ideas of the project sponsors into an outline definition of the LNG plant which can be used to call for bids from the contractors for the FEED study. Before moving into the conceptual engineering, the project sponsors will have decided on the approximate size of the plant based on assessment of the requirement for LNG in the market and of the size and producibility of the gas reserves. During conceptual engineering, the targets for plant capacity will be turned into firm plans to produce the required volumes of LNG. Conceptual engineering will generally be carried out by a team of engineers drawn from the project sponsors or from one of the sponsors appointed as technical leader. Contractors may be used to provide specialist expertise and initial contact will be made with equipment manufacturers, including licensors of liquefaction technology.

As conceptual engineering progresses, decisions will be made on the number of trains, the design capacity of each train and the basic layout of facilities on the plant site. Storage requirements are also likely to be determined in consultation with the team working on shipping requirements. The preferred liquefaction process will probably be identified at this stage. It is possible to defer this decision but delay is likely to result in additional costs since it will be necessary to run with two (or more) alternative plant designs in parallel. Having identified the preferred liquefaction process it will be possible to work with the licensor of the technology to determine the number and size of the turbines needed to provide compression in the plant. It is also likely at this stage that a decision will be made on whether to use air or water cooling for the plant. One of the key factors to be taken into account in designing the plant is the specification of the feedgas. This will determine what facilities are needed to treat the gas before it enters the liquefaction process. It will also be an important factor in determining the heating value and the constituents of the LNG which will be produced.

The specification of the LNG will be important in the marketing since prospective buyers will want to be confident that the LNG received from the project will be compatible with their facilities and meet the requirements of users of the regasified LNG. For example, each buyer will want to know the heating value of the LNG it will receive. If it is higher than LNG (or pipeline natural gas) it already receives from other sources then it may be necessary to install nitrogen injection facilities to reduce the heating value. Conversely, LNG with a low heating value may have to be spiked with LPG to bring it to a similar level to its other supplies. The density of the LNG will also be important to the buyer. If LNGs of different densities are stored in the same tank there is a risk that the contents could roll over—a phenomenon whereby the lighter contents rise to the top of the tank. If this happens rapidly there is the possibility of a rapid build-up of gas pressure which could cause the tank to fail. Consequently, if the LNG offered by the project has a very different density from other LNGs that the buyer receives, then it may be necessary for the buyer to segregate the LNG to be received from the project by building new tanks or by installing mixers on the existing tanks.

If condensate and LPGs are to be extracted from the feedgas and sold as separate product streams then facilities will have to be included for their handling, storage and export from the plant. The need to load products other than LNG on to ships will impact on the design of the berthing facilities. The LNG plant must be able to berth, load and dispatch the LNG ships with a minimum of delay. Any disruption to the scheduling of the LNG fleet could have a major impact on the project's ability to supply the LNG in the volumes and on the schedule agreed with the buyers. Therefore, it may be necessary to provide separate berthing facilities for condensate and LPG ships, although on some projects LNG and LPGs are loaded from the same berth.

The output from the conceptual engineering will be a statement of requirements (SOR) for the LNG plant. This document will provide the basis for the production of a new cost estimate which will be the first in which some confidence can be placed. Even so, at this stage the range of uncertainty of the estimate is likely to be wide—probably plus or minus 30 per cent around the base case estimate. The project sponsors will use the SOR as a basis on which to prepare bid packages to call for proposals from contractors to carry out the FEED work. The selected FEED contractor will prepare a more detailed design of the plant. The requirement for all major pieces of equipment will be identified during FEED and final decisions will be made on such key issues as the number, size and type of storage tanks and the number and size of turbines. The appointed FEED contractor will work closely with a team from the project sponsors (or the appointed technical leader) since final choices will be made on key aspects of the plant design. It is possible that contracts may be awarded during the FEED process for major items of equipment which have the longest lead times and hence could impact on the overall project schedule. The storage tanks often fall into this category and it may also be necessary to place orders for the heat exchangers and the turbines.

Completion of the FEED will allow a new cost estimate to be made with a reduced level of uncertainty—possibly a range of plus or minus 20 per cent around the base case estimate. It should also be possible, at this stage, to develop a schedule for construction of the plant which will provide a basis for estimating the phasing of capital expenditure. This will be an important issue in both the economics of the investment and seeking finance for the project. The objective will be to keep early expenditure as low as possible since the sponsors will want to minimise the time interval between the spending of the capital and the receipt of revenues. However, it will also be important to ensure that capital expenditure is scheduled in a way which minimises the risk of a delay to startup of LNG production.

One of the main outputs from the FEED work will be the bid documents which will be used to invite contractors to tender to carry out detailed engineering, procurement of equipment and construction of the plant—the so-called engineering, procurement and construction (EPC) contract. The EPC contact will normally be awarded to a single main contractor or a consortium of two or more contractors brought together for the purpose of working on a particular LNG project. There are only a small number of contractors around the world with capacity or experience to build a large-scale LNG plant so at this stage there are unlikely to be more than three or four bidders. The main contractor may be asked to bid on a lump-sum, turnkey basis under which the engineering, procurement and construction is carried out for a fixed sum of money. The contractor agrees to deliver to the project sponsors, by an agreed date, a plant ready for startup and meeting the specifications set out in the EPC contract. The lump-sum fee has to cover the cost of equipment and labour and the contractor's own costs and profit. Under this type of contract the project developers can have some confidence in the final cost of the plant, although variations to the design during the construction can lead to changes in the lump-sum payment. There will also normally be penalty clauses in the EPC contract requiring the contractor to compensate the sponsors in the event that startup is delayed for other than *force majeure* reasons or changes to the plant specification by the sponsors after award of the EPC contract.

An alternative approach is to use a reimbursable contract under which the contractor charges the project developers for the actual cost of equipment and labour. The contractor receives a fee which may be a fixed amount or a percentage of the final cost. As for a lump-sum, turnkey contract, there may be penalty clauses if the plant is not ready for startup as agreed in the EPC contract. Whichever route is chosen for the EPC contract, the sponsors will be looking for a cost estimate for the plant which they can use to make a final decision on whether to commit to the project. The signature of the EPC contract will normally be co-ordinated with the signature of other project agreements. These will include the LNG sale and purchase agreement (SPA) with the buyers, any agreements with the host government covering fiscal issues or land use, agreements for the acquisition of the LNG ships and any financing agreements.

A team of engineers from the project sponsors (or from the appointed technical leader) will work closely with the contractor to ensure that decisions affecting the design and construction of the plant can be made quickly and effectively. The main contractor will use a number of sub-contractors to carry out work on the plant. The contractor will probably take over responsibility for any orders for long lead time equipment made by the project sponsors during the FEED stage of the work. The schedule for designing and constructing the LNG plant will vary with location and with the size of the plant. Figure 3.3.5 illustrates a possible schedule for a two-train project. The total time from commencement of work on the conceptual engineering to ready for startup of the first train is of the order of six to seven years with two to three years of design work (conceptual engineering and FEED) preceding an EPC contract of around four years. It is possible to reduce this time-frame by overlapping work, particularly during the conceptual engineering and FEED stages. For example, the bid packages for the EPC contract may be released in stages so that preparation of EPC bids by contractors can commence before FEED is complete. The early ordering of the long lead time equipment can also contribute to the shortening of the time-frame. However, it is unlikely that the schedule can be compressed into much less than five years.

In Figure 3.3.5 the second train is shown as being ready for startup six months after the first train. This would allow the contractor to build the two trains in parallel, making optimum use of labour by transferring them between trains. It also avoids the costly process of demobilising and then remobilising the workforce. Overall, costs are likely to be optimised with this approach. However, if the build-up of LNG deliveries agreed by the buyer is relatively slow then this would result in facilities remaining under-utilised and it may be more efficient to delay startup of the second (and any subsequent) trains until their production is needed by the market.

Figure 3.3.5   LNG Plant Development Schedule

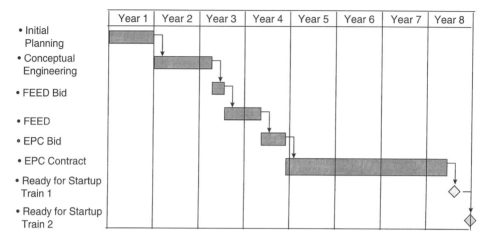

Costs will generally be higher with this approach, but the delay in incurring capital expenditure should more than compensate in terms of the overall project economics. The scheduling of plant design and construction has to be closely co-ordinated with work on other parts of the project. The marketing of the LNG will be particularly important in determining the LNG plant schedule. In some circumstances the lack of an immediate market opportunity for the project may provide extra time for work on planning the plant. However, it will be important to ensure that unnecessary early expenditure on plant design is avoided since this can have a significant negative impact on the profitability of the project.

3.3.6   LNG Plant Capital and Operating Costs

Each LNG plant is designed and built to meet the specific requirements of the project and costs vary widely depending on such factors as location, production capacity, liquefaction process and the number of tanks and the total volume of the storage facilities. The state of the contracting industry at the time bids are called can also have an impact. At a time when activity in the industry is low, contractors may be willing to put in a very competitive bid in order to win the business. In contrast, if the world economy is buoyant, with construction activity in the oil, gas and chemical industries high, then the contractors may not be as anxious to obtain the business and bids may be priced higher. However, there are broad trends in LNG plant costs as is shown in Figure 3.3.6. The costs of constructing LNG plants in real 1997 US dollars per tonne of installed production capacity have been estimated, based on reported costs for the LNG plants in operation in 1997 and those under construction. An average cost has been calculated for five-year periods commencing with the period from 1965 to 1970. Included in the cost estimates are all the plant facilities—site preparation, gas treatment, heat exchangers, utilities (power, cooling water, etc.), turbines, storage tanks and berthing facilities. The estimates are based on reported figures for each plant, but the information is, in some cases, limited and in others the basis for the quoted costs is not clear. For example, there may be uncertainty as to whether such items as the cost of site preparation or loading facilities have been included. Therefore the numbers have had to be adjusted to bring the estimates, as far as is possible, on to a consistent basis.

As Figure 3.3.6 shows, costs declined in the 1970s and early 1980s as technology advanced. During this period, average train sizes increased from 1 mtpa to over 2 mtpa and gas turbines replaced steam turbines. The late 1980s were dominated by the Australian North-West Shelf project which proved to be a high-cost plant partly because of its remote location in a country where labour costs tend to be higher than those for some of the earlier LNG plants. There was some decline in costs in the early 1990s but the biggest reduction is being seen in the plants due to come into operation between 1995 and the year 2000. The reported cost estimates for these plants suggest we are seeing a return to the cost trends established before 1985. Plants under construction in the late 1990s are estimated to be costing between US$250 and US$300 per tonne of installed capacity. This means that a 7 mtpa plant being constructed to come onstream around the year 2000 would cost of the order of US$2 billion. The phasing of the capital expenditure on the plant is an

Figure 3.3.6   Liquefaction Plant Costs

$_{96}$ / tpa Capacity

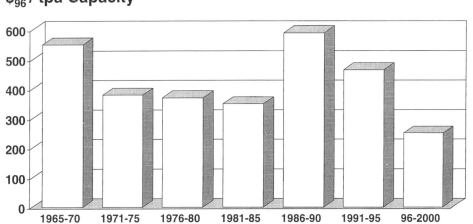

important input into the evaluation of project economics. Generally expenditure will build up rapidly, peaking around 12 months before startup when the size of the workforce on the plant site is likely to be at its maximum level.

The operating costs of LNG plants are very dependent on their location. Many of the operational plants have been built in areas remote from major centres of population and, hence, accommodation and other facilities for the workforce have had to be constructed. Furthermore, the staff operating such plants have had to be paid wages which encourage them to move to a remote location. In addition, costs will be incurred in maintaining the plant and ensuring that it is available to operate as near as possible to full capacity, 24 hours per day, 365 days per year. There will be unscheduled downtime as equipment fails, but experience shows that plants can be operated for well over 95 per cent of the available time. Regular maintenance will involve each LNG train being taken out of service for a full overhaul about once every three years. These routine overhauls generally take around a month and are scheduled so that the other trains remain in operation while the work is carried out. Dry-docking of the ships is co-ordinated with plant maintenance to minimise the impact on deliveries to the buyers. As far as possible the periods of planned maintenance are scheduled to coincide with times of the year when the buyers' consumption of natural gas is at a low point. For example, for buyers in Japan, this tends to be in April/May and September/October, outside the periods of peak demand for heating in the winter or air conditioning in the summer. In total, the annual operating and maintenance costs generally average around 3 per cent to 5 per cent of the plant capital costs. This means that a 7 mtpa LNG plant will involve operating costs of US$60–100 million per year.

3.3.7   Transportation

The shipping phase of an LNG project provides the link between the LNG sellers and the LNG buyers. It is the single point where their facilities come together, whether it is the sellers' LNG ships delivering LNG to the buyers' receiving terminals in an ex-ship or CIF sale or the buyers' LNG ships arriving to lift cargoes at the sellers' liquefaction plant in an FOB sale. Consequently, transportation is a key part of the feasibility study for any LNG project, but its treatment will be very different depending on whether the sale is on an FOB or a CIF basis. In the case of an FOB sale the capital and operating costs of the ships are for the account of the buyer so these costs will not feature in the feasibility study. However, the project sponsors will want to be sure that the buyers are committed to providing a fleet of

LNG ships with sufficient capacity to lift the volume of LNG it is planned to produce. For a CIF or ex-ship sale the operating and capital costs of the LNG ships will be a major factor for the project sponsors in evaluating the economic viability of the overall project.

Whether the buyers or the sellers are responsible for the LNG ships, the first stage in any feasibility study will be to determine how many ships are needed to deliver the volume of LNG produced by the plant to the buyers' receiving terminal (or terminals). This will be mainly a function of three variables: the size of the LNG ships, their speed and the distance between the LNG plant and the buyers' facilities. However, the production capacity of the LNG plant, the number of berths, the amount of storage capacity at the LNG plant and the receiving terminals and the risk of delays at both the loading and unloading ports also have to be taken into account in determining the number of ships. At this stage, the choice of design (supported spherical tanks, as licensed by Moss-Rosenberg, or membrane tanks) will not be a factor since either type of ship can be designed to meet the requirements of a particular LNG project. In some projects the water depth and the size of the berths at either the loading or the unloading port may place a restriction on the size of the LNG ships. Generally the economies of scale will dictate that the project chooses the largest ships which are acceptable at both the loading and discharge ports. Often the capacity of the buyers' facilities is the limiting factor since many new projects are likely to be delivering some, if not all, of their production to already established terminals. The project sponsors may also want the flexibility to access alternative receiving terminals in the case of problems at one of the terminals it normally uses or to sell to other buyers in the event of the main buyers being unable to take the whole of the project's production. This will probably dictate that the ships have to be a similar size to those already in operation on other projects.

Most of the LNG ships brought into service in the 1980s and 1990s (and most of those under construction in 1997) have the capacity to carry around 135,000 cubic metres of LNG. Designs exist for larger ships (up to 200,000 cubic metres) and some projects have sought to take advantage of the savings in unit transportation costs resulting from the additional LNG such ships could deliver on each voyage. However, buyers have been reluctant to accept larger ships since it would require additional investment in their terminals and, in some cases, local port authorities restrict the size of ships which can enter their waters. Ships with a smaller capacity to carry LNG may be appropriate for some projects. For example, ships with a capacity of around 20,000 cubic metres are being used to supply LNG to medium-sized gas companies in Japan (the large gas utilities, Tokyo Gas, Osaka Gas and Toho Gas, can all receive 135,000 cubic metre ships). These medium-sized gas utilities have a limited daily demand for gas and the smaller ships are more closely matched to their requirements.

The faster the speed of the LNG ship the larger the volume of LNG it can deliver each year and, hence, providing larger-sized engines can reduce the number of ships needed. However, it will also increase the cost of each ship and its fuel consumption and, hence, the operating costs will be higher. Most of the LNG ships in operation have average service speeds of around 17 or 18 knots with a maximum speed some two or three knots higher which can be used to overcome delays at the loading or unloading ports or during the voyage. The options for the size and speed of the ships are inputs into a simulation programme which will determine the number of ships needed by the project. The distance between the LNG plant and the buyers' receiving terminals and, where two or more terminals are to be used, the volumes of LNG to be delivered to each terminal will also be key inputs to the simulation model. The time taken to berth, prepare the ship for loading, load the LNG and dispatch the ship will be incorporated into the model as will similar information with respect to the unloading port. The risk of delays will have to be assessed. Delays can arise through congestion at either the loading or unloading port. For example, where the buyer is receiving LNG from more than one LNG project at the terminal it may be necessary to take into account, in the simulation model, the priority rules for receiving LNG ships from different projects.

Weather conditions can also affect the shipping, particularly if high winds or rough sea conditions might restrict access to the loading and unloading ports. Weather reports over a number of years will generally be available and can be used to estimate the risks of delays due to adverse weather conditions. The model can be programmed to simulate random delays to the ships in line with the type of delays which, historical data suggests, the project can expect to experience in actual operation. The availability of sufficient LNG to load the ship when it arrives at the LNG plant will also be important in scheduling the LNG fleet. The model will have to take into account both the daily (and even the hourly) rate of LNG production and the risk of plant shutdowns. The LNG storage tanks at the plant should provide the stocks needed to load an arriving ship. The amount of storage capacity will, therefore, be a further input into the simulation model.

The model is run many times varying key assumptions such as the size of each ship, the average speed of each ship, the volume of storage at the LNG plant and the number of berths. Each run simulates the operation of the LNG chain over a number of years—at least 10 and often for the full 20 years or longer life of the project. Each run produces information on the average amount of LNG that can be delivered each year. In addition, the simulation will provide estimates of the maximum and minimum volumes which can be delivered in any year together with data on the utilisation of the LNG berth, the potential delays to the LNG ships and the use made of the plant storage capacity. Figure 3.3.7 illustrates the type of information on the delivery capacity of the fleet of LNG ships which might be obtained from several runs of a simulation model with the ship size, the number of ships and the average service speed varied. This is based on an LNG plant delivering to a single LNG receiving terminal 8000 kilometres (5000 miles) from the LNG plant. Two different sizes of ship have been assumed— 135,000 and 165,000 cubic metres—and two average service speeds—17 and 20 knots. The number of ships has been varied in each case. For the purpose of this simulation it has been assumed that the LNG plant can produce sufficient LNG to load the fleet of ships. Thus in each case the output from the simulation is the average volume of LNG the fleet can deliver on an annual basis. For example, the output shows that nine ships of 135,000 cubic metres capacity and an average service speed of 17 knots would be required to deliver 7 mtpa to the customer. In contrast the same volume could be delivered by six ships of 165,000 cubic metres capacity with an average service speed of 20 knots.

The decision on the number of ships will have a significant impact on the overall project viability. Ships with a capacity of 135,000 cubic metres had a capital cost of around US$225 million in 1997. The cost of a 165,000-cubic metre ship would probably be around US$250 million. Providing excessive transportation capacity will have a significant negative impact on the project's overall economic viability. At the same time, the fleet of ships has to be able to meet the sellers' contractual commitments to supply the buyers' requirements for LNG , in terms of both the total annual volumes and the reliability of deliveries to the buyers' facilities. A failure to satisfy the contractual commitments will result in the loss of revenue and could involve penalties for the LNG sellers. To avoid this

Figure 3.3.7   LNG Ships Required to Deliver 7 mtpa of LNG over a Distance of 5000 miles (8000 km)

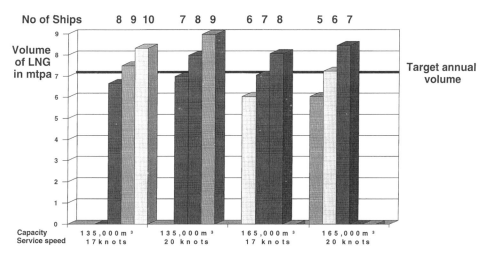

risk some surplus delivery capacity will normally be built into the shipping fleet. There is only a limited number of LNG ships not dedicated to operating projects so there is no certainty that any shortfall in the capacity of the fleet can be made up by chartering spare ships. The only long-term solution to a shortfall in delivery capacity may well be to order the construction of an additional ship, which would take at least three years.

Looking again at Figure 3.3.7, it can be seen that for this theoretical project there are a number of choices of fleet configuration which would have the capacity to deliver over 7 mtpa These are listed in Figure 3.3.7A. As the size and the speed increase the number of ships required reduces from nine through to as low as six. However, some of the outcomes would not be ideal. For example a fleet of seven 165,00 cubic metres capacity with a service speed of 17 knots could deliver marginally over 7 mtpa. This would probably not provide sufficient slack in the system to overcome any interruptions to the operation of the fleet of ships. Therefore, it is unlikely to be a basis on which to go ahead with the project. On the other hand, eight 135,000-cubic metre ships with a service speed of 20 knots have a delivery capacity of nearly 8 million tonnes which is probably well in excess of the spare delivery capacity needed to overcome any problems in operating the project. Clearly other sizes and service speeds can be considered which could result in a shipping fleet more closely tailored to the project needs. In the process of making the decision on the configuration of the shipping fleet, the buyers' position on the size of ships they are prepared to accept in their terminal facilities can be taken into account.

The model can also be used to determine the optimum size of storage capacity to be provided at the LNG plant. By running the model with different sizes of storage capacity it is possible to measure the impact on the overall ability of the project to deliver LNG to the buyers. This

Figure 3.3.7A   Options for Delivering 7 mtpa over a Distance of 5000 miles (8000 km)

Size in Cubic Metres	Average Service Speed in Knots	Number of Ships	Total Anual Delivery Capacity
135,000	17	9	7.5
135,000	20	8	8.0
165,000	17	7	7.1
165,000	20	6	7.3

information can then be used to decide whether the additional capital expenditure to provide extra storage capacity would be repaid by the increase in the volume of LNG which can be delivered to the customers each year. Similarly, it is possible to use the simulation model to consider the effect of providing additional berthing capacity at the LNG plant. This could reduce the potential delays to the ships and thereby increase the volume of LNG that can be loaded and delivered to the buyers. Running the simulation model with an additional berth will give an estimate of the impact on the amount of LNG loaded and delivered each year (and hence the additional revenues generated). This can be compared with the extra cost of constructing the berth to determine whether the additional capital expenditure can be justified.

In projects which are selling LNG on an FOB basis, the final decision on the number of ships and their design will be made by the buyers. However, they will have to work closely with the project sponsors in making the decision. The sponsors will want to be confident that the risk of the buyers' being unable to lift LNG as agreed in the sales contract is minimised. Furthermore, the design and the size of the ship will have to be taken into account in determining the storage capacity at the LNG plant and the number of berths to be provided. The cost of providing the shipping will almost certainly be a factor in negotiating the FOB price for the LNG. The buyer will want an FOB price which, after adding the cost of transport to its receiving terminals, produces a delivered price for the LNG competitive with the price of alternative fuels.

The operating costs of the fleet of LNG ships can also be a significant cost to the project. The costs will include crewing, port dues at both the loading and unloading port, dry-docking, insurance and fuel costs. The ships generally use the natural gas which boils off during the voyage as fuel. They also use fuel oil as a supplemental fuel source, particularly when berthing. An indicative operating cost for each ship is of the order of US$12 million per year. The actual costs can vary widely between projects depending on factors such as the nationality of the crew, port charges at both the loading and discharge ports and the extent to which boil-off natural gas is used to fuel the ships. At this level, the total annual operating cost for the fleet of ships used by a project can be similar to the operating cost for the LNG plant.

In the case of a CIF or ex-ship sale, the capital and operating costs of the LNG ships will be a major part of the project sponsors' commitment, potentially accounting for 25–40 per cent of the total capital costs and as much as 50 per cent of the operating costs. The method of acquiring the vessels will have an impact on the way the ships are treated in the project economics. If the LNG ships are to be owned by the project sponsors, then they will be treated as capital expenditure which has to be remunerated, along with other capital costs, by the project revenues. If the ships are acquired on a time charter or bareboat charter basis, then it may be possible to treat the costs as annual operating expenses. This will probably depend on the guarantees the project sponsors are required to make to the owners of the ships. In many cases, the shipowners will be looking for guarantees directly from the project sponsors that charter payments will be made whether or not the plant is producing LNG or delivery is being made to the buyers. In some cases this can result in the charter payments having to be capitalised in assessing the project economics.

The time required to construct LNG ships is around two and a half years. This is much greater than the construction time for a similar-sized oil tanker because of the time taken to construct the aluminium tanks in which the LNG is carried. To this must be added the time taken to prepare the outline design and to call for and evaluate bids from the shipyards which can take a further 12–18 months. Since this is significantly shorter than the time to design and build the LNG plant, the ships are unlikely to be on the critical path for the development of the project. However, the phasing for the design and construction of the ships will have to be integrated into the overall project schedule. For example, contracts for the construction of the ships will probably be let around the same time as the EPC contract for the LNG plant. Consequently, decisions on the number, size, speed and design of the ships will have to be made well in advance of this point in the project schedule.

The phasing of delivery of the ships will be timed to fit in with the build-up of deliveries to the buyer. With each ship costing of the order of US$225 million, the project sponsors will avoid ships being delivered earlier than they are needed. Payment for each ship is normally phased over the construction period with the timing of payments agreed in negotiation between the shipyard and the shipowners. The first payment (usually around 5–10 per cent) is made when the keel is laid with further staged payments (possibly two of around 20–25 per cent each) made during construction. A final payment (usually the largest) covering the balance of the cost is made on the delivery of the ship to the project.

3.4   THE MARKET

The previous sections of this chapter have looked at the major costs of developing any LNG project: gas production, the LNG plant and the ships. It is now time to turn to the market which has to provide the revenues to remunerate these costs. It is the market which will ultimately determine whether and when the project will be developed. Without a market for the LNG, the project will not go ahead no matter how good the design or how well the costs have been controlled.

In the very early stages of the project the sponsors will want to identify potential customers and make contact with them as the start of a process aimed at securing their commitment to purchase the project's planned output. Indeed, marketing will probably start as soon as the sponsors have confidence that they will be able to prove up sufficient natural gas reserves to support an LNG project and the initial technical and economic assessment suggests that a project is viable. The project sponsors will be looking for a contractual commitment from reliable buyers to purchase the planned output of the project for 20 years (or longer). They will need this commitment in the form of a signed SPA at the time they sign the EPC contract for the construction of the plant, agreements to purchase (or charter) the LNG ships, finalise finance agreements and make all the other commitments which mark the point of no return in developing the project.

For most projects the identification of potential markets is driven entirely by the location of the reserves. The cost of transportation means that projects will look to the closest potential markets. For projects in the Asia-Pacific region, this means Asian markets (currently Japan, Korea and Taiwan) while those projects located in the Atlantic Basin and/or North Africa will mainly target Europe, although the United States may provide a secondary market. The only projects with a real choice of markets are those in the Middle East which are approximately equidistant from southern Europe and eastern Asia. However, the level of LNG demand in Asia and the higher prices in that market have led to Middle Eastern-based projects looking primarily to existing markets in Japan, Korea and Taiwan to sell their LNG production. The Middle East is also very well placed to meet any LNG demand which might emerge in the Indian subcontinent.

Until the mid-1990s, securing a market in Japan was the key to success for LNG projects in the Asia-Pacific region. It was the only market with the level of demand which could underpin a greenfield project development. Indeed, the eight LNG plants in operation in 1997 supplying the Asian market were all developed to meet the demands of Japanese customers. Korea and Taiwan entered the market in the mid-1980s and the beginning of the 1990s, respectively, by purchasing their supplies from plants already in operation—either spare production capacity in plants which were built to supply Japan or the output from new LNG trains built at these plants. By 1995 demand in Korea had grown to the stage where its sole buyer, Korea Gas Corp. (KGC), was able, for the first time, to contract for supplies from a new greenfield project and provide the level of demand needed to underpin the development. Contracts with the Oman and Ras Laffan projects were finalised in 1996 and 1997, allowing construction of both these projects to commence. The impact of the financial crisis in Asia in 1997 may result in Korea's position as an LNG buyer having to be reassessed by potential sellers.

New projects in Asia-Pacific are likely to continue to look to Japan as one of the main potential markets for a major part of their planned production. The role of Korea has been made much more uncertain by the financial crisis in 1997 but it is the second largest market for LNG in Asia and as such is likely to remain a target for new projects. The market in Taiwan is not yet large enough to provide the main outlet for a new project but it is potentially an important secondary market. As we move beyond the year 2000, additional new markets for projects in the region may emerge. India and China are probably the most likely new markets with a number of proposals being made to construct receiving terminals in both countries. However, it is taking time for such proposals to be brought to fruition so both the timing of the first imports into these countries and the possible rate of build-up of demand are both uncertain. The Philippines, Pakistan and Thailand are possible new LNG importers, but the uncertainty here is well illustrated by the case of Thailand. An agreement for the import of LNG from Oman was close to final ratification in 1997 and plans were well advanced for the design and construction of an LNG import terminal. However, economic problems in 1997 caused the Thai government to defer the import of LNG until 2007 or later. It seems likely that the Asian LNG market will develop and diversify in the future. This will present sponsors of new LNG projects with the challenge of bringing together customers from two or more markets to create the demand needed to underpin their proposed investment.

Southern Europe is likely to provide the main market opportunity for projects in the Atlantic Basin and in Northern Africa. For nearly 30 years following the startup of the first LNG project in Algeria (in 1964), only Libya, with a small-scale scheme, entered this market as a new supplier. However, in the mid-1990s commitment was made to both the Trinidad and Nigerian LNG projects. The former project found customers in Spain and the US while the latter has a number of customers in southern Europe (in Italy, Spain, France and Turkey). Future projects in this region will probably have to follow a similar pattern of bringing together buyers from two or more countries to create the demand needed to underpin the proposed investment.

There is no fixed process for marketing LNG. Each project is likely to take its own approach based on the needs of the sponsors and the potential buyers. The sponsors will be looking to increase their confidence that a market opportunity exists for the project's LNG production in line with their increasing expenditure on the project. If it looks as though the market opportunity may be delayed, then the sponsors may decide to wind down or even suspend activity until a need for LNG emerges in the market.

The first stage in finding a market is likely to be initial contact with the identified potential buyers to introduce the project. A number of prospective buyers in several countries will probably be approached with the objective of establishing whether they have any potential interest in purchasing LNG from the project. At this stage the project sponsors are unlikely to be able to present more than an outline description of their planned development, but it will provide a basis on which an initial dialogue can take place. The sponsors will be looking to the buyers for an indication of the level of their interest and when they need the LNG. This should then lead to an identification of the buyers who are most likely to purchase LNG and with whom more detailed discussions can be held. The aim will be for both sides to gain confidence that there is a real prospect of a long-term agreement to buy and sell LNG. As part of the building of the relationship between the parties, the project sponsors will probably invite the potential buyers to visit the planned plant site and to meet representatives of the host government.

In parallel with the discussions with potential buyers, the project sponsors are likely to be entering into the early stages of conceptual engineering and other work on the planning of the project. As these studies progress they will be able to share additional information with the potential buyers, thereby increasing confidence that the project will be developed. Similarly, the buyers are likely to provide more information on the expected development of the market and their plans for the import of LNG. The project sponsors will be looking for an early expression of the buyers' interest in the project. In Asian markets this has often come through a letter of interest. There is no standard form for such a letter which is usually sent by the intended buyer to the project sponsors. However, its contents will almost certainly have been agreed between the parties before it is sent. The project sponsors will be looking at this stage for an indication of the amount of LNG the buyer proposes to buy and the potential timing of its demand. Although a letter of interest is not a legally binding commitment to purchase LNG, it should serve to provide the sponsors with confidence to continue expenditure on progressing the project.

3.5 SALE AND PURCHASE AGREEMENT

The next stage for the project sponsors is to turn the expression of interest by the potential buyers, in whatever form it has been given, into a more binding commitment to purchase the LNG. It is probably too early for either side to finalise the full details of an SPA but they may be in a position to record the main terms of such a contract. This has often resulted in the negotiation of a heads of agreement (HOA), a memorandum of understanding (MOU) or a letter of intent (LOI)—all terms which have been used in the past for an agreement which covers the outline terms for the sale and purchase of LNG. In this section, the term HOA will be used for this type of agreement which will include some or all of the following terms:

(1) timing of startup;
(2) length of build-up and volumes in each year of build-up;
(3) annual contract quantities at plateau;
(4) whether the sale is on a CIF, ex-ship or FOB basis;
(5) take-or-pay arrangements, i.e. the minimum volume of LNG the buyer undertakes to pay for each year even if its actual requirement for LNG is below this level;
(6) annual flexibility to increase or decrease volumes;
(7) any seasonal flexibility.

All these are issues of importance to the project sponsor in assessing the feasibility of the planned project. The other market issue of critical importance is the price to be paid for the LNG. However, with the HOA likely to be finalised five years or more before the project starts up, it may be too soon to agree details of the pricing arrangements. Consequently, HOAs may outline the broad principles under which the pricing provisions will eventually be negotiated. In addition, the HOA may define a timetable for finalising the price. Although the HOA will probably be a legally binding document, it is usually signed at a stage of the project development when significant uncertainties remain for both the sellers and the buyers. As a result, there is likely to be provision for either side to withdraw if agreement cannot be reached on the details of the SPA. The consequences for both sellers and buyers if the project does not proceed because of a failure to agree on the terms of the SPA are so serious that both sides will undertake, in the HOA, to use every effort to overcome any problems and only withdraw as a last resort.

The project sponsors will generally be seeking a signed HOA before they commit to FEED and to further work on the shipping and gas production phases of the project since such activity represents a step-up in the level of expenditure on the project. It is also possible that during this stage of the project orders may be made for long lead time equipment for the LNG plant such as the storage tanks or the heat exchangers. Commitments may also have to be made to shipowners, shipbuilders and other key players such as the host government. The degree of commitment by the buyers inherent in the signed HOA will be an important factor in determining the extent to which the sponsors are prepared to incur additional costs at this stage of the project. Furthermore, the HOA will define more closely the buyers' LNG requirements. This can be taken into account in the FEED and other related work when decisions will have to be made on such issues as the production capacity of the upstream production facilities, the sizing of the LNG plant and the number of ships. When the FEED stage is completed it will usually be too late to make major changes to the design of the project without incurring significant additional costs and, possibly, delaying the startup.

The next stage in the marketing of the LNG is to turn the HOA into a full SPA. This agreement will define the terms under which the buyers and sellers will work together throughout the 20 or more years of LNG production. It will incorporate the main terms for the sale of LNG which were included in the HOA and will probably define them in more detail. It will also include clauses covering issues such as those listed below, all of which are important to the operation of the project:

(1) *force majeure*;
(2) invoicing procedures;
(3) quality of the LNG;
(4) measurement and testing of the LNG;
(5) procedures to deal with any LNG paid for but not taken under the take-or-pay provisions of the agreement;
(6) procedures for arbitration in the case of a dispute between the buyers and sellers;
(7) processes for determining the programme for the delivery and receipt of cargoes each year (the annual delivery programme).

The annual delivery programme (ADP) is a key document for both buyer and seller in determining how they will work together over the life of the project to achieve the efficient delivery and receipt of cargoes. It is normally agreed between the parties before the beginning of each contract year. For an ex-ship sale, the ADP deals with the dates on which the sellers' LNG ships will deliver LNG to the buyers' terminals. For an FOB sale, the ADP will cover the dates of arrival of the buyers' ships at the LNG plant. Whether the sale is ex-ship or FOB, the ADP will provide a basis for decisions on how buyers and sellers will operate their facilities during the contract year which it covers. Hence, it is important to both sides that the procedures to be adopted to develop the ADP are agreed in the SPA.

A critical clause in the SPA is likely to cover how the LNG is to be priced. In some cases, buyers and sellers will agree the base price and the adjustment provisions in the SPA with the intention that it will provide a basis on which the LNG can be priced throughout the life of the project. The aim of the adjustment provisions is to maintain the price of the LNG at a level which ensures its competitiveness with other energy supplies in the buyers' market. This has usually been achieved by linking the price of the LNG to other fuels. Crude oil or oil products were the most common factors used to adjust the price in contracts in place in the 1990s. However, experience over the last 30 years of the LNG trade has shown that adjustment provisions negotiated in the expectation of gradual changes in energy prices may not be effective when there are large and sudden movements in prices. Most of the projects in operation have experienced one or more major price negotiations, usually in response to the changes in oil prices such as those which took place in the 1970s and 1980s. As a result, the SPAs for some of the LNG projects developed in recent years have included a change of circumstances clause which allows either side to call for a review of the pricing provisions if it is believed that they no longer reflect the realities of the market. The SPA is generally finalised at least four years before LNG production starts. In some cases buyers and sellers, recognising the uncertainty in energy markets, have agreed to defer finalising the pricing arrangements (both the base price and the adjustment provisions) until just before LNG production starts.

The signing of the SPA represents a commitment for both buyers and sellers to proceed with the project. Consequently, the sellers will have to be confident that all the other key arrangements will go ahead as planned. These will include the EPC contract, financing, ship charters (or construction contracts for the ships) and agreements with the host government. Similarly, the buyers will want to be sure that they have, or will receive, the necessary permissions (and have the finance available) to construct receiving terminals and the power stations or gas reticulation systems to consume the regasified LNG. If any of the agreements needed to allow the project to proceed is not in place at the time the SPA is signed, then that agreement may include conditions precedent which allow either party to withdraw if the agreements are not finalised by an agreed date. Any right to withdraw would only be exercised after the party concerned had made every effort to overcome the obstacles to the project proceeding.

As buyers and sellers progress through LOI and HOA to the full SPA, more detailed information will be generated on some of the key variables which impact on the economic feasibility of the project. The start date, the build-up of offtake, the annual contract quantities when the project is at plateau and the duration of the contract are all key factors in assessing the economic feasibility of an LNG project. The HOA and SPA should also define some of the upsides and downsides on the volume of LNG to be produced and sold. The take-or-pay commitment will provide a guarantee of the minimum volume of LNG for which the project can expect payment each year (as long as it is in a position to produce and supply that volume). The clauses in the agreements covering the arrangements for the project to supply and the buyers to take volumes over and above the annual contract quantity may also help define some of the upsides on sales volumes and, hence, the project revenues.

The other key variable in determining the expected project revenues is the price of the LNG. As discussed above, the process of negotiating the

HOA and the SPA may provide detailed pricing provisions in the form of a base price and a price adjustment clause. However, the agreements may defer final agreement on prices until closer to the date of startup. Even where there is a fully defined pricing clause in the SPA, the price of the LNG will be a major uncertainty in assessing the economic feasibility of the project. It will depend on the way in which the factors included in the price adjustment clause move over time. Almost invariably the price of crude oil or oil products are used as factors to adjust the price and experience has shown how difficult it is to forecast these prices.

3.6   GOVERNMENT

Host governments have an important role to play in the development of any LNG project. Natural gas reserves are a key resource for most countries and governments will want to be sure that they are developed in a way which maximises the benefit to the nation. They will want to be confident that producing the gas and exporting it as LNG represents the best option, especially where the alternative may be using natural gas to satisfy local energy demands. Support from the government will be a key factor in turning the plans for the development of an LNG project into a reality. Governments will want to ensure that they receive a fair share of the rewards from the project, but at the same time they need to set a fiscal regime which ensures that LNG is an attractive investment option for the project sponsors. Creating the appropriate balance between sharing the rewards and creating incentives to invest can make a major contribution to the successful implementation of any LNG project.

There are many other ways in which an LNG project impacts on the country in which it is located. The high level of capital investment means that the inflow of funds during construction can affect the economy of the host country. When the plant is in operation, the revenues from the export of LNG can be an important factor in the country's balance of payments. The project is also likely to have a major effect on the region close to the plant site. During construction, and to a lesser extent during operation, it will generate employment both directly in the LNG plant itself and in local companies which provide services to the project. Skilled labour may well have to be brought in to construct and operate the plant and this creates the potential for the transfer of skills to the local population.

Many LNG plants are in remote and relatively undeveloped areas where considerable investment is required to build infrastructure (housing, roads, airstrips and port facilities). National and local governments will inevitably be involved in developing such facilities. The host government may also have a key role to play in helping to develop the market.

Its relationship with the governments of the potential buyers can provide an important support to the commercial discussions between buyers and sellers. Certainly, any LNG buyer will want to be sure that the host government fully supports the project and will facilitate its development by expediting approvals for construction of the plant and for its operation and by granting export licences for the LNG. Support from the host government may also be a major factor in raising the finance for the project. Lenders will look at the risk profile of the project and one of the issues they will have to consider is the extent of the country risk. Assurances from the government on their support for the project can help mitigate this risk and can help the project to secure loans from commercial banks, multilateral institutions and other potential lenders.

The involvement of governments in LNG projects takes many forms. In many of the projects brought into operation between 1965 and 1997 and those due to come onstream by the year 2000, governments are direct investors in the project. Usually their involvement is through the national oil company which, in many cases, holds a majority stake in the gas production and the LNG plant. Even where the government or a government agency is not a direct investor (for example, in the Australian North-West Shelf project and the Kenai project in Alaska), it has a significant financial interest through the taxes and royalties charged against the project revenue. Discussions between the project sponsors and the host government are likely to take place from the very earliest stages of the project development. Indeed, the project sponsors will probably have worked closely with the government in the bid and award of the exploration acreage. Often the fiscal terms set for the development of any hydrocarbon discovery are on the assumption that oil will be found. However, the cash flow characteristics of an LNG development are very different from those of an oil development, as is illustrated in Figure 3.6. This figure is meant to be indicative. It is not based on actual LNG or oil projects, but it is intended to be reasonably representative of the very different profiles of cash flows which the two types of projects might generate.

The capital investment to develop oil production and export is usually much lower than for an LNG project producing a similar amount of energy. The construction period for an LNG project tends to be longer than for an oil development and, once onstream, the build-up of production may well be slower and the level of the plateau lower. Consequently, it is likely to take much longer to repay the capital investment in the case of an LNG project. For an oil project the production profile depends mainly on the producibility of the reservoir and the capacity of the installed facilities. Working within these constraints, the operator will want to build production up to maximum capacity as quickly as possible. The oil market is sufficiently flexible to absorb the production from most projects so it will not place a constraint on the

Figure 3.6   LNG v Oil—Illustrative Annual Cash Flows

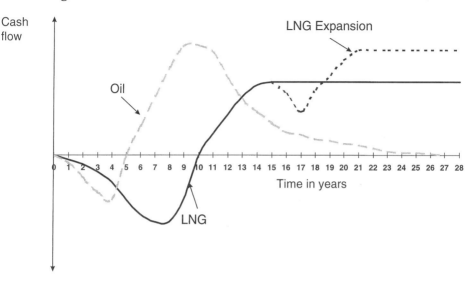

level of production. For an LNG project it is the market which will be the main factor in determining both build-up and the plateau production. The buyers will generally be looking for a plateau level of production which can be sustained for 20 years or more. As a result the cash flows from an LNG project will generally be sustained at a high level for much longer than an equivalent oil project. Furthermore, experience has shown that the plateau for an LNG project can be extended and may also be increased as the project is expanded through the construction of additional trains.

It is therefore not surprising that fiscal regimes designed to share the rent between project investors and the host government for an oil develop-ment frequently do not provide the incentives needed to promote investment in an LNG development. Consequently, governments in many of the countries where LNG projects have been developed have been prepared to modify their fiscal regimes or provide other incentives to the project sponsors. There are many ways in which governments may take a share in the rent from an LNG project. They include:

(1)   a royalty on the production of the natural gas;
(2)   a share of the gas production;
(3)   a carry of the state oil company's share of investment in the project;
(4)   corporate taxes on profits;
(5)   specific taxes on hydrocarbons;
(6)   resource rent taxes;

(7)   property taxes;
(8)   local government taxes;
(9)   contribution to the development of local infrastructure not directly related to the LNG plant (e.g. hospitals, community centres, sports facilities, roads, etc.);
(10) duties on the import of materials or equipment and/or on the export of LNG.

Modifying any of the charges to the project may provide incentives for its development. Indeed, in nearly all of the LNG projects brought into operation since 1965 and those under construction in 1997, some form of incentive has been provided to the project sponsors by modifying the prevailing tax regime or even developing a special regime for the project in question. Examples of the incentives given in the past include:

(1)   increasing the share of profits an upstream producer is allowed to retain in a production-sharing contract when natural gas is being produced to supply an LNG plant;
(2)   granting a tax holiday which exempts the LNG project from paying taxes (and possibly royalties) for a specified number of years;
(3)   reducing the level of corporate or hydrocarbon taxes the project pays;
(4)   accelerating the rate at which the project is allowed to depreciate capital expenditure for tax purposes;
(5)   granting investment allowances to the project or allowing an uplift on the capital costs which can be charged against tax;
(6)   reducing (or eliminating) duties on equipment imported for the construction of the facilities.

It is unlikely that fiscal change will, on its own, turn a fundamentally uneconomic project into a profitable investment opportunity for the project sponsors. However, modification of the fiscal regime can improve the attractiveness of the project for potential investors. This can be crucially important in a world where there are many competing opportunities for each investment dollar.

While it is the government take from the project which will have the most impact on the economic viability, there are numerous other areas where government actions (or inaction) can affect the project. One area of growing importance in an increasingly environmentally conscious world is the environmental standards the project has to meet. LNG projects are comparatively benign in their impact on the environment since they are processing natural gas which is a relatively clean fuel. However, they are often located in remote regions where building a large industrial facility may be seen as an unwelcome intrusion, especially since it will bring an influx of people to construct and operate the plant and to provide the services and the facilities needed by the workforce. Furthermore, around 10 per cent of the natural gas is consumed as fuel in the plant and the resultant carbon dioxide emissions are being seen as a major environmental concern especially for projects where carbon dioxide extracted from the natural gas supplied to the plant is also vented to the atmosphere.

The environmental and other regulations (for example, the need to maximise the use of local labour and locally produced materials and equipment) imposed by a government before giving permission for development can also have a significant impact on project costs. Clearly, any project sponsor will want to satisfy the legitimate concerns of host governments and their populations to minimise the effect on the environment of the development and to maximise the benefits to the national and regional economy. However, it has to be recognised that meeting such regulations may add to capital and operating costs and, at the extreme, could make a project uneconomic.

In any project the time between incurring expenditure and earning revenue will be one of the key factors in the economics of the investment. This is particularly true for LNG projects where time-frames are often much longer than for other oil or gas developments. It is important, therefore that governments help expedite the development by ensuring the timely provision of permits for construction and operation of the facilities and the export of the LNG.

3.7 PROJECT STRUCTURE

Each LNG project consists of a chain of activities, gas production, liquefaction and shipping, which have to be developed and operated together if the project is to be successful. The way in which the project is structured will determine how the parties work together and how each link in the chain relates to the others. The structuring of an LNG project will have to take into account the aspirations of individual investors, the policies of the host government and the requirements of the buyers. The project will involve a number of companies, some of whom may want to participate in all parts of the chain while others may feel that their skills and experience are such that they want to limit participation and investment to only one of the phases.

The policy of the host government on the participation of foreign companies in the hydrocarbon business in their country may also restrict the roles companies may play in the various phases of the project. For example, in some countries the ownership of natural gas reserves and their development is entirely the responsibility of the national oil company. On the other hand, in Indonesia, while foreign investors participate in the exploration and development of the natural gas reserves as production-sharing contractors, it is government policy that LNG plants are owned by the national oil company, Pertamina. The production-sharing contractors do, however, participate in the operation of the LNG plants.

The way in which the project is structured will determine the role each participant takes, the risks it faces and the rewards it is likely to receive. Since each potential participant will have its own aspirations for the project and its own views on each of these issues, finding a structure which satisfies everyone, including the host government, or, at least, provides a basis for everyone to proceed with the development, can be a very complex and time-consuming exercise. There is no single answer to the question of the best structure for an LNG project. The structure of each project will be determined on a case-by-case basis, taking into account a host of factors the most important of which are likely to be the conditions set by the host government and the needs of the participants. This is well illustrated by the projects which were in operation or under construction in 1997. Each has a unique structure reflecting its own particular circumstances.

The two main issues to be answered in structuring the project are which companies will be shareholders in the individual phases of the project and what will be the relationship between the phases. In some ways, the simplest structure is an integrated one where each participant has the same share in each part of the LNG chain. This is illustrated in Figure 3.7. One of the main advantages of such a structure is that the potential for a conflict of interest between parties is limited. Since each partner has the same share in each element, it will be largely indifferent

Figure 3.7   LNG Project Structure—Integrated

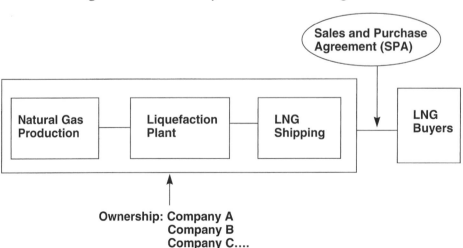

to the part of the chain in which the profit is earned. The question of transfer prices between, for example, the gas producers and the LNG plant or between the LNG plant and the transporters should not be a major issue since the effect on each participant should be the same. Similarly, there should not be a need for arm's-length agreements between the natural gas producers and the LNG plant owners or between the LNG plant and the shipowners. As shown in Figure 3.7, the main agreement for such a project is the SPA with the LNG buyers. Despite the simplicity of an integrated structure in terms of the contractual arrangements needed to control the chain, there will still be many agreements which have to be put in place. The most critical of these is likely to be the shareholders' or participants' agreement which will govern how the project is run and how key decisions are made. Since this agreement has to cover all the phases of the project, it will be of major importance for each of the participants. In addition, arrangements will have to be put in place to manage each phase of the project and operating procedures will have to be agreed to ensure that the various parts of the chain work together in an optimal way.

The alternative to an integrated structure is one in which the shareholdings in the links of the chain differ. This is illustrated in Figure 3.7A. In this structure some participants may choose not to participate in one or more phases of the project. Even companies which participate in all phases may have different shares across the chain either through choice or because there are limitations on the size of the shareholding they can own. In the example shown in Figure 3.7A, company A has shares across the chain, but a different percentage in each of the phases. Company B is shown as participating in natural gas production and the liquefaction plant, but not the shipping. Company C only participates in the natural gas

Figure 3.7A LNG Project Structure—Non-Integrated

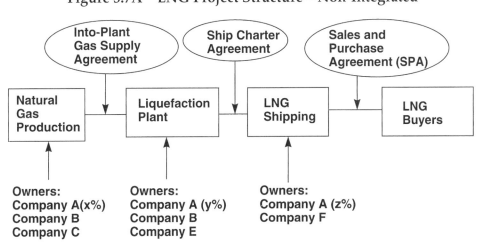

production, company E is only in the liquefaction plant while company F participates only in the shipping. This is an illustrative example not based on a real project, but the complexity created is typical of that which can occur in real projects. This type of structure creates interfaces within the project and potential conflicts between the parties. For example, company C, which is involved in gas production but not the LNG plant, is only interested in the income from selling natural gas to the LNG plant and will be looking for as high a price as possible for the gas at the LNG plant gate. On the other hand, company E, which is in the LNG plant but not the gas production, will want to keep that price as low as possible. There are similar interface problems between the LNG plant and the shipping phase where company F will want to maximise the income from its involvement in the shipping whereas all the other partners (with the possible exception of company A) will probably be looking for the lowest possible transportation costs.

The way in which transfer prices move in the future may also be an issue for the parties. For example, company E, which is only involved in the LNG plant, runs the risk of its income being squeezed by payments to the natural gas producer and to the transporters. To minimise this risk it may be looking for all prices in the chain to be linked to the LNG price paid by the LNG buyers. This may be a risk which investors in the natural gas production or the shipping are not prepared to take. Investors in the natural gas production may feel that the price of the LNG is outside their control and, therefore, may want to see the price of natural gas delivered to the plant set in a different way. The investors in the shipping phase may be looking for fixed charter payments which would be more closely in line with the traditional arrangements in the shipping industry. In a non-integrated project, interface pricing is only one of the issues which will have to be included in the contracts needed to govern the relationship between the phases of the project. A legally binding agreement will be required between the natural gas producers and the LNG plant owners for natural gas supply and a ship charter agreement will have to be negotiated with the companies involved in the shipping phase. It is critically important that the terms and conditions in these agreements are consistent with the SPA with the LNG buyers since no LNG buyer will be prepared to accept constraints on the project's ability to satisfy its commitments to supply LNG.

Many factors will drive the choice of structure chosen by a project. One of the most important will be the regulations and requirements of the host government. For example, the right to participate in gas production may be reserved for the national oil company or there may be a limit on the share a foreign company can hold. The government may also require the national oil company to hold a majority share in the LNG plant which may restrict the options open for structuring that part of the project. The host government's fiscal regime can also have an impact on how the project can be structured. The way in which taxes and royalty are charged on gas production may require that phase to be separated from the LNG plant and an arm's length agreement negotiated for the transfer of natural gas to ensure that the price is not set in a way which might be seen by the host government as reducing the level of tax payments. In some countries oil and gas production is only allowed under a production-sharing contract. Incorporating the other parts of the project into such an arrangement may not be appropriate or possible and, consequently, the LNG plant part of the chain may have to be organised separately from the natural gas production.

The investment motives of each of the participants will also be a factor which has to be taken into account in determining the project structure. Some investors may, for example, not want to participate in the LNG shipping phase of the project because they consider that shipping can best be provided by dedicated shipping companies. As a result, in some projects the LNG ships are chartered into the project from independent ship-owners. In other projects it is provided by one or more of the companies participating in the other parts of the chain. The requirements of the buyers may also have to be taken into account in finalising the structure. For example, if the buyer insists on an FOB sale then the interests of the project sponsors will be limited to the natural gas production and LNG plant phases of the project. Finally, the structure of the project will be important to lenders since they will have to be certain that nothing in the way the project is organised and nothing in any of the interface agreements will impact on the smooth operation of the project and the flow of cash to repay the loans.

The structuring of the project may provide the opportunity to include additional companies into the project to strengthen the partnership or to bring in additional skills or interests. Several projects have brought in companies who can strengthen the link with the market. In the case of Japan this has resulted in trading houses, such as Mitsui, Mitsubishi and Marubeni, participating in several of the operational projects (for example, Malaysia, Brunei, Australian North-West Shelf and Qatargas). In the case of Korea, the government has made it a policy to give preference to LNG supplied by projects in which Korean companies participate. As a result, Korean companies own a 5 per cent share in the Oman project and in 1997 they were negotiating a similar share in Qatar's Ras Laffan development. In the Atlantic Basin, the two main buyers of LNG from the Trinidad project, Cabot in the USA and Repsol in Spain, are shareholders in the LNG plant.

There are other choices to be made in the organising the project. One of the key ones will be whether the project is to be arranged as an incorporated or unincorporated joint venture. In the case of an incorporated venture, a company is formed to manage and control the project (or a particular phase of the project). The company may be funded by equity injections from the shareholders and by loans from third parties or from the shareholders themselves. The shareholders will receive income from their equity investment through dividends paid by the project company. It is possible that separate companies may be formed covering, say, natural gas production, the liquefaction plant and the shipping. In an unincorporated joint venture there is no project company. The participants directly control their share of the project and can fund it as they choose. This could include funding it from internal sources or from loans they raise themselves using the project itself as security. Income from the sale of LNG (and other products such as condensates or LPGs) flows directly to the participant. This has the advantage of income from the investment being received immediately, thereby avoiding the potential delays in receiving dividends from the project company. However, an unincorporated joint venture may make it more difficult to raise finance for the project and may add complexity to the relationship with the buyers. For example, each of the joint venturers may have to sign a separate SPA with the buyers and raise separate invoices for their share of each cargo delivered.

The key objective in the structuring of a project is to work within the constraints set by partner aspirations, host government regulations and requirements and the needs of buyers and lenders to implement a project which can operate successfully to produce and deliver LNG. A successful project structure is likely to be one which gives a fair balance of risk and reward to each of the participants, including the host government. The structuring of the project should be seen as a way of sharing rewards when there are sufficient available to meet the aspirations of all the participants. It is unlikely to create extra rewards to overcome the problems of a fundamentally unsound project.

3.8 FINANCE

As discussed briefly in the section above, finance will probably be one issue which has to be taken into account in structuring the project. For example, the choice between an unincorporated and an incorporated joint venture may be driven by the need of some or all of the partners to raise funds on a project rather than individual participant basis. It is also possible that decisions on the degree of integration along the chain could depend on whether it is felt that it is easier to raise finance for each phase of the project separately or whether a single, larger-scale, financing would be preferable.

If the project is organised as an unincorporated joint venture then it becomes the responsibility of each of the partners to fund its own share of the project. This may be the easiest way to raise the cash needed to cover the project costs, provided that all the partners have a strong balance sheet and are prepared to put in equity or use the strength of their balance sheet to raise finance. It is also possible for the partners in an unincorporated joint venture to work together to raise finance jointly, but the need for co-ordination between the parties may make it a more complex exercise than raising funds through a jointly owned company.

Some partners may be unable to raise the money required for the project against their own balance sheet or may prefer to use finance raised jointly for the project. In such cases, the use of an incorporated joint venture with the project company (or companies) raising the finance may be the preferred option for the project structure. A project company will be able to deal with financial markets on behalf of the project participants, but it has to be recognised that lenders will probably look behind that company to the strength of its shareholders before agreeing to lend funds to the project.

3.9   THE ECONOMIC MODEL

The final decision to develop the upstream natural gas production, construct the liquefaction plant and acquire the LNG ships involves the commitment to the expenditure of several billions of dollars for the typical LNG project. Although the costs will be shared between a number of companies, it will represent a major commitment for each of them, probably running into hundreds of millions, and possibly into billions, of dollars. Certainly the decision is one that will only be made if all the participants are confident that the project will operate safely and reliably throughout its life. They will also want to be satisfied that the expected returns on the capital investment are commensurate with technical, commercial, political and other risks that are being taken. For some, if not all, the participants there will be alternative investment opportunities available and they will want assurance that the project offers returns which are at least as good as, and preferably better, than those on offer elsewhere.

The final 'go or no-go' decision will be taken when all the contracts for construction of the facilities have been finalised, when the SPAs with the buyers have been agreed and when arrangements with the host government and lenders have been put in place. However, reaching this stage involves considerable financial commitment—US$200 million or more can easily be spent in arriving at the final decision point. Perhaps more important are the moral commitments which are made to the many parties involved: other participants, buyers, engineering contractors, shipbuilders and shipowners, governments and lenders. Walking away from a project at a late stage in its development could create considerable damage to these relationships and potentially to a company's overall reputation unless the reasons for leaving the project are clear and are understood and accepted by all the other parties.

This means that an economic model of the project's expected cash flow is an important tool to have available as the project is developed. It will allow the economic returns of the project to be monitored as work progresses on the design and engineering of the facilities, as negotiations progress with the LNG buyers and as arrangements with the host government and lenders are put in place. There may also be changes in the external environment which participants want to evaluate and take into account as project planning progresses. The design of the model will be very specific to the project itself, reflecting, at least in part, the particular way in which the project is structured. The needs of the individual participants will probably differ in terms of the information each wants to obtain from the model, the criteria it wants to use to assess the economic feasibility and the assumptions it makes on the economic environment. Therefore, it is likely that each participant will maintain its own model of the project especially if the way in which the project is structured results in companies having different interests across the chain. However, there is also likely to be a common project model which can be used jointly by the sponsors as a tool to aid decision-making during its development. For example, a joint model can be used to evaluate proposals from the buyers during the negotiation of the SPA. This can help frame responses on issues such as volumes, build-up and price.

Whether the economic model is maintained by an individual participant or is a common model run for the project as a whole, it is likely to start life as a very simple representation of the possible cash flows. At this stage, the estimates of costs, production levels, revenues, etc. will be no more than ballpark figures. For example, capital cost estimates may be simply calculated using an estimate of the dollar per tonne of installed capacity based on the cost of projects recently developed. As the project progresses and the available information increases, the model will be expanded into a detailed representation of the project cash flows. At the same time, the quality of the data will improve as the design of the proposed facilities is better defined, information becomes available from the buyers on the level of offtake and the fiscal regime is finalised with the host government. Through this process the confidence in the project's economics will increase and the range of uncertainty on the expected outcomes will decrease.

Much can change over the life of any LNG project which extends into several decades (when the time for planning and construction are added to the 20 or more years of operation). Any economic assessment can be no more than an estimate at one point in that long time-frame and the potential for change can be large, especially in the early stages when critical decisions may have to be made. In addition to the information specific to the particular development, the model will require the input of a number of variables exogenous to the project itself. These will include factors such as forecasts of inflation rates, interest rates, exchange rates and energy and other prices. The source of such information may be the participants themselves, but external forecasting agencies may be used to obtain a consensus view.

The measures of the project economics which may be used in assessing its feasibility are numerous and will probably include:

(1)   internal rate of return (IRR);
(2)   net present value (NPV) calculated at a chosen discount rate which may be in real terms (i.e. adjusted for inflation) or in nominal terms;
(3)   time taken to repay the capital investment;
(4)   ability to service loans (interest and debt repayment);
(5)   efficiency of the investment in terms of the NPV earned for every dollar invested;
(6)   average return on capital employed when the project is in operation.

Each participant will have his own views on the measures which should be used. There may also be differences on how the measures should be calculated. The way in which finance is treated is one example of the different approach companies may take. Some will treat third party finance as off the balance sheet and will therefore measure rates of return on equity after taking into account the cost of servicing the debt. Others will look at the return on the total investment arguing that that is the only true measure of the project's underlying economic feasibility.

The differences in the way companies look at the economics of an LNG project can lead to tensions amongst the partners. One partner may be looking for improvements in the returns whereas others may consider the expected returns acceptable and want to go ahead on that basis, avoiding the potential delays which could be incurred in achieving improvements. For example, a review of plant design may be proposed to identify areas for savings in capital cost, but this will inevitably take time. A key skill in bringing a project to fruition is the ability to manage partner relationships so that differences of views are resolved in a way which allows the project to proceed with the minimum of delay and in the interests of all the parties involved.

3.10 SUMMARY

The sections of this chapter have described many of the issues that have to
be addressed in establishing the feasibility of an LNG project and bringing
it into operation. Each project will have its own particular problems to
solve so it is not possible to produce an exhaustive list of all the factors
which may have to be taken into account. It is clear that a number of
complex issues have to be considered, often in parallel, if a project is to be
brought to fruition. This is a time-consuming exercise which, as was discussed briefly in the introduction to the chapter, can take as long as three
decades. The time-frame varies considerably from project to project so it is
impossible to give a definitive schedule. Conditions in the LNG markets,
the relationship between the project sponsors, host government policies,
the speed of decision-making and the ability to raise finance are all factors
which will impact on the time schedule. Even if all the problems are solved
quickly and the parties involved work together effectively, the time taken
from discovery of reserves to first delivery of LNG is unlikely to be much
less than a decade. Figure 3.10 gives a representative time schedule for an
LNG project. It is not based on an actual project, but is intended to illus-
trate how the various activities in establishing the project feasibility,
appraising and developing the reserves, marketing the LNG, designing
and building the LNG plant, acquiring the LNG ships and arranging
financing might be brought together.

The schedule in Figure 3.10 starts with the discovery of the natural gas
reserves, which may well be preceded by several years of exploration
effort. It shows a 10-year time-frame from this point to the delivery of the
first cargo of LNG to the buyers. This is certainly an achievable time-
frame, but past experience suggests that it may be optimistic. The
schedule in Figure 3.10 shows the initial feasibility study as the first activity
after discovery of the natural gas reserves. It is possible that at the same
time discussions may commence between the sponsors on the structure of
the project. This activity, which is not shown in the schedule, will probably
continue until full commitment is made at the end of year 6. Once it is
established that the proposed project is likely to be economically and
technically viable, it is possible to start expenditure on appraisal of the
reserves and to commence the marketing effort. Initially, informal
approaches will be made to possible buyers to register the project as a
potential source of LNG supply in the longer term. This will lead to a
phase of active marketing during which the project will be seeking an
increasing level of commitment from prospective buyers. Full commitment will be achieved with the signing of the SPA which is shown as
occurring at the end of year 6. It is possible that the SPA might be
finalised and signed earlier but it is only likely to become effective once

Figure 3.10   LNG Project Schedule

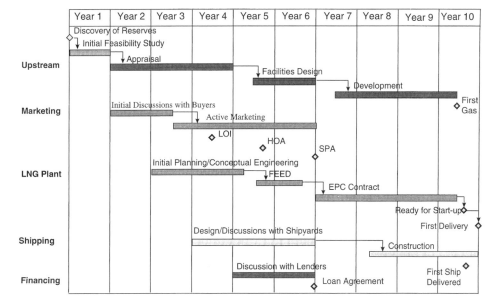

full commitment has been made to the investment through the signing of other key agreements.

Work on the initial planning of the LNG plant and on its conceptual design is assumed to start at the beginning of year 2. This work should be sufficiently developed to allow the award of the FEED contract during year 5. At this time it is assumed that the natural gas reserves will have been fully proved and sufficient progress will have been made in marketing the LNG to give the sponsors the confidence they need to commit to the additional expenditure on FEED. Work on the design of the LNG ships and initial discussions with the shipyards and shipbuilders are likely to be underway at this time, as will negotiations with potential lenders of funds for the project. All the work should come together at the end of year 6 when full commitment to the project is made. At this time the SPA will be signed, the EPC contract for the LNG plant will be let, commitments will be made to the shipbuilders and the loan agreement will be finalised with the lenders. The plant should be ready for startup around the middle of year 10 at which time the first gas production should be available to allow testing and commissioning of the LNG plant and other facilities. The first LNG ship should be delivered during the second half of year 10, allowing loading and first delivery of LNG to the buyer at the end of that year.

Even in this relatively optimistic case the schedule extends over 10 years and during this time a number of complex agreements have to be negotiated involving many parties—project sponsors, buyers, lenders, shippers, governments and contractors. This requires a level of cooperation amongst organisations, and amongst individuals within those organisations, which is not often required in other types of energy projects. The reward for success is an LNG project which will be generating income and providing natural gas supplies to customers for at least 20 years. Experience has shown that most projects will be extended for many years beyond the initial term of the SPA, thereby prolonging and increasing the benefits for both the project sponsors and the LNG buyers.

Chapter 4

The Chain of LNG Project Contracts

Peter P. Miller

4.1 INTRODUCTION

Recently I told one of my favourite clients that I was writing a chapter for a book on the LNG industry. He asked what my topic would be and I told him 'The legal aspects of developing an LNG project'. His deadpan reply was 'Are there any?'

I should explain that this is a gentleman with whom I have worked for many years. In fact, I was his counsel during the very first LNG transaction in which he was involved. Therefore I took his reply as a friendly poke at lawyers and the legal profession (an increasingly popular pastime these days), rather than an expression of serious doubt that there are legal aspects to the LNG business.

It is the intention in this chapter to discuss those legal aspects. The approach will be to identify the more significant agreements that document the development of a project, to explain the function each serves and to discuss the interplay among them. We will start at the beginning with what are often referred to as the 'concession' arrangements, when a project may be no more than an explorationist's fantasy. From there we will proceed to a study of the contractual arrangements among the participants in the venture and the internal and outside contractor activities that are conducted up to the point when a development decision is made. Assuming there has been a gas discovery and approvals to proceed have been obtained, we will then turn to the construction phase and examine the engineering, procurement and construction (EPC) contract. Financing and shipping issues will be discussed along the way to the extent that they arise in the context of our survey of the other project documents.

Finally, we will examine the LNG sale and purchase agreement (SPA), the goal of all other efforts, the determinant of whether there is a project, and thus the most important document of all. Actually the marketers, who surpass even the explorationists in their ability to fantasise, will probably have been negotiating this document for years prior to contract award, perhaps starting the moment the presence of an exploitable resource is discovered. One does not normally commit to the construction phase until a sale justifying the cost has been completed. In sequence, therefore, a study of the SPA could reasonably precede our review of the construction documentation. However, because of the unique features of the SPA and its pivotal role in the development of an LNG trade,[1] we will save the discussion of this document for dessert.

The list appearing in Figure 4.1 shows the 'links' in the chain of documents typically utilised in LNG projects. Figure 4.2 portrays the manner in which the various agreements interrelate and bind the respective project participants together. During the course of our review we will address each of the documents identified, although special emphasis will be placed on those items appearing in bold letters in Figure 4.1. Some of the items are duplicative. For example, a venture might be initiated pursuant to a licence or lease, a production-sharing contract (PSC) or what I shall refer to as a development agreement (DA), but not by more than one of those arrangements. Our review will look at each of them, pointing out what they have in common and how they differ. It should also be said that the list is not exhaustive. Each project is different, and special circumstances may call for other types of agreements. The financing arrangements alone may entail a multitude of agreements and other documents; but fortunately we do not need to discuss them here, except as they may dictate provisions that will appear in the other project documentation.[2]

4.1.1 Hallmarks of an LNG Trade

As we go through the discussion of the various links in the chain of documents, the reader should bear in mind a number of defining features, or what might be called 'hallmarks', of the LNG industry. These hallmarks

---

[1] In this chapter, the expression 'LNG trade' is used to denote an individual SPA between a particular buyer and a particular seller. 'LNG industry' is used when referring to all LNG trades or the LNG business generally.
[2] The financing of LNG projects is treated in detail in Chapter 6.

Figure 4.1   The Links in the Chain of LNG Project Contracts

	Related Documents
• 'Concession' Arrangements	
Licence / Lease	Licence / Contract Area
Production-Sharing Contract /	Operating Agreement
Contract for Work	
Development Agreement	Joint Venture Agreement
• Operating/Joint Venture	Contract Area
Agreements	
Operating Agreement	Accounting Procedure
Joint Venture Agreement	Incorporating Documents
	Accounting Procedure
	Project Services Agreements
• From Discovery to Development	
Data Acquisition Agreements	Information Purchase, Exchange
Exploration Agreements	Seismic Programmes
	Appraisal, Delineation Drilling
Analyses-Studies	Enhancement, Interpretation
	Agreements
	Simulation, Feasibility,
	Optimisation, Technical Studies
Front End Engineering	
and Design (FEED)	
Contract—Plant, Field	
• **Engineering, Procurement and**	Technology Licensing
Construction (EPC) Contracts	**Long-Lead Items**
	Insurance Arrangements
Production and Pipeline	
Facilities	
Drilling Contracts	Offshore Services
Terminal Facilities	Port Use Arrangements
Land and Other Property Use	Land Leases
	Cooperation and Co-ordination
	Agreements
• **Sale and Purchase Agreement (SPA)**	LOIs/MOUs
	Transportation Arrangements
Condensate SPA/Offtake	
Agreements	
• Financing Arrangements	

characterise virtually every trade and are reflected in the related project documents. They, in large part, determine why things are the way they are, and we ignore them at our peril.

4.1.1.1   Integration

The first of these hallmarks is the 'integrated' nature of the LNG business. By 'integrated' we mean that the various and multiple aspects of a trade, such as the volumes of available gas, the gas production and pipeline throughput capacities, the LNG plant capacity, the storage tank capacities, the LNG volumes being sold, the cargo-carrying capacities of LNG tankers and the capacities of buyers' receiving and regasification facilities must all be co-ordinated, so that the trade may operate as an efficient, uniform whole. Each and every link in the contract chain will therefore be influenced by, and must reflect, this integration.

Integration is also a fundamental characteristic of the way LNG plants are operated.

Gas and LNG are fungible commodities. It is impossible to identify the specific facilities responsible for the production, transportation, processing, storage and shipment of a given molecule of delivered product. This inability to identify genealogy has often been expressed by the saying 'There is no purple and no yellow LNG'. Where a seller has more than one trade, therefore, no buyer may lay claim to specific volumes destined for delivery to him alone.

This is fortified by the fact that no one can say with precision what the capacity of a given facility, such as an LNG production train, might be. True, each train has a design, or 'nameplate' capacity. But that is only a capacity the EPC contractor guarantees under specific test conditions, failing which it would have to pay liquidated damages or suffer possible rejection of the train. One assumes that the contractor will have built some contingency into the design and manufacture so as to avoid any liquidated damages or other penalties. This would argue that the true capacity is something more than nameplate. On the other hand, no one ever operates a train under test conditions for a sustained period of time; and nameplate does not take into account actual operating conditions, such as scheduled maintenance and unscheduled downtime. The 'stream' capacity is therefore likely to be something more than nameplate but less than the maximum possible running rate. One can only determine the latter rate by pushing the facility to the break point, which a prudent operator would ordinarily not do.

In a situation calling for the construction of multiple trains to support multiple sales, the principles of integration would normally call for the uniform sizing and rateably even operation of all production trains. The Arun plant in Indonesia is an example. There, the first three trains were built in response to a sale to buyers in western Japan, the next two trains in response to a sale to buyers in eastern Japan and the sixth as a result of the first sale to Korea. But that does not mean that the individual buyers have claim to the production from specific trains. They recognise that they will be supplied from the overall, integrated capacity of the plant, a principle that is borne out in the allocation provisions of their respective SPAs.

4.1.1.2   *Size*

Another hallmark of the LNG industry is the sheer size of each undertaking. A greenfield venture cannot be launched comfortably unless sales involving the construction of two or more production trains are in hand. The attendant offshore and onshore facilities, infrastructure, port facilities and shipping will normally serve more than a single train, and a second train contributes to security of supply by providing necessary flexibility for scheduled maintenance and unscheduled downtime. Later expansions calling for additional trains and attendant facilities may be projects of a justifiably smaller size; but the greenfield project requires a substantial base if it is to succeed.

4.1.1.3   *Cost and Financing*

A natural consequence of the aspect of size is cost. It is often difficult for newcomers to the industry to appreciate how much money is involved in the development of an LNG project. The required investments on both the seller's and the buyer's side will amount to billions of dollars, and shipping will cost billions more. Presumably, the sales proceeds from the investment will, over time, exceed the seller's costs and yield an acceptable return, so billions more are involved. To paraphrase Everett Dirkson, a former United States senator known for his wit and eloquence, 'A few billion here, a few billion there, and pretty soon it begins to add up to real money'. Under the circumstances, it is not difficult to understand why it may take three to five years to negotiate and finalise an SPA. Virtually every word of the document receives close scrutiny when such vast sums hang in the balance.

   Over the years, costs of development have risen significantly, while LNG prices have remained fairly constant in real terms. This has forced sellers to seek ways to reduce development costs. With increasing frequency, they are no longer willing and able to fund development costs through borrowings on their own credit and reflected on their balance sheets. New approaches to financing are dealt with in Chapter 6. These new approaches are having an impact on the provisions of agreements throughout the chain of project contracts.

4.1.1.4 Security of Supply

Security of supply has always been one of the hallmarks of the LNG industry. It is vital to buyers, enabling them to meet their obligations to provide needed electricity or fuel to their customers. It is vital to sellers that there be a constant revenue stream, thereby enabling them to service their debt and obtain the anticipated return for their risks and investments. It is vital to the party responsible for shipping, to ensure that vessels are utilised in the most efficient manner. And with the advent of limited recourse project financing, it has become vital to lenders, whose lending decisions have been based not on the creditworthiness of the project participants, but on projected project revenues and lender access to the proceeds from LNG sales.

Concerns for the security of supply (and the receipt of the proceeds thereof) have been addressed in a variety of ways in the history of the industry. Some of those ways, typifying trades begun some 30 years ago when the industry was in its infancy, have become less prevalent today due to a number of trends discussed below. It is nonetheless worthwhile to mention the historical practices, since they have long proven their value and still characterise most existing trades.

4.1.1.4.1   Role of Governments

In the early years of the industry, when LNG was in its pioneering phase, those of us at the 'working level' always knew that the LNG project, which was taking all of our waking hours (and sometimes more), was a 'government to government' deal. Somewhere, at some earlier point in time, those in authority had met and decided there was to be a sale. For the buyer, it was a matter of keeping one's population powered, illuminated and warm. For the seller, it was a matter of exploiting one's national resources as a means of developing one's economy. That made our marching orders rather clear. Whether there was to be a sale was not within our purview. Our task was to determine when deliveries would begin, in what volumes, at what price, whether arbitration should be in Paris or The Hague, and all the remaining details. No one had a brief to walk out of a negotiating session, and no one ever did. Negotiations would carry on in intervals of weeks at a time, and in three or more years they would come to a conclusion. Meanwhile all other aspects of the project would have been put in place. Whatever else might be said for such an approach, it imparted a certain sense of security that this would be an arrangement that would endure over time, and it would work.

4.1.1.4.2 *Nature of Sellers and Buyers*

In those early years, the identity of the participants led to further assurances of security of supply. Sellers were usually major companies of sound financial strength and with significant experience in all aspects of the petroleum industry, often backed by state entities that could marshal the support of their parent governments. Buyers were usually major utilities with monopoly markets and top credit ratings, and were based in developed countries with relatively low political or currency exchange risk. The ability to finance the costs of a development was therefore not a matter for major concern, and one could embark on a costly, long-term project with considerable confidence that it would endure.

4.1.1.4.3 *Term*

Knowing that it would take perhaps 10 or 12 years to repay the financed portion of these projects, the economics dictated that the sales arrangements continue for at least 20 years, with the possibility of renewal at that time. This presumed, of course, a supply source that would continue to produce over the period, which in turn helped determine which reservoirs were viable candidates to support a project. A substantial term also adds to the stability of supply in that it permits sellers and buyers to make long-range plans without having constantly to be searching for new customers or sources of supply.

4.1.1.4.4 *Volumes*

It is not surprising that, given the critical mass required to mount a project and the long-term nature of the resulting sales, significant volumes of producible natural gas would have to be available. Independent experts would be required to certify such reserves initially and on a continuing basis as the seller made additional sales commitments. Both the presence of these volumes, and the practice of sellers to build some spare capacity into their LNG production facilities for operating flexibility and unforeseen contingencies, contributed to security of supply.

4.1.1.4.5   Scheduling

Ideally, an LNG plant should be designed, constructed and operated in such a manner that all its component parts may function in co-ordinated fashion and at their most efficient level. Debottlenecking and other adjustments may be necessary to achieve this. However, all would be for naught if LNG delivery schedules were not synchronous with production rates or consistent with storage and shipping capacities. Since rateably even production and delivery is the seller's ideal, take obligations ideally should coincide. This is why sellers have traditionally asked buyers to utilise LNG for their 'base-load' requirements, with seasonal, medium and peak load requirements being satisfied from other fuel sources. Some flexibility in take patterns is allowed in the scheduling provisions, of course; but these are intended primarily to cater for unusual or unforeseen circumstances, and not as a concession to the seasonality of buyers' requirements. Seasonality is, after all, a buyer phenomenon; and sellers traditionally maintain that buyer use of alternative fuels beyond base-load needs should certainly provide greater flexibility at less cost than the building of spare LNG production capacity that would receive full use only if seller could find another buyer for the off-season.

4.1.1.4.6   Take-or-Pay

Take-or-pay provisions in LNG SPAs have to do not so much with security of supply as they do with sellers' security of revenue. They have been a hallmark of the LNG industry since its inception. Despite the fact that they have always attracted extensive discussion, they have remained basically unchanged through the years. A possible explanation is that actual experience has shown take-or-pay clauses to pose more of a theoretical threat to buyers than a real one. They have been invoked only on exceedingly rare occasions, and usually without success, the parties finding other ways to treat a delay in a scheduled delivery. It is reasonable to assume that take-or-pay obligations will take on added importance as limited recourse project financing becomes more popular.

4.1.1.4.7   'SMUT'

'SMUT' does not refer to what the *Oxford American Dictionary* defines as 'a small flake of soot' or, secondarily, as 'indecent talk or pictures or stories'. Rather, SMUT is what has become one of the favourite acronyms in the business, innocently resulting from an oft-repeated admonition, usually by buyers, that the parties entering into an SPA should do so in a 'spirit of mutual understanding and trust'. Another thought very often repeated is that an LNG trade is analogous to a marriage, the only difference being that divorce is unthinkable. These sentiments may bring a wry grin to some; but they have traditionally been one of the elements that have brought sellers and buyers together, and part of the glue that has kept them there. Despite all the negotiations and discussions and careful selection of words and phrases in the documents, when all else is said and done, the security of supply and therefore the success of an LNG trade depends on the determination of the parties to make it work. The relationships developed and the goodwill thus engendered have proved themselves over the years. Difficult contretemps between the parties have often been amicably overcome because of this reservoir of good will.

4.1.2   Future Trends

The foregoing reflects the perspective of past experiences and trades already in existence, as a backdrop to the analyses of the LNG project documents that are to follow. But what of projects in the future, some of which are already underway with negotiations in progress? Some observers say we have already entered into an era of 'second generation' LNG projects. With increased privatisation of the energy business, the role of governments is expected to decline. More and more parties, often with limited experience, having taken no exploration risk and with no long-term stake in the success of the host country's development, are seeking to join ventures on the seller's side. Even buyers and those traditionally associated with buyers want to become sellers. Buyers are also proliferating, many of whom have reduced financial resources, creditworthiness and governmental backing. Country, currency and exchange risks are on the increase, at the same time as rising costs have driven investors to seek limited or non-recourse project financing from lenders who are notably risk-averse. Diversity of demand and supply has caused sellers and buyers to seek markets on a number of continents with divergent price structures. Shorter-term sales and less than train-size volumes are being widely discussed. Requests for greater flexibility in scheduling, reduced take-or-pay requirements and lower prices, competitive with pipeline gas, coal or other commodities, are on the increase. And as if this weren't enough, as will be seen later in this chapter, SMUT may have seen its better days.

4.1.3   Paradigm

It would be too complicated, and perhaps too lengthy, to discuss in detail in the chapter sections that follow each and every type of venture and project contract in existence today. It would also suggest that every such detail is personally known to this writer, when we all know that confidentiality arrangements do, on occasion, operate as they are intended.

For present purposes, therefore, the paradigm case to be discussed is a new venture consisting of a state entity and private parties authorised to explore for and, if found, develop hydrocarbon resources, including gas that could support an LNG project. The authorising document will be either a PSC or a DA, with indications of how they differ when appropriate. Likewise, the venture arrangements will be governed by either an operating agreement (OA) or a joint venture agreement (JVA).

We will assume that there has been a gas discovery that could support sales from at least two, and possibly three, LNG production trains. The relevant authorities and the boards of the respective parties believe a viable project is at hand and grant all requisite approvals to proceed. The marketers, meanwhile, are already scouring the world for buyers. A potential sale that would justify the construction of two trains is identified, so a front end engineering and design (FEED) contractor is engaged. Development of the bid package for the EPC contract for an onshore LNG plant, as well as packages for offshore production and pipeline facilities and long-lead items, then gets underway. Pre-award discussions narrow the EPC contractor field to two candidates, with the actual award timed to follow completion of LNG sales negotiations.

At this point the focus shifts to conclusion of the SPA itself, in the minds of many the most difficult step of all.

4.1.4   Legal Perspective

Much of what has already been said and will be said in the pages that follow is of a technical, or engineering, planning, financial, marketing, managerial or administrative, nature. A business and commercial lawyer's business is part business and commercial, and part lawyering. The number of times that the lawyer is chided by business persons for getting into their business is exceeded only by the number of times business persons have chided their lawyer for not understanding the business implications of the lawyer's work. It is a perpetual-motion, no-win proposition that I have found can be resolved only by taking the position that a lawyer is the best judge of what is a legal issue; and since every one of the issues arises in the context of a contract, which is a legal document, every matter dealt with in the chain of project documents is, at least to some degree, a legal issue.

That, anyway, is the answer I gave to my marketing colleague who expressed doubt that there were any legal aspects to the LNG business.

There is another, less facetious, justification for a lawyer's credential in discussing LNG project development through the lens of the contracts involved. It goes back to the thought that certain themes and principles transcend the various phases of a development and ought to be reflected on a consistent basis throughout the contract chain. The number of contributors who participate in every aspect of the development, from concession grant to completion of construction to implementation of the SPA, are very few indeed. Yet lawyers often do; and some even survive to tell about it.

4.2 'CONCESSION' ARRANGEMENTS

4.2.1 Early Concessions

The reader will observe that quotation marks appear around the word 'concession' in the title of section 4.2. This is intended to signify that, in today's world, relationships between sovereign powers and petroleum industry developers are no longer governed by the traditional concession arrangements that prevailed in earlier times. Simply put, those earlier

Figure 4.2 Contractual Framework for Project Documentation

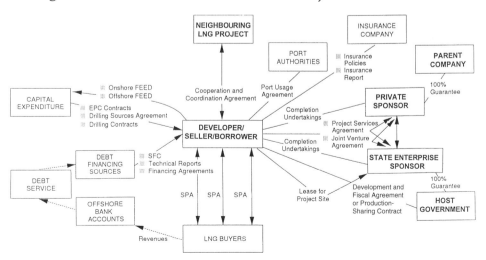

arrangements purported to vest in the concessionaire ownership rights in natural resources in the ground; and if and to the extent such resources actually existed and could profitably be produced, they belonged to the concession holder, to be disposed of as he thought fit. The newer thinking, as states have gained their independence from colonial rule, is that the resources belong to the people, and should be developed by the state on behalf of the people for their benefit. Instructive in this regard is the following passage from the Explanation accompanying Indonesia's Law No. 44 of 1960, which among other things created Pertamina as a state enterprise:

> This Law ... is of an entirely different spirit if compared to the principles which form the basic thinking of the Netherlands Indies Mining Act and the other regulations applicable up to now. Striving for a just prosperity for the Indonesian people, this Law ... abandons the point of view which gives priority to the individuals' rights. This regulation does not justify the view that the happiness of an individual can be achieved in a proper way by the individuals themselves with their individual rights, and cannot accept that the riches of a citizen accumulated in full freedom really means national riches as well. For this regulation, the way to establish a prosperous and just Indonesian community is not through and by emphasising the individual but through efforts which primarily lay obligations to the State of the Republic of Indonesia. ... The [former] Mining Ordinance and the regulations resulting from a liberal, capitalist and individual line of thinking <u>must therefore be eliminated as quickly as possible</u>, in order to obviate the existence of two conflicting ways of thinking during the process of achieving a new life for the Indonesian people. (emphasis added)

This puts the sentiment rather well, and goes a long way toward explaining why PSCs contain many of the provisions they do.

4.2.2   Licences and Leases

Of course, not all petroleum-producing countries are former colonies, and it is not every jurisdiction that purports to deny to developers an ownership interest in resources. Licensing and leasing arrangements, prevalent in most countries (or subdivisions thereof) that are not newly independent and that have well-developed petroleum laws, grant to the licensee or leaseholder certain rights in respect of a specified area, including the right to explore for, produce, transport, process and sell petroleum recovered from that area. Licence groups may or may not include a state oil enterprise or other public entity, while leases are normally issued by states or individuals to private interests. The licence or lease is usually a rather cryptic and standardised document, containing such basic terms as a description of the specified area, the licence or lease term, the party or parties to whom issued, their payment obligations, and otherwise incorporating the provisions of applicable laws, including those imposing royalties and taxes.

4.2.3 Production-Sharing Contracts/Contracts for Work

The production-sharing contract, or PSC, enables the state to exercise nominal control over the development of its natural resources. Private interests are invited to participate as the contractor, or agent, of the state for two primary purposes:

(1) to make available the benefit of their technological expertise and experience; and
(2) to provide a needed source of financial backing for the enterprise.

Contracts for work, as they were known in Indonesia before the advent of the PSC, were similar to the traditional concession in that the contractor 'managed' all operations. The 'management clause' in the PSC assigns this role to Pertamina. In their latter-day form, contracts for work are a means for governments to engage skilled assistance for particular petroleum operations, without in the process giving up any ownership interest in the related natural resources.

4.2.4 Development Agreements

A relatively recent addition to the range of agreements between governments and petroleum resource developers is the development agreement (DA) or one of its varieties, such as the development and fiscal agreement (DFA) or development and production-sharing agreement (DPSA). These arrangements have been devised to address the situation where there is a known resource capable of development to support an LNG project, and government participation is to take the form of equity participation by the state enterprise in a joint venture organised for the project upon basically the same terms as equity investors from the private sector. In the discussion that follows, a combination of DA and PSC terms will be reviewed as the model for the government-to-developer arrangements providing the starting point for the chain of LNG project contracts.

4.2.5 Standard (and Not So Standard) Terms

4.2.5.1 *Scope*

A clear objective of any government, when authorising private energy companies to seek for and produce the state's natural resources (either with or without the participation of a state enterprise), is to establish the scope or range of the activities that the venture is authorised to conduct. In cases where there is not yet a discovery, the authorised petroleum operations will normally be wide enough in scope to cover both upstream (exploration and production) and downstream (processing and sale) operations, and will extend to oil, gas and any other hydrocarbons or non-hydrocarbon substances produced in conjunction with hydrocarbons. Where a discovery has been made, however, the scope of authorised operations may be more restricted, depending on what future activities the government may wish to reserve for its state enterprise and/or other developers. The state may, for example, wish initially to establish limits on the size of the project, with the possibility those limits may be expanded at some future time when the project has demonstrated its commercial viability.

The concession agreement, whatever form it takes, constitutes the 'charter' or foundation document whereby the state grants to the venturers the governmental authority they need in order to conduct their operations in a lawful manner. Since it is intended that the parties have reciprocal rights to enforce the agreement terms, both the state and the venturers are signatories to the document.

If one of the venturers is a state entity, the agreement provisions specify the nature of the relationship that is to exist between that entity and the other venturers. Normally there is an assurance that whatever participant is to be responsible for the actual conduct of petroleum operations, whether it be a production-sharing contractor or a joint venture company formed by the participants, it shall have the authority to conduct the full range of petroleum operations, to the exclusion of any other parties or interests. By the same token, if the government has made any prior commitments with respect to the contract area or the reservoirs involved, the scope provisions should reflect that fact in order to avoid any possible collision of interests.

Since the scope provisions will define those rights and activities that are within the ambit of the parties' authority, they will also serve to delineate what is *ultra vires* to the venture. Participants, and especially those from the private sector, will thus want to make every effort to fashion scope provisions that are as expansive as possible, lest operations be unduly hindered or opportunities for ancillary activities, not specifically mentioned in the enabling provisions, be lost. Project lenders, too, will one day be looking for expansive powers, since the assignment to them of such powers will form part of their security. From the very outset, therefore, venturers should be sensitive to this factor, which could ultimately affect the project's financibility.

4.2.5.2 *Effective Date and Term*

In addition to circumscribing the scope of operations authorised to the venture, the state will normally place a temporal limit on the parties' authority. The charter document will usually establish a date upon which the agreement is to become effective, which may be the date of execution or a future date when a condition precedent, such as the obtaining of further requisite governmental approvals, has been satisfied. The 'term' of the agreement will extend over a stipulated period of time commencing with the effective date and ending either on a date specific or upon the occurrence of a specified event, such as the completion of all LNG sales permitted to the venture.

One may assume that the fundamental purpose of the state in establishing a limit on the term of the arrangements is to afford to the state (and/or its participating entity) the opportunity one day to take over the venture. Though this prospect may not be expressly stated in the chartering document, it is usually implied. The language normally provides that the term of the venture may be extended, without forfeiture, if the parties mutually agree. This may afford to private parties some hope that they may be permitted to continue to benefit from a successful venture, although it is just such a venture that would be the most likely candidate for state take-over. Under the circumstances, private investors would be wise to harbour their hopes, but to base their project economics only on a term that is certain.

As discussed in section 4.2.5.12 (Termination), the charter document or its related operating or joint venture agreement usually provides for early termination in certain circumstances, such as voluntary withdrawal or the occurrence of a material breach of the agreement terms.

4.2.5.3 *Licence/Contract Area*

A further limitation normally appearing in the chartering document relates to the geographic location in which venture operations may be conducted. The metes and bounds of the 'licence area' or 'contract area' are usually set out in detail. Limitations may also be placed on the specific reservoirs or geologic formations with respect to which petroleum operations may be conducted. Venturers will naturally try to obtain access to the widest possible geographic location and geologic structures, and to this end should make every endeavour to secure the agreement of the state to permit future expansions of the contract area to the extent necessary to permit the venture to fulfil all of its LNG sales commitments. Buyers, under the terms of their SPAs, and possibly lenders under financing arrangements, will require initial certification as to available gas reserves as well as periodic updates when additional sales are made. To avoid possible breach of the venture's sales and financing commitments, the state should be prepared to allow access beyond the initial contract location and formations should that become necessary.

4.2.5.4   *Operator*

The charter document, or in some cases the operating agreement or joint venture agreement attached to and forming part of the charter document, identifies the person or party who is to act as the operator for the venture. Hopefully the operator has been selected or staffed on the basis of experience, expertise and other such qualifications, since it will be the operator who will be responsible for the day-to-day conduct of all venture operations.

Where the charter document is a PSC, the operator is normally one of the production-sharing contractors. The operator under a DA is a joint venture company organised pursuant to the provisions of the DA and in which the respective co-venturers own equity participating interests, represented by shares.

Since the joint venture company is owned by the participants and directed by them through board and shareholder decisions, it would not be appropriate to allow the operator voluntarily to withdraw from the operatorship. Nor would forced removal be an appropriate remedy for a breach of operator obligations. Instead, the DA normally provides that the remedy available against the operator for breach of its obligations is monetary damages. The operator may be held liable to third parties for losses resulting from the operator's negligence or wilful misconduct and is required to indemnify the government against any such claims. For actual damages resulting from the uncontrolled loss of petroleum in the contract area (or of LNG at the LNG plant, if LNG plant operation is within the scope of the joint venture's activities), the operator will be liable to the government only in cases of gross negligence or wilful misconduct. All of the venturers in the project bear their proportionate share of these potential liabilities through the share structure of the joint venture company.

By contrast the operator in the PSC context, being a volunteer from among the PSC contractors entitled to recover its operatorship costs but not to receive any profit for its efforts, may voluntarily resign and may be removed for cause. It is normally expected to conduct its operations 'prudently' and 'in a workmanlike manner'. Due to the 'no profit–no loss' feature, however, only a demonstration of gross negligence or wilful misconduct will be cause for removal. The operator is normally indemnified by its fellow PSC contractors, in the proportion of their participation interests, against claims by third parties arising from the operator's ordinary negligence.

Additional discussion regarding venture operatorship appears in section 4.3.2.3.

4.2.5.5 Fiscal Regime

Equal in importance with the petroleum rights provisions of the concession document are the provisions of the PSC or DA establishing the fiscal regime for the venture. This 'regime' includes the provisions establishing the percentage participations of the respective parties, the taxes, royalties and other payment obligations to which the venture parties are subject, the budget and accounting rules that shall apply, and the enumeration of other obligations, not necessarily of a monetary nature, that will apply to venture operations. The state's overall 'take' is essentially a combination of two factors: the share and role accorded to the state enterprise in the venture, and the details of the fiscal regime in the charter document.

The venture will normally be liable for taxes on income at a specified rate. Similar taxes, such as taxes on dividends, interest and royalties, may also apply. The charter document usually provides details on how these taxes are to be calculated, including depreciation rules, rates and schedules, how to distinguish between capital costs and operating costs, and which costs are 'cost-recoverable' or chargeable to the venture. The document may also provide for tax relief, such as through a tax holiday or a government undertaking to pay a participant's taxes for a specified period of time.

The charter document should also specify those taxes that will not apply to venture operations, such as income taxes in respect of services performed for the venture by its participants, or in respect of capital employed, or on the distribution or repatriation of dividends, equity invested or other property. The right of the venture, its participants, its contractors and subcontractors and their respective employees to import, utilise and re-export venture and personal property without duty or other tax should also be provided for.

Royalties are another significant contributor to the government 'take'. The charter document will therefore specify which types of royalties (e.g. royalties on gas, condensate and/or crude oil) shall apply to petroleum operations, the relevant rates, and the manner of their calculation.

Other payment obligations may apply to the venture or its participants and may appear in the charter document. PSCs, in particular, may include a 'signature' bonus, an obligation to compensate the state for exploration activities and data furnished to the venture, and one or more bonuses based on volumes produced during the production phase. Other obligations, not involving payments as such but nonetheless constituting a cost to the venturers, may take the form of a requirement to market the state entity's share of production, a requirement to supply the domestic market with a portion of production (often at prices below those that could be realised through export), a requirement to refine a portion of production locally or an obligation to use local goods and services in petroleum operations even though they may cost somewhat more than comparable imported goods and services.

Essential for the proper administration of the fiscal regime are accounting standards, rules and procedures. These are normally contained in an accounting procedure forming an attachment to the operating agreement or joint venture agreement that is to govern the venture's operations, which in turn is attached to (and thereby becomes a part of) the PSC or DA. The accounting procedures specify record-keeping and reporting requirements, procedures for the establishment of work programmes and budgets, rights of the participants and the government to receive reports of venture operations, to have access to the venture records and to audit the venture accounts, and rules regarding the disposal of venture property.

4.2.5.6 *Title*

The issue of who has title to petroleum produced, and to the assets utilised to produce the petroleum, gives rise to some fundamental and rather interesting differences between PSCs and DAs.

As discussed earlier, participants under a PSC regime are not normally accorded title to resources in the ground. In keeping with the notion of national sovereignty over those resources, the participants are said to have an 'economic interest' in the produced petroleum and the proceeds from its sale while the production remains within the country of origin. Title passes to the participants at the point of export (or at the point of delivery, for domestic sales), thereby enabling the participants to pass title onward to their purchasers. In the Indonesian LNG context, this mechanism includes an added twist in that sales are effected by the state enterprise, on behalf of the PSC participants. For that enterprise to be able to pass clear title, the participants enter into a supply agreement with the enterprise whereby the participants convey their ownership interest in the LNG to the enterprise immediately prior to passage of title from the enterprise to the customer. The LNG sale document normally describes these supply arrangements, thereby recognising that the sale is, in part, being made on behalf of the participants and that they have an economic interest in the related proceeds.

By contrast, the DA specifically provides that ownership in and title to the produced and processed petroleum resides with the joint venture, and thus is indirectly owned by the joint venture participants through their shareholdings.

The PSC approach to asset ownership is similar to that pertaining to petroleum. All of the project assets are 'owned' by the state enterprise even though the participants must pay their PSC 'share' of the costs, either directly or through borrowings that are amortised from the proceeds of LNG sales (thereby reducing the funds available for distribution as PSC shares of the project income). The DA, on the other hand, also consistent in its approach, provides that all project assets are the property of the joint venture.

LNG buyers, and in recent times lenders to LNG projects, take a keen interest in these title issues and will seek assurance that the seller is able to convey unencumbered title to its purchasers. To the buyer it is a matter of getting what it has paid for; to the lender it is a matter of security for the repayment of its loan. For this reason the language of the charter document should clearly describe whence title derives and how it flows to the seller and its purchaser.[3]

4.2.5.7 'Work' Obligations

The PSC or DA provides a logical setting for the government to set out the exploration, development and other obligations to be performed by the participants through the operator or joint venture company. The most fundamental of these requirements, often referred to as 'work obligations', are designed to encourage the parties to proceed diligently and in substantial measure to explore for and develop the state's hydrocarbon resources in the contract area. In the case of a known gas discovery, the work obligation may be framed as a directive to determine the commercial feasibility of developing the field, possibly as an LNG project if the source of supply is too far removed from potential customers to warrant the construction of a pipeline.

---

[3] Lenders also seek ways to obtain the assignment of an ownership interest in project assets as a further security measure. It is perhaps too soon to tell whether these efforts are enforceable and therefore serve their intended purpose, especially in jurisdictions where the assets are owned by a government or state enterprise, or where local law prohibits the foreign ownership of real property.

Work obligations in PSCs usually specify in detail the types of activities the operator is to undertake (e.g. the conduct of seismic investigation or the drilling of exploration wells), the time-frame within which each phase of exploration and development must be completed, and minimum expenditure levels for the various activities.[4] Termination of the PSC is usually the remedy for a failure to complete work obligations within the allowed time limits.

Development agreements, on the other hand, have greater application to situations where there is a known gas discovery. In this case, exploration activity is of lesser importance, although some reservoir delineation and additional definition may be called for. The emphasis in this case is on determining the feasibility of a development, such as an LNG project, and the conduct of marketing activities to identify potential customers. Since the decision as to feasibility would normally precede the obtaining of commitments for the sale of LNG, marketing activities may be assigned time limits and minimum sales volume requirements. Failure to achieve these objectives could either result in a curtailment of the size of the project or lead to its abandonment.

4.2.5.8   Use of Local Goods and Services

It has long been the objective of states not only to develop their natural resources, but also to realise other 'ripple effects' in the development of their economies. Therefore, charter documents normally contain a variety of provisions designed to maximise indigenous participation in all phases of a project's development. For example, the operator may be required to give preference to suppliers of local goods and services, usually with the proviso that such goods and services are 'competitive' with regard to such matters as price, credit and other purchase terms, quality, workmanship, availability in the quantities desired and timely performance. In some instances, local suppliers are given a slight edge by stipulating that a price somewhat higher (say, 10 per cent or 15 per cent more) than that charged by non-national suppliers is deemed competitive.

Additional requirements in this vein include an obligation to hire, educate and train nationals at all levels of the organisation charged with development activities; the providing of training for employees of the state enterprise, if it is a participant; the use of indigenous lending institutions, insurance companies and marine service companies to the

---

[4] PSCs are especially detailed in describing the minimum requirements for crude oil exploration, providing for periodic relinquishments of portions of the contract area and surrender of any portion where 'reasonable exploration efforts' have not been undertaken within a specified period. These relinquishment and surrender provisions do not apply to areas known to be underlain by hydrocarbons, such as a proven gas reservoir.

extent reasonably possible; and, in the case of certain PSCs, the require-ment to offer a percentage of participation in the development to local investors.

4.2.5.9 *Environmental Requirements*

Charter documents generally provide that the participants shall comply in every respect with all applicable laws, rules and regulations, including those relating to the environment. It is often the case, however, that local environmental laws are in the developmental phase, and may lack precision as to what is permitted and what is not. In at least one case, a DA provides that the government and the other parties shall discuss and agree on environmental guidelines prior to the commencement of LNG deliveries.

Most experienced operators come to a project equipped with their own, internally adopted set of environmental guidelines and standards, which they apply wherever they conduct their business. Despite public percep-tions, the guidelines and standards the petroleum industry applies to itself are generally rather demanding and of a quality that will meet the require-ments of most governments and international organisations concerned with the environment.

As new projects begin to turn to limited recourse project financing, one can reasonably expect that lenders and export credit agencies (ECAs) will require that projects comply with environmental standards established by the World Bank, the Organisation for Economic Cooperation and Development (OECD) or the ECAs themselves. Thus, despite the fact that the environmental undertakings in a PSC or DA may be of a limited nature, developers should be prepared to require of themselves and their contractors and subcontractors standards sufficient to satisfy the requirements of their potential lenders.

4.2.5.10 *Government Obligations*

In the charter document governments take on a number of obligations in addition to the basic grant of the right to explore for and develop petroleum resources. These obligations relate to the development activities required to be carried on by the operator and are essential to the success of those activities. Among other things, the government ensures access to the contract area, onshore areas where petroleum operations are con-ducted, government-owned facilities and other locations as needed. The government undertakes to provide easements, rights of way and surface rights for production facilities and to assist in the leasing or other acquisition of property. It also undertakes to provide assistance in the obtaining of visas, work permits, licences and other required authorisations, in dealing with governmental entities, and in the obtaining of insurance and financing for the project.

Additionally, the government may warrant that the rights accorded the parties under the charter document, including exclusive rights in respect of the contract area and the production therefrom, shall be free and clear of any encumbrance, backed by an indemnity against third party claims in respect of such rights. Finally, the government may offer a 'stabilisation clause' providing that if any governmental action has a material adverse impact on petroleum operations, the government shall take such remedial steps as are necessary to restore the economic or other benefits contemplated under the charter document.

4.2.5.11   *Applicable Law and Dispute Resolution*

Both PSCs and DAs normally provide that the charter document shall be governed by and construed in accordance with local law. In the event of a dispute that cannot be resolved amicably, the normal recourse is a reference to arbitration in a foreign, neutral jurisdiction under the rules of one of the internationally recognised arbitration associations, such as the International Chamber of Commerce (ICC) or the United Nations Commission on International Trade Law (UNCITRAL), unless reference to an expert has been provided for as to specified technical matters. Expert decisions are usually advisory in nature, however, and are not finally binding on the parties. PSCs sometimes provide that if an arbitration tribunal is unable to resolve a particular matter, it may be referred for decision to the courts of the local jurisdiction.

Participants (and ultimately lenders) may wish at some time to enforce one or more of the charter provisions against the government, and to this end a waiver of sovereign immunity should be included in the document. This is a feature of recent DAs, and indeed the immunity waiver is repeated in the context of the arbitration clause. PSCs, on the other hand, are known to provide that nothing in the agreement, including the arbitration provisions, shall prevent or limit the government from exercising its inalienable rights. One can only imagine how this might be received by future lenders of limited recourse financing to projects where such PSCs apply.

4.2.5.12   *Termination*

PSCs are normally not terminable during an initial period, after which the parties may relinquish their rights and be relieved of any further obligations if continuing with petroleum operations is not warranted. In any event, however, the agreement may be terminated by a party after a specified notice period in the event of a major breach by another party, which must be established by arbitration. The DA, on the other hand, is stated to be co-terminous with the JVA entered into by the co-venturers at the same time as the DA is executed. Under the JVA, the parties may terminate the arrangements at any time by mutual agreement. In the event of a breach by a private party, the non-defaulting parties may buy out that party's shares at a discount to their book value, while a breach by the participating state entity entitles the non-defaulting parties to 'put' their shares to the state entity at a premium.

4.3   VENTURE ARRANGEMENTS

4.3.1   Types of Ventures

Investors seeking to develop a nation's resources, perhaps in conjunction with an oil company that is an instrumentality of that nation, often form themselves into consortia for this purpose. This approach may stem from the oil industry's time-honoured practice of attempting to spread risks by seeking safety in numbers ('I'd rather have 10 opportunities for participating in 10 per cent of a discovery than one opportunity for owning 100 per cent of a dry hole'). Often, however, this multi-party structure is dictated by the concession terms of the host country.

Joint operations may take a variety of forms. Where petroleum rights are granted under a licence issued by the state, 'licence groups' organise themselves under an 'operating agreement' or 'joint operating agreement', with one of their number designated as the operator charged with the conduct of petroleum operations on behalf of the group. A state enterprise may or may not be a participant. Under PSC arrangements, the private participants (contractors) and a state enterprise form themselves under an 'operating agreement', with one of the private participants normally being selected as the operator. Under a DA, normally involving a state enterprise, the parties enter into a 'joint venture agreement' calling for the establishment of a joint venture company, the shares of which are held by the respective participants and which serves as the operator. Project development may also be undertaken by a group of companies or joint ventures organised as a new joint venture, with the operator being either one of the constituent members or a new joint venture company. Operations may also be undertaken among groups of the foregoing on a unitised basis pursuant to a 'unitisation and unit operating agreement', with one of the constituent members being designated as the unit operator.

While all of the agreements mentioned above have a great deal in common, the ensuing discussion of the relationships among parties to a development will focus on the form of operating agreement normally accompanying a PSC and the form of joint venture agreement normally accompanying a DA.

4.3.2   Common (and Uncommon) Principles

4.3.2.1   *Effective Date, Term and Termination*

Operating and joint venture agreements normally enter into effect at the time of their execution but may, as noted in section 4.2.5.2, require the satisfaction of a condition precedent to effectiveness such as the obtaining of necessary government approvals. The agreements have a term that in no case extends beyond the term of the PSC or the DA to which they relate,[5] but which may be limited to a specified time period or a date when a specified event occurs, such as the completion of the last sale under the last remaining SPA entered into by the venture. The parties are always free to terminate their arrangements by mutual agreement, and provisions for early termination by way of withdrawal, abandonment or upon material breach by another party are usually included.

4.3.2.2   *Nature of Participating Interests*

Each participant in a joint operation is said to have a 'participating interest' in the venture. In the case of a PSC, this is represented by a percentage of the total rights and obligations under the agreement, while the interest of a member of the joint venture under a DA is represented by a percentage of the shares. Aside from the specific rights, duties and obligations assigned to an operator in the context of a PSC or to certain rights and privileges that may be assigned to a state enterprise in the context of both PSCs and DAs, participation interests in joint operations normally entitle each participant to rights and obligations of the same nature and quality. They may vary in quantity, of course, depending upon the percentages of interest held by the respective participants.

A new development in this area is the creation of differing interests among participants in a joint venture, represented by different classes of shares. The holders of each class of shares are entitled to participate in

---

[5] Interestingly, the term of one joint venture agreement is not tied to the term of its related DA. Instead, it is the DA that terminates upon termination of the joint venture.

some, but perhaps not all, of the activities of the joint venture, depending upon the nature and extent of their contributions to the project. This approach has been developed to reward parties who were not among the original investors but who bring value to the project in such ways as purchasing LNG, performing marketing activities or providing financial support. At the same time, the approach enables the original investors to avoid undue dilution of their participation interests while preserving the availability of equity for possible offer to future project contributors.

4.3.2.3 Designation of Operator: Rights, Duties and Obligations

Under a licence or PSC regime, one of the participants is designated in the operating agreement as the operator charged with conducting the day-to-day operations of the venture. This function is performed by the joint venture company in the context of a joint venture agreement. The operator carries out the venture operations in accordance with policies, programmes and budgets approved by the operating committee pursuant to the operating agreement or by the board of directors of the joint venture company pursuant to the joint venture agreement. The operator conducts its activities utilising its own employees, employees of its affiliates, employees seconded to the operator by co-participants in the venture, or by contractors and subcontractors.

Both operating and joint venture agreements require that the operator perform its obligations in compliance with applicable laws and with standards set forth in the relevant venture document. These standards, as well as the operator's rights to resign or the conditions under which it may be removed, are set out in section 4.2.5.4.

The duties of an operator do not vary significantly between operating and joint venture agreements. In each case it is required to keep accounting records in accordance with an agreed accounting procedure; to furnish to all parties information regarding the operations, including technical reports and periodic statements of activities and progress reports; to allow to all participants reasonable access to operations; to prepare and submit to the operating committee (in the PSC context) or the board of directors (in the DA context) work programmes consistent with the chartering document, annual or semi-annual budgets, requests for approval of budget over-runs, and authorisations for expenditure (AFEs) for individual projects; to enter into contracts as required; to issue cash calls and pay venture costs and expenses; to deliver for and on behalf of the participants their respective shares of petroleum or petroleum products; and, in the context of joint venture arrangements, to distribute dividends, other distributable cash and property and to retire equity in the venture. The operator is usually given special powers to act in the event of emergencies even if such actions would ordinarily require approval of the operating committee or board of directors.

The operating agreement or joint venture agreement may relegate certain functions to special committees composed of representatives from various of the co-participants. Marketing activities, shipping matters and the arranging of insurance and financing for the project are items often relegated to such committees.

4.3.2.4   *Operating Committee or Board of Directors*

The operating or joint venture agreement provides for the establishment of an operating committee or board of directors to establish overall direction for the venture and to oversee the activities of the operator. Each participant is normally represented on the operating committee or board by one or more representatives or alternates. The parties may also be assisted by advisors at committee or board meetings.

The operating committee or board establishes, reviews and revises the policies, programmes and budgets that govern venture operations. It may appoint technical, financial, accounting, legal and other committees to assist in its work as it deems appropriate. Normally any participant is entitled to call for a meeting of the operating committee or board. Notice, quorum and agenda requirements are usually specified. Voting requirements may vary depending upon the composition of the venture, the identity of the participant or the subject to be considered. Thus, an operator under a PSC is often given a deciding vote. In joint ventures, the affirmative votes of the major shareholders may be required for the adoption of certain measures, and unanimity may be required in respect of matters that would affect the fundamental structure or powers of the entity. The operating committee or board may take action without a meeting provided that certain procedures are followed. All decisions normally must be in writing and are binding upon all the co-participants if taken in accordance with the required procedures.

4.3.2.5   *Work Programmes and Budgets; Sole Risk*

As has been stated, the operator is charged with submitting to the oversight body periodic work programmes and budgets proposing future activities for the venture, presumably with a view towards project development. The operating committee or board reviews these programmes and budgets and either approves them as submitted or modifies them. If a commercial discovery has been made and a development project appears to be feasible, any party may advance a development proposal if the operator has not done so. The other parties may either agree to the proposal, perhaps with amendments, or decline to participate. In the latter case, those parties wishing to proceed may do so on a 'sole-risk' basis.

Even though not everyone may have chosen to participate in a particular activity, it remains the function of the operator or joint venture company to prepare a development programme and budget for that activity. Those who have chosen to participate may either approve the proposed programme and budget or modify them as they see fit. In the production-sharing context, separate approval of the state enterprise may also be required. The operator also conducts the sole-risk operations on behalf of the participating parties, and may use assets in which all parties have an interest upon reimbursement of allocable costs for such use. The operator must make reasonable efforts to prevent sole-risk activities from impeding general operations, and the sole-risk parties may be required to indemnify the non-participating parties against damages or disruptions of this nature. Non-participating parties in sole-risk operations are usually given an opportunity to elect at some future time to participate in the sole-risk activity. Should they so elect, they are usually required to pay a premium over the costs which they would otherwise have borne had they participated from the outset.

4.3.2.6 Disposition of Production

Participation in a development venture normally entitles each participant to its participating interest share of all production. With respect to crude oil or condensate, the parties may have an offtake obligation and may actually lift their share of produced volumes for their own use or onsale. Otherwise, the operator may effect sales and attribute the proceeds to the respective participants according to their participation shares. LNG volumes delivered to buyers, and the proceeds from such sales, are allocated among the participants in similar fashion. LNG sales invoices are normally payable to an offshore account with a paying agent, who is instructed to channel the proceeds to various accounts for the payment of royalties and taxes, project operating costs, shipping costs (if applicable) and debt service costs before paying over any remaining amounts to the operator for further disposition or directly to the participants.

4.3.2.7 Abandonment, Surrender, Extension, Renewal

Joint activities that are to be abandoned or otherwise terminated normally require the same approval procedures as applied to the initiation of such activities. Those not wishing to abandon or terminate an activity may be given the opportunity to continue it on a sole-risk basis. It has been previously noted that PSCs normally provide for the systematic surrender of portions of the contract area, but that this applies mainly to crude oil and not to areas overlying proven hydrocarbon reserves. The operating or joint venture agreement, or its related PSC or DA, may allow for extensions and renewals; but these normally require the consent of the state enterprise and/or the government, both of which carefully refrain from giving any pre-assurances that such consent will be granted. Any party may initiate the request for extension or renewal, and those not wishing to join in the request are free to withdraw.

4.3.2.8 Transfers of Interests

Because the participants in a petroleum venture have usually been carefully selected by the host government for their ability to lend technical expertise and sound financial backing to the enterprise, the operating or joint venture agreement normally contains a variety of restrictions on the ability of the parties to assign or otherwise dispose of their interests. Assignments to affiliated companies may usually be made, although parent company guarantees of performance by the assignee may be required, as may the obtaining of consents from certain of the other parties, such as those holding significant participation interests. Transfers of interests to third parties usually require the consent of the government and/or the state enterprise, and transfers may be limited to companies that fulfil specified technical and financial criteria. Also, the transferring party may be required to guarantee the performance by the transferee of its obligations under all applicable project documents. Rights of first refusal are another feature, found in joint venture agreements, that provide limitations on a party's ability to assign its interests to third parties.

4.3.2.9 Withdrawal

Parties to an operating agreement under a PSC are normally allowed to withdraw from a venture once the minimum work obligations they have undertaken have been fulfilled. If they have not, withdrawal is not permitted. Under DA and joint venture arrangements, a party may withdraw if the government or the state entity takes any action that is materially prejudicial to the interests of that party, and an amicable resolution cannot be reached. In such a case, the withdrawing party may 'put' its shares to the state entity at a premium over their net book value.

4.3.2.10 Relationship of the Parties and Taxes

Those who have entered into joint operations with United States companies are aware that such companies are normally subject to US tax laws, as well as those imposed by the jurisdiction where the venture operates. This has the potential for putting the US partner in an unenviable tax position. Often the proposed remedy is a request to the other participants that the venture elect to be treated as a partnership for US tax purposes. This gives rise to no increased exposure or liability to taxes for the non-US participants, and the US party is normally prepared to provide assurances to the other participants in this regard. It does, however, entail the making of the election and of periodic filings of US tax returns on behalf of the venture, which the US party is fully prepared to do.

4.3.2.11 Dispute Resolution and Applicable Law

The method for resolving disputes under operating or joint venture agreements is normally the same as that specified in the relevant PSC or DA, and for this purpose reference is made to section 4.2.5.11. The law governing operating agreements is usually the same as that governing the related PSC, while joint venture agreements do not automatically adopt the same governing law as that applicable to the related DAs.

4.3.2.12 Additional Provisions

Operating and joint venture agreements generally contain additional provisions designed to facilitate cooperation among the parties and the smooth conduct of joint operations. Among such provisions are *force majeure* clauses, provisions designed to cater to potential conflicts of interest, confidentiality clauses, specifications for the making of public announcements, and 'good faith' and waiver of sovereign immunity provisions. The latter two of these assume some degree of importance when a state enterprise is involved; and although a private party may not ever choose to invoke one of these provisions, let alone attempt to enforce it, its very presence in the agreement serves to set a tone for the manner in which the parties treat each other in the conduct of their business.

4.4   FROM DISCOVERY TO DEVELOPMENT

4.4.1   Data Collection and Analysis

The potential project developers have organised themselves and are ready to commence venture operations. They have obtained the necessary government charter, setting out the scope and authority for their activities, the applicable fiscal terms and the other rights and obligations that are to govern their relationship with the state. They have also entered into a government-sanctioned agreement establishing the interrelationships among the participants and have taken such legal and corporate actions as may be necessary to found and organise the entity through which they will operate. They are ready and eager to begin business.

In most instances the government or, where appropriate, the state enterprise participating in the venture will have furnished to the venture all existing geological and geophysical data pertaining to the formations found in the relevant contract area. Additional data pertaining to adjacent areas may also be provided if that would assist in the venture's analysis of the contract area reservoirs. This data, which may be merely the results of seismic surveys but could include well logs, core samples, interpretive studies or any other information resulting from past exploration activities, may be offered free of charge or, in the case of PSCs, at a cost to be reimbursed to the provider.

The new venture will study the available data and perhaps seek to upgrade it or expand on it through computer enhancements, new interpretive techniques or other available means. It may decide, or may by the terms of its undertaking to the state be required, to supplement the data through additional seismic and the drilling of additional exploration, appraisal and delineation wells. The performance of this analytic and data collection activity can in large part be performed utilising the capabilities available to the venture through the operator or its other constituent members. Alternatively, it may require the hiring of services from drilling companies and other contractors specialising in exploration activities. The related contract arrangements and documentation that would apply in the context of a potential LNG project, such as the one under consideration here, do not differ in any significant way from the contract arrangements applicable to other exploration ventures and will therefore not be the subject of detailed discussion in this chapter.

4.4.2   Studies and Other Pre-FEED Activities

Assuming that the data collection and analysis activities described above indicate the presence of a commercially exploitable reservoir, additional studies and analysis will be required with a view to formulating a development plan. Reservoir feasibility, optimisation, simulation, engineering and other technical studies are all means of arriving at a plan for the most effective and efficient exploitation of the resource, while identifying the requisite production facilities and their size, optimum location and potential cost. Corporate and government approvals will be required before the venture may proceed to development. The development plan, including an estimate of project development costs, a proposed project schedule and budget, a comprehensive work plan and a forecast of project return, is the means by which the requisite approvals will be solicited and obtained.

With the approvals in hand, there are a number of additional activities the venture will have to undertake before engaging a FEED contractor. Decisions as to the desired liquefaction technology and process design must be made. The size and number of liquefaction trains required for the overall project must be determined. 'Order of magnitude' cost estimates and a detailed project execution and contract strategy must be developed. The FEED bid package must be prepared and bidders prequalified. Finally, after bid analysis and negotiation, the FEED contract is ready for award.

4.4.3   The Front End Engineering and Design (FEED) Contract

4.4.3.1   *Function of the FEED Contract*

The single most important function of the FEED contract is to provide the maximum possible definition for the work ultimately to be performed by the EPC contractor. This will enable the potential EPC contractors to submit bids on a lump-sum basis, with the least possibility that the contract cost will change through undefined work requiring compensation on a cost-reimbursable basis or through claims for unanticipated changes in the work. Clear definition of contract costs is important not only for cost control purposes, but also for purposes of project financing. Project lenders will normally limit their lending commitment to a specific percentage of forecast project costs, and cost overruns will have to be covered by the borrower's equity investment.

The FEED contractor provides definition for the EPC contractor's work by performing the initial engineering and design work in respect of the facilities to be constructed. The FEED contractor also provides procurement assistance, including the initial procurement of long-lead items. These are items with respect to which procurement commitments must be made before the EPC contractor has been selected, and in the context of an LNG project normally include site preparation, the construction of storage tanks and the manufacture of compressor packages and of the main cryogenic heat exchangers. Through its initial engineering and design work, the FEED contractor is uniquely positioned to provide maximum definition for the work and facilities to be provided by the EPC and long-lead item contractors and to assist in the development of the bid packages for these contracts.

It is therefore not surprising that qualified FEED contractors are usually the same internationally recognised engineering and construction companies that would be qualified to bid for the EPC contract. Indeed, some firms are willing to bid on the FEED contract on terms that are quite favourable to the developer, believing this will give them an inside track for the EPC contract award. Practice has shown, however, that this strategy provides no special advantage, and that the company submitting the lowest evaluated bid is the party destined to win the EPC contract award.

4.4.3.2 FEED Contract Terms

The format and contents of the FEED contract follow along the lines of contracts widely used in the international engineering and construction industry. Familiarity with the usual provisions of such contracts will be presumed for present purposes, and the discussion that follows will focus only on items deserving of special comment in the FEED contract context.

The FEED contractor's obligations to provide front end engineering and design in respect of specified facilities, as well as procurement assistance, are spelled out in detail in the contract and its attachments. The contractor is also obligated to provide all services, personnel, equipment and materials needed for its performance of the work, to the end that its compensation will be limited to the maximum extent possible to its lump-sum bid. It is the obligation of the developer, however, to provide to the contractor all necessary technical and process data, to obtain from third parties all necessary licences for proprietary processes, and to specify which equipment and materials the FEED contractor is to purchase.

While the lump-sum portion of the contract price is intended to cover all identifiable costs, taxes, duties and expenses, it is recognised that certain exceptions will have to be made due to the impossibility of assessing those costs at the outset or to the inability of the contractor to control the developer's project task force (PTF) costs.[6] The contract price therefore makes provision for various items compensated on a reimbursable basis, such as costs generated by the developer's inhouse activities at the contractor's home site, costs associated with certain testing work and other activities at the field site, the cost of purchases made on a reimbursable basis and increased costs due to changes in the work. Change order procedures should be clearly established, with the developer having final approval authority over the changes, lest this become an avenue for the contractor to expand the work scope and claim additional compensation.

The timing of commencement and completion of the FEED work are of key importance. The award of the EPC and long-lead item contracts are dependent on completion of the FEED contractor's work. Sufficient time must be allowed for completion of construction to permit first deliveries of LNG at the time required under the LNG SPA. It is at this point in the project that the interdependence of the provisions of the various project documents is very graphically demonstrated. Large expenditures are on the horizon, and delays anywhere along the line could entail serious financial consequences.

Various measures may be provided for to foster timely performance and completion. The FEED contract should establish specific milestones and dates as a means of monitoring progress, with the achievement of milestones tied to the payment schedule. A provision that 'time is of the essence' is sometimes used to convey the sense of urgency that should attach to the progress and completion schedule, although contractors in certain jurisdictions resist such provisions for fear they will serve to define what is a material breach, entitling the developer to terminate the agreement.[7] Experience has shown that the most effective measure to ensure timely performance is to include in the work description an obligation by the contractor, at its sole expense, to work such additional shifts and to furnish such additional personnel and other resources as are

---

[6] It is a feature of FEED contracts that a fairly large staff of developer personnel from a variety of disciplines (often referred to as a project task force, or PTF) be assigned to work alongside the FEED contractor at the latter's engineering offices. A multitude of decisions affecting every aspect of the development will be made during this period. The FEED contractor has very little scope to limit this involvement by the developer and will therefore require compensation on a reimbursable basis for the costs of providing office, transportation, communications and other support for the PTF.

[7] Contractors often do not appreciate that developers are rarely inclined to view termination as a viable remedy, since it would necessitate the engaging of a replacement contractor and would almost assuredly result in schedule disruptions and increased costs.

necessary to enable the contractor to meet its scheduled milestones and completion dates.

The quality of the contractor's performance is regulated through representation and warranty clauses, regular monitoring and inspection of the work, and completion provisions that afford the developer opportunities to inspect and test the work and require the contractor to remedy any defects at its cost. During a warranty period extending beyond the date of final completion the contractor remains responsible for the reperformance, at its cost, of any defect that may become manifest.

Title issues play an important role in FEED contracts, since a large part of the contractor's work involves the development of designs and drawings and the specification of equipment and processes to be provided by others. The developer will have paid for this work and will therefore expect to receive from the contractor full title to all drawings, engineering work, computer disks and other documentation generated by the contractor. In addition, the contractor will be required to indemnify the developer against all claims in respect of patents, trademarks, copyrights and the disclosure of trade secrets insofar as they concern apparatus patent rights that the contractor has specified or are based on the design, construction or operation of any plant or unit specified by him. The contractor is obligated to disclose promptly and assist the developer in obtaining rights to all inventions the contractor conceives or reduces to practice that are wholly or in part based on proprietary information given to the contractor by the developer, and to grant to the developer a non-exclusive licence to use any patents owned by the contractor. All of these rights are of course important to protect the EPC contractor in its construction of the facilities and the owner in their ultimate operation.

4.5   ENGINEERING, PROCUREMENT AND CONSTRUCTION (EPC) CONTRACTS

4.5.1   Scope

A greenfield LNG project development entails a wide variety of design, engineering, fabrication and construction work far beyond the capabilities of any single contractor. Those having the expertise to build and lay subsea pipelines may or may not have the skills and experience required for the fabrication of offshore production facilities. Offshore facilities contractors may be capable of building an onshore LNG plant, but limitations on their availability due to prior commitments or a shortage of qualified manpower may prevent them from doing both. A company perfectly capable of building the plant will nonetheless have to turn to major subcontractors for the provision of specialty items, such as turbines or heat exchangers. And certain aspects of the project, such as offshore drilling and the provision of related offshore services, may involve such a large number and variety of service providers that it would be impractical to gather them all under a single umbrella.

The reasonable solution for a project developer is to divide the work into a number of segments, each one being the subject of an engineering, procurement and construction contract. In a development currently in progress, there is a separate EPC contract for the onshore LNG plant and related infrastructure, for the offshore production facilities, and for the pipeline from the offshore location to the plant site. Drilling and offshore services are separately contracted with each supplier; and specialty long-lead items relating to the onshore facilities were initially contracted directly with the suppliers and subsequently assigned to the onshore EPC contractor as subcontracts, for which the EPC contractor has assumed full responsibility.

4.5.2 Long-Lead Items

The discussion that follows will focus on the EPC contract for the onshore liquefaction facilities, since that agreement (including the assumed contracts for long-lead items) covers a wider range of activities than the others, and it requires contractor assistance pertaining to the project financing that is not a feature of the others. Before turning to an analysis of the onshore EPC contract, however, it would be useful to consider the contracts for the long-lead items and observe certain differences among them.

The differences arise mainly from the fact that the design, engineering and fabrication or construction elements of each vary in emphasis and content. The site preparation contract deals mainly with civil engineering work not involving significant mechanical engineering content and proprietary designs and processes. The contract for the LNG storage tanks places somewhat more emphasis on engineering and design, but it is still primarily an onsite construction contract. On the other hand, the contracts for the refrigerant compressor packages and the main cryogenic heat exchangers provide for the supply of discrete components manufactured in the contractor's own facilities, involving minimum site work and utilising proprietary designs, components and processes.

Due to this progression of emphasis from onsite, non-proprietary construction work to offsite fabrication entailing proprietary, licensed designs and processes, the related contracts range in form from construction contracts favoured by the developer to what in essence are purchase orders provided by the supplier.

4.5.3 EPC Contractor Selection

We discussed above how, with the assistance of the FEED contractor, the project developer can bring maximum definition to the EPC bid package with a view to obtaining firm, lump-sum quotations for as much of the work as is possible. The EPC contractor selection process adopted by the developer can make a significant contribution to this objective through a number of means, including:

(1) development of a detailed bid evaluation process, including the solicitation of initial and final unpriced proposals and priced proposals;

(2) allowing sufficient time for an orderly and thorough implementation of the evaluation process;

(3) providing for interim bid clarification meetings with the bidders and timely publication of bid supplements;

(4) maintaining strict confidentiality as to every aspect of the process; and

(5) preserving competitiveness through impartial treatment of bidders and by keeping at least two, and preferably three or more, bidders in the process until contract award.

For all concerned it is less confusing and more likely to yield reasonable price quotations if bids are initially solicited on an 'unpriced' basis. The focus of such bids should be contractor's technical qualifications and how it proposes to perform the work. Initial bid solicitation, clarification meetings with the bidders and the publication of bid supplements can add significantly to the obtaining of bids that are based on the same understandings and assumptions. Being able to compare apples with apples during the evaluation process for both unpriced and priced proposals is in the best interests of everyone concerned.

The evaluation process for unpriced proposals will be based on such matters as the contractor's:

(1) proposed organisation, including its management and staffing structures, the proposed project manager's experience and authority, the identification of other key personnel, the proposed project procedures, contractor's workload and the availability of manpower, and the locations where work is to be performed;

(2) engineering skills with respect to each aspect of the work, including its technical knowledge, the quality of its work, its loss prevention and control procedures and its track record on other, similar projects;

(3) construction management experience;

(4) procurement organisation and procedures; and
(5) subcontract administration skills and procedures.

The evaluation should also take into account the projected impact on the project of those items of the bid solicitation to which the contractor has taken exception in its bid.

Following the submission of unpriced bid proposals, bidders will be asked to submit their priced proposals. These will be broken down by category as required by the bid solicitation, and the individual quotations will be compared with the other bids and with the developer's own estimates. Quotations significantly out of line may indicate a misunderstanding that can be remedied. In addition to the actual price quotations, the evaluation of the priced proposals will take into account such matters as the contractor's proposed deviations from the payment schedule specified by the developer and the costs assigned to any technical or commercial exceptions to the bid specifications taken by the bidder.

If bidders have been asked to provide financing in respect of the work they are to perform under the EPC contract, a separate financing bid will be solicited. The evaluation of such bids will take into account such matters as the costs (including interest and fees) of such financing, currency risks, the impact of any prepayment requirements and an assessment of the strength of the underlying commitments for the provision of such financing.

The various bids will be compared based on all of the above evaluations. Award will be based on the lowest evaluated bid. The entire bidding process described above, which can reasonably be expected to take at least nine to 12 months, must be completed in time to permit award and completion of the EPC contract so as to permit timely commencement of deliveries of LNG.

4.5.4 EPC Contracts for LNG Plants

Building on what has been said about major international construction contracts in general and FEED contracts in particular, the discussion that follows will highlight some of the more significant features of the EPC contract for the onshore LNG liquefaction facilities. It will be assumed that the EPC contractor has accepted the assignment of contracts for all long-lead items, and that they have thus become part of the scope of his work for which he will be compensated at the agreed lump-sum prices for those contracts, for onward payment to the subcontractors. It will also be assumed that the EPC contract does not cover the land on which the facilities are to be located, which will be separately leased from the owner; it does not cover the port and loading facilities for LNG, condensate, sulphur and other by-products and for equipment and supplies, for which the LNG project developer will pay a user fee to the developer or owner of such facilities; it does not cover infrastructure, facilities and other property that may be common to any neighbouring LNG development, the cost sharing of which will be provided for in a cooperation and co-ordination agreement among the respective project owners; and it does not cover developer-provided insurances, such as builder's all-risk and marine insurances.

4.5.4.1 Contract Price

Every effort will have been expended to define the scope of the contractor's work in as detailed a manner as possible, assigning a fixed lump-sum price to the whole with but few tightly controlled exceptions. Among these exceptions might be:

(1) unforeseen changes in work directed by the developer, at pre-agreed schedules of rates;
(2) the cost of materials the developer may direct the contractor to purchase on a reimbursable basis;
(3) the cost of 'option' items, such as an additional production train, at pre-agreed option exercise times and prices;
(4) substantial changes to the cost of the work due to changes in law subsequent to contract execution;
(5) documented costs arising from a developer-directed acceleration of the construction schedule; and
(6) pre-agreed cancellation costs for specified portions of the work.

It should go without saying that stringent cost and scheduling controls are necessary to preserve the project economics and because cost overruns most probably will not be covered by the project financing.

4.5.4.2 Project Scheduling

As in the FEED contract, detailed project scheduling, including pre-agreed dates by which the contractor is to have completed specified portions of the work, will be a feature of the EPC contract. The contractor is responsible, at its cost, to adhere to the master schedule and the developer, at its cost, may require accelerated completion. Though the schedule for payment of the contract price will probably be linked to the percentage of overall completion, providing some financial incentive to the contractor to keep on schedule, this is not adequate to ensure that each phase of the construction proceeds at its own assigned rate with proper sequencing for a co-ordinated completion of the whole project. As an added incentive for timely completion, the contractor may be subject to liquidated damages, such as a pre-agreed percentage of the total contract price for each week of delay. It is usually a feature of all liquidated damages, however, that they are set at a low rate that falls far short of offsetting the financial impact of the delay or failure to meet specifications giving rise to their imposition.

4.5.4.3   Completion

The contractor is obligated to complete the work in accordance with the master schedule, as it may be adjusted due to approved changes, the exercise of options for additional work items, delays directly attributable to the developer or acceleration directed by the developer. Completion in timely fashion and in accordance with contract specification is of tremendous importance to the project. The developer will have undertaken to the LNG buyer to commence deliveries of LNG within a very narrow time window. Although failure of the contractor to complete the facilities in time to meet this delivery obligation may be an event of *force majeure* under the LNG SPA, the absence of revenue will certainly disrupt project economics and will be a matter of concern to the project lenders. Completion within a set time may have other far-reaching consequences for a limited recourse project financing, since it is upon completion that the completion guarantees of the developer's shareholders expire and the borrowing becomes non-recourse as to them.

4.5.4.4   Testing and Acceptance

The EPC contract will normally contain detailed testing and acceptance provisions providing for a staged and orderly transfer of custody to the developer and a clear definition of when and to what extent the contractor's guarantees shall apply. Mechanical completion occurs on completion of construction (less punch-list items) and pre-startup of mechanical testing of the facilities in accordance with the contract requirements. Operational acceptance occurs after commissioning of the facilities, completion of all punch-list items not completed at the time of mechanical acceptance, and delivery of all documentation. Final acceptance follows on the successful completion of all test runs. Detailed test run specifications and procedures are designed to measure whether and to what extent the facilities meet contract requirements for such items as LNG production capacity, LNG quality, sulphur capacity and specifications, field and plant condensate specifications, refrigerant make-up specifications and auto-consumption. Liquidated damages may be established for minor deficiencies in a given test category. Major deficiencies will normally entitle the developer to reject the facilities, with the contractor being obligated at its expense to remedy or replace the work to the extent required to bring them within allowable tolerances.

The EPC contractor's warranty obligations commence upon final acceptance and extend for a specified period (say, two years) thereafter. Differing warranty periods may apply to long-lead items. During the warranty period, the contractor is obligated at its expense to rectify any deficiency in the facilities that may arise.

Final completion occurs upon the expiration of the warranty period, provided that all warranty obligations have been satisfied.

4.5.4.5 *Provisions Relating to Financing*

As project development costs have increased and developers have become increasingly unwilling or unable to finance their projects on their balance sheets, new borrowing sources and methods are gaining popularity. Contractors may be requested to assist the developer in its financing efforts in a variety of ways. The following types of contractor assistance have been included in some EPC contracts:

(1) contractor agrees to cooperate with the developer in developer's efforts to arrange financing by providing information regarding contractor's organisation and by furnishing various certificates, legal opinions and other documents requested by the project lenders;

(2) as part of lenders' security, the contractor agrees to 'step-in' clauses or other assignment arrangements allowing the lenders to take over the developer's EPC contract rights and obligations under certain conditions;

(3) contractor agrees to source materials and goods from suppliers and locations other than those specified in its bid if requested by the developer to improve its access to financing opportunities provided by ECAs; and

(4) contractor agrees to obtain underwritten commitments for financing in respect of its work under the EPC contract either through banks or other credit providers or guarantors, such as ECAs. As noted above, contractor's ability to obtain such financing and the lending terms may form a portion of contractor's bid and determine which bidder will win the contract award.

4.6 THE LNG SALE AND PURCHASE AGREEMENT (SPA)

4.6.1 Marketing

The EPC contract discussed in the preceding section would not, chronologically, be awarded without first having a firm LNG sales commitment in hand. The SPA is the *sine qua non* for proceeding to development, if for no other reason than it is required to produce the revenues that make development possible. The developer's marketing team will have begun their LNG sales activities almost from the moment the venture has been organised and a potentially commercial reservoir has been defined. For a greenfield development, identification of a suitable buyer and negotiation of the sales terms will have taken years of concentrated effort, begun long before the development decision is taken and the search for a FEED contractor has begun.

A 'suitable' buyer, in this instance, is one which has an identified need within the appropriate time-frame for LNG in sufficient quantities to justify the project's development. This almost certainly means the needed volumes would require the construction of at least two trains. Although one-train projects have been built, they are not 'optimal'. A single-train development provides half the income, no opportunities for economies of scale and less security of supply, and for these reasons would be more difficult to finance. Project success and the ability to obtain financing is also enhanced if the buyer is a major utility with a sound credit rating from a developed country having minimum political and currency risk.

4.6.2 Preliminary Steps

Once the suitable buyer has been identified, the signing of a letter of intent (LOI), memorandum of understanding (MOU) or similar document has been the usual next step. In earlier days this had considerable meaning, since it was assumed that such an instrument, no matter how preliminary, would not be entered into without some measure of encouragement from the buyer's and seller's respective governments. Unfortunately the trend today represents a devaluation of the LOI/MOU currency. In today's documents, very little is said of the outline or substantive terms of the proposed arrangements, those matters being left to negotiation of the final SPA. Indeed, the practice of late has been to provide in express terms that the document is not legally binding; and since they are normally of limited duration, it has become increasingly expedient for a party to let them lapse rather than risk embarrassment by walking away from a negotiated transaction.

Assuming our willing seller and suitable buyer are in earnest, however, the signing of a confidentiality agreement is often the next step. Such agreements are important, at least in theory, since the parties will be revealing considerable information about themselves, their marketing strategies and the terms upon which they would be prepared to sell or purchase LNG. This information could be 'shopped' among the other party's competitors as a means of improving the bargaining position of the disclosing party. As a practical matter, however, one has to assume that occurs, and there is no readily identifiable way to prevent it.

4.6.3   The SPA Terms

Each agreement for the sale and purchase of LNG, being the result of long and arduous negotiation in differing circumstances and contexts, is unique. All, however, deal with similar issues. These common elements, and the various ways parties have dealt with them in their SPAs, will be addressed in the discussion that follows.

4.6.3.1   Term

LNG sales arrangements requiring the construction of new production facilities have terms of at least 20 years. More recently, terms of 25–30 years are the rule rather than the exception. The contract term is measured from the time sales reach their 'plateau', or even annual delivery rate, following an initial 'build-up' period during which sales levels increase in steps up to the plateau. Long-term sales are necessitated by project economics, since heavy capital investments (including vessel costs) are incurred early on, beginning several years before deliveries commence and revenues begin to flow. Debt service will consume most of the revenues for the first 10–12 years, and it is only when payout has been reached that the investors begin to realise their return in full measure. Theoretically, the ideal would be to arrange sales having a duration approximating the useful life of the facilities constructed for the sale. That life is difficult to predict at the outset, however, and the parties may want to have a new look at the market once the initial project objectives have been achieved. SPAs do envisage the possibility of extension by mutual agreement, and they may provide for limited extension for the delivery of cargoes that may not have been delivered during the initial term due to the exercise of 'downward flexibility' rights[8] or to 'make up' for take-or-pay volumes.[9]

Once the liquefaction facilities are up and running, the rate at which they are operated can be increased rather rapidly up to their design capacity. For this reason, and because a seller's cash flow will be at its lowest levels during the initial years, the seller would prefer to minimise the duration of the build-up period and maximise the volumes taken during that period. Buyers, on the other hand, may maintain that they need to phase in the volumes under the new purchase arrangements, since their taking of additional quantities may have to be harmonised with the tapering off of purchases from other suppliers or with a gradual build-up of demand. This is a matter that always requires discussion and mutual accommodation.

A related matter is the timing of the commencement of deliveries. Buyers will seek as much definition as possible for the date when the first delivery of LNG is to occur in order to synchronise their demand requirements and to avoid disruption to their lifting schedules. The seller, on the other hand, is reluctant to commit several years in advance to a specific first delivery date, given the massive and complex construction activity that must occur in the interim. Accommodation is often reached in this instance by providing for a 'target' date, which may be advanced or deferred within a specified time band, or for a 'window' during which deliveries are to commence, perhaps narrowing as the target date or window approaches and the parties are able to predict more accurately when the production facilities will come onstream.

4.6.3.2   *Quantities, Rates of Taking and Adjustments*

LNG contract quantities are normally measured in terms of British thermal units (Btu),[10] rather than by volume, since it is the heating value of the commodity in its delivered state that is of primary interest to the buyer when considering its energy requirements and comparing LNG's cost to other energy sources. The SPA may also state the contract quantities in metric tonnes, but normally these values are indicative only and are not controlling for contract purposes.

It is usually the seller's objective that the buyer take deliveries of LNG on a rateably even basis over time, and provision for this is included in the SPA. Even taking implies even deliveries and even rates of LNG production, which in turn imply the most efficient use of production

---

[8] These rights are discussed in section 4.6.3.2.
[9] See section 4.6.3.6.
[10] A British thermal unit (Btu) may be defined as the amount of heat required to raise the temperature of one avoirdupois pound of pure water from 59 to 60 degrees Fahrenheit at an absolute pressure of 14.696 pounds per square inch.

facilities and vessels. If the rate of taking shows marked peaks and valleys, it stands to reason that investment in higher capacity levels will be required to accommodate the peaks, and there will be idle capacity during the valleys. This represents less than optimum utilisation of such costly facilities. The buyer, on the other hand, will point out that its demand for energy is not constant. Not only do the seasons affect its requirements, but customer demand may also vary. How may these apparently conflicting approaches be reconciled?

Historically, when the LNG business was in its youth, buyers could be enjoined by sellers to use this energy source to accommodate their base load requirements. They were encouraged to use other sources available in spot energy markets to achieve greater flexibility in deliverability that responded to their medium and peak load requirements. The SPAs in those earlier years reflected very little swing in offtake rates on a quarter-to-quarter basis and rather stringent allowances in shifting deliveries from one year to another. Today, reliance on LNG has grown to the point where it is being used ever more frequently to satisfy medium and sometimes peak load requirements. If a seller wishes to sell its commodity, it is going to have to grant increased flexibility in lifting patterns to be competitive with other available energy sources. This trend is already noticeable in latter-day SPAs.

SPAs still reflect the efforts of the parties to level, as much as practicable, the pattern of LNG deliveries. A hint of seasonality, however, is evident. As to additional flexibility, there are a number of mechanisms in current-day SPAs that permit less than even taking.

Foremost among these is the right of 'downward flexibility' afforded the buyer (and sometimes the seller). By this mechanism, the buyer may take (or the seller may deliver) one or more fewer cargoes during a given contract year than the buyer's annual or quarterly contract commitment would otherwise require. Period, and sometimes overall, limits on this right of downward flexibility are established. The quantities not taken due to an exercise of downward flexibility will often be required to be 'made good' within a set period of time, at the contract price then prevailing, subject to the availability of LNG for this purpose. If no production is available, the time during which the make good must occur will be extended. If it has not occurred prior to the end of the SPA term, the agreement may either provide for an extension of the term or that the make good obligation terminates.

Another element of flexibility is introduced by the manner in which the parties agree to treat cargoes that cannot be delivered or received due to an event of *force majeure* affecting the seller or the buyer. Any such cargo will operate either as a reduction to the basic contract quantity to be taken by the buyer during a relevant period, or as an exception to the buyer's 'take-or-pay' obligation for the period. Usually, the buyer is expected to 'restore' the undelivered quantities in a subsequent period, subject to restoration limits and the availability of LNG for restoration purposes. The SPA provisions normally require the parties to try to schedule the delivery of restoration cargoes before the end of the contract term. Inability to do so, however, normally does not operate automatically to extend the contract term; and all obligations in respect of quantities remaining unrestored at the agreement's expiration will terminate. The parties are free, of course, to agree otherwise, and are likely to do so if they choose to extend the original term of the SPA. The price payable for restoration quantities is usually the price prevailing at the time the quantities are actually delivered.

The SPA may go on to provide that if the *force majeure* event, such as the loss of a vessel, can be expected to prevent deliveries over a stipulated, prolonged period of time, the party who otherwise could perform its SPA obligations may elect to reduce the contract volumes by an amount equivalent to the projected *force majeure* deficiency quantities, thereby enabling it to seek alternative sources or markets for the LNG.

Flexibility also arises from provisions that require the seller to deliver, and the buyer to take, LNG in 'round cargo lots'. What constitutes a full cargo for purposes of the SPA is a provisionally stipulated quantity and is subject to future adjustment based upon actual experience as the trade matures. The objective of this requirement is to encourage optimum and safe utilisation of vessel capacity. It is understood that the contract quantities (stated in Btu) required to be taken and paid for (or paid for if not taken) in a given period will not precisely coincide with the quantities (in cargo lots) actually delivered during that period. To the extent that any projected shortfall is less than a full cargo, the buyer is normally given an opportunity to 'round down' the volumes required to be taken during the relevant period without penalty. The amount of the shortfall will then be added to the quantities required to be taken in the succeeding period. The buyer may also be accorded an opportunity to 'round up' its nominations for a period to the next full cargo lot; and subject to availability and to buyer's taking the additional volume, the excess over its contract obligation may be deducted from its take obligations in the succeeding period.

A somewhat analogous approach is taken with respect to deliveries occurring immediately prior to or after the end of a given contract year. Such deliveries may be deemed to have occurred during the subsequent or prior year, respectively, if that would operate to help reconcile contractually obligated quantities with actual quantities delivered during a particular period.

Finally, the buyer's obligation to take specified quantities of LNG during a given period will normally be reduced by any quantities the seller fails to deliver or make available for delivery during that period for reasons that are not otherwise permitted the seller under the terms of the agreement. This results in a lost sale for the seller, with no opportunity to require the buyer to take a commensurate amount of LNG in any future period.

All of the above mechanisms operate to impart added flexibility in the delivery and take patterns of the parties, with a view to accommodating their respective requirements. In the process, they assist in enabling the buyer to reconcile the quantities he is contractually obligated to take during a given period with the volumes actually taken, thereby minimising the possibility of having to pay for quantities not taken. The adjustment mechanisms are administered through a scheduling process, discussed further below, in which the buyer nominates in advance his projected lift-ings, and the seller accommodates those nominations to the best of its ability within physical and contractual constraints. Quantities taken during a contract year are usually assigned a priority, with the first deliveries being deemed to represent the buyer's satisfaction of its basic annual contract quantity obligations, as adjusted by the various mechanisms described above. Once these have been satisfied, additional volumes are deemed to represent the restoration of quantities not taken due to *force majeure*, the making good of quantities not taken due to the exercise of downward flexibility, and the making up of quantities previously paid for but not taken. The actual priority ordering of these categories is a matter of contract negotiation and may vary among SPAs.

4.6.3.3   *Programmes and Schedules*

To foster even lifting of LNG throughout the contract year, and to enable the seller to co-ordinate production rates, LNG and condensate storage tank levels, shipping schedules and delivery requirements to its various customers, the SPA provides that the seller shall prepare an annual programme of deliveries several months prior to the end of each calendar year. The seller also calculates each buyer's contract quantity obligations for the ensuing year and advises the buyer of those quantities, together with a proposed schedule of deliveries. The buyer is then required to advise the seller as to whether and to what extent the buyer wishes to take additional quantities representing make good quantities, restoration quantities and make-up quantities. Seller, in consultation with the buyer, then prepares a final annual programme taking into account nominations made by all of its buyers and seller's forecast of the quantities of LNG that can actually be produced and will be available for delivery during the ensuing year.

In addition to annual programming, the SPA will normally require the seller to prepare, each month, a rolling three-month forward plan of deliveries (the '90-day schedule'), based on and consistent with the annual programme to the maximum extent possible. Seller and buyer are then required to co-ordinate actual loading and delivery dates so as to implement, as nearly as possible, the annual programme and the 90-day schedule.

4.6.3.4 *LNG Quality and Other Technical Provisions*

SPAs and their attachments contain a number of provisions of a technical nature relating primarily to the quality specifications of the LNG, procedures and devices for the testing and measurement of volumes delivered, and how to derive the Btu content of the volumes delivered for purposes of invoicing and determining whether the parties' sale and purchase obligations have been met. These technical provisions do not vary significantly among SPAs, although there will always be some discussion about such details as the number, types and degree of accuracy of measuring devices that will be required, who is to pay inspection costs under various circumstances, and what adjustments to past invoices should be made if it is determined that measuring devices are inaccurate. Much will depend on whether the sale is made on an ex-ship[11] or FOB[12] basis, since this will determine where testing and measurement is to be performed and therefore who is responsible for performing the measurement and testing procedures. To minimise areas of disagreement, the parties normally stipulate the specifications and procedures that are acceptable to them by reference to standards established by reputable third parties, such as the Gas Processors Association or the American Society of Testing and Measurements. They also often provide that disputes of a technical nature are to be referred to an independent, mutually acceptable expert, rather than by reference to arbitration.

A particularly nettlesome issue that could arise in this area is how to treat LNG that does not meet technical quality specifications, either because it does not fall within the agreed range of gross heating values or it contains too little methane or too much of another component. This could be of rather serious concern to a buyer, whose turbines or other equipment may be adversely affected.

The first inkling of possible 'off-spec' cargo could occur at the seller's loading port, where preliminary testing occurs. If detected early enough to prevent loading, remedial action at the loading port may be possible. However, it is usually not possible for the seller to take remedial action in respect of volumes already loaded on board the tanker, since the loading

---

[11] Under terms published by the International Chamber of Commerce (*INCOTERMS 1990*), a DES or ex-ship sale is one in which the seller is required to make the goods available to the buyer *at the port of destination* named in the sales contract, where title and risk pass to the buyer. The seller bears the cost of carriage and risk of loss to the cargo en route to the port of destination.

[12] An FOB sale, according to *INCOTERMS 1990*, is one in which the seller delivers the goods on board the buyer's vessel *at the seller's loading port*, where title and risk pass to the buyer.

port is usually not equipped to return LNG to the storage tanks. The only
remedy may then be to ship the LNG to the buyer's receiving terminal,
with the buyer taking remedial action such as dilution of the off-spec LNG
with on-spec LNG in the buyer's storage tanks or 'spiking' the LNG with
components of the type that are deficient. SPAs are notably silent about
what remedial action may be required and usually provide that the parties
are to consult on the matter. This suggests that the appropriate remedy
will vary on a case by case basis. It may also suggest that the buyer should
be entitled to recover its costs in bringing the LNG within specification,
perhaps by way of a discount from the LNG contract price for the off-spec
cargo. One remedy that does not appear feasible is outright rejection of
the cargo without there being an alternative taker readily available. Absent
such a person one has visions of the LNG tanker, like the *Flying Dutchman*
of opera fame, sailing the seas indefinitely waiting for its cargo to boil off
or be consumed as fuel.

4.6.3.5 Price

LNG price theories abound and have evolved significantly over the years.
Pricing in North America, where LNG prices must compete with prices for
readily available domestic gas, differs from pricing in Europe, where
reference is often made to a variety of competing fuels including heating
oil, gas oil, pipeline gas and sometimes coal. This in turn differs from
pricing in the Asian markets, where the major purchasing countries have
scant, if any, indigenous energy resources and prices must compete with
landed prices for imported crude oils. Sellers to, and buyers in, each of
these regions have their own favoured pricing theories, not only as to that
portion of the price relating to the energy value of the commodity, but also
as to transportation costs. Each region has its own favoured basket of crude
oils or cocktail of reference energy sources, and each seller and buyer has
its own preferred indices for escalation.

It is not the intention here to undertake a detailed comparative analysis
of the prices applicable in the world's existing trades. Instead, the discussion will focus on the various and rather unique factors that make up the
price for LNG, and to describe how those factors have been dealt with in
various sales.

The LNG contract price, usually stated in US dollars per million British
thermal units (US$/mmBtu), reflects a number of elements. The first, and
without doubt the most important, of these is the energy element, which is
seller's compensation for the fuel that it is providing. The energy element
will be negotiated and determined by reference to competing LNG trades
and/or competing fuels. At times an incrementally higher value has been
accorded to LNG over the value of competing solid and liquid fuels, as a

premium for the clean and efficient burning properties of gas. This premium has diminished over time as improvements in technology have permitted the cleaner and more efficient burning of competing fuels.

If it is an FOB sale, with the buyer providing the LNG transportation, determination of the LNG energy element comes close to determining the LNG sales price. However, a number of adjustments may be appropriate, as explained below.

If, on the other hand, it is an ex-ship sale, with the seller being responsible for the LNG transportation, a second element must be added to the LNG contract price to compensate seller for this service. This transportation element may represent a pass-through to the buyer of seller's actual costs for the transportation, based on a forecast of such costs in advance of a given year and a later adjustment when actual costs have been determined, or it may represent a negotiated and predetermined value per mmBtu, based on an educated forecast of carriage costs. As in the case of an FOB sale, determining the transportation element is not necessarily the end of the story, and additional adjustments may be provided for.

The first of the adjustments referred to above, applicable to FOB sales, relates to the phenomenon known as 'boil-off'. This is the tendency of LNG to warm at the surface of its mass in an LNG ship's tanks and consequently to vaporise. Some of this revaporised gas may be recooled through agitation and returned to a liquefied state.[13] That which cannot be reliquefied can usually be used to power the vessel. In an ex-ship sale the seller absorbs the loss of LNG through boil-off, since the amount of LNG actually delivered to the buyer at the buyer's receiving terminal is less than the amount that had been loaded at seller's loading port. In an FOB sale, it is the buyer who would ordinarily absorb this loss. However, in some cases, the seller agrees to take on the loss (thus placing the buyer in the same position it would have been had it been an ex-ship sale) by way of according to the buyer a 'boil-off allowance'. This allowance is calculated by reference to an agreed daily boil-off rate for the duration of the voyage, which operates as a downward adjustment to the volumes actually delivered to the buyer's vessel. This, of course, results in a reduction to the energy element of the sales price.

A second adjustment to the energy element that is seen in some SPAs for FOB sales relates to transportation costs. The theory behind such an adjustment is that a seller geographically far removed from a buyer must be competitive with suppliers who are not so far removed. Because the buyer will incur higher transportation costs when purchasing from the more distant seller, that seller should accord to the buyer a transportation allowance so that the landed cost to the buyer will not be substantially higher than its

---

[13] LNG tankers could be built with an onboard LNG liquefaction capability; but so far there is industry consensus that the resulting economic benefits are insufficient to justify the high costs associated with this approach.

cost for purchases from its closer neighbours. The allowance is applied as a reduction to the energy element of the LNG sales price.

Another adjustment, applicable to the energy element of both FOB and ex-ship sales, is designed to keep the LNG price competitive with selected other energy sources. All or a portion of the energy element will therefore be subject to adjustment based on a formula that maintains, over time, the same relative prices of the LNG and the reference sources as existed during an agreed base period.

Yet another adjustment, applicable to both FOB and ex-ship sales, is designed to offset the effects of inflation. A portion of the energy element is subject to annual upward adjustment either at a mutually agreed escalation rate or by reference to a mutually agreed index, such as the US Consumer Price Index.

Escalation of the transportation element in an ex-ship sale is not necessary if the actual transportation costs can be passed through to the buyer. However, where the parties have based the transportation element on a forecast of carriage costs, it is reasonable to assume that at least a portion of those costs will increase over time due to inflation and should be subject to escalation. In a number of trades, however, the parties have agreed to periodic renegotiation of the contract sales price in part to correct for variations in transportation costs, including inflation. This approach, in theory, is said to ensure competitiveness with other ex-ship trades. There are disadvantages to the approach, however, not the least of which are:

(1)   it ensures repeated rounds of price renegotiations, which could consume considerable energy, cost and goodwill; and

(2)   it lends a note of future uncertainty with regard to the contract sales price, which could adversely affect the parties' ability to obtain needed financing for the project.

Having calculated the energy and, if appropriate, the transportation elements of the sales price and made the agreed adjustments described above, there may be another step in the calculations that is required before the final contract sales price is determined. While this step technically is not an additional 'element' of the price, it will have a direct impact on the sales price calculation where the parties have agreed to its inclusion. I am referring here to the concept of 'minimum price' or a variation of that concept, such as the floor and ceiling price or the 'S' curve.

Stated simply, the minimum price approach establishes a benchmark price level, usually determined by reference to historical LNG prices applicable over a base period in the relevant buyer's market, and subject to escalation to maintain the level of the minimum price in 'real terms' over time. As the seller prepares the invoice for each cargo of LNG delivered, it compares the price calculated for the energy element of the sales price (with such adjustments as may apply) with the escalated minimum price. The energy element of the sales price to be invoiced will be the higher of the two compared prices. In this manner the minimum price provides a floor below which the energy element of the contract sales price will not fall.

The minimum price concept, as originally devised, was meant to address two important considerations especially applicable to greenfield projects. The first of these is the issue of project viability. Can the seller or its shareholders be convinced that the project has a reasonably certain chance of providing an acceptable rate of return on investment, even if there should be a significant drop in energy prices? The risk of such downturns is inherent in the business, and one which the players presumably faced when getting into the business. In the context of major LNG developments, however, involving massive investment and obligations extending over 20–30 years, some assurance of at least a minimal return takes on considerable significance. Without that assurance, the investors may well decide to spend their money elsewhere, with the result that there will be no project. Should buyers be concerned about this? Most certainly they should, if they wish to have supply sources in the future and a sufficient diversity of such sources to provide some degree of competition among sellers.

The second consideration in advancing the concept of minimum price is intended to address the issue of financing. As new methods of financing are developed in response to developers' concerns about massive debt appearing on their balance sheets, lenders will increasingly look to a project's cash flow as the source of their security. Limited recourse project financing is less concerned with the developers' financial standing than it is with having a secure access to LNG sales revenues that are assured to provide sufficient returns to cover the borrower's debt-service obligations. Lenders are not 'players' in the petroleum industry and are not particularly well equipped, let alone willing, to take on the risks that are inherent in that industry. There are banks and other financial institutions that are willing to forego the opportunity for high rewards (with its attendant high risks) in exchange for the assurance of a sound, solid and steady flow of revenues as security for repayment of their loans. Their lending models are fashioned on the assumption that project revenues will always exceed, by safe coverages, debt-service requirements. A minimum price provides the assurance they need; exposure to the volatility of energy prices does not. Once again, is this solely a seller's concern? Once again, it is not. If the seller cannot obtain needed financing on acceptable terms, the project will not be developed, and the addition of new LNG supplies will not occur.

Some would argue that a minimum price is not essential, as some sellers maintain, because it is not a feature of many existing LNG sales contracts, and in recent instances where sellers have argued for its inclusion, they have eventually yielded on the point. The response to this is that historical practice is not particularly appropriate as a precedent for today's project economics and lending requirements; and that in those cases where sellers may have yielded on the point, one may assume the project lenders have sought and achieved alternative means for backstopping the price assurances that a minimum price would otherwise have provided. These means are not transparent to the uninvolved, but may become so as buyers press ahead with their desire to become equity participants in the seller's organisation and as they gain insights into what is necessary in order to obtain limited recourse project financing.

It should be pointed out that it is not, or should not be, a seller's objective to use the minimum price as a means of structuring a 'heads I win, tails you lose' sales arrangement. The principal problem seller should be addressing is those periods of time when, due to falling energy prices, the project revenues fall below the level of debt service requirements or what may be considered a reasonable project return. These shortfalls are more in the nature of timing differences, which in some fashion may be offset in other periods when energy prices rise above minimum price levels. A great deal of creative thought has been given to how these offsets might be realised.

One possibility sometimes advanced by buyers is to institute a ceiling price as a counter to the floor. The seller would thus be protected against serious declines in energy prices, while the buyer would be protected against severe price hikes and would share in the benefits such a climate would provide. A variation of this approach is the 'S' curve, which would operate to soften the curves of escalation between the floor and the ceiling through adjustable escalation rates that decline as the lower and upper limits are approached and that increase within an intermediate band.

There is certainly a challenge and an opportunity for creative thought in this area. For those willing to listen to and accommodate the needs of the other party, there ought always to be 'a pony in there somewhere. It's just a question of finding it'.

4.6.3.6   *Take-or-Pay*

The basic undertaking of a buyer in most SPAs is to 'purchase, receive and pay for, or to pay for if not taken, LNG'. Take-or-pay has been a hallmark of LNG sale and purchase arrangements since their inception. It is a device to ensure that the buyer does not fail to take its contractually required quantities, thereby depriving seller of the constant flow of revenues needed to cover its costs (including debt service) and to realise a return on its investment. The buyer may argue that the seller has not really lost anything when a cargo is not lifted, since the seller still has the LNG (or the natural gas in the reservoir) and can dispose of it in some other fashion. In this case, however, if the buyer does not take its full contract quantities during a given period, it is problematic whether and when the seller will have an opportunity to recover the resulting lost revenues. Historically there has not been an active spot market for LNG, and organising a distress sale on the spur of the moment would be extremely difficult. It may be just as difficult for the buyer to 'make up' the deficiency in a future period, even though a limited mechanism for this will likely be provided in the SPA, since the seller is not obligated to maintain spare capacity for this purpose and may not have such capacity if its production is already committed to other sales.

The quantities for which a buyer must pay, even if not taken, is the difference by which the quantities actually taken by the buyer during a given period are less than the quantities the buyer was contractually obligated to take during that period, as adjusted for the various reasons described in section 4.6.3.2. Aside from such adjustments, the SPA may provide for additional instances when the take-or-pay obligation will not apply, such as a lifting shortfall that is less than a full cargo.

Take-or-pay quantities are usually calculated based on adjusted annual contract quantities and actual deliveries. Shorter take-or-pay periods, such as calendar quarters, appear in some SPAs where the seller has felt a tighter control on buyer liftings is warranted, and the buyer has acceded to this request. In such cases there is an adjustment mechanism whereby the buyer's take-or-pay obligation is recalculated at the end of each quarter on a cumulative basis as the year progresses. Quantities lifted in excess of a quarterly obligation are credited against quantities previously underlifted and paid for, and appropriate adjusting payments are made.

The price the buyer is required to pay for take-or-pay quantities is either the price prevailing at the time the quantities should have been taken or, more often, the price prevailing at the end of the year or quarter when the deficiency occurred.

If the buyer in a subsequent period is able to take, as make-up LNG, delivery of quantities in excess of the quantities it was contractually obligated to take in that period, it will be given a credit for the price previously paid as take-or-pay. The SPA will provide either that the credit is to be valued in absolute US dollars (by comparing the value of the LNG when the take-or-pay deficiency arose to the value of the make-up quantities when actually delivered), or in quantity terms. Adjusting payments either will or will not be made, depending on which method has been chosen.

4.6.3.7 *Invoices and Payment*

Under normal SPA terms, the seller submits to the buyer an initial or preliminary invoice upon completion of each delivery of LNG, based on a calculation of the LNG volumes delivered and converted into Btu according to a mutually agreed formula. The invoice is normally a preliminary one and subject to later adjustment because the calculation of the applicable price for the month in which the delivery is made requires the availability of certain published data relating to energy values, used in the escalator for the energy element of the price. That data is often not yet available at the time the delivery price is being calculated. The preliminary invoice may be sent by electronic means, such as facsimile or telex, to be followed up with a hard copy accompanied by documentation as to volumes delivered and the calculations for converting those volumes into Btu.

Invoices are normally payable within an agreed number of business days from the buyer's receipt of the invoice. What constitutes a 'business day', which holidays are to be recognised, the number of business days given to the buyer to make payment and how the business days are to be counted are all matters that should be agreed in the SPA. Invoices in respect of other payments under the SPA, such as take-or-pay payments, are usually assigned a somewhat longer period for payment than that applicable to LNG invoices. Invoices under the SPA are stated in US dollars, since sellers are unwilling to assume currency and exchange risks associated with other currencies.

Invoices not paid when due attract penalty interest at an agreed rate. The rate is normally set sufficiently high to discourage the parties from using each other as a source of convenient financing. If a buyer fails to pay an LNG invoice within an agreed period of time, the seller may suspend further deliveries and may apply against the unpaid invoice amount any amounts that may then be owing by the seller to the buyer. Further delays in payment will normally entitle the seller to terminate the SPA.

It is usually provided that either party may dispute an invoice. However, unless the invoice is patently in error (such as an obvious arithmetic miscalculation or a misplaced decimal point), the amount in dispute must normally be paid either to the invoicing party or into an escrow account pending resolution of the dispute. Upon such resolution, any overpayment or underpayment is paid to the party making such overpayment or who was underpaid, normally with interest at the agreed penalty rate.

Payments owing by the buyer to the seller are normally directed to an offshore trust or payment account stipulated by the seller. The trustee or paying agent allocates the proceeds to such other accounts (e.g. for the payment of seller operating costs, taxes, royalties and debt service) in accordance with directions given by the seller and/or its lenders.

4.6.3.8 Sources of Supply

The SPA specifies, by reference to a specific contract area and/or reservoir, the source of the gas that is to be used as feedstock for the manufacture of the LNG deliverable under the agreement. To assure buyers that there are sufficient gas reserves to provide the necessary feedstock, the seller is normally required to deliver to the buyer a certificate as to the proved recoverable reserves[14] in the area or reservoir, issued by an internationally renowned firm of independent petroleum experts. The certificate should reflect the existence of sufficient proved recoverable reserves to enable the seller to fulfil its LNG delivery requirements under the SPA. As the seller enters into each new sales arrangement, it may be required to deliver to its various buyers supplemental certificates showing that the proved remaining recoverable reserves are sufficient to cover the seller's gas requirements in respect of all of its commitments for the sale of LNG manufactured from gas supplied from the same contract area or reservoir.

Sellers generally do not, however, guarantee their reservoirs or commit that they will obtain gas from sources other than the specified contract area or reservoir in order to fulfil their LNG delivery obligations. Indeed, loss of, damage to or failure of the reservoir(s), or depletion of the proved remaining recoverable reserves 'that can economically be produced'[15] by the seller for purposes of the SPA, may be specified in the SPA as an event of *force majeure* for which the seller is excused its delivery obligations absent seller's wilful misconduct. Under such circumstances, the seller would be required to take such remedial action as it can to remedy the situation. This might include attempts to seek from the host government an expansion of the contract area or access to additional areas or reservoirs, or the use of gas from other contract areas or reservoirs currently available to the seller. The buyer cannot be guaranteed, however, that such other sources will be made available; and since the use of such other sources may have implications with respect to the quality of the alternative feedstock, the costs involved in its use or other factors, it is not necessarily a matter of right that the seller may turn to such other sources.

4.6.3.9 Transportation

The liquefaction of natural gas by purification and cooling, thereby reducing its volume approximately 600 times, and the transportation of the resulting LNG by specially designed tankers, are among the most important features that distinguish this industry from any other. The liquefaction process is clearly a seller responsibility, as the ultimate regasification is clearly a buyer responsibility, and the SPA does not contain detailed provisions as to how these responsibilities are to be fulfilled. The transportation

---

[14] 'Probable' and 'possible' recoverable reserves are given no consideration for this purpose.
[15] What reserves can economically be produced is a matter for the seller to determine. The seller is not expected to produce gas to fulfil LNG commitments under circumstances that in its opinion cannot be justified from an economic standpoint.

link, on the other hand, is of vital concern to both parties. It is this sea-going link, otherwise served by a pipeline, that determines whether, when and how the seller is to perform its supply obligations and the buyer is to perform its take obligations. The determination of who is to assume the responsibility for transportation under the SPA will affect almost every provision of the document, including its technical provisions and attached schedules. It is helpful, therefore, to determine early on whether the supply is to be on an FOB or an ex-ship basis.

This decision is not made easily, affected as it is by numerous seller and buyer considerations. Both parties tend to focus on the sale and purchase of energy as their 'core' business, and neither tends to view transportation as an additional opportunity for profit. Given the large costs involved in tanker construction and the absence of an ongoing spot market in LNG, few vessels have ever been built on the speculation that there may one day be a need for them. Most fleets, therefore, are specially designed and sized with specific trades in mind, and are 'dedicated' to that trade to ensure continuity of supply throughout the SPA term. And since sellers and buyers are not experts in the transportation business, they generally turn to third party vessel owners and/or operators, who provide the necessary carriage through time charters or other transportation arrangements.

Early on, the preponderance of sales were consummated on an ex-ship basis. By controlling transportation, sellers wished to add to their assurance that deliveries would occur without interruption and on schedule. Sellers' access to favourable vessel financing, resulting in lower transportation costs, also played a role in some cases. The seller might occasionally have regarded transportation as an opportunity to benefit local shipping interests; but for the most part LNG exporting countries have not been powers in the shipbuilding or maritime industries. LNG importing countries, on the other hand, often are active in those industries, and over time FOB sales have become more frequent as buyers have sought to benefit their nations' economies through the ripple effects gained from taking on shipbuilding, transportation, financing and insurance obligations. As new buyers with such aspirations come into the market, one can expect there will be added impetus for FOB sales. To the extent these new buyers are lacking in extensive maritime traditions and experience, however, sellers will once again become concerned about security of supply. Project lenders may also attempt to influence the decision as to who is to provide transportation, as security of supply and the relative abilities of the seller and the buyer to incur and repay debt become factors in their lending decisions.

Let us assume that the parties have weighed the foregoing factors and arrived at a decision to sell and buy on an FOB basis. This is normally the simplest solution for the seller, since delivery of the LNG will occur at the seller's loading port. The exact point of delivery is normally stated to be the outward flange of the seller's loading arm where that flange theoretically[16] joins the loading manifold onboard the buyer's LNG tanker. The SPA provides that title to the LNG, and all risk of its loss, pass to the buyer at the delivery point. All requisite measurements and tests of the delivered LNG occur at the point of loading, and the volume, density and gross heating value are calculated for purposes of determining the Btu quantity delivered for invoice purposes. The seller is the party responsible for these procedures, since they occur at its port. It is the buyer's responsibility, on the other hand, to ensure that its tanker has berthed at the appointed time; that the vessel configuration and specifications comply with the port and berth requirements and the loading equipment's technical specifications; that the buyer or its agent has arranged for all necessary permits, approvals and port assistance with regard to piloting, tugs, escort and other support vessels; that the vessel is sufficiently cooled down to accept delivery of LNG; and that it is capable of receiving LNG at a specified rate so that delivery can be completed and the vessel can clear the berth within a specified time. Failure of the buyer or its tanker to comply with any of these obligations could cause it to be liable for expenses or penalties.[17]

Completion of FOB delivery to the buyer would normally end the seller's responsibilities with respect to a particular cargo. As has previously been noted, however, one or more adjustments to the invoice price may be required. One such adjustment, referred to as the 'boil-off factor', attempts to compensate the buyer for the fact that a portion of the LNG will vaporise during the voyage to the port of destination and cannot be used to power the vessel. What the buyer actually receives at its unloading

---

[16] It has long been a matter of conjecture what would happen if the flange coupling were not properly made, leading to a spill of LNG. Since the 'point of delivery' in both the FOB and the ex-ship cases is on board the tanker, and the vessel crew is responsible for making the coupling, it is reasonable to argue that the loss of LNG should be borne by the party responsible for providing the transportation. This would be consistent with the notion that in an FOB sale the LNG has been delivered, and title and risk have passed to the buyer (the provider of transportation), since the LNG has passed the outward flange of the seller's loading arm; and in an ex-ship sale the LNG has not been delivered, and title and risk have not passed to the buyer (who is not the provider of transportation), since the LNG has not passed the flange coupling of the unloading arm at the buyer's receiving terminal.

[17] A typical expense would be compensation of the seller for excess boil-off due to a delay in arrival time or excess time at berth. Penalties may be in the form of 'demurrage' at an agreed daily rate for delays caused to the vessel by the seller (in an FOB sale) or by the buyer (in an ex-ship sale), or an excess berth occupancy charge for failure to complete loading or unloading within the allotted time assessed against the buyer (in an FOB sale) or the seller (in an ex-ship sale). Arguably, the excess berth occupancy charge is also a demurrage charge, in that it is payable in anticipation of the payee having to pay demurrage charges to a transporter under another trade whose vessel suffers delay due to the payer's excess time at berth. Actually, in most cases it is questionable whether any party will be liable to any transporter for demurrage, since one would not normally expect demurrage to be a feature of long-term LNG charter arrangements, where transporters are fully compensated for capital and operating costs, plus a reasonable return, whether or not they incur temporary delays at ports. Nevertheless, the demurrage and excess berth occupancy charges do serve the function of encouraging the parties to proceed diligently in berthing, loading and unloading LNG tankers.

port will be somewhat less than the Btu quantity invoiced by the seller, which would not be the case had the delivery been made ex-ship.[18]

It is this 'wasting' nature of the LNG cargo that has led to the use of ex-ship terms, rather than cost, insurance and freight (CIF or C&F), where title and risk pass to the buyer at the seller's loading port upon delivery of the bill of lading for the LNG cargo. When the seller provides the transportation, the easiest way to determine what the buyer has actually received in terms of Btu is to conduct all measurements and tests at the unloading port, and in the ex-ship context the performance of these operations becomes a buyer obligation. The actual point of delivery in such cases is said to be the point at which the flange coupling of buyer's unloading arm joins the flange of the discharge manifold of the seller's tanker at the buyer's unloading port. Contrary to the FOB sale, all of the tanker obligations with regard to arrival, configuration, arrangement of port permits and assistance, delivery rates and time at berth become seller obligations, with similar expenses or penalties in the event of failure to fulfil such obligations. There is no stated obligation on the part of the seller to retain a 'heel'[19] sufficient to ensure that the vessel, upon its return to the seller's loading port, remains 'cooled down' to a temperature that would permit commencement of loading, since it will be the seller itself, through use of its own LNG and otherwise at its cost, who will have to cool down the vessel in such cases.

4.6.3.10   Facilities Construction and Co-ordination

With each signing of an SPA leading to a new greenfield development, the seller, and in most cases the buyer, will be required almost immediately to undertake massive construction efforts in support of the new trade. The construction progress of the various facilities must be closely co-ordinated, the ideal being that each link in the supply chain, including the requisite

---

[18] It is an intellectual curiosity that most sellers seem to have accepted the notion that buyers in FOB sales are to be compensated for boil-off occurring during the cargo voyage and for transportation differentials (see section 4.6.3.5). One wonders why sellers should always bear such differentials. If a buyer can argue that the seller's price must be competitive with the prices of the buyer's other suppliers, why may not the seller argue that the buyer should pay a price that is competitive with the prices paid by the seller's other customers? Why is it axiomatic that the remote supplier must receive a smaller return than the supplier who happens, as a geographic accident, to reside closer to the seller? Is a Middle Eastern supplier any further away from a Far Eastern buyer than the Far Eastern Buyer is removed from the Middle Eastern supplier? It is suggested this order of things reflects an historic imbalance attributable to the respective geographic locations of the world's largest LNG consumers and suppliers, and that if and when, for example, the Far Eastern buyer must rely on ever-more remote sources for the preponderance of its energy supplies, these issues may be revisited.

[19] A 'heel' is a quantity of LNG left in each tank of an LNG tanker after delivery in order to keep the tank cold during the return voyage to the loading port.

tankers, be completed or delivered neither earlier nor later than required for the timely commencement and build-up of deliveries. The SPA therefore provides for the creation of a joint co-ordinating committee, composed of representatives from both parties having knowledge and expertise in all the appropriate disciplines. The committee should meet regularly and with increasing frequency as the targeted date for first delivery approaches in order to co-ordinate progress and to ensure the compatibility of all aspects of the construction. In this regard, ship–shore meetings are essential to ensure that vessels and port specifications coincide. An added aspect of these meetings, not addressed in the SPA, is the development over time of the mutual confidence and relationships so essential for a secure, timely and efficient LNG trade.

Prior to the commencement of deliveries, the parties may also wish to discuss and agree upon detailed procedures for the implementation of the SPA terms. These implementation procedures are intended not to amend the basic SPA terms, but rather to provide precise guidelines as to how the agreement obligations are to be fulfilled. Typically, the emphasis in these supplemental guidelines is on matters pertaining to scheduling and custody transfer, such as prioritisation for the berthing and loading/unloading of vessels; detailed port procedures; specification of acceptable measuring devices and their tolerances, calibration and rectification; details regarding testing procedures, including the taking and preservation of LNG samples; and invoicing procedures, including the specification of invoice formats. Trades that address these matters before deliveries actually commence are far more likely to experience a smooth implementation of the SPA terms than those that wait until events give rise to questions for which there are no predetermined answers.

4.6.3.11   Conditions Precedent

Most SPAs contain a provision listing a number of conditions, which the parties undertake to fulfil as soon as is reasonably possible following execution of the agreement. These are usually referred to as 'conditions precedent' and traditionally relate to such matters as the obtaining of necessary governmental approvals and of requisite financing on acceptable terms. As a new generation of buyers emerges, sellers, responding to requirements of their potential lenders, may seek additional conditions as security for the buyer's performance of its purchase obligations, such as the obtaining of government or third party performance guarantees or monetary guarantees in respect of such matters as foreign exchange reserves, access to hard currencies, currency exchange rates and the remittability of currencies outside the buyer's country.

It is a matter of conjecture how the 'conditions precedent' provisions originally developed. Viewed from a present-day perspective, however, it would seem that the conditions ought to be regarded as 'conditions subsequent' or, in the case of the obtaining of government authorisations and approvals, as matters of representation and warranty, with the remedy of termination and the possibility of damages if the representations and warranties turn out not to be true. This is so because of the significant costs incurred by both parties in initiating a greenfield LNG project, the large risks involved, and the timing of the events that normally occur following SPA execution.

Buyers typically are unwilling or unable to make firm commitments for their energy needs many years in advance. One also suspects that they prefer to forestall committing to an LNG sales price as long as possible, hoping in that way to take advantage of any downward trend in market prices. These are not unreasonable positions to take. They do, however, have the tendency to prolong the conclusion of SPA negotiations until the very minimum time possible for the seller to complete project construction in time to permit commencement of deliveries on the buyer's preferred target date.

Sellers, meanwhile, are reluctant to make any commitment for the commencement of construction until they have a firm LNG purchase commitment in hand. Theoretically the risk of commencing early can be lessened by negotiating cancellation rights with manageable penalties in their EPC contracts. Few developers, however, are prepared to approve a greenfield project on this basis. The seller is therefore in the position of having to proceed apace almost from the moment of the SPA execution in order to complete on time.

Under these circumstances, it would be somewhat imprudent to sign an SPA and commit to EPC contracts subject to an SPA 'condition precedent' that necessary government approvals be obtained, with protracted periods allowed for obtaining such approvals. Such approvals should be obtained before SPA signature and made a matter of representation and warranty. This should not be revolutionary, since as a practical matter both parties' governments are known to be actively aware of proposed LNG transactions; and most buyers and sellers would be reluctant indeed to execute a firm commitment for a long-term sale and purchase of LNG without assuring themselves that all necessary authorisations and approvals are in hand.

Buyers have often taken the position that the seller's ability to obtain requisite financing on reasonable terms is a seller problem having nothing to do with the buyer. This is not a particularly far-sighted view, however, when one considers that the inability to finance a project may mean there will be no project at all. A potential source of energy, and the related enhanced competition with other suppliers, will be lost to buyers whose need for energy is undeniable. Traditional buyers may view these issues somewhat differently from sellers, in that they normally are regulated utilities directly or indirectly supported by their governments through strategic energy policies and government-approved rate structures. They benefit from an assurance of a return on sales to their customers that is not available to sellers, which in turn provides a basis for financing that sellers do not enjoy. Buyers should understand that sellers are unable to obtain firm financing commitments before an SPA and related EPC contracts have been executed, and that any such financing commitments may require various forms and degrees of assistance from the buyer, such as government or third-party monetary and performance guarantees.

4.6.3.12   Allocation

Buried in the SPA, usually among the provisions dealing with sales quantities and the various permissible adjustments to such quantities, one often finds a provision calling for the allocation of sales among buyers in the event production of LNG should be curtailed for certain reasons. Normally these reasons relate to events of *force majeure*, preventing the seller from delivering on time the full quantities it is obligated to deliver under its respective SPAs. In such instances, it is often provided that the quantities available for supply to each long-term customer shall be in the proportion that that customer's annual contract quantity bears to the annual contract quantities of all long-term customers. A 'long-term customer', for these purposes, is normally considered to be a buyer under an SPA having an initial term of 15 years or more. The SPA may or may not provide that the quantities not delivered due to these allocation provisions are to be treated as *force majeure* deficiencies and subject to restoration at some future time when the seller is able to deliver and the buyer is able (or required) to take restoration quantities.

Allocation of available quantities among buyers in these circumstances is consistent with the concept that LNG is fungible and that LNG production facilities are operated on a fully integrated basis, with no 'ownership' of particular facilities implied by the mere fact that those facilities were constructed in response to a specific SPA or trade. It is also consistent with the approach, often adopted in the petroleum industry, that risks are to be shared among all the parties in interest. This approach is clearly evident in new exploration ventures, where there is significant risk no hydrocarbons will be discovered. In the LNG context, this translates into an opportunity to share in at least a portion of the full plant production should there be a curtailment, rather than require an individual buyer to suffer the full brunt of the curtailment by identifying the affected facilities with that buyer. Hitherto, the principle has been that all of the seller's facilities are available to all of the seller's buyers.

This principle may come under challenge as new methods of financing become popular. Lenders and other financial institutions, such as ECAs, are experienced participants in limited recourse refinery and power plant financings and expansions. In those contexts, security arrangements usually apply to the specific facilities financed through the lending arrangements. Should those facilities cease to function because of an unforeseen incident, no claim is made against the production or supply attributed to an owner's pre-existing facilities. But by the same token, should an untoward incident affect the owner's pre-existing facilities, the lenders would not entertain any claim for a share of production or supply attributable to the facilities financed by the lenders. This all-or-nothing approach is obviously at odds with the allocation approach traditionally typifying many LNG trades. It is reasonable to assume that at some point the two approaches may come into conflict, and appropriate accommodations will have to be made if there is to be financing available for projects and projects available for financing.

4.6.3.13   *Governing Law and Dispute Resolution*

The substantive and procedural laws chosen to govern SPAs have usually been laws that are neutral to both the seller and the buyer. New York or English law are most often selected since they are particularly suited to interpreting English language agreements, and outcomes are largely predictable due to the guidance provided by extensive codification and voluminous case precedents available under these systems.

It is also usual for SPAs to specify arbitration as the means for resolving disputes as to interpretation or performance, with perhaps certain technical matters to be decided by specified experts. The arbitration may be conducted either according to rules to be adopted by the arbitrators selected by the parties, or according to the rules of an established arbitral association or other institution, such as the ICC or UNCITRAL.

Presumably, the practice of preferring arbitration to court proceedings reflects the belief that arbitration is more private, it is less costly, and it provides for a speedier resolution of the issues. While these benefits may have accurately portrayed the expectations of the past, they do not necessarily comport with the outlook for the present or the views of those who have actually endured an arbitral process. The supposed virtues of privacy, cost-efficiency and speed have not only proved illusive in some cases, but parties believing in their cases and willing to accept an 'up or down' decision on the merits have sometimes been frustrated by arbitrators who see their role as mediators and who decide to 'split the baby' in order to mollify both parties.

There may, however, be a virtue in all this; for the greater the prospect of prolonged, costly proceedings without satisfactory result, the less inclined will be the LNG seller and buyer to resort to that process to resolve their differences. Instead, they will exert greater efforts to reach an amicable resolution of their differences without recourse to outside parties. It is submitted this is a preferred course for parties involved in a commercial relationship the success of which is very much dependent on a cordiality that must endure over the decades.

4.7 TRENDS AND PROSPECTS

Certain trends characterising what is sometimes called the 'second generation' of LNG projects were noted in section 4.1.2, and the potential impacts of these trends have been noted in the ensuing discussion of the various links in the chain of LNG project contracts. It is not possible, of course, to anticipate the outcome of negotiations yet to be held and the shape of the resulting SPAs. It is possible, however, to identify issues that sellers and buyers are likely to encounter if current trends persist. Indeed, some of these issues have reared their heads in negotiations that are currently under way; and because that is so, in certain cases it would be generous to describe those negotiations as being 'in progress'.

4.7.1 New Sources

Those who have been active participants in the development of LNG projects over the years know how potentially rewarding the business can be. Drop-outs are rare, while those eager to join the fray are rife. At this point in the history of the industry the reserves available to some traditional suppliers have begun their decline; but they are being more than replaced by new sources. For the foreseeable future, these new discoveries and potential developments can be expected to be more than adequate to meet forecast demand, creating a climate rather more favourable to buyers than to sellers. In the nature of things, this means that buyers can be expected for the short term to use their leverage to exact ever more favourable terms of purchase. For the longer term, one might expect buyers to place a premium on sources that are renewable far beyond the initial SPA, but so far there has been no concrete manifestation of this approach.

4.7.2 Emerging Markets and New Buyers

At the time of this writing the traditional purchasers of LNG, usually being monopoly utility and energy companies of sound financial condition from developed countries and having some degree of governmental backing, have already experienced the build-up of their purchases of LNG to strategically acceptable levels. Many of them now feel constrained in committing to additional LNG purchases, either because government policies encourage diversification of energy sources or because privatisation efforts are under way and there is relative uncertainty as to who tomorrow's purchaser will be. This adds to a softening of demand in the market, which may at some point be offset by emerging markets.

These markets are expected to appear in countries that have not traditionally been consumers of LNG, but whose development creates a vast potential for energy demand. In these countries, as well, the winds of deregulation are expected to result in substantial privatisation of the power industry and a proliferation of new buyers. Progress has been sporadic, however, as these new players feel their way toward sound energy policies and an orderly development of their local industries.

As these trends continue, new buyers will differ significantly from their more traditional predecessors. They will have relatively little industry experience. Competition will be the order of the day and they will not be able to rely on monopoly status. Being new to the business, they cannot be expected to be of particularly sound financial condition. Government backing may either be unavailable or of relatively little value in securing the cash flows and assurances as to foreign exchange reserves, convertibility of currency, exchange rates and remittability that lenders to projects may require.

A further, significant feature of the new buyer is the absence of an existing and substantial demand base for the quantities of LNG it requires. As the buyer is new, so too is its customer, with whom there may be no proven history of constant demand and reliable payment. Under these circumstances the new buyer may feel constrained to allow flexibility in the take obligations of its customer, which the buyer in turn will attempt to build into its SPA with the seller.

And as if all this were not enough, new buyers can be expected to appear in an ever-diversifying range of geographic locations quite apart from those where traditional buyers reside. As the bulk of LNG sales shifts from the Far East, western Europe and North America to such places as east, central and south Asia and possibly South America, sellers increasingly will be confronted with the difficulties of pricing and transporting their product on terms that are competitive at the new destinations yet reconcilable with the terms already established with their traditional buyers.

4.7.3   Trends and Prospects

The impact of these trends is already being felt. Potential buyers have mounted assaults on some of the principles described as hallmarks of the industry in the introduction to this chapter. For example, buyers are now heard to argue that take-or-pay should not apply to quantities scheduled for delivery during the build-up period, and that the obligation to take such quantities should be on a 'best efforts' basis. Buyers have also argued that less than 100 per cent of the quantities to be taken during the plateau period, after build-up, should be subject to the take-or-pay provisions. Either position, if accepted, would operate to reduce the seller's assurance of the constant, relatively even cash flow that is normally considered essential to its project economics and the expectations of its potential lenders.

A somewhat related trend is buyers' insistence on ever-increasing levels of flexibility in take patterns, which would impact not only on cash flows but on the amount of spare production capacity sellers may have to build into and maintain in their facilities, thereby increasing the unit cost of LNG production. Buyers are also challenging the 'priority provisions' to permit make-up quantities, representing quantities previously not taken but paid for, to be taken before make good quantities (in respect of exercised downward flexibility) or restoration quantities (in respect of *force majeure* deficiencies). Once again, cash flows could be adversely affected were this position to prevail.

Without revealing too much about negotiating positions in respect of trades currently under consideration, suffice it to say that attacks on what had long been considered 'settled' SPA terms have proliferated on many other fronts. To some degree, in a period when market demand is soft, this is natural. Presumably sellers will have their say if and when the demand–supply picture changes. What is not natural, however, is the appearance of other disturbing trends, which could bode ill for the future.

One such trend is the growing number of projects in which deliveries have commenced before the parties agreed on price. Price is normally considered to be a key element of any contract, and the absence of this key element, in some circumstances, could be so profound as to affect the very enforceability of the agreement. Perhaps just as significantly, the ability to finance the project could be prevented or severely impaired. Lenders, and especially those whose security lies in the project revenues rather than the creditworthiness of the borrowers, regard price as fundamental to their lending decision. At the present time it is safe to say that a project without an agreement on price is not financeable on a non-recourse or limited recourse basis, which is as much to say that if this type of financing is essential to the seller, there will be no project at all.

Another such trend, which may or may not have to do with the inability of parties to agree on price, is what might be called the 'demise of

SMUT'. This may be merely a matter of perception; but the perception is increasingly shared. Some 'negotiations' today are of a different nature from those of the past. Parties not only seem willing to take 'hard' positions, on a take-it-or-leave-it basis without apparent avenue for compromise; they also, ever more frequently, couch their language and deliver their terms in ways that appear ill-suited to reaching mutual, amicable solutions. Refusals to meet, or excuses for not meeting, or conditions placed upon meeting have occurred. Meetings, once agreed, have been prematurely terminated to make a point, which is of course no way to make a point. The language used in meetings and correspondence is sometimes confrontational, and sometimes plainly intemperate. One hardly recognises the climate that used to prevail in these matters, and one wonders how in the world a smooth, long-term relationship can safely rest on such a foundation.

The uncertainties that characterise today's industry, the new directions it is taking, the increasing difficulty in justifying and mounting greenfield projects, the challenge of responding to new buyers' appeals for improved terms at a time when project economics and financing opportunities demand the opposite, and the deteriorating climate in which all this is taking place, represent challenges for the future of the industry. Yet this is an industry that has always faced challenges, and has always shown the resourcefulness to surmount them. For those who have had the will, there has always been a way. That will has always relied on the participants' willingness to listen, as well as talk; to recognise that the other party's concerns must be one's own; and that, together, buyers and sellers have the opportunity to make a profound contribution to the wellbeing of their respective nations and peoples.

Chapter 5

The LNG Transportation Link

*Richard G. Eddy**

5.1 UNIQUE FEATURES OF LNG TRANSPORTATION

In many ways, the transportation of LNG by ship is similar to shipping of other commodities such as oil, containers or iron ore. In all cases, facilities must be made available at the loading and discharge ports to handle the ship properly and the cargo safely and expeditiously. There are also many features of LNG transportation which are unique to the trade.

5.1.1 Dedication to the Trade

LNG ships are typically constructed specifically to serve a particular project for long periods, typically 20 to 25 years. At the end of the LNG sale and purchase agreement (SPA) for that project the SPA, if renewed for an extended period, may continue to be served by existing ship(s) or existing ship(s) may be replaced by newbuilding(s). When replaced, existing ships have mainly found new employment in other projects, in one case resulting in a total expected ship life of 51 years. Since the oldest ship currently in service is only 32 years old, ultimate physical proof of the suitability of service for these

* With thanks to Alain Vaudolon for his review of the chapter text and a number of his constructive and helpful suggestions included herein.

long periods cannot be demonstrated for another 20 years or so, but all indications are that such periods of service life should be possible.

A number of LNG ships were built on speculation in the late 1970s, and since then there have been a few of these ships which could not find employment and have been available for substitution in case of problems with a dedicated vessel. As of 1997, almost all of these ships have found long-term employment, so that the prospect of substitution of another vessel in case of problems is practically non-existent.

5.1.2   Extreme Reliability Requirement

The reason why so much emphasis has been placed on reliability is that if any one component of the LNG chain is out of action it cannot easily be replaced. If a liquefaction plant fails, there is little prospect of obtaining LNG from another LNG plant which also has dedicated customers. There might be a possibility of some surplus LNG production capacity being made available, but the current tendency is to market this capacity if possible in order to improve project economics.

In the case of LNG ships, those not in service are usually in a laid-up 'mothballed' state requiring a minimum of two months for reactivation. This is even more reason to do all that is possible to avoid having unscheduled downtime for ships in service. The reliability record for LNG ships is, as a whole, extremely good. Many ships operate for years without any unscheduled downtime. The fleet average of the Gotaas-Larsen Shipping Corporation is typically measured in hours (i.e. less than one day) per year. Several other LNG ship operators have similar very high reliability records.

5.1.3   Outstanding Safety Record

The safety record for LNG ships has been exemplary. As of 31 December 1996, a total of 24,788 voyages had been performed, delivering almost 2 billion cubic metres or 900 million tonnes of cargo, since the *Methane Pioneer* first arrived on Canvey Island in 1959. During this period there has not been a single operating ship lost, nor has there been any significant loss of cargo. There have been two serious groundings of LNG ships; one in the Straits of Gibraltar in 1979 and the other in Tobata, Japan in 1984. In both cases, the outer hull was seriously damaged, but the inner hull remained intact.

The high standards of safety and reliability are expected to be maintained regardless of the length of the ship's life, which places a considerable technical and financial burden on the LNG ships' owners and managers. Painstaking attention to detailed maintenance requirements is the key to success in this area.

5.1.4   Custody Transfer System Acceptance

LNG ships are fitted with high-accuracy liquid level, temperature and vapour pressure measuring equipment. This equipment is periodically recalibrated to maintain its accuracy. The cargo tanks are calibrated by an independent measurer so that the volume of cargo can be determined accurately. This shipboard custody transfer measuring system (CTMS) is accepted by the buyer and seller of the cargo as the basis for the quantity purchased or sold.

Samples of the LNG cargo are taken ashore and analysed on a mass spectrometer to determine the cargo's chemical composition from which the heating value can be calculated. The heating value is then multiplied by the volume loaded or discharged from the ship to obtain the British thermal unit (Btu) content of the delivered cargo. Accuracy is important, since the quantities determined are used as a basis for cargo invoices, import duties and fiscal accounting.

5.2   DESIGN AND CONSTRUCTION OF LNG SHIPS

5.2.1   History of Development

All of the LNG ships currently in operation (as of December 1997, numbering 103 vessels) except one, as well as all of those under construction, utilise one of four basic cargo containment system designs. The cargo-handling systems for all of these designs are similar in most respects. These four containment systems (and their licensors) are:

(1)   Self-Supporting Prismatic Type 'B' (Conch/IHI);
(2)   Dual Membrane (Gaz Transport);
(3)   Single Membrane (Technigaz);
(4)   Self-Supporting Spherical Type 'B' (Kvaerner Moss).

Ships built to all four of these designs have operated successfully since they were first introduced. The construction costs of these designs appears to be similar, in that when competitive tenders are sought the responses are within a very narrow range. The selection of one design over the other is for reasons other than the capital cost of the ships. The extent and cost of financing plays an important part in the decision-making process. Often the desire to continue with the same containment system as for previous vessels in a fleet is a factor when the cost difference of an alternative is minimal.

The one vessel which is not built to one of these designs was one of the first three commercial LNG ships. She was built in 1965, and is still trading today under the name *Cinderella*. The tank design is somewhat similar to the spherical type, with a conical centre section and supported at the bottom rather than the centre.

This section will include a description of the features of each of the four designs, followed by the history of their development.

5.2.1.1   Self-Supporting Prismatic Type 'B'

The Type 'B' designation is an International Maritime Organisation (IMO) 'leak before failure' criterion which permits the tank to be constructed with only a partial secondary barrier (i.e. a drip tray beneath the tank). The criterion states that these tanks are 'tanks designed using model tests, refined analytical tools and analysis methods to determine stress levels, fatigue life and crack propagation characteristics'. The high-strength aluminium alloy tank is divided longitudinally into two separate compartments to improve stability and avoid sloshing. It is keyed into the ship and supported by special blocks which are also thermal barriers. The foamed plastic insulation is applied to the outside of the tank, which is completely accessible for inspection. This containment system was the first to be developed as a result of a need to demonstrate that the carriage of LNG by sea was a safe and practical means of transporting this energy between continents.

Figure 5.2.1.1   SPB LNG Tank Construction

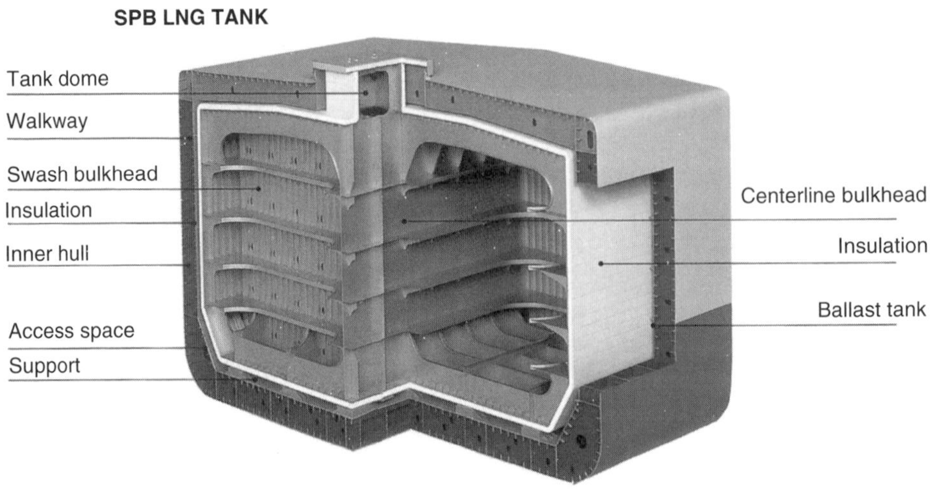

SPB LNG TANK

Tank dome
Walkway
Swash bulkhead
Insulation
Inner hull
Access space
Support

Centerline bulkhead
Insulation
Ballast tank

Early in the 1950s, the Union Stock Yards of Chicago initiated a research investigation into the possibility of liquefying natural gas in Louisiana and transporting the LNG by barge up the Mississippi River to Chicago where it could be regasified and used as fuel in the meat packing business. If successful, the vaporised LNG was expected to be cheaper than the natural gas supplied by pipeline from the local gas distribution company.

A small liquefaction plant and LNG storage tank were built at Lake Charles, Louisiana and although no LNG was ever shipped to Chicago, this facility provided the product for the first transatlantic cargoes.

In 1954, this research effort came to the attention of the British Gas Council. The Council was actively looking for a means to supplement the manufactured gas supply which was being stretched severely by industrial expansion and home heating requirements. In 1956 Union Stock Yards teamed up with Continental Oil Co. to form Constock Liquid Methane Corp., and early in 1957 an agreement was made with the British Gas Council to convert a World War II dry cargo vessel into a 5000-cubic metre LNG carrier. An LNG unloading, storage, vaporisation and send-out facility was constructed at Canvey Island, near London, concurrently with the ship conversion. In February 1959, the first LNG cargo was transported in the *Methane Pioneer* and the Canvey Island methane terminal was subsequently successfully commissioned. A further six transatlantic voyages were performed and the project was deemed to be a complete success. This prototype differed from the Type 'B' described above in that the insulation consisted of laminated balsa wood panels attached to the inner hull, rather than polyurethane foam panels attached to the cargo tank.[1]

At this stage Shell joined with the Constock shareholders to form Conch International Methane Limited. The prototype project was the stepping stone which led to the Algeria–UK project in 1964. Two 27,400-cubic metre ships were built in British shipyards and dedicated to the trade for 15 years.

The next ships built to this design were constructed in the Avondale Shipyard in New Orleans, and were intended for service in the El Paso project to import LNG to the United States from Algeria. Whereas the prototype vessel and the two previous ships had used balsa wood as the insulation, these 125,000-cubic metre ships used a polyurethane foam system which failed during cold trials of the ships in 1979. These three vessels never entered service as LNG ships. Finally, the Type 'B' system described earlier was incorporated into two ships built by Ishikawajima Harima Shipyard in Japan for the Alaska–Japan trade. These vessels were completed in 1993–94 and are now the only two operating vessels which are basically the same design as the original prototype. (See Figure 5.2.1.1.)

---

[1] Roger Ffooks, *Natural Gas By Sea* (Witherby & Co. Ltd, 1993), pp. 45–54, 121–137, 149–154.

5.2.1.2   Dual Membrane

The dual membrane containment system is known as the Gaz Transport design. The primary barrier in contact with the LNG is a 0.7 millimetre thick sheet of 36 per cent nickel steel called Invar. Invar has an extremely low coefficient of thermal expansion so that expansion joints in the membranes are unnecessary. This is formed in 0.5 metre strakes which are welded together and attached to plywood boxes filled with Perlite, a volcanic ash used as an insulating material. These boxes are in turn attached to an identical secondary barrier of Invar and a further set of insulated plywood boxes which are fastened to the inner hull. The thickness of the plywood is 200 millimetres or more, if a lower boil-off rate is required.

Initial research and testing of the system took place in the mid-1960s by a group which had been formed from Gaz de France and Worms, later to become Gaz Transport. An experimental tank was installed on the forward deck of the *Jules Verne* and carried liquid nitrogen for 10 months between Arzew and Le Havre. A very thorough testing programme was reviewed and evaluated by the American Bureau of Shipping and the US Coast Guard, as well as Phillips Petroleum Company and the Kockums Shipyard in Sweden.[2]

Figure 5.2.1.2   GAZ TRANSPORT Membrane Construction

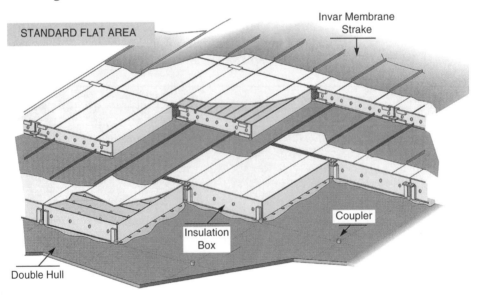

[2] *Ibid.*

In 1966 Phillips (and Marathon Oil Co.) ordered two 71,500-cubic metre ships which served the Alaska–Japan trade for 25 years. They were then purchased by British Gas and subsequently chartered to Enagas of Spain for service on another long-term LNG sales contract. These two ships will be 51 years old when their time charter is completed. The main difference between these ships and the current design is that the thickness of Invar is 0.5 millimetres and the strake width is 0.4 metres.

The Gaz Transport system has been popular and several ships were built in France in the 1970s, 1980s and 1990s to this design. In 1995 the first Korean-built membrane vessel, the 131,000-cubic metre *Hanjin Pyeong Taek*, was delivered for trade between Indonesia/Malaysia and Korea. There are currently 30 ships of the GT design trading worldwide. (See Figure 5.2.1.2.)

5.2.1.3 Single Membrane

The single membrane system, known as the Technigaz design, consists of a primary barrier of stainless steel, having raised corrugations or waffles to allow for thermal expansion and contraction. In the original Mark I design the primary membrane was supported by panels of laminated balsa wood with a sealed plywood face which acted as a secondary barrier. These panels were then secured to the inner hull of the ship. In the latest Mark III design, the balsa/plywood panels have been replaced by reinforced cellular foam. Within the foam there is a fibreglass cloth/aluminium laminate secondary barrier.

Development of this system was undertaken by a French LPG shipping company called Gazocean which formed a subsidiary, Technigaz, to develop the system in 1963. In 1964, a 605-cubic metre ship was fitted with two cargo tanks of this design having a secondary barrier with an identical waffled membrane construction. This vessel, the *Pythagore*, delivered two LNG cargoes for demonstration purposes and then went into LPG/ethylene service. Gazocean and Conch collaborated for a time and developed the Mark I system with Technigaz membrane and the Conch plywood faced balsa panel secondary barrier and insulation system. In 1968, a 50,000-cubic metre ship, the *Descartes*, was ordered to this design.[3]

A total of 14 ships were built to this design in the 1970s. In the 1980s the Mark III system was developed and finally introduced in an 18,900-cubic metre ship, the *Aman Bintulu*, delivered by the NKK shipyard in 1993.

[3] *Ibid.*

198

Figure 5.2.1.3   Technigaz Mark III Membrane Construction

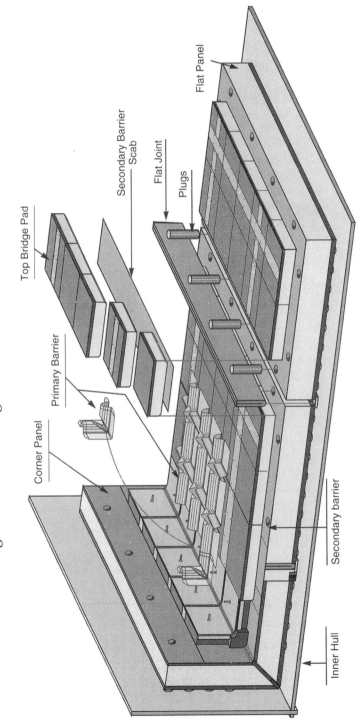

In 1996, the first 137,500-cubic metre ship to the Mark III design was ordered to be built by Samsung in Korea for service in the forthcoming Oman to Korea project. (See Figure 5.2.1.3.)

5.2.1.4   Self-Supporting Spherical Type 'B'

The spherical tank system, better known as the Kvaerner Moss design, consists of high-strength aluminium alloy tanks, supported at the equator by a continuous cylindrical skirt. Because of detailed stress and crack propagation analysis and investigation of fatigue life, the Type 'B' tank requires only a partial secondary barrier in the form of a drip tray at the bottom of the tank. The Type 'B' criteria is the same for the prismatic and spherical tank designs. The tank is insulated with cellular foam which is covered with a vapour barrier, and the whole tank is protected by a steel weatherproof cover.

In the mid-1960s the Kvaerner Group, in association with the advisory group of Det Norske Veritas, began an intensive investigation of this spherical tank possibility.

One of the Kvaerner shipyards had already built LPG ships to this design which were very successful in service. Enough confidence was gained from this experience and the thorough technical evaluation to permit Kvaerner to offer 88,000-cubic metre vessels without the benefit of prototype testing, as had been done with the other designs. Two of these 88,000-cubic metre ships were ordered in 1970, both of which are still in active service and one, the *Norman Lady*, is now dedicated to the Trinidad–Spain project until 2020 for an expected working life of at least 47 years. Orders for 125,000-cubic metre ships were booked in 1973, and the use of this design expanded rapidly thereafter. It is currently the most widely used LNG ship technology with 55 vessels in service out of a total LNG fleet of 103. (See Figure 5.2.1.4.)[4]

5.2.1.5   Future Size Development

Certainly the ship's capacity can easily be increased provided that the LNG ports are ready to accommodate larger vessels. There has been a certain amount of resistance in Japan to vessels larger than 138,000 cubic metres, but this may be overcome for selected ports if the economic advantage is sufficient. One logical limitation might be the maximum practical size which can be powered economically by a single-screw steam turbine. This is

[4] *Ibid.*

Figure 5.2.1.4   MOSS Independent Spherical Tank System

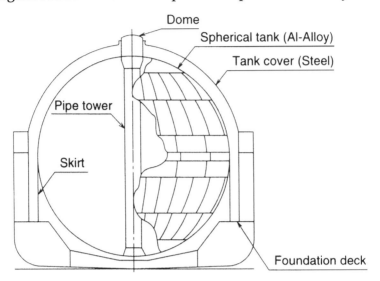

Figure 5.2.1.5A   200,000 m³ GAZ TRANSPORT Type LNG Carrier—Principal Characteristics

Length Overall	318.00 m
Length B.P.	310.00 m
Moulded Beam	48.50 m
Depth to trunk deck	28.30 m
Full-load draft	12.50 m
Horse power 100%	40000.00
Engine type: steam turbine	
Trial speed	18.5 knots
Displacement (long tons)	139540.00 LT
Deadweight	98200.00 LT
Cargo tank capacity at 100%	200115 m³
Tank Design:Gaz-Transport Type	NO-96.2
Cryogenic Insulation Thickness	500 mm
Number of cargo tanks	5 unit
Boil-off rates (IMO basis):	
—Nominal (with pressurised insulating spaces)	0.145%

probably up to 200,000 cubic metres, as indicated in Table 1. Note that the 40,000 hp steam plant, which is a common size used in a number of LNG ships built since the late 1970s, is enough to produce a trial speed of 18.5 knots or service speed of, say, 17.5 knots. All of the containment system designers have similar proposals for ships up to 200,000 cubic metres in size.

The next increase in vessel size from 137,500 cubic metres is likely to be about 160,000 cubic metres which will fit well with some of the projects currently in the planning stage.

If we look at the spherical tank design, the comparison of principal characteristics between the existing 125,000-cubic metre ships, the more recent 137,500-cubic metre vessels and a proposed 168,750-cubic metre vessel looks like the following:

Figure 5.2.1.5B   Vessel Comparison

Ship Capacity m^3	125,000	137,500	168,750
Length Overall—m	287.6	290.1	335
Length B.P.—m	274	275	321
Moulded Beam—m	43.4	48.1	48.1
Depth—m	25.0	27.0	27.0
Full Load Draft—m	11.3	11.3	11.2
Horsepower 100%	40,000	40,000	40,000
Service Speed—knots	19.7	19.5	19.0
Displacement—tonnes	98,760	103,000	126,900
Deadweight—tonnes	69,260	73,000	89,600
Tank Design	Sphere	Sphere	Sphere
Number of Cargo Tanks	5	4	5
Boil-Off Rates—%/day	0.25	0.15	0.15

An interesting feature of the 168,500-cubic metre ship is that the draught is only 11.2 metres compared with the 11.3 metres for the 137,500-cubic metre and the 125,000-cubic metre ships. One of the main restrictions for larger ships is the draught and this in fact can be accommodated by lengthening the hull without altering the beam and depth of the ship.

Another possible method of increasing capacity of the spherical tank ship is to install a cylindrical section at the equator of the sphere, increasing the capacity of a 137,500-cubic metre ship by 5000 cubic metres by installing such a section in the three aft tanks. This would increase the draught to about 11.5 metres.

5.2.2 Role of International Maritime Organisation (IMO) and Classification Societies

Since inception, the liquefied natural gas shipping industry has developed an enviable safety record. This is, in large part, because of the application of legislation, standards and codes which are largely promulgated by the IMO and the classification societies.

5.2.2.1 *International Maritime Organisation*

The IMO is an agency of the United Nations with headquarters in London. In 1967 the United States requested that the International Maritime Consultancy Organisation (IMCO) (the predecessor of IMO) develop international standards for ships which transport chemicals and liquefied gases in bulk. This request eventually led to the adoption of two IMO Codes which pertain to the transportation of liquefied gases:

Code for the Construction and Equipment of Ships Carrying Liquefied Gases in Bulk, IMO Resolution A.328 (IX)

This standard is known as the 'Gas Tanker Code' , contains detailed standards for the design, construction, equipment requirements and operation of a liquefied gas tanker and applies to new gas tankers. In November 1975, the IMO adopted the Code and recommended that governments incorporate the contents into national regulations as soon as possible. In 1983, the Code was adopted as an amendment to the International Convention for the Safety of Life at Sea 1974 and thus became mandatory for governments (countries) which are parties to that convention. At the same time it became the 'International' Code or IGC Code.

Code for Existing Ships Carrying Liquefied Natural Gases in Bulk, IMO Resolution A.329 (IX)

During the development of the Gas Tanker Code it also became obvious that a separate code would be required for existing ships. A number of ships in service or under construction at the time would not meet all of the requirements of the new Code, but at the same time could be operated safely according to a somewhat less rigorous standard. Part of the reason for the Code for Existing Ships was to set a time limit for certain improvements to be made, so there would be a more universal acceptance of existing ships according to a common standard.

These codes are part of the 'umbrella' maritime safety standard which is titled: *International Convention for the Safety of Life at Sea 1974 (SOLAS)*. SOLAS contains the basic international regulations for ship safety including life-saving equipment, fire protection systems, radiotelegraphy and navigation equipment. The SOLAS Convention has been amended several times and has been ratified and implemented by all of the major maritime countries.

5.2.2.2   Classification Societies

Classification societies evolved from the desire of insurance underwriters to be assured that ships are adequately constructed and maintained. They play an important role in publishing rules containing standards for hull integrity, seaworthiness and machinery reliability, based on SOLAS and other IMO Conventions. They approve designs and conduct surveys during the construction and/or repair of ships. Additionally, they make periodic surveys during a vessel's life to ensure that the society's rules are being observed and that the ship is being maintained in a safe and seaworthy manner.

The major classification societies, e.g. the American Bureau of Shipping, Lloyds Register of Shipping, Det Norske Veritas, Bureau Veritas and Germanischer Lloyd, have included the IMO Gas Code(s) in their rules. They also provide technical assistance to governments, including conducting surveys and issuing Convention certificates on their behalf. For example, the Gotaas-Larsen LNG ships are registered in Liberia and their SOLAS Certificate and Gas Carrier Code Certificate of Fitness are issued by Det Norske Veritas on behalf of the Liberian Administration.

5.2.3   Role of Licensors

The proprietary technology which has been developed by each of the four basic containment system design groups has been licensed to a large number of shipyards, as may be seen in Figure 5.2.3. These licensees normally pay a modest fee to acquire the technology and a more substantial amount for each vessel built under licence. The shipyards which have actually constructed an LNG ship or have LNG ship(s) under construction comprise a much shorter list, as follows:

Moss

Finland
  Kvaerner-Masa Yards Inc.

Japan
  Kawasaki Heavy Industries Ltd
  Mitsubishi Heavy Industries Ltd
  Mitsui Engineering & Shipbuilding Co. Ltd

South Korea
  Hyundai Heavy Industries Co. Ltd

Germany
  Howaldswerke-Deutsche Werft AG

IHI/SPB

Japan
  Ishikawajima-Harima Heavy Industries Co. Ltd

Gaz Transport/Technigaz

France
  Chantiers de l'Atlantique

Italy
  Fincantieri SpA

Japan
  Nippon Kokan KK

South Korea
  Daewoo Heavy Industries Ltd
  Samsung Heavy Industries Ltd
  Hanjin Heavy Industries

These shipyards are the ones most likely to respond to requests for tender and the list is not likely to expand substantially because of the extensive investment and training required to qualify as a potential LNG shipbuilder.

5.2.4 Construction Time Required

The actual minimum construction time for an LNG Ship is about 31 months after ordering the cargo tank material. In order to allow

Figure 5.2.3   Cargo Containment System Licensees

Moss

Finland:	Kvaerner Masa-Yards Inc
Japan:	Kawasaki Heavy Industries Ltd
	Mitsubishi Heavy Industries Ltd
	Mitsui Engineering & Shipbuilding Co Ltd
South Korea:	Hyundai Heavy Industries Co Ltd
USA:	Avondale Industries
	Newport News Shipbuilding
Germany:	Howaldswerke-Deutsche Werft AG
	Bremer Vulkan AG
Belgium:	Boelwerf SA
France:	Chantiers de l'Atlantique
Italy:	Fincantieri SpA
Spain:	Astilleros Espanoles SA

IHI/SPB

Japan:	Ishikawajima-Harima Heavy Industries Co Ltd
	Sumitomo Heavy Industries Ltd
Italy:	Fincantieri SpA
USA:	Newport News Shipbuilding

Gaz Transport/Technigaz

Belgium:	Boelwerf SA	GT
	Cockerill	TGZ
Canada:	Davie Shipbuilding	GT
France:	Chantiers de l'Atlantique	GT/TGZ
	CMR (Repair Yard)	GT/TGZ
Germany:	Bremer Vulkan AG	TGZ
	Howaldswerke-Deutsche Werft	GT/TGZ
Italy:	Fincantieri SpA	GT/TGZ
Japan:	Mitsubishi Heavy Industries Ltd	GT/TGZ
	Mitsui Engineering & Shipbuilding Co Ltd	GT/TGZ
	Kawasaki Heavy Industries Ltd	GT/TGZ
	Nippon Kokan KK	GT/TGZ
	Hitachi Zosen	GT/TGZ
	Sumitomo Heavy Industries Ltd	TGZ
	Ishikawajima Harima Heavy Industries Ltd	GT/TGZ
	Sasebo Heavy Industries Ltd	TGZ

Figure 5.2.3 *(cont'd)*

Korea:	Daewoo Heavy Industries	GT/TGZ
	Samsung Heavy Industries	GT/TGZ
	Hanjin Heavy Industries Co	GT/TGZ
	Hyundai Heavy Industries	GT/TGZ
	Halla Engineering & Heavy Industries	TGZ
Netherlands:	Verolme	TGZ
Poland:	United Polish Shipyard	TGZ
Singapore:	Jurong Shipyard	GT
Spain:	Construccion Naval del INL	GT
Taiwan:	China Shipbuilding Corp	GT/TGZ
USA:	Ingalls	GT
	Newport News Shipbuilding	GT/TGZ
	Avondale Industries Inc	GT

adequate design time, especially if the ship is non-standard, a total time of 36 months from placing the order until ship delivery would be preferred by most shipyards. A typical shipyard construction schedule for an LNG ship with independent cargo tanks is shown in Figure 5.2.4. The critical path is the cargo tank construction, and the total construction time is about the same for ships with either independent or membrane tanks.

5.2.5 Establishing Ship Requirements

Part of LNG project planning consists of estimating the transportation capacity required for the trade, taking into account the time necessary for each function in the chain of events which compose the typical round voyage:

Loading port events
    Port entry (potential delay)
    Berthing (potential delay)
    Tie-up (potential delay)
    Line connection (potential delay)
    Cooling of LNG tanker cargo tanks, if necessary
    LNG cargo transfer
    Cast-off from berth
    Port departure (potential delay)

Voyage time to discharge port

Discharge port events
    Port entry (potential delay)
    Berthing (potential delay)
    Tie-up (potential delay)
    Line connection (potential delay)
    LNG cargo transfer
    Cast-off from berth
    Port departure (potential delay)

Random events en route
    Weather
    Breakdown
    Deviation
    Night-time transit restrictions

This simulation, combined with contract quantity, expected loading schedule throughout the year and related factors, leads to an estimate of shipping capacity in terms of number of vessels, size of vessels, operating speeds of vessels, etc. On the basis of these estimates, the project can calculate its transportation requirements. As a practical matter, the normal turnaround time of both loading and discharge ports can be estimated to be one day. Ships normally arrive at the loading port with cargo tanks fully cooled ready for loading.

The sizes of LNG newbuildings are nearly always at the maximum considered to be possible in order to reduce unit transportation costs. This maximum capacity is currently at 137,500 cubic metres gross, 135,000 cubic metres net LNG loaded quantity. The difference is due to the shrinkage of the tank and the design allowable filling limit of 98 per cent. In practice, the allowable filling limit can be increased up to 99.5 per cent in some cases, depending on the shape of the tank top and configuration of relief piping.

The service speed of the ship as defined by the shipyard is normally based on light weather conditions. This speed may need to be reduced for purposes of estimating voyage time, ship capacity and horsepower requirements, depending on the anticipated weather conditions en route. Since schedule implementing long-term LNG SPAs do not normally allow for weather delays, the ship needs to have an adequate margin of speed and power to meet these schedules in at least moderately severe weather. Wind conditions above Beaufort Force 5 (i.e. wind 17–21 knots, waves 1.8–2.5 metres) will reduce speed capability of a large 125,000 to 137,500-cubic metre LNG ship by at least half a knot. A 10-degree roll can reduce speed by three-quarters of a knot. Hull fouling in tropical waters can also reduce speed, and this can often be restored by underwater hull brushing and propeller polishing.

208

Figure 5.2.4 LNG Ship Construction Schedule Self Supporting Cargo Tanks

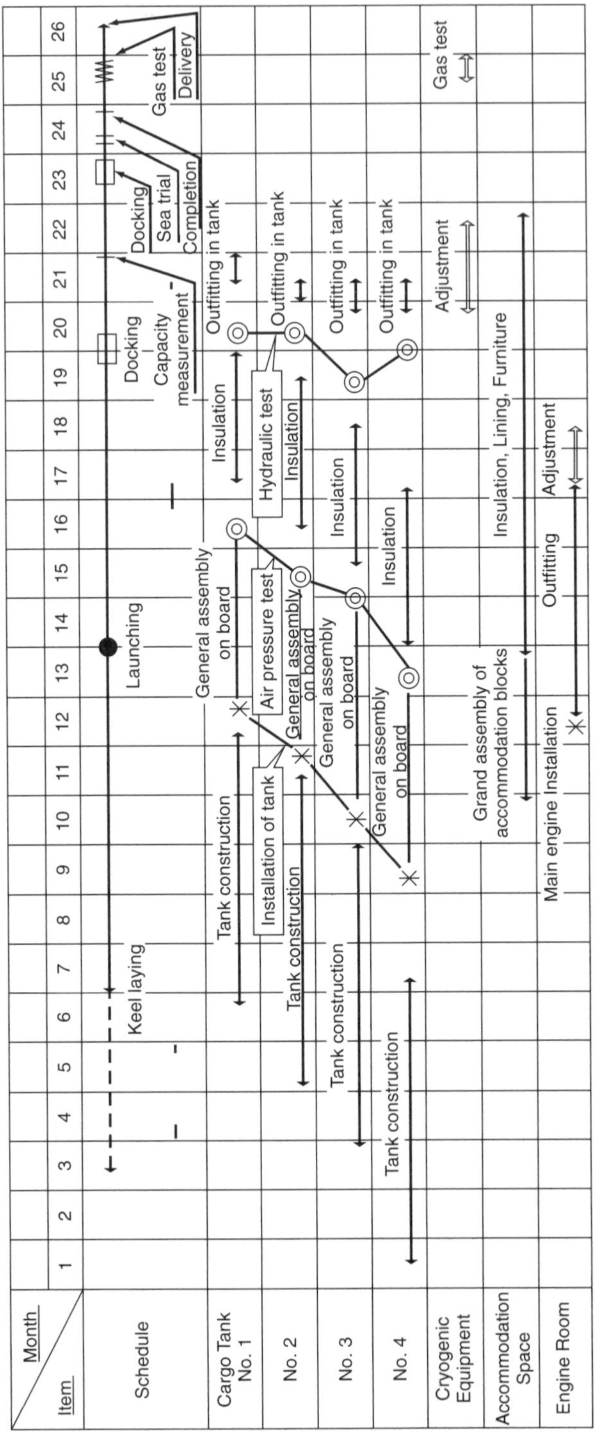

If project transportation requirements indicate a need for, say, four and a half standard 137,500-cubic metre vessels, it may be less expensive to build five standard-size ships and downsize the main engine for a service speed of less than 19.5 knots, rather than design a 123,750-cubic metre ship to meet the exact transportation requirements. When determining project transportation needs, it is important that capacity is adequate to transport the anticipated maximum production capacity of the plant during the normal round trip voyage time. Allowance must also be made for heel remaining in the cargo tanks after discharge.

A typical deliverability calculation for a 137,500-cubic metre ship might be:

One-way distance	6000 nautical miles
Ship 'service'speed	19 knots
Sea days (round trips)	26.31
Port days (round trips)	2
Total days in voyage	28.31 or 29
Operating days in year	350
Voyages per year	12.07
Ship capacity (net)	135,000 m^3
Less: heel	3000
Discharge quantity =	132,000 m^3
Annual delivered quantity =	132,000 x 12.07 = 1,593,103 m^3.

LNG specific gravity varies depending on gas composition, but is typically about 0.45 which means the annual deliverability of the vessel is $0.45 \times 1,593,103 = 716,896$ metric tonnes.

If the maximum output of the liquefaction train is, say, 3.3 million metric tonnes per annum this would equal a maximum daily production of 10,000 tonnes over the 330-day annual operating period. The deliverability of the 137,500-cubic metre ship is 59,400 metric tonnes which means it can cater for a daily production of 2048 metric tonnes on this route, or five ships can carry 10,240 tonnes, slightly more than maximum production. Note that in this example the ship 'service' speed has been estimated at 19.0 knots rather than 19.5, to cater for poor weather during part of the year, without reducing project deliverability.

5.2.6 Preliminary Cost Estimates

Once the basic size and speed requirements are known, the LNG ship-builders can be approached for a preliminary estimate of the ship's cost. The cost provided by the shipyard is normally the contract price of the

Figure 5.2.6 LNG Ship Capacity vs Cost

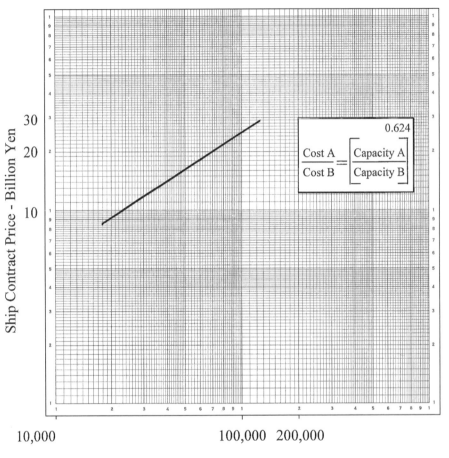

Ship Contract Price - Billion Yen

$$\frac{\text{Cost A}}{\text{Cost B}} = \left[\frac{\text{Capacity A}}{\text{Capacity B}}\right]^{0.624}$$

Ship Capacity - Cubic Meters

completed vessel which is paid in a series of progress payments during construction. To the contract price, the other predelivery costs must be added including the interest on progress payments, plan approval, construction supervision, initial inventory of spare parts, extra cost allowance and legal and bank fees. For a standard 137,500-cubic metre ship the typical predelivery costs are about 16–17 per cent of the contract price. For smaller ships the percentage is higher, since interest costs are proportional to contract price and the other costs do not vary much with ship size. Actual shipbuilding costs will vary depending on the shipbuilding market at the time the tender is issued or order is placed. One useful circumstance took place in 1990, when LNG ships of three different sizes were ordered in Japan at about the same time.

The costs of the three vessels were:

Capacity (CM)	Contract Price (YEN)
18,800	8,725,000.000
87,500	22,000,000.000
125,000	29,000,000.000

The relationship between the costs and capacities of similar assets of varying size can be approximated mathematically as follows:

Cost A/Cost B = (Capacity A/Capacity B)^x

A smaller exponent means that the economies of scale are greater than they would be using a larger exponent. Shipyards use an exponent of about 0.6 for making preliminary estimates and this method is also applied to the petroleum industry generally.[5] The exponent based on the 1990 cost data for the three vessels built in Japan suggests the appropriate exponent is 0.624. Figure 5.2.6 is a graph of this relationship. If the contract price of a ship is known, the graph can be used for scaling to a smaller or larger size within the range of 10,000 cubic metres to 137,500 cubic metres.

5.3 UNIQUE FEATURES OF THE LNG SHIP

The main feature of the LNG ship which distinguishes it from any other ship is the temperature of the cargo. Liquid natural gas, or LNG, mainly consists of methane and some heavier hydrocarbons, such as ethane and propane, which boil at slightly above minus 163 degrees centigrade at atmospheric pressure. The cargo is loaded, transported and discharged at this temperature, which requires special materials, insulation and handling equipment.

The insulation surrounding the cargo is extremely effective in maintaining the temperature of the liquid cargo. Some heat leak keeps the cargo surface constantly boiling. However, the quantity of vapour which is released from the tanks in a modern LNG ship is less than 0.15 per cent per day. The rate of boil-off can be adjusted at the design stage by increasing (or decreasing) the thickness of the cargo tank insulation. The thickness is normally predetermined to be such that the rate of boil-off during the loaded passage is less than the total fuel consumption at the service speed and corresponding power of the ship (i.e. no venting).

---

[5] W.L. Nelson, *Cost-imating* (Petroleum Publishing Co., 1957), p. 36.

The balance of fuel is provided by heavy fuel oil (HFO). During the ballast passage the boil-off rate is typically about half that of the loaded condition, but additional boil-off is often available when using LNG to spray-cool the cargo tanks prior to the subsequent loading, or to provide LNG vapour for boiler fuel rather than use HFO for ship's power.

A second distinguishing feature of an LNG ship is that the cargo boil-off vapour is used to power the ship and thereby no gas is wasted. The boil-off vapour is compressed, heated and sent to the ship's boilers which produce steam for the turbine which drives the propeller (see Figure 5.3). Methane is lighter than air at ambient temperature and is the only gaseous fuel allowed to be used to power a ship's machinery. The steam turbine is an extremely reliable and low maintenance machine, but the efficiency of the diesel engine is so much better that there are almost no steam turbine-powered ships in the world, except for LNG carriers.

5.3.1   LNG Cargo Systems

Cargo piping on LNG ships is all stainless steel material and located above deck. Piping, except for vapour relief lines, is insulated with preformed polyurethane or similar insulation sealed with glass cloth and epoxy resin and jacketed with a stainless steel or preformed fibreglass cover.

The liquid system consists of manifolds, usually four, on either side of the ship which receive cargo from, and discharge cargo to, shore. These manifolds are located approximately amidships and are connected via crossover pipes to fore and aft pipelines or 'headers', which are branched to individual cargo tank domes. The penetrations through the tank consist of separately valved filling, discharge and spray lines for each tank. The fill line extends to the tank bottom, and discharge is via submerged electric cargo pumps, usually two in each tank. The spray system is normally a series of nozzles located at the top of the tank, which are used to cool the tank prior to loading. The evaporation of the sprayed liquid has a cooling effect. This spray system can also be activated by a small submerged electric pump located in one or more cargo tanks in order to cool the tank while the ship is underway, or provide LNG vapour via the vapour vent system to be used as main propulsion fuel.

The vapour system consists of a single manifold on either side of the ship which is, in turn, connected to a fore and aft vapour header. LNG vapour passes from the dome at the top of each cargo tank through the vapour header to shore during cooldown and loading. Two pressure relief valves are also located on the dome of each cargo tank and in the event of tank over-pressure, relieve gas to a relief header and thence to atmosphere via a relief riser. The vent risers are located at a safe height and distance from the accommodation.

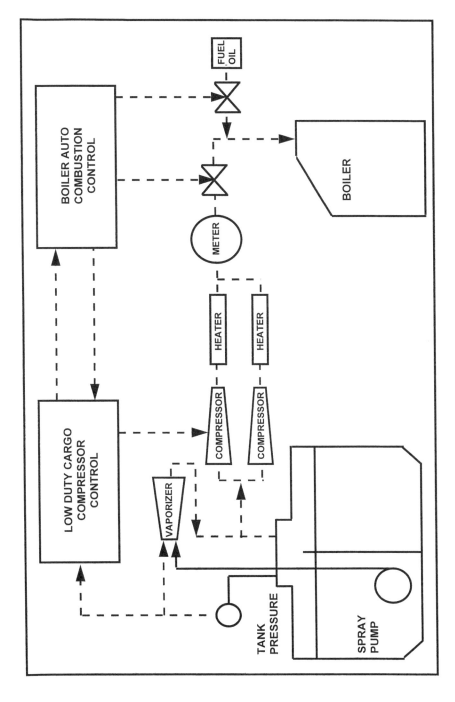

Figure 5.3   Cargo boil-off handling system

Gas normally boiled off during the passage is compressed, heated and piped to the engine room to be burned as fuel for ship propulsion. Piping in the engine room is jacketed and the annular space between the pipes is purged with nitrogen as a safety measure.

The ship is also fitted with one or two high-capacity compressors to send displaced gas to shore during loading operations. A heavy-duty heater is used in conjunction with these compressors to heat LNG vapour for warming cargo tanks prior to inerting.

Two other vaporisers are also installed; one to vaporise LNG from shore during gas purging of the cargo tanks to displace inert gas with LNG prior to cooldown; the other a forcing vaporiser to provide make-up gas to the boilers to permit 100 per cent gas firing, particularly on the ballast voyage. All the vaporisers and heaters are shell-and-tube-type heat exchangers supplied by steam from the main boilers in the engine room.

All cold piping is fitted with expansion bellows or, if space permits, is looped to allow for contraction of the piping when cooled.

5.3.2   Instrumentation

Instrumentation is an important component of the LNG cargo system for both safety reasons and custody transfer purposes. It consists of equipment to measure cargo level, pressure and temperature as well as gas detection. Considerable attention is given to maintenance and periodic recalibration and testing.

5.3.2.1   *Liquid Level Gauges*

The capacitance gauge is widely used on LNG ships as the primary device for cargo level measurement. It measures the change in electrical capacitance between two probes as liquid rather than vapour is detected between them. The probes extend to the full depth of the tank and provide a continuous indication of liquid level to a readout in the cargo control room.

The float gauge is normally fitted on all cargo tanks as a back-up for the capacitance probe. It consists of a float attached by a tape to an indicating device which reads the tank level both locally and in the cargo control room. The gauge is fitted in a tubular well extending to the bottom of the tank. The gauge is normally mounted on the top of a gate valve on the dome of the cargo tank so it can be completely removed and serviced, if necessary. Float gauges are only activated in port during cargo operations.

Another level gauge type which shows considerable promise for LNG ships is the radar gauge. The gauge is mounted on the tank dome and has the advantage of no moving or electrical parts within the cargo tank. These gauges are widely used on oil tankers and shore tanks and could be a useful alternative to the capacitance probe.

5.3.2.2   High and Low Level Alarm and Shutdown Systems

All cargo tanks are also fitted with high level audible and visible (in the cargo control room) alarms which warn of high level. Warnings are usually given in three stages; a high level, followed by a high-high level which automatically closes the valves at the tank dome, followed by a very high level alarm which activates the Emergency Shutdown System (ESD). Low level alarms are also fitted which automatically stop or prevent start of the cargo and spray pumps. These alarms are usually of the capacitance type, activated when contacted by LNG.

The high-high and very high level alarms are independent and fixed whereas the high and low level alarms are adjustable.

5.3.2.3   Pressure and Temperature Gauges

Pressure gauges, alarms and relief valves are fitted throughout the cargo system, including the cargo tanks, and liquid and vapour lines. If liquid is trapped in a pipe when valves are closed, the pressure will be relieved into the relief header to avoid pipe rupture from overpressure.

Cargo tanks are fitted with accurate temperature sensors (usually platinum resistance thermometers) which measure within 0.2–0.3 degrees centigrade at LNG temperature. This accuracy is required for custody transfer purposes. There are typically five in each tank, spaced at intervals of 25 per cent of the tank height, which are duplicated for redundancy. They are also used for monitoring temperature differences during cargo tank cooldown operations in order to avoid excessive thermal stress.

Resistance thermometers are also fitted to the inner hull of the ship on the transverse bulkheads, the double bottom and drip pan. These are connected to an alarm in the event of a drop in temperature to near the lowest temperature the hull steel can tolerate. An abnormal drop in temperature is a sign of a liquid or vapour leak from the cargo tank.

5.3.2.4   Gas Detection System

All LNG carriers are fitted with a fixed continuous gas detection system with audible and visual alarms. These alarms must be fitted in the wheelhouse and in the cargo control room. Detector heads are normally fitted in any place where gas is likely to accumulate including:

(1)   cargo compressor room;
(2)   cargo compressor motor room;
(3)   cargo control room;
(4)   hold spaces and interbarrier spaces;
(5   airlocks;
(6)   burner platform vent hoods and engine room gas supply pipelines. (The gas supply pipeline is a double pipe with the space between the pipes purged with nitrogen. The gas detector is in this inter pipe space.)

Gas samples are drawn sequentially from each detector head and passed through an infra-red or catalytic combustion type analyser, usually located in the cargo control room. Alarms are activated when the LNG vapour concentration reaches 30 per cent of the lower flammable limit.

Ships are also equipped with a number of portable gas detectors and oxygen detectors which are used when entering spaces which have been purged with air, such as cargo tanks and hold spaces normally containing inert gas or nitrogen, as well as ballast spaces.

5.3.3   Nitrogen/Inert Gas

Inert gas is required on LNG ships for purging cargo tanks of air prior to introducing methane vapour or purging them of methane vapour prior to introducing air. These operations are carried out before and after the periodic dry-docking of the ship. Individual tanks are sometimes inerted at sea during the ballast passage when repairs to in-tank equipment are required.

This inert gas is normally supplied from a combustion type generator on board, using gas oil as fuel. After combustion the gas is cooled and dried to a dewpoint of less than minus 45 degrees centigrade and contains less than 1 per cent oxygen. The generator on modern vessels is sized to be able to purge the ship to these conditions in about 20 hours (i.e. 12,000–15,000 cubic metres per hour). A number of ships trading to Tokyo Bay do not have inert gas generators, but rely on similar barge-mounted equipment or liquid nitrogen also supplied by barge for inerting.

Smaller quantities of nitrogen are also required on board for inerting hold spaces and interbarrier spaces. Combustion-produced inert gas is not suitable for this purpose as the carbon dioxide would freeze out as dry ice at LNG cargo temperatures. This gas used to be supplied from liquid nitrogen tanks on board the ship, but modern vessels use a membrane-type air separation unit instead. Air is compressed, filtered and passed over the hollowfibre membrane which divides the air into nitrogen (containing up to 3 per cent oxygen) and oxygen, carbon dioxide and other trace elements which are exhausted to atmosphere. The typical capacity of the on-board generator is 60 cubic metres per hour.

5.3.4 Ship–Shore Interface and Emergency Shutdown Systems (ESD)

The cargo transfer between ship and shore is accomplished by a series of shore-based articulated loading arms, usually three or four liquid arms and a single vapour arm. The configuration is very similar at both the loading and discharge terminals. These arms have flexibility in three directions to allow for relative motion between the ship and shore. If this allowable motion is exceeded, alarms sound on the ship and shore. Cargo transfer is automatically stopped, either by the ship's pumps shutdown during unloading or shore pumps shutdown during loading.

If the motion continues to increase, the valves of the ship's end of the articulated arm automatically close. The arm disconnects from the ship and swings clear by the counter-balance with the outer valve attached to the ship's manifold flange.

The ship and shore are also linked by ESD via an intrinsically safe electrical connection and, in the new ships, a fibre optic connection as well. All ships have a pneumatic back-up system.

The ESD system is divided into two circuits:

The ESD-1 system is normally tested before cargo operations commence. ESD-1 is activated by:

(1) melting plugs in cargo machinery room, tank domes and loading manifold;
(2) push buttons located at strategic positions on the ship at very high level in any cargo tank;
(3) low pressure in cargo hydraulic system, control air system, or pneumatic ship–shore link;
(4) electrical power failure in ESD system;
(5) ESD signals from shore.

When initiated either onshore or onboard, ESD-1 initiates the following actions:

(1) low-duty and high-duty compressors stop;
(2) all cargo and spray pumps stop;

(3) manifold valves close in 30 seconds;
(4) master boil-off gas valve closes;
(5) inert gas generator blowers stop;
(6) spray nozzle valves close.

ESD-2 is a separate system, normally operated from shore, which first activates the ESD-1 system and after a time delay gives a warning and then disconnects the ship's loading arms.

5.3.5 Heel

Normally, sufficient cargo is retained in the ship after discharge to provide for spray cooling the tanks to the allowed loading temperature before the ship's arrival at the loading terminal. Sometimes all of the heel is kept in one tank; and on some ships which have a spray pump in each tank, some heel is retained in all tanks.

In some trades, where LNG production capability is in excess of sales requirements, gas burning is used for nearly 100 per cent of fuel requirements. In this case, spray cooling or forced vaporisation is used to supply boiler requirements during the ballast passage.

The quantity of heel can be substantial; in the order of 3500 cubic metres for a typical 125,000-cubic metre spherical tank ship on a 14-day ballast passage. For membrane ships, where spray cooling is not required, less than 1000 cubic metres are required for a six-day passage, and for passages of 14 days or more, no heel is needed. The membrane tanks can be cooled from ambient temperature to loading temperature in about 12 hours.

5.3.6 Firefighting

LNG ships are normally fitted with a number of fire extinguishing systems which are described as follows:

5.3.6.1 *Water Fire Extinguishing System*

Salt-water fire hydrants and hose boxes are located at regular intervals around the outside deck spaces and in and around the accommodation and machinery spaces. These are supplied by firemain pumps in the engine room.

Water is not a suitable medium for fighting an LNG fire directly, as it will cause a massive vaporisation of gas from any spilled liquid. Water spray is used as a cooling medium for the areas surrounding an LNG fire and to protect personnel who may need to approach the fire. Water is essential for protecting steel work from the effects of the extreme cold (i.e. cracking) in the event of an LNG spill.

5.3.6.2 Dry Powder System

An LNG ship usually has four individual dry powder systems located in the cargo area. Units are positioned so that any part of the cargo deck can be reached by two hand-held hose nozzles. A remotely activated fixed monitor is aimed at each cargo manifold (port and starboard). The dry powder is normally sodium or potassium bicarbonate and is quite effective in extinguishing small LNG fires.

5.3.6.3 CO_2 System

The CO_2 system consists of a series of pressurised bottles or a large storage tank which can be released into enclosed spaces. These spaces include the cargo machinery room, engine room and emergency generator and switch-board room.

It is essential that all personnel are evacuated from the enclosed space before CO_2 is introduced, because asphyxiation is almost immediate when breathing an air–CO_2 mixture.

5.3.6.4 Water Spray and Water Curtain Systems

The water spray system consists of a spray pump in the engine room, a distribution manifold with valves which are accessible outside the dangerous area and various distribution pipes and spray heads. The areas covered are:

(1) all cargo tank domes;
(2) port and starboard cargo manifolds;
(3) cargo compressor and motor room bulkheads;
(4) accommodation front and side bulkheads;
(5) both lifeboat embarkation areas.

The water curtain system is operated by a separate pump and supplies a sheet of water under the cargo manifolds which protects the ship's side from accidental splashes of LNG during cargo operations.

5.4 LNG TRANSPORTATION CONTRACTS

Almost all LNG transportation contracts are now in the form of the time charter which is essentially an operating lease. A time charter party, which is the contract between owner and charterer, identifies the salient characteristics of the ship and obligations of the shipowner (which is to provide a ship capable of the specified performance, and to operate the ship according to that performance when requested by the charterer) and the charterer (which is to pay the hire on time). The charterer also has a due diligence obligation (but not an absolute warranty) to ensure that the ship trades between safe ports. LNG time charters are based on conventional oil tanker charter provisions, such as appear in Shelltime 4, with additional clauses relating to cryogenic performance. Some of the important aspects of the time charter from an operational point of view are briefly described in the following sections.

5.4.1 Ship Characteristics and Classification

The chartered vessel must conform to a detailed physical description, (commonly called a 'Form B') which includes:

(1) classification society and class;
(2) country of registry;
(3) dimensions, displacement, deadweight and canal tonnages;
(4) cargo capacity;
(5) speed, propulsion machinery, fuel consumption, bunker capacity;
(6) cargo system design;
(7) cargo pumps, spray pumps, gas compressors, inert gas generators and nitrogen generators;
(8) boil-off rate;
(9) cargo loading and discharge performance.

The owner has an obligation to deliver the ship in the condition described in the Form B and to exercise due diligence to maintain the ship in that condition throughout the period of the charter. Performance penalties are also measured against the specifications described therein.

One of these obligations is to maintain the ship in class which means a periodic inspection by the classification society surveyors to be sure the condition of the ship and its equipment does not deteriorate below an acceptable standard.

5.4.2 Hire and Off-Hire

Charter hire which is paid monthly in advance provides funds for the owner's return on his investment in the vessel and the payment of the operating costs which include the crew, provisions, stores, spare parts, maintenance, insurance and overheads. The time charter hire includes all the costs required for ship's operation and maintenance, except for fuel, port charges and (Suez or Panama) canal dues. These latter items are referred to as voyage costs which are the responsibility of the charterer.

For short-term contracts of up to about three years, the hire is based on an all-inclusive daily rate which applies for the entire period. For longer-term contracts, the hire is divided into the 'capital element', which remains fixed, usually for the full term of the charter, and the 'operating element'which varies with the actual cost of ship operation and takes cost escalation into account. The capital element includes loan repayments and financial return on invested equity. The operating element is adjusted annually to reflect historic or anticipated cost changes.

Three methods are commonly used to adjust the operating element:

(1)   Cost pass-through.
In this method all of the costs incurred are passed through to the charterer. An estimated operating element is established at the beginning of the year, and a lump sum credited or debited to the shipowner at the end of the year based on actual costs.

(2)   Fixed escalation.
Costs are increased each year by a fixed percentage based on the anticipated cost escalation.

(3)   Index-linked.
Costs are adjusted annually depending on changes in specific published indices. These can be consumer price indices in the country where crew and stores or spares originate, and/or specific labour and machinery cost indices. When indices are for currencies other than US dollars, there is often a currency compensation factor, since LNG ship charters are normally denominated in US dollars.

The ship is normally paid hire throughout the charter period, except when the ship is not available to the charterer for reasons due to the shipowner or to the state of the ship. For longer-term charters the periodic dry-docking time is also often off-hire.

Events which will lead to off-hire claims are listed in the off-hire clause and include:

(1)   deficiency of personnel or stores, repairs, dry-docking, collision, stranding, accident or damage to the vessel and breakdown of machinery;

(2)   industrial action by the crew, refusal to sail, or neglect of duty by sea-going personnel;

(3)   deviation, except to save life, or avoid bad weather;

(4)   detention by authorities due to infraction of local law by sea-going personnel, or legal action against the vessel or owners;

(5)   failure to meet performance undertakings;

(6)   engagement of the vessel's flag state in hostilities, such that charterers cannot employ the vessel.

5.4.3   Penalties for Non-Performance

Penalties for the ship's failure to perform in accordance with Form B requirements typically include:

(1)   failure to sail at guaranteed minimum speed, in which case hire is reduced to the percentage of actual to guaranteed minimum speed;

(2)   excess fuel consumption, in which case the shipowner pays for actual fuel used in excess of the guaranteed maximum consumption at the guaranteed minimum speed;

(3)   boil-off in excess of the guaranteed maximum, in which case the shipowner pays for the excess at the sales price agreed between the charterer and the LNG buyer or seller, as the case may be;

(4)   excess loading or discharge time, in which case hire is reduced by the number of hours used in excess of the guaranteed loading or discharge time.

One of the sometimes controversial performance-related subjects in the time charter negotiation is the conversion of the heating value of boil-off gas to its fuel oil equivalent. Boil-off gas is composed of methane and nitrogen. The quantity of nitrogen in the boil-off is measured from mass spectrometer analysis during loading and discharge. This quantity can be deducted from the liquid volume of boil-off calculated from custody transfer readings.

The calculation of the equivalent heating value for heavy fuel oil and methane needs to take into account the difference in boiler efficiency for the two fuels.

The efficiency for a typical 70 tonnes per hour boiler (two of which supply a 40,000 shp power plant) when burning methane is about 96 per cent of the efficiency when burning fuel oil at 100 per cent load. At the more likely operating condition of 75 per cent load the efficiency is about 97 per cent.

The other pertinent data is:

	Btu/1b
Higher Heating Value —HFO—	18,060
—Methane	23,892
Methane Specific Gravity	0.425

The conversion of cubic metres of LNG to equivalent HFO (after deduction of nitrogen) is therefore:

$$1 \text{ m}^3 \text{ LNG} = \frac{0.425 \times 23,892 \times 0.97}{18,060}$$
$$= 0.545 \text{ tonnes of HFO}$$

When using the conversion factor in fuel consumption calculations, it must be remembered that the total fuel consumed includes that required to power the boil-off gas compressor and heater, typically 12 tonnes of HFO per day for a 40,000 shp power plant. This amount is to be added to the guaranteed maximum consumption, based on fuel oil only, before this calculation of HFO plus equivalent boil-off is made for guaranteed consumption purposes. In some charters, the conversion factor is reduced from the 0.545 level, where nitrogen is not deducted by calculation or to give some performance margin to the shipowner.

5.4.4   Exceptions

The exceptions clause of a time charter is, in effect, the *force majeure* clause which excuses a party from its performance of time charter obligations to the extent that such performance is prevented or lessened due to enumerated causes. In the early days of maritime commerce, each voyage was seen as a separate enterprise which could be frustrated by any number of man-made and natural events and the ship and shipowner were excused from their performance obligations for these reasons. Over time, the charterer has also been excused from his obligations (i.e. mainly to pay hire) for some of the same reasons. This is known as 'extending the mutuality of exceptions'.[6]

A typical exceptions clause for a time charter could read as follows:

'The Vessel, her Master and Owners shall not, unless otherwise in this Charter expressly provided, be liable for any loss or damage or delay or failure arising or

---

[6] Mocatta, Mustill and Boyd (eds.), *Scrutton on Charterparties and Bills of Lading* (Sweet & Maxwell, 1984), p. 209.

resulting from any act, neglect or default of the Master, pilots, mariners or other servants or agents of Owners in the navigation or management of the Vessel; fire, unless caused by the actual fault or privity of Owners; collision or stranding; dangers and accidents of the sea; explosion, bursting of boilers, breakage of shafts or any latent defect in hull, equipment or machinery; provided, however, that Clauses (relating to ship's condition and owner's performance) hereof shall be unaffected by the foregoing. Further, neither the Vessel, her Master or Owners, nor Charterers shall, unless otherwise in this Charter expressly provided be liable for any loss or damage or delay or failure in performance hereunder arising or resulting from act of God, act of war, seizure under legal process, quarantine restrictions, strikes, lock-outs, riots, restraints of labour, civil commotions or arrest of restraint of princes, rulers or people.

The Vessel shall have liberty to sail with or without pilots, to tow or go to the assistance of Vessels in distress and to deviate for the purpose of saving life or property.'

Most LNG charterers follow this model and although the exact scope of the mutual exceptions (i.e. the second sentence in the clause) is subject to negotiations, the final wording is likely to be similar to the above.

It is important to note that the hire clause requires the continued payment of hire by the time charterer even when the shipowner is excused due to an event listed in the exceptions clause unless the off-hire clause or other clause in the charter excuses the payment of hire in such circumstances. However, most off-hire clauses are drafted in terms wide enough to cover almost any loss of time to the charterer.

As noted in the second paragraph of the exceptions clause, the vessel is at liberty to deviate from the voyage directed by the time charterer in order to assist vessels in distress and save lives and property. This feature of the time charter is in recognition of the master's traditional obligation to render assistance to others who are in peril.

A feature of the LNG time charter which is unique to the trade is the tendency of the charterer to try to persuade the shipowner to accept a portion of the *force majeure* risk provided for in the LNG sales and purchase agreement. Whereas in the conventional shipping trades the charter hire is paid in full, whether the ship is being used or not (except for operating cost savings which can be passed on to charterer), some charterers of LNG ships attempt to have shipowners accept off-hire time due to problems with production or receiving of cargo. Needless to say, this sort of proposal is strongly rejected by shipowners and particularly by the financiers of the ship who will reject any delay in debt service payments for reason of LNG buyer or seller *force majeure*.

5.5 LNG SHIP OPERATIONS

The major functions of LNG ship operations are similar to other types of ships, with perhaps more emphasis on crew training for steam turbine plant and cargo handling operations, as well as planned maintenance procedures and spare parts control. A brief description of the various operating functions follows.

5.5.1 Crewing

The crew complement of a typical LNG ship numbers about 28–30 persons.

Deck officers
Master
Chief officer
Second officer
Third officer
Cargo engineer

Deck ratings
Bosun
Able-bodied seaman (5)
Ordinary seaman (2)
Repairman

Engine officers
Chief engineer
First assistant engineer
Second assistant engineer
Third assistant engineer
Electrician

Engine ratings
Donkeyman
Repairman
Fireman (3)
Oiler (1)

Catering Ratings
Chief cook
Messman (2)

Ships are normally on automatic steering unless in congested waters or in harbour, so that during the day there is only a single officer on watch on the bridge. All other deck personnel are on day work. At night an able-bodied seaman is also on watch with an officer.

The engine room is also operated unmanned so the engine officers and ratings are all on day work. At night an alarm sounds in one of the engine officer's cabins in the event of malfunction in the engine room.

Cargo handling operations are mainly carried out by the chief officer with the assistance of the cargo engineer. The officer on watch looks after ballasting and mooring. It is important to keep adequate personnel on board in port to cope with emergencies and sail the ship if necessary.

There is no longer a requirement to have a radio officer on board since the introduction of the Global Maritime Distress Safety System (GMDSS) which is also a communications mode. At least two of the deck officers must be qualified to operate the system.

Ships have planned maintenance systems on board which define a detailed programme of periodic maintenance for all of the ship's machinery. This system is often combined with spare parts control so that parts are automatically resupplied when used.

Dry-docking of the ships is typically done at two- to three-year intervals. Dry-docking out-of-service time is between 20 and 30 days which includes deviation to the dry-docking port, gas freeing prior to dry-docking and cargo tank inerting, return to the loading port, purging and cooldown prior to the subsequent loading. The dry-docking is normally timed to coincide with liquefaction plant shutdown for periodic maintenance.

The main reason for the dry-docking interval of two to three years is the deterioration of the outside hull paint system. There has been some improvement in paints recently, and the goal is to achieve a five-year docking interval which would coincide with the five-year special survey (including tailshaft inspection) required by the classification societies.

5.5.2   Crew Training

Considerable crew training is carried out on board by spending the required sea time to qualify for the examination to the next upward rank. Shoreside courses, such as those in advanced firefighting, medical first aid and survival craft rescue boat, are mandatory for officers. LNG training can be carried out at on-board seminars, or at shoreside courses in a number of locations in England, Japan and the United States. There is also an LNG training ship, the 35,500-cubic metre *Annabella*, which carries out this training in conjunction with normal LNG trading. Many crew members take advantage of opportunities to take specialised courses ashore during their leave periods.

5.5.3   International Safety Management and Standards for Training, Certification and Watchkeeping

The International Maritime Organisation has introduced two important measures which are intended greatly to improve the standards of safety of operation and competence of marine personnel. These two measures are briefly described as follows:

5.5.3.1   *International Safety Management Code 1994 (ISM)*

The fact that more than 80 per cent of marine accidents are caused by human error has been addressed by the Assembly of the International

Maritime Organisation. To remedy this situation the ISM Code was incorporated into the Safety of Life at Sea Convention as a new Chapter IX in 1994. It will affect almost every passenger ship, tanker and bulk carrier and their owners or operators as compliance is mandatory by 1 July 1998. The objectives of the Code are to ensure safety at sea, prevention of injury or loss of life, and avoidance of damage to the environment and to property. The Code requires a compulsory quality assurance system of ship management with policies and procedures in place which identify potential problems and take corrective action before an accident or failure takes place. Classification societies have a major role in the implementation of the ISM Code by assisting shipowners in setting up the proper systems and issuing necessary certificates on behalf of the flag states. Ships not having proper ISM certification are liable to be prohibited from entering, or to be detained in, port until such certification is in place.

5.5.3.2 *International Convention on Standards for Training, Certification and Watchkeeping for Seafarers (STCW) 1978 (revised 1995)*

The STCW Convention of 1978 contains the basic qualifications for ships' officers and crews and includes specific training requirements for crew members of liquefied gas tankers. It is the principal international treaty regulating seafarers' training, certification and watchkeeping arrangements and forms the basis of national standards worldwide. Three concerns about the existing 1978 Convention have been identified, which the 1995 amendments are intended to address:

(1) The 1978 Convention did not contain precise standards of competence required to obtain certification of candidates, and evidence that required knowledge had been absorbed was left to individual administrations (i.e. member countries) to define.

(2) Neither the ratification process nor the provisions of the 1978 Conventions have provided sufficient guarantees that STCW requirements have been implemented or sufficiently enforced. There has been a loss of confidence in the reliability of STCW certificates issued by certain governments.

(3) The 1978 Convention was written in terms of conventional shipboard work organisation based on traditional divisions between deck and engine departments. This has proved to be too restrictive and hinders safety-enhancing redistribution of work load during periods of intensive activity.

A crucial date for implementation of the 1995 amendments will be 1 August 1998 when training must be carried out according to the newly adopted standards and governments will have to submit documentary evidence of compliance with the new requirements.

Sea staff who have commenced training before this date can continue to have their STCW certificates issued and renewed under STCW 1978 requirements until 1 February 2002, but all sea staff commencing training or sea service after 1 August 1998 will have to be documented according to the new requirements. It is expected that most LNG ship operators will be in a position to comply with these IMO requirements before the relevant deadlines.

5.5.4   Port Requirements

Most LNG ports have been designed for a particular project which caters to the ships specified for that project. Now that there is more interchange of ships between ports, it will be useful if the following can be considered for new LNG terminals:

(1)   It is extremely useful if the port can accept a range of 20,000 to 137,500-cubic metre ships, or larger, especially on the long-haul routes.

(2)   Breasting dolphins and mooring points should be spaced and sized to accept the complete range of ship sizes.

(3)   Mooring points should be strong enough to take maximum ship's wire tension and be of quick release design. Wire tension monitors should be fitted.

(4)   Width and depth of approach channels and turning basins should have adequate margin to accommodate the largest ship which might serve the port.

(5)   Ship's approach speed indicators, which are visible from the bridge, should be fitted.

(6)   Ship–shore interface connections including the Emergency Shutdown and Communication Systems should be a standard design.

(7)   Loading and discharge articulated arms should be designed to accommodate all ship sizes and should be equipped with insulating flanges and dry-break coupling.

(8)   ESD-2 limits should be calculated for all ship sizes.

(9)   The ship–shore gangway should be a flexible design to accommodate a range of ship types and sizes.

(10) Clear and well-defined weather operating limits to be established.

(11) Anti-surge devices should be fitted in LNG pipelines.[7]

---

[7] McGuire and White, *Liquefied Gas Handling Principles on Ships and in Terminals* (Witherby & Co. Ltd, 1996), pp. 141–150.

5.5.5 Insurance

Ships are normally insured for both damage to hull and machinery and the total loss of the ship. Separate policies are written for damage caused during normal marine operations and those resulting from war risks. Protection and indemnity cover gives protection against third party liabilities.

Hull and machinery marine and war risks are insured by groups of underwriters located mainly in London, Bergen, Oslo, New York and Paris, but also in other cities worldwide. The cover is for the physical or mechanical damage that may be caused to the vessel in the course of operations by unusual 'fortuitous' events (i.e. perils of the sea). There is normally a deductible amount for the first part of the claim which reduces the annual premiums, but apart from this, the policy covers t he cost of repairs up to the insured hull value. The insured value of the vessel for total loss (for example, sinking) or constructive total loss (irreparable damage, or damage costing more to repair than the value of the ship) is usually the replacement value when the replacement ship is delivered, and declines over time according to the greater of book or market earning values. There has been a recent trend to insure LNG ships for their replacement value, even after the ships have been in service for a long period. This means that the insurance cover can increase if shipbuilding costs are rising over time after delivery of the LNG ship.

Protection and indemnity insurance is provided by 'mutual clubs' which are groups of shipowners who mutually share the risk of third party claims against an individual owner. The claims are funded by 'calls' against the individual shipowners in the group. The amount of protection and indemnity (P&I) cover at one time was unlimited, but now is limited to about US$4.25 billion, and US$750 million for oil pollution. In the case of very large claims, funds are provided by a combination of club calls, reinsurance and calls on the International Group which consists of most of the P&I clubs worldwide.

Off-hire insurance is also available to reimburse owners for charter hire lost during the repair period for hull and machinery claims. Cover is normally available from 15 to 180 days in any one incident and costs about one to two days of hire per year. LNG ship out-of-service time is very rarely more than 15 days for any single damage event, so that claims for this type of cover are unusual, and some shipowners do not take this type of cover.

An important aspect of insurance premiums as an operating cost is their unpredictability. Insurance costs can vary substantially from year to year, depending on individual claim history and fluctuations in the market as a whole. Time charters which have a fixed or index-linked escalation in the operating element can give rise to ship owners' costs when insurance premiums exceed the estimate used in the original calculation, or can give rise to 'profit' for shipowners should costs decrease.

5.6 EXTENDED SHIP LIFE AND EXISTING SHIP AVAILABIILTY

In the late 1970s a number of newly-built LNG ships were laid up without immediate prospects of future business because the Algeria–USA projects collapsed. Other vessels were built on speculation for projects that never materialised. A few of these vessels were scrapped and the rest remained in lay-up throughout the 1980s.

In the early 1990s, LNG project developers, particularly Shell on behalf of the Nigeria project, began to consider these existing ships for new greenfield projects. The cost of these little-used vessels was a fraction of that for a newbuilding. The Nigerian project itself would not have been economically viable unless unit transportation costs were reduced by using existing ships.

In 1993 the Brunei–Japan LNG project was extended for an additional 20 years. After careful evaluation of the condition and life expectancy of the ships serving the original 20-year term of the project, the ships were allowed to continue trading as long as there is no important deterioration in vessel condition.

Similar studies of life expectancy of existing LNG ships have been carried out by Det Norske Veritas, Lloyds Register of Shipping and the American Bureau of Shipping for a number of LNG shipowners. The common conclusion from all of them is that LNG ships show very little sign of deterioration in the first 20 years of their service life. If maintenance is continued at the same high standard, the useful life of such ships may be extended to allow them to trade successfully up to 50 years of age without significant reductions in reliability and safety—more than enough for these ships to be utilised in a second 20 to 25-year project.

The Trinidad LNG project may not have been economically viable with newbuildings. LNG purchasers acquired one little-used vessel which had been laid up since 1981 and three vessels which had been in service, two of them for 25 years in the Alaska–Japan trade. All of these ships are expected to trade until 2020 which is the expiry date of the relevant project sales agreements.

Six of the ships currently serving the Japanese Western LNG buyers on delivered ex-ship (DES) contracts from Indonesia have been extended until 2015.

In summary, then, the ships that have been extended on long-term trades are:

Route	Ship Size (m³)	No.	Expiration of Contract Life
Brunei–Japan	70,000	7	40 years
Nigeria–Europe	125,000	7	42 years
Trinidad–US	126,540	1	40 years
and Europe	70,000	2	51 years
	87,500	1	47 years
Indonesia–Japan	125,000	6	35 years

These 24 existing ships have been fixed on charter in the period since 1993, when the Brunei–Japan project was extended.

There are very few existing ships remaining available. Only seven 125,000-cubic metre vessels are available from the year 2001–02, and only two available at the end of 1997.

Name	Ship Size (m³)	Available from
Arzew	126,540	1997
Hilli	125,000	2001
Gimi	125,000	2001
Khannur	125,000	1998
Golar Freeze	125,800	2001
Aquarius	125,000	2001
Aries	125,000	2002

It is not clear at present if and when any more existing ships will become available, although the first possibility could be about 2005 when four 125,000-cubic metre ships could be released by the Arun, Indonesia to Japan project because of declining gas resources.

The overriding advantage of using existing ships is that the capital element of the charter hire can be less than half that of new ships. Many of the recent fixtures of existing vessels have been at about US$15 million per year, but this figure is liable to increase because of the scarcity of these ships.

5.7 FUTURE DEVELOPMENT PROSPECTS

Most of the liquefaction plants constructed to date have had a production capacity which is in excess of the delivered quantity sold under the project LNG sales contract. Transportation capacity is generally sized to match the total plant capacity which means there has been a certain amount of built-in redundancy in the system. For this reason, there has also been a tendency to burn gas rather than heavy fuel oil (HFO) in both the loaded and ballast legs of the voyage. More recently, there has been a trend towards matching the contract quantity with the maximum capability of the liquefaction plant in order to improve overall project economics. Since the value of delivered LNG (ex-ship) is generally considerably higher than the cost of HFO, there is now some impetus to reliquefy the boil-off onboard and deliver the maximum possible quantity of LNG.

If onboard liquefaction is a viable alternative to burning boil-off as fuel, consideration can then be given to replacing the steam turbine drive with diesel engines. A modern diesel or diesel electric power plant uses about 60 per cent of the quantity of fuel of a steam turbine. A single, slow-speed diesel engine is a common means of propulsion for a wide variety of ships including oil tankers, bulk carriers and container ships. However the diesel engine requires more frequent periodic maintenance than a steam turbine. Scheduled or unscheduled stops for maintenance are an anathema to an LNG project which is one reason why there is reluctance to consider a diesel engine even with the very substantial potential fuel savings.

The answer could be the diesel electric power plant which would have four diesel generators driving a single motor for main propulsion. A brief analysis of both of these possibilities follows.

5.7.1 Steam Turbine plus Reliquefaction

This concept would involve installation of a reliquefier in the space which would normally be occupied by the cargo compressor and motor room on the outside deck. All LNG (except nitrogen in the boil-off which would be separated and vented) would be returned to the cargo tanks.

Figure 5.7.1 illustrates the system whereby boil-off gas from the cargo tanks is compressed and liquefied in a plate fin heat exchanger. Nitrogen is then separated from the methane and vented through the relief riser, and the liquid is returned to the cargo tanks. A nitrogen expansion loop consisting of a three-stage compressor and expander-driven fourth-stage compressor and sea water coolers provide the required refrigerant duty.

Figure 5.7.1   Kvaerner Maritime Reliquification System

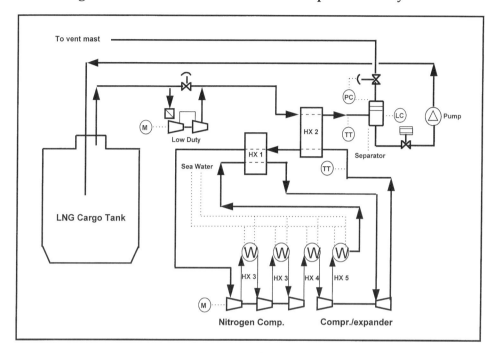

For the Abu Dhabi–Japan trade, which is typical of the long-haul LNG trade, the economics would be as follows:

Ship size	135,000 m^3 (net)
Boil-off (average)	0.125%
Sea days per year	320
Boil-off per year	54,000 m^3
Additional revenue:	
@ US$4.00 per mmBtu	US$5,140,000
and 23.8 mmBtu per m^3	

The cost of the additional HFO to replace boil-off, now delivered as extra cargo, must be deducted from the benefit. The conversion from the heating value of LNG to fuel oil is a factor of about 0.545 tonnes of HFO per cubic metre of LNG (see Section 5.4.3).

In addition, an average of 12 tonnes of HFO per day must be added as the net additional fuel required to power the reliquefaction plant, after deducting fuel requirements for boil-off compressors and heaters.

On this basis, and for a typical cost of HFO of US$100 per tonne, the extra cost of fuel is:

US$100 x 54,000 x 0.545 =   US$2,943,000
US$100 x 12 x 320 =   US$ 384,000

                              US$3,327,000

The annual operating cost saving is therefore:

Additional revenue   US$5,140,000
Less extra fuel cost   (US$3,327,000)

Annual saving   =   US$1,813,000

Kvaerner-Maritime have designed and costed a reliquefaction plant to fit the 135,000-cubic metre ship with the boil-off indicated and determined that the net additional installed cost, when allowing for the savings in cargo compression machinery and related equipment, is in the order of Nkr30 million (US$4 million at 1997 exchange rates). This plant consists of two identical units, each capable of reliquefying all of the boil-off; in other words, 100 per cent redundancy. The pay-back period for the additional investment is about 2.2 years.[8]

5.7.2   Diesel Electric Propulsion plus Reliquefaction

Diesel electric propulsion has been in existence since the 1930s. In recent years diesel electric has mainly been used for icebreakers and modern offshore vessels because of its high reliability and passenger ships because they are designed to be relatively vibration free, and redundancy can be built in by using multiple diesel generator units. A possible configuration for an LNG ship would be four diesel generators producing about 31 megawatts, supplying electricity via a frequency convertor to a single motor driving the propeller (see Figure 5.7.2). Having four generators would allow for periodic servicing with only a temporary reduction in speed, if such service were to be done while the ship is underway.

The LNG shipbuilders that are also passenger shipbuilders are:

Kvaerner-Masa, Finland
Chantiers de L'Atlantique, France
Fincantieri, Italy

---

[8] Kvaerner Maritime AS, *LNG Reliquefaction* (Kvaerner Internal Document, 1996), pp. 11–13.

Figure 5.7.2   Diesel Electric Propulsion System

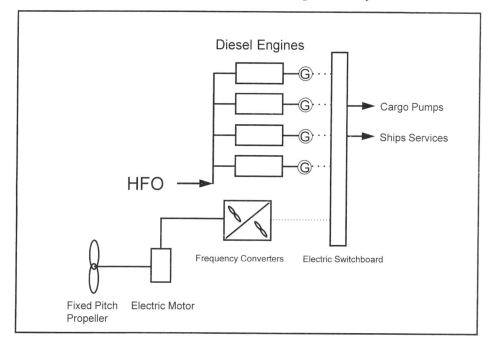

Any of these shipyards would be prepared to offer a diesel electric plant for LNG ships. Kvaerner-Masa has estimated the additional capital cost of such a plant, including the two 100 per cent capacity reliquefaction plants, to be about Nkr37 million (US$5 million).

The total annual fuel cost saving for the diesel electric alternative, on the Abu Dhabi–Japan example, would be:

Fuel consumption:	tonnes per day
Steam turbine	180
Diesel electric	110
Saving	70

Cost saving:
US$100 per tonne × 70 × 320   =   US$2,240,000

The cost/benefit for the diesel electric plus reliquefaction case compared with the gas/HFO fire boiler will then be:

	Million US$
Reliquefaction saving	1.81
Fuel saving (diesel electric)	2.24
Net annual saving	4.05

In other words, the annual cost savings will pay for the extra investment in about 15 months of operation. There will be some extra maintenance costs for the diesel electric plant versus the steam turbine which have not been quantified in this brief analysis, but it would be conservative to consider a total benefit in the order of US$4 million per year per ship for this alternative. The advantage of this particular combination as compared to other ideas, such as the dual fuel diesel or gas burning diesel, is that the technology is well established and can easily be introduced in the next generation of LNG ships.[9]

Prospective charterers need to appreciate that a slightly higher charter rate can easily be justified by the additional cargo deliverability and the substantial voyage (i.e. fuel) cost savings which can be achieved. If fuel costs increase and/or the differential between HFO costs and delivered LNG value widens, this will give project planners more incentive to introduce such an innovation.

---

[9] Torill Grimstad Osberg, *Technical and Economical Evaluation of the Machinery Plant in an LNG Carrier with Diesel Electric Propulsion using Gas Fuelled Engines* (Det Norske Veritas, 1996), pp. 44, 49.

Chapter 6

LNG Project Finance: Sharing Risks with Project Lenders

Gerald B. Greenwald

Worldwide trading of liquefied natural gas began in 1964, grew rapidly in the decade of 1975–85 and after 30 years stands on the threshold of what has been called the 'second generation'of LNG projects. In these high-cost LNG projects, money talks. As we enter the second generation of LNG project development, money will be talking even louder than previously as sponsors of greenfield LNG ventures increasingly seek to shift project risks to their project lenders. Financing the first generation of LNG projects was relatively straightforward. LNG producers benefited from preferential credit terms made available in Japan to projects exporting LNG to Japan, and relied upon the credit available to project sponsors. For state owners of gas resources, this meant access to financing by export credit agencies, government loans from banks and international capital markets. For international oil companies bringing LNG technology and transportation skills to their gas resource base, this meant self-generated funds and balance sheet borrowings from commercial banks.

Over the past 30 years, the capital cost of implementing LNG projects has risen steadily due to both substantial rates of inflation and increasingly larger project facilities designed to exploit economies of scale. Greenfield projects have developed larger gas reserves to feed larger liquefaction plants in order to produce larger quantities of LNG that were transported by larger LNG ships to more distant markets. Notwithstanding steady increases in technical efficiencies and economies of scale, the overall costs of greenfield projects continued to increase. The second generation of greenfield LNG projects face significant challenges, both in raising billions of dollars of debt financing needed to implement these projects and in shifting from recourse loans to non-recourse or limited recourse project finance.

6.1   FINANCING A PROJECT IN SEGMENTS

Given the competition for financial resources worldwide, gas faces difficult competition against other fuels for finance. World Bank commentators noted:

> In relation to other fuels, gas has often found it difficult to compete for financing. Oil projects have always been seen as easier to finance, due to oil's flexibility, international marketability and relatively low costs. In the power sector, coal has lower capital costs than gas for supply over long distances, and also benefits from more flexible marketing opportunities. Gas projects by their nature are inflexible. Most gas projects require the supply, transportation and utilization phases to be developed concurrently. Financing for one part of the chain is tied to all the others.[1]

LNG project functions can be divided logically into three:

(1)   upstream development of the natural gas supply that provides feedgas to the LNG plant;
(2)   downstream development of liquefaction, storage and loading;
(3)   marine transportation of LNG to market.

The first two are essential aspects of an LNG project; the third, marine transportation, will depend on the terms of LNG sale. If LNG is sold on the basis of ex-ship delivery to the purchaser's receiving terminal, then transportation is a project function. If LNG is delivered at the loading port, as in the case of a free on board (FOB) sale, then transportation is the responsibility of the LNG purchaser. While LNG is sold both ex-ship delivery to the buyer and FOB, liquefaction site, most project developers begin with the intention of controlling transportation to the buyer's LNG receiving terminal. For one project under development, the complete integration of shipping into the project was considered 'to be essential for obtaining the highest standards in design, construction and optimised operation of the fleet, which are prerequisites for ensuring continuous safe and reliable transportation of LNG cargoes'.[2] Each project creates its own

[1] Levitsky and Nore, 'Financing LNG Projects in Developing Countries', *Proceedings, LNG 10* (1992).
[2] D. Fleming, 'The Oman LNG Project', *Proceedings, GasTech 94* (1994).

allocation of capital costs among project segments. As a generalisation, almost half of the project investment may be applied to downstream development costs. The balance may be divided about equally between:

(1)   upstream development;
(2)   ocean transportation; and
(3)   pre-operation project development expense and capitalised interest during construction.

Notwithstanding that the LNG project is a unified activity encompassing upstream, downstream and transportation functions, each function can follow its own path to financial markets. Projects have been organised on the basis that both upstream and downstream investment are shared in the same proportion by each sponsor in the project. But this is not always the case. In fact, each project seems to develop its own project investment structure quite aside from finance considerations. When ownership of the gas resource is allocated differently from ownership in the downstream liquefaction stage, then separate structures for each stage and agreements between them seem likely. Different ownership or ownership percentages can force finance into separate upstream loans and downstream loans. Also, there may be opportunities for better access to financial markets by splitting the upstream financing from the downstream financing, although at the cost of more complicated intercreditor issues which must be sorted out before both financings are firmly in place.

6.1.1   Upstream Development of Gas Supply

The expense of gas field development to produce feedgas to the LNG plant in sufficient quantities to produce base-load LNG quantities for 20 or more years is very substantial. A large amount of this investment will take place during the development of the project, before first LNG deliveries are made. Further sums will be spent throughout the sales contract period to maintain deliverability of the gas by drilling new wells. The latter may be funded from project cash flows or separate borrowings anchored in these cash flows, but the former must be financed as part of the initial project development. Condensate recovery during production of natural gas supply for the LNG plant opens the door to financial markets and techniques used to finance oil field development. But unlike an oil field financing, the upstream lenders will also assume the integrated project risk, that is, there will be no condensate revenues if LNG production or LNG transportation fails. The LNG industry has created several different models for financing upstream development.

6.1.1.1 Unified Ownership

Projects, such as those in Algeria and Australia, have unified ownership throughout all stages of the project. In such cases, the identity of borrowers' interests in each stage permits the project to be financed on a unified basis so that upstream and downstream can be part of a single financing plan.

6.1.1.2 Production-Sharing Contract

The Indonesian LNG project development relies totally for upstream development of gas supply upon Pertamina's production-sharing contractors. The funds required for development of the Badak and Arun gas fields, including the construction of relevant gas production facilities, were provided by the Huffington Group for Badak and Mobil Oil Corporation for Arun.

6.1.1.3 Upstream Separation

The North Dome gas field offshore Qatar is rich in condensate which is produced together with natural gas and is readily marketable in the manner of crude oil. Thus, the Qatargas project will enjoy two separate income streams, one from condensate sales and the other from LNG sales. This permitted the LNG project to be organised into two separate projects, each with separate financing. The condensate cash flow in Qatargas was used to support a separate financing to fund gas field development for the LNG project.

6.1.1.4 Upstream Ownership

When the gas resource owners differ from the sponsor of the liquefaction facilities, transfer pricing of upstream gas supply to downstream liquefaction or pre-agreed percentage shares in LNG sales revenue can create independent profit centres for the upstream and downstream segments of the LNG project.

6.1.1.5 Separate Finance

The system of Japanese import finance provided to LNG projects by Japanese government agencies has largely benefited the downstream development, leading resource owners to obtain upstream finance by other means.

6.1.2   Financing Downstream Development of Liquefaction, Storage and Loading

Segmentation of a single integrated LNG project by separate financing of upstream and downstream development is illustrated in the Qatargas project. This project provides a good text for discussion because Qatargas financing is structured as a chain of projects, that is the upstream, downstream and transportation each pursued separate finance structures in order to achieve non-recourse project debt. A key factor was the sale of the full LNG production of two trains, 4 million tonnes per annum (mtpa), to a single Japanese buyer, Chubu Electric Power Company in Nagoya, Japan.

To understand a separate downstream finance strategy, it is necessary to shift focus from Qatar to Japan. Almost every project delivering LNG to Japan has relied upon the Export-Import Bank of Japan's (JEXIM's) co-financing as a principal funding source. Moreover, Japan National Oil Co. (JNOC) guaranties and Ministry of International Trade and Industry (MITI) insurance against political risk have provided credit enhancement for the Japanese commercial banks that finance resource development for energy imports. (This Japanese financial support for LNG imports is discussed in section 6.5.1.2). In the case of Qatargas, the 70 per cent debt portion of about US$3 billion of total investment in the downstream LNG plant development was provided by a US$1.6 billion untied direct loan arranged through Japan's Export Import Bank and US$250 million by Japanese commercial banks, with repayment solely from revenue derived from the sale of LNG to Chubu Electric.

Qatargas, however, is an example of a project with identical sponsors participating in both the upstream and downstream developments (though in slightly different equity percentages). Equally common is the case where upstream development is pursued by a separate sponsor group, and therefore depends on separate finance of its capital investment in LNG facilities. Early LNG projects in Brunei, Abu Dhabi and Indonesia, and their successive expansions all focused solely on downstream finance, reflecting the separate ownership arrangements for the natural gas supply to the LNG plant.

6.1.3   LNG Transportation

Just as LNG projects exhibit a variety of ownership structures, so do LNG ships. Independent shipowners build, finance and lease (charter) ships to an LNG project, as in the case of Qatargas. Project sponsors do the same, as in the case of Australia North-West Shelf. Tax-advantaged lease finance can produce a structure in which ownership is in one entity, operation in another and use in the third, as in the case of the Burmah fleet serving the Indonesia–Japan LNG trade. In no case has a project company established as the LNG producing entity been the owner and operator of the LNG ships used in its project. However, well before project startup, Shell acquired a fleet of existing LNG ships on behalf of the Nigerian LNG project company. There has been some movement toward LNG buyers, rather than sellers, owning, or taking ownership interests in, the ships transporting their FOB purchases of LNG, notably Tokyo Gas Co. and Osaka Gas Co. in the Pacific trade and Cabot Corp. in the Atlantic trade.

Ship financing is a special financial niche involving a movable asset in international waters that makes periodic contact with numerous (and unpredictable) littoral states. Moreover, ships are generally subject to admiralty and maritime laws that differ from customary commercial laws. Long-standing markets for ship financing have adapted to the unique legal aspects of maritime trades. Independently owned oil tankers have long been financed on a project basis by lenders such as national export credit agencies of shipbuilding countries, commercial banks and placement of debt privately with institutional investors or in public bond issues on capital markets. LNG ship finance has tended to stay within these marine finance grooves. This probably best explains the practice of financing LNG transportation outside of the perimeters of the financing for other functions of the LNG project. Ship financing is available in different configurations. Short-term (about three years) predelivery construction loans from commercial banks are subject to full repayment on delivery. Combined construction and term loans amortised over 10 or 12 years after ship delivery can be based on straight-line debt amortisation or level-payment debt- service. Ship loans are fully paid down at maturity or mature with a balloon payment that is expected to be refinanced thereafter. The objective of shipowners is to spread debt-service expense over as long a term as possible in order to minimise the capital recovery factor contained in the unit transportation cost of the LNG cargo, thereby offering charters on 'competitive' terms.

The sources of finance are primarily commercial banks and national export credit agencies. For ship loans from commercial banks of the magnitude required for newbuild LNG ships, the hurdles are high. Nevertheless, large money-centre commercial banks can be a source of international ship financing by syndicating loans with smaller banks. A syndicated bank finance of an LNG tanker may finance up to 90 per cent of capital cost, repayable in 10–12 years after delivery at floating interest rates tied to the London Inter-Bank Offered Rate (LIBOR). ECAs will combine construction and term financing for up to 80 per cent of capital cost at a fixed or floating interest rate, repayable over a maximum of 10 years. Nations participating in the OECD Arrangement, except the United States, agreed in 1994 to extend the repayment period to 12 years after delivery and charge commercial interest rates. For the time being these new terms are in abeyance pending American acceptance.[3]

Not all LNG ships are built for export. Japan and Korea are active builders of LNG ships employed to transport LNG imports to those countries. These ships have been owned and operated by domestic shipping companies and fly the national flag. The financing of these ships draws upon domestic credit markets and is supported by national policies relating to energy imports, shipping and shipbuilding. For example, the Qatargas fleet was financed under a programme of the Japan Development Bank which extended 10-year yen loans to construct the LNG ships in Japanese shipyards. The finance was repayable in US dollars, the currency in which the Japanese shipowners will earn charter hire from Qatargas, thereby relieving the shipowners of foreign currency exchange risk. Capital markets (public issue of bonds or private placement of debt with institutional investors) have not yet been a source of LNG ship finance.

As a separate project finance of only one of the various functions performed within an LNG trade, the credit evaluation of LNG tanker finance will run the gamut of due diligence investigation. The focus is not only the borrower, but also the LNG seller and buyer. Country risk attaches not only to the flag state of the ship, but also to the states of the LNG exporter and importer. The transit route between loading port and unloading port will be examined for choke points such as canals, narrow straits and potentially dangerous waters. Physical risk analysis includes both the loading port and LNG terminal and the unloading port and LNG receiving terminal. Moreover, potential technical risk inheres in the LNG ship design and its dimensions. The cost of transportation has undergone very substantial economies of scale in their 30 years of operation and further scaling-up is contemplated. The drive to reduce unit transportation costs leads to consideration of innovations in LNG ship propulsion and other features. Cargo containment and insulation systems undergo change to reduce boil-off loss of LNG cargo. Each newbuilding LNG ship is evaluated on criteria of technical reliability and operating cost/efficiency by shipyards and their customers, and also by lenders. The construction risk focuses on the shipyard and its previous experience constructing LNG ships; the operations risk focuses on the tanker operator and its experience and efficiency in operating LNG ships. Legal analysis of lenders extends beyond the long-term lease (charter) into the chain of project contracts which affect the charterer's ability to make monthly lease (charter hire) payments. Contract analysis will also focus on containment of construction costs and operating costs and pricing

---

[3] US shipping laws include a programme known as Title XI which authorises sovereign guaranty of up to 87.5% of a ship's capital cost, repayable over up to 25 years. This programme has been the stumbling block to US agreement. Although the TitleXI programme financed 13 American-built ships in the 1970s, it is not regarded as a current source of LNG ship finance.

mechanisms for charter hire and LNG sales revenue. Finally, conventional financial analysis must support the viability of debt service payment.

The loan that surmounts these hurdles is usually secured by assignment to the lenders of the long-term charter and charter hire and insurance proceeds from various marine insurances. The LNG tanker itself is mortgaged to lenders, and perhaps the shares of stock ownership in the shipowner (often a single ship, special purpose corporation) as well. A conventional time charter will include provisions that excuse hire payments to the shipowner when the ship is unavailable for service. The cash flow to the shipowner reflects these uncertainties. Also, the LNG sales and purchase agreement will include *force majeure* events that excuse failure of LNG delivery or purchase. The interruption of hire payments or project cash flow is a risk that must be evaluated. The time charterer may try to share the project's cash flow risk with the shipowner or increase the scope of off-hire events. The ship finance lender seeks assurance of consistent cash flow to service debt. In LNG ship finance a delicate balance must be struck among the three parties concerned.

Seven LNG ships were required to deliver 4 mtpa of Qatari LNG to Chubu Electric in Nagoya, Japan. The cost of these vessels was estimated at US$2 billion. Treating LNG transportation as a separate finance in the LNG chain, Qatargas was able to achieve off-balance sheet finance by entering into an operating lease in the form of a long-term time charter of newbuild LNG ships from Japanese shipowners. In this regard, Qatargas followed an innovative procurement strategy. Qatargas prepared a detailed technical specification for a uniform seven-ship fleet sized to transport 4 mtpa of LNG from Qatargas's loading terminal to Chubu Electric's receiving terminal. The specification was issued for tender by 12 preselected shipyards worldwide. After tender, negotiations were initiated with three Japanese shipyards. In parallel, Qatargas invited preselected shipowners to tender for ownership and operation of the seven LNG ships, and three Japanese shipowners were selected. The lease, rather than ownership, lessened the financing burden of the overall project by shifting the LNG tanker finance burden to the Japanese shipowners. While the lease rate incorporated the capital costs of the ships, their financing was effectively 'off-balance sheet' for the Qatargas project.

6.2   EXTENDING THE LNG CHAIN TO THE ELECTRICITY GRID

As noted above, for purposes of finance the LNG project can be viewed as the three projects of upstream development, downstream development and transportation or can be viewed as a single integrated project, depending upon the structure and financing plan of the project sponsors. Another determinant of financing strategy can depend upon the nature of the LNG purchaser. The dominant LNG market is Japan, but Japan is increasingly being viewed as a mature market in which future growth opportunities are limited, at least well into the first decade of the 21st century. New LNG import markets are expected to emerge during the intervening period in China, Thailand and India. Each economy has increasing need for new electric power, most efficiently generated by combined cycle turbines fuelled by natural gas. The twin competitive forces of privatisation of state-owned power production and the market for electricity produced by independent power producers (IPPs) are opening a large potential market for LNG. The development of ground rules for IPP project development in China, Thailand, India, The Philippines, Taiwan and Korea, is at an early stage. Fuelling electric power production can fill some of the market potential for LNG. The large volumes of natural gas consumed in electricity generation and long economic life of generating plants can anchor the demand which is needed for construction of new LNG production facilities. But IPP developers are themselves dependent on non-recourse or limited recourse project finance of independent power generating plants. Consequently, their LNG purchase contracts cannot bring to the LNG project the robust credit support of LNG buyers heretofore found in large franchised electric power and natural gas utilities in Japan, Taiwan and Korea. IPP credit support must ultimately rest upon the power purchase agreement (PPA) entered into between the IPP project and its customer, the host country's electric power distribution company.

The question, then, is whether the financing of an LNG chain can be supported upon the creditworthiness of the purchaser of electricity from the IPP. The answer seems to be: only with difficulty. The root of the difficulty is that the best credit these electricity markets have to offer is sovereign credit. While that may be sufficient to sustain the magnitude of finance required for both power generation and imported fuel supply, there is uncertainty as to whether sovereigns will wish to make their credit available for these purposes, particularly in the current rush to reduce demands for government credit through privatisation, deregulation and attraction of foreign investment. Another factor to be considered is the willingness and ability of financial markets to support a 'project finance based upon a project finance' or, more properly, to co-ordinate the non-recourse finance of two projects which share a common ultimate collateral (the PPA) and a common cash flow (the price paid for electricity to the IPP which includes the price paid by the IPP to the LNG project for fuel supply).

6.3 THE ECONOMIC FEASIBILITY OF LNG PROJECTS

The economic returns of LNG projects depend ultimately on the long-term stream of revenue generated by the sale of hydrocarbon energy in the form of natural gas. The volatility of hydrocarbon prices, both crude oil and refined products, adds an element of conjecture to the prediction of this revenue stream. It is for this reason that costs become as critical as revenue in determining the economic feasibility of the project. The cost side of the calculation is awesome.

6.3.1 Capital Cost and Lead Time

Total capital investment for a project relying upon economies of scale is between US$4 and 8 billion, depending upon inflation rates and site-specific factors, such as cost of natural gas recovery, remoteness of plant site and port development and shipping requirements based on distance to markets, etc. The length of the construction period is between three and four years. This adds a substantial amount of interest during construction which will be capitalised. Moreover, all of the capital investment will be made before the LNG project produces the first cash flow. LNG sales and purchase agreements have historically started deliveries at volumes considerably less than full plant production capacity, building up volume over several years to nameplate production. Cash flows are thereby reduced during the critical early years of the project.

6.3.2 Payout Periods and Leverage

The magnitude of the indebtedness, the construction period before starting repayment and the decade or more for amortisation of debt impose high financing costs on the project. Debt is generally regarded as less costly to project sponsors than equity, so that debt:equity ratios have a material effect on project economics. To the extent that project finance markets seek to reduce project leverage, the calculation of project returns becomes problematical.

6.3.3 Borrowing Costs and Equity Returns

The economic sensitivity of LNG projects depends upon the terms offered by the financial markets in response to the LNG project's financing plan. Market interest rate levels and added risk premiums can overwhelm an energy project seeking to enter the market in an environment of low expectations for rising oil prices. If some degree of interest rate 'management' is left to the borrower of commercial bank funds, interest rate options in various short-term debt maturities and hedges through devices such as interest rate swaps, caps and collars can add expense and uncertainty to the calculation of financing cost. Equity generally is invested before debt, and therefore is longer at risk. Equity generally receives cash flow only after the lender is paid its debt-service. Moreover, equity investors tend to evaluate project risks in a manner similar to lenders because equity is in the first loss position and increased equity investment may be required in order to avoid a loss of the original investment. As a result, equity is valued at a higher 'cost' than debt, i.e. the sponsors demand returns on investment considerably higher than the lender's interest rate.

6.3.4 Take-or-Pay Quantity and Energy Price

The comment is frequently made in LNG circles that sellers take the price risk and buyers must take the quantity risk, that is buyers must take delivery of all of the sales contract quantity (which may include flexibilities that permit minor reductions) or pay the contract price for any quantity that is not taken. Take-or-pay terms of sale to creditworthy buyers are seen by producers as the essential requirement for loan repayment and investment returns. Moreover, producers believe that lenders are not prepared to take volume risk and will expect the LNG purchaser to commit fully to the contracted volumes. 'Take-or-pay' and 'limited flexibility' are seen as essential for project finance. Price risk for LNG can be tolerable for both lenders and borrowers. Lenders can be expected to accept a certain sales price risk to the extent that the level of equity investment, debt-coverage ratios and loan repayment periods are compatible with their perception of the downside risk of LNG sales prices.

Energy price risk is inherent in the oil industry. Oil companies traditionally take exploration risks. Price risk is the other side of the reward coin. Lenders and oil companies have developed models for 'predicting' or assuming energy prices. Whether or not predictive models actually predict, they do offer a means of making current decisions to keep the wheels of commerce turning. Markets, however, usually offer both price risk and quantity risk. Often they are inverse, that is when prices rise, quantity (demand) declines. In such cases, the economic reward is measured by the aggregation of reduced quantity multiplied by increased price. This is the case for crude oil revenues during periods of rapid price rise. Producers do not accept this view of an LNG market. The magnitude of upfront investment, long-term contractual sales and the volatility of hydrocarbon prices lead them to the conclusion that quantity offtake should be stable regardless of price. In other words, quantity risk is shifted to the purchaser. From another perspective the take-or-pay obligation in the sales contract is an effective device by which lenders capture in their net the credit strength of the project's buyer. During the first decades of the LNG industry, credit support was provided by both project sponsors as borrowers and the size and stability of project buyers. As the industry embraces project financing, the buyers' credit becomes the sole credit support available to project lenders.

6.4   THE FINANCING PAST WILL NOT BE PROLOGUE

6.4.1   Japanese Import Finance

Japan imports almost all of the hydrocarbon energy needed to fuel its economy. This energy dependence has spawned an array of government policies and programmes which support private importation of energy. The LNG industry has been a major beneficiary of these government supports. After the 1973 Organization of Petroleum Exporting Countries (OPEC) oil price shock, importation of natural gas offered to Japan an opportunity to diversify energy imports by substituting natural gas for some crude oil imports and by supplementing Middle East sources of oil supply with Pacific Basin LNG. Japanese government support was provided in a number of areas.

Funds are provided in the form of joint financing by JEXIM with associated commercial banks. (In the case of government-to-government loans, the Overseas Economic Cooperation Fund (OECF) provided funding.) JEXIM is a Japanese governmental financial institution established in 1950 as a state-owned export promotion vehicle, mirroring the United States Export-Import Bank. Over time, JEXIM differed from other national export credit agencies in that its banking operations have been very much diversified in parallel with expansion of the nation's economy and Japan's role relative to the world economy. JEXIM operations cover not only export and import financing, but investment, development and other financing such as project loans untied to procurement from Japan. It should be noted that JEXIM has been playing a key role in securing Japan's natural resources, and particularly energy resources. For LNG, JEXIM has been involved as a primary financier to almost all of the projects exporting LNG to Japan.[4] The application of this array of Japanese government programmes to finance early LNG project development was decisive. Investment insurance is provided in the form of export proceeds insurance or overseas investment insurance through the Export Insurance Department of MITI; insurance by the Department of Insurance of MITI covers the risks of Japanese companies' investment involved in overseas natural resource development projects

[4] S. Tsukakazi and S. Madono, 'The Role of the Export-Import Bank of Japan in LNG Projects', *Proceedings, LNG 9* (1989).

(overseas investment insurance), insuring against the damage caused to investors, either shareholders or lenders, by political as well as commercial risks.[5] JNOC finances hydrocarbon exploration through investment and soft loans and supports Japanese companies by providing guarantees of their loans for gas field development. Overseas investment credit provides Japanese investors with the funds necessary for:

(1) capital investment in, or loans to, foreign enterprises;
(2) loans to foreign governments or corporations which may in turn distribute the funds to joint venture companies in the form of either capital investment or loans.

JNOC can provide guarantees for up to 60 per cent of the total credit amount. Recently, JNOC was empowered to invest in groups of Japanese companies that participate in joint ventures to create foreign LNG chains deemed important to Japan's gas supply security, and to grant such groups low-interest loans.

Shipbuilding finance of the Japan Development Bank (JDB) provides Japanese shipping companies with a part of the funds necessary for building Japanese LNG ships. To utility companies that purchase LNG, JDB provides a part of the funds necessary for the construction of LNG receiving terminals, process and distribution facilities and power plants. In 1994, JDB made its first dollar-denominated loan to build in Japan seven LNG ships which will transport LNG to Japan from Qatar. The ships are owned by Japanese shipping companies and operated by them under time charters to the Qatargas project. The JDB, working with the Japanese Ministry of Finance, loaned dollars rather than yen in order to shield participating Japanese shipowners from potentially massive foreign exchange risk.

6.4.1.1 Brunei LNG Project

The LNG plant in Brunei began operating commercially towards the end of 1972. In order to implement this project, a joint venture was established to construct a liquefaction facility. The equity investment was allocated 24 per cent for the Brunei government, 34 per cent for Japanese investors and 42 per cent for foreign investors. The total investment cost for the plant construction was reported to be approximately US$250 million. The capital to cover the cost was raised in the form of 16 per cent equity investment and 45 per cent shareholders' loan, with the remaining 39 per cent covered by outside financing. Specifically, this 45 per cent of shareholders' loan can be broken down into foreign and Japanese investments of 20 per cent each, with the Brunei government providing the final 5 per cent.

---

[5] See T. Iizuka, 'Financing LNG Plants', *Proceedings, LNG 6* (1980).

In this particular case, the Japanese investors were able to provide their shareholders' loans through JEXIM and associated commercial banks by utilising the overseas investment credit programme.

6.4.1.2   Abu Dhabi LNG Project

The first LNG shipment from Abu Dhabi's Das Island to Japan was made in May 1977. In this project, like that at Brunei, a joint venture was established in the form of a liquefaction company with equity participation of 24.5 per cent by Japanese investors, 24.5 per cent by foreign investors and 51 per cent by the Abu Dhabi government. The total investment outlay of the LNG plant was reported to be approximately US$500 million, of which 20 per cent was raised in the form of equity investment, while the remaining 80 per cent was financed by loans arranged by the Abu Dhabi government (14 per cent) and by shareholders' loans (66 per cent). Breakdown of the shareholders' loans was:

Foreign investors	1%
Abu Dhabi government	17%
Japanese investors	48%

The repayment of that portion of the Japanese shareholders' loan which exceeded the Japanese equity share was guaranteed by the foreign investors and the Abu Dhabi government. The Japanese funds, comprising 53 per cent of the total investment cost, were financed by JEXIM and associated commercial banks utilising the overseas investment credit programme.

6.4.1.3   Indonesia LNG Project

LNG was first imported from Indonesia to Japan in August of 1977. The total investment cost is said to have been approximately US$1.5 billion for the construction of the two independent LNG plants at Bontang in east Kalimantan (Badak field) and at Lhok Seumawe in North Sumatra (Arun field). The financing in 1974 of Indonesia's first LNG export project was a dramatic example of the application of these Japanese government programmes. Financing of the project was segmented. Mobil Oil Indonesia and the Roy M. Huffington Group, as production-sharing contractors of Pertamina, financed the upstream development through loans and self-generated funds. Project transportation was financed upon the credit of Burmah Gas Transport utilising the Ship Mortgage Insurance Program

(Title XI) of the United States government. Japan provided the finance for the downstream segment.

The financing for the liquefaction phase of the first Indonesian project was unique in that:

(1)   the majority of the funds were provided by Japan, while the project itself was owned and implemented directly by Pertamina, Indonesia's national oil company;

(2)   the Japanese buyers participated by arranging finance of nearly 80 per cent of the total capital required through JEXIM and its associated banks in the form of an import credit loan. The Japanese buyers combined with JNOC to extend a guarantee directly to JEXIM and the associated commercial banks;

(3)   a government-to-government loan was extended through Japan's Overseas Economic Cooperation Fund (OECF) to cover infrastructure costs in Indonesia.[6]

JEXIM financing of the upstream cost of early Indonesian LNG projects was enormous:

	Startup	Total Cost US$ million	JEXIM Finance US$million
Badak/Arun	1977	1,547	1,130
Badak Expansion	1983	1,043	996
Arun Expansion	1984	785	761

6.4.1.4   Malaysia LNG Project

Malaysia's Bintulu LNG plant began deliveries to Japan in January, 1983, with Japanese trading company participation in the project company. The Malaysian government had a substantial position in the project's financing. JEXIM provided credits not only to the Japanese trading company participating in the downstream investment, but also to Petronas, Malaysia's national petroleum company. The Japanese trading company held an equity share and contributed a shareholder loan based on its equity share. Petronas obtained a direct loan from JEXIM. The direct loan to Petronas, guaranteed by the government of Malaysia, was JEXIM's first direct lending to a foreign governmental petroleum company for the purpose of natural resource development. Still, the bank's financial

---

[6] See R.O. Hutapea, 'The Development of Project Financing for the Indonesian LNG Trade', *Proceedings, LNG 7* (1983).

involvement in this project was limited to US$248 million of the total investment cost of US$1.5 billion.[7]

6.4.1.5 *Australia North-West Shelf LNG Project*

LNG exports from Australia to Japan started in August 1989. The North-West Shelf LNG project was an integrated development from the offshore gas field to the onshore gas supply system and LNG liquefaction and export terminal site. Six joint venturers established an unincorporated joint venture, each with one-sixth ownership interest. Neither the national nor state government was a project participant. A company equally owned by two major Japanese trading companies, Mitsui & Co. and Mitsubishi Corp., participated, along with Australian companies and international major oil companies' affiliates. The Japanese partner's financial requirements were met by JEXIM. JEXIM also extended a direct loan to one of the foreign participants of this project on a commercial basis, the first transaction of this kind made by the bank. JEXIM financing accounted for about 20 per cent of the project's total cost.

These greenfield Asia-Pacific LNG projects in Brunei, Abu Dhabi, Indonesia and Australia all benefited from Japanese government energy import finance programmes. In each case loans were made with full recourse to the borrowers, often with credit support of government loan guarantees. Only in the 1990s were these programmes extended to project finance with limited recourse to borrowers. This development is discussed in section 6.4.3.

6.4.2 *Balance Sheet Finance*

Each LNG project had its own unique strengths and its own access to financial markets. In the main, projects that have not had access to Japan's system of import finance support have been financed in the traditional manner with recourse loans from commercial banks to the borrower. Algeria, the pioneer in the LNG trade, constructed extensive gas supply, liquefaction and LNG transportation capacity on its sovereign credit, utilising recourse financing supplied by national export credit agencies and sovereign Eurodollar loans. International oil companies supported their participation in LNG projects with self-generated funds and balance sheet borrowings. This is the path followed by Phillips Petroleum and Marathon Oil in the early Kenai, Alaska LNG project, and more recently by Shell, British Petroleum, Chevron and BHP in Australia's North-West Shelf

---

[7] S. Tsukakazi and S. Madono, *op. cit.*, note 4.

project. Balance sheet financings made two positive contributions to past LNG project development. The first benefit was the access to financial markets that is available to strong borrower credits. Major energy companies based in industrialised nations with their portfolio of worldwide operations in large-scale developments minimise or eliminate lenders' concerns with country-risk or country lending limits. The second benefit is lower cost-of-borrowing. An LNG project investment financed by strong corporate borrowing will bear less interest expense than a standalone LNG project, thereby improving the project's economics and its economic feasibility for development. Notwithstanding these benefits, the trend is definitely toward non-recourse project finance of LNG projects by international energy companies. And there are some good reasons.

6.4.3 Sharing Risk with Project Lenders

In its narrowest sense, project finance is any financing so structured that the lenders must look solely (or at least principally) to the cash flows of the project itself for repayment. If the project fails, the lenders will have no recourse to the non-project assets of the borrower or to the assets of the sponsors of the project. For this reason, project finance is often described as 'non-recourse'. True 'non-recourse' financing, however, is extremely rare, and most project financings are more accurately described as 'limited recourse'. The distinguishing characteristic is that the borrower's obligation to repay is limited in time or amount, the precise limits being defined by the allocation of risks between the lender and the borrower. While most sponsors of LNG projects are risk-takers by the nature of their business activities, they still may find some appeal in risk-sharing with lenders in high-stakes projects. LNG production can be sited in geopolitical areas that are sufficiently stable at the time of project development to attract investors and lenders, but remain subject to potentially volatile national or regional tensions over the long term of the LNG trade. Notwithstanding safeguards such as political risk insurance, national investment or even international institutional participation, the utilisation of project finance does shift some of this geopolitical risk from sponsors to lenders.

In a project involving more than one sponsor, project financing may be an attractive option. When one party is financially stronger than its partner, the strong party may seek project finance for the whole project to ensure that the weaker partner has access to sufficient funds for its share of the capital costs. Perhaps unexpectedly, project finance can have its own attractiveness to lenders. Lenders to a project finance obtain greater participation in the structuring of the total transaction, increasing their understanding and therefore their level of comfort, but also permitting the tailoring of debt service to project earning expectations and thereby identifying the exact source of repayments before the loan is made. Not the least of the attractiveness is the benefit to lenders of up-front fees and interest rate spreads.[8]

The advantages of project finance to the borrower must, however, be weighed against several disadvantages, including increased costs. Lenders will expect a higher interest rate in return for assuming risks that in conventional corporate lending would be left with the borrower. The requirements for an initial detailed technical review and for increased monitoring of project performance during the life of the loan will lead not only to higher loan management fees, but also to increased fees for technical consultants to the lenders, all at the expense of the borrower. Similarly, the complexity of the documentation will usually result in higher legal fees. The negotiation of a project financing will focus on the allocation of risks between the sponsors and the lenders. While the lenders will, in return for a higher rate of return, accept some risks which they would not accept in an ordinary corporate financing, they will not accept risks which they view as properly attributable to the equity interest in the project, the best example being completion of the project and initiation of its cash flow. The nature of the risks to be allocated will vary, depending on the project. However, the risks can generally be categorised under three headings: technical, commercial and political.

Technical risks will relate to gas reserves, facilities design and engineering, facilities operation and environmental liabilities. Commercial risks include sales volume, price and other sales contract terms and scope of facilities insurance. (Foreign currency convertibility and exchange rate fluctuation have not yet been risk factors in LNG projects because both loans and revenues have been fixed in US dollars.) Finally, there is political risk. At the most fundamental level, political risk includes any aspect of political or financial instability in the host country. Other negative impacts arise from potential 'government take' issues. This would include nationalisation or expropriation of the project, but would also include any change (such as an increase in taxes or import or export duties) which would increase the government take from the project at the expense of project cash flow available for debt service. Similarly, revocation of licences or other necessary governmental consents can be a risk that could devastate the project.

Pertamina, the national oil company of Indonesia, has been particularly successful in attracting project finance of its expanding LNG production. Indonesia is the world's largest exporter of liquefied natural gas, mostly to Japan. Indonesia delivered its first LNG cargo in 1977, a time when Pertamina's finances were at a low ebb and the International Monetary Fund was imposing strict limitations on new Indonesian debt. Pertamina

---

[8] J. Mitchell, *Project Financing—The Banker's Approach to Project Risk* in *Energy Law in Asia and the Pacific* (Matthew Bender, 1982).

pursued complex LNG financing structures for its early LNG production, relying mainly upon Japanese import finance and credit support from LNG buyers in Japan in order to achieve 100 per cent finance of its upstream development, while 100 per cent of downstream investment was borne by its production-sharing contractors. As expansion of Indonesian LNG production continued with LNG sales to Taiwan in 1987, Pertamina entered other financial markets for the first time with syndicated bank loans for its Badak Train E which achieved project finance on a non-recourse basis. This was followed by project finance of Train F production sold to Japanese natural gas companies in 1990, supported by partial loan guarantees provided by five Japanese trading companies. At about the same time, Malaysia achieved project finance of three expansion trains to its LNG complex at Bintulu. These three transactions in recent years, each involving expansion of production by an experienced LNG seller to support sales to creditworthy LNG markets (Japan, Korea and Taiwan), mark the beginning of project finance for LNG production.

Qatargas succeeded in obtaining a project finance extended wholly from Japanese financial markets in 1994. The first shipment of LNG from Qatar reached Japan in January 1997. JEXIM, in co-financing with commercial banks, financed 70 per cent of the downstream development of the Qatargas project.[9] JEXIM co-financing, together with guaranties by Japan National Oil Corp. and political risk insurance from Japan's MITI, prompted loan participation of Japan's commercial banks and supported equity investment of two Japanese trading companies. The entire loan is a project finance to be serviced solely from revenues generated by LNG purchases of Chubu Electric Power Co., a triple-A-rated Japanese electric utility located in Nagoya.[10] The Japanese financing of the Qatargas downstream development consists of a loan of almost US$2 billion for 12 years of which US$1.6 billion is supplied through JEXIM and backed by MITI political risk insurance. Four Japanese commercial banks have approximately US$250 million of uncovered loan exposure. The Qatargas financings could be encouraging to future project developers because as a greenfield project sitting in the middle of the politically volatile Gulf, Qatargas seems exemplary for project finance of other newcomers to the LNG trade. But there were special factors at work in Qatargas, namely a Japanese electric utility as LNG purchaser, a Japanese EPC contractor for construction of downstream facilities, Japanese ship construction and Japanese ship operation. This concentration of Japanese interests, coupled with Japan's import finance programmes and sizeable capital market, enabled the project finance to succeed.

---

[9] W. Aoki, 'The Japanese Approach to Financing LNG Projects', *Proceedings, First Annual Doha Conference on Natural Gas* (1995).
[10] *Euromoney* (June 1995).

Qatar's newest greenfield project, Ras Laffan, financed 70 per cent of its upstream and downstream capital cost on project finance terms, raising loans in worldwide markets. This was also the financing path initiated by the Nigerian project, but not all LNG project finance succeeds. Nigeria LNG experienced extreme difficulty in attracting project finance during a period of political turmoil in Nigeria and subsequently announced that it would rely solely on equity investment and shareholder loans. In any event, LNG project sponsors are now developing their financial planning with emphasis on potential lenders that will accept a greater allocation of project risk than found during the first 30 years of the international LNG trade.

6.5 NEW PRIORITIES FOR LNG PROJECT FINANCING

The ways in which multilateral development banks (MDBs) can best promote the development process that seeks to alleviate poverty and encourage economic growth are being re-examined. Developing the private sector for market-oriented growth and fostering greater private sector involvement in the creation and operation of infrastructure are becoming MDB mantras. Working with the private sector to increase private capital flows by combining public money with private investment has become a chosen process. Sovereign ownership or guaranties are being exchanged for MDB co-financing, equity investment or syndication of debt. The transition from balance sheet debt to project finance has in turn placed some pressures upon public institutions to play a significant assisting role. During the 1980s, it was the national export credit agencies (ECAs) that became the institutions to take some of the risks of limited recourse borrowing. In the 1990s, MDBs initiated project finance programmes. Moreover, during the same period, international capital markets offered greater scope for finance through so-called asset securitisation. Thus, it was inevitable that the financial planning of LNG project sponsors should look to ECAs, MDBs, capital markets and commercial banks for loans on project finance terms.

There are three distinct challenges in arranging project finance debt for energy projects in developing countries. The first is the obstacle of political risk, the second is the familiar barrier of commercial risk and the third is liquidity (that is the availability of sufficient capital at reasonable cost to fund the debt portion of project costs). Applying these challenges to the development of multi-billion dollar projects in developing countries, attention is quickly focused on the role played by multilateral institutions (such as the International Bank for Reconstruction and Development (World Bank), International Finance Corporation of the World Bank Group, (IFC), Asian Development Bank (ADB) and European Bank for

Reconstruction and Development (EBRD)) and on ECAs of developed nations, notably Export-Import Banks of the United States (USExIm) and Japan (JEXIM), Britain's Export Credit Guarantee Department (ECGD), Germany's HERMES, France's COFACE and Italy's SACE.

The political risks of project investors and lenders can include a multitude of scenarios:

(1) political violence;
(2) expropriation;
(3) foreign exchange restriction;
(4) revocation of sovereign contractual rights or licences;
(5) confiscatory taxation;
(6) material adverse changes in laws and regulations;
(7) breach of sovereign agreements.

Insurance against political risks provided internationally (e.g. World Bank Group's Multilateral Investment Guarantee Agency (MIGA)), nationally (e.g. United States' Overseas Private Investment Corporation (OPIC)), or commercially is limited as to both amount and scope. Consequently, there is a growing effort by multinational institutions and ECAs to stimulate greater private sector debt finance by offering programmes which reduce political risks of lenders. There is a common perception that the mere presence of institutional participation in a loan package reduces political risk because of the host government's reliance upon continued access to resources provided by the institution.

6.5.1 National Export Credit Agencies

Given the size and complexity of international energy projects seeking project finance on limited recourse terms, a variety of financing sources is needed to provide the required capital. ECAs have played an increasingly important role in project financing packages for LNG projects. An ECA is a government agency whose mission is to facilitate the export sale of goods and services by providing credits which are more attractive than those available commercially and by providing security for credit risk and political risk which may not be available at an economic cost from private finance sources. ECAs of the United States, European countries and Japan have been consistent contributors to financing LNG projects. The reason is apparent. LNG projects are front end capital-intensive efforts to construct in developing countries the sophisticated facilities and services that are supplied by vendors in industrialised countries with established export credit programmes. Since these loans are by their nature international, the ECAs play a crucial role by accepting political risks inherent in any cross-border financing.[11] Historically, the ECAs provided insurance to sponsors, suppliers, and commercial bank lenders protecting against political risks such as war, revolution, expropriation or nationalisation and non-convertibility of local currency or discriminatory exchange risks. Later, their role extended to guarantees of banks making loans to an exporter, first requiring sovereign counter-guarantees for the full loan, and more recently instituting project finance programmes to assume pre-completion political risk and both political and commercial risks after completion of project construction. In this way, the ECAs attract commercial bank syndicates lending alongside ECA-supported finance. The premium charged by ECAs for taking political risks is set by each ECA individually. The percentage of loan exposure covered also varies.

When tendering for engineering, procurement and construction (EPC) bids to build the liquefaction phase of the Ras Laffan project, the project company required bidders to include in their bids a proposal for project finance of capital costs. Contractor-arranged financing was seen by Mobil Corp. as having a number of advantages for Ras Laffan's project finance. Each of the bidders was compelled to align itself with commercial bank syndicates for the finance portion of its bid, with the effect that each contractor applied to ECAs for export finance of the relevant portion of its bid. The bank participants in the bid in turn obtained needed credit committee approval of participation as part of the bid process. Thus by the bid deadline there was early evidence of project finance support and distribution of banking support from a number of ECAs and all of the banks involved in all of the syndicates aligned with all of the bidders.[12]

JEXIM, the UK's ECGD and Germany's HERMES each established a project finance department in 1988, Italy's SACE in 1990. In 1994, France's COFACE, Canada's EDC and USExIm each established separate project finance departments. ECA project finance credits offer a number of advantages. Interest rates are sometimes fixed and potentially subsidised. Often ECA project financing has no per project limit and finances the maximum allowed under the OECD consensus, based upon the amount sourced from the country. ECAs generally make financing available to more countries than commercial banks and capital markets. Their participation in a project finance can attract increased participation by commercial banks and capital markets to complete the financing of the project. As providers of political risk cover, ECAs have become the single most important source of finance for exporters. Yet, in the area of project finance, ECAs differ in the type of cover, when it is available in the course of project development, percentage covered, foreign content rules and risk premiums. As a result, the overall

---

[11] See Parish, 'Project Finance and the Role of Export Credit Agencies', *Oil & Gas Law and Taxation Review*, 13 (June 1995), p. 222.

[12] Minyard, 'Financing the LNG Project in Qatar', *Proceedings, Euro Forum Project Finance Conference* (17 April 1997).

debt package for an LNG project can be complex as each participating ECA facilitates export credit based on its own policies and practices. Commercial sources of financing for the project then accommodate to the particular national requirements for underwriting each ECAs tranche. Nevertheless, the combination of multiple ECAs in a single project financing provides unparalleled access to limited recourse finance of LNG projects. While all of the ECAs provide significant credit support for large-scale energy projects, two have played substantial roles in LNG project finance, namely the Export-Import Banks of the United States and Japan.

6.5.1.1   The United States Export-Import Bank

USExIm enables US exporters to compete in overseas markets by matching the effect of export credit available from other governments and by absorbing credit risks that the private sector will not accept. Over its 60 years, US ExIm introduced cover for both commercial risks and political risks of non-payment of 85 per cent of the US export value included in the contract sales price. Direct loans are made at fixed interest rates or LIBOR floating interest rates to foreign buyers of US goods and services and export finance loans to foreign buyers made by commercial lenders are guaranteed. Political risk cover generally includes war risks, cancellation of export or import licences, expropriation, confiscation or foreign currency transfer risks. Maximum repayment term depends on the nature of the project and the OECD classification of the buyer country. For LNG projects the term is likely to run up to 12 years after first disbursement of funds. Until recently, USExIm credit enhancement required the support of a sovereign guaranty issued by the importer's government. Responding to government reluctance to issue sovereign guarantees of export credits extended to private buyers and to the increasing availability of project finance in other financial markets, USExIm initiated its programme for limited recourse project finance which makes repayment dependent solely upon revenues generated by the project. Comprehensive USExIm review of the project includes the financial commitment of the project's equity shareholders, experience and capacity of project participants (including suppliers and offtakers), project cash flow coverage of US dollar debt service and security structures. Project sponsors are required to fund this review of project proposals by bearing the costs of outside financial consultant, legal counsel, engineers and insurance advisers retained by USExIm to perform due diligence investigation and assess project risk. During project construction, political risk cover is available, but commercial risks are not accepted. In other words, precompletion commercial risks must be borne by a creditworthy source arranged by project sponsors. All projects financed by USExIm must comply with host government environmental guidelines and permit requirements and meet the bank's own determination of the environmental soundness of the project. Environmental guidelines issued in February 1995 by USExIm are incorporated in third-party consultant reports to lenders covering environmental aspects associated with project construction and operation offshore and onshore.

The primacy in US manufacture of major components of liquefied natural gas plants (heat exchangers, turbines, compressors, etc.) led USExIm into export financing for early LNG plants built in Algeria in the 1970s. USExIm continued for the next 20 years to issue cover for export sales to LNG projects against the security of government guarantees. In the 1990s, the Qatargas project and Ras Laffan project in Qatar and Trinidad's Atlantic LNG project have benefited from the new project finance facility of USExIm.

6.5.1.2   Export-Import Bank of Japan

JEXIM offers a wide array of programmes to support finance of developing energy projects. The traditional export credit co-financing with commercial banks, when supplemented by related Japanese government programmes, covers substantially all of the political risk and commercial risk. Of significance for LNG project development in Asia and the Middle East are three other JEXIM programmes: credits to support Japan's energy imports, overseas investment credits to support Japanese overseas investment in energy production and loans untied to Japanese sourced exports. Since the 1980s, these three programmes have accounted for more than half of JEXIM's total commitments. JEXIM's expansion of its role as a co-financier with multilateral institutions (e.g. World Bank Group and ADB) and other ECAs is also significant. The most notable example is JEXIM's co-financing with the World Bank for Pakistan's Hub River Power Project in which its support of guarantees to private lenders against political risks was backed up by indemnities issued by the government of Pakistan.

JEXIM has been, and probably continues to be, the most significant source of financing for the liquefaction phase of LNG project development in Asia and the Middle East. In early LNG projects developed in Abu Dhabi and Malaysia in the 1970s, JEXIM finance was extended through the participation of Japanese trading companies included within the group of project sponsors. For Indonesian project development, JEXIM made a loan to the finance vehicle of Japanese LNG buyers which then extended the loans to Pertamina, Indonesia's state hydrocarbon corporation. The Australian North-West Shelf LNG project was launched as an unincorporated joint venture in which JEXIM supplied funds to the Japanese co-venturers, for the first time financing the Japanese sponsor portion on the basis of project finance. More recently, JEXIM co-financed with commercial banks on project finance terms 70 per cent of the costs of liquefaction trains developed by the Qatargas project for LNG sales to Japan.

Japanese commercial banks and Japanese sponsors of LNG projects are supported in their LNG projects not only by JEXIM co-financing, but also by related Japanese government programmes such as guarantees provided by the JNOC and insurance provided by Japan's MITI which can cover pre-completion commercial risk of up to 90 per cent of bank loans as well as post-competition political risk insurance for up to 97.5 per cent of loans. As the Japanese LNG market matures, it has become increasingly clear that the launch of new LNG projects can no longer depend primarily on LNG sales to Japan. As LNG marketing efforts of new projects extend their range to existing importers such as Korea and Taiwan, and to prospective importers from Thailand, India, Pakistan, China, or The Philippines, the question arises as to whether JEXIM and related Japanese government pro-grammes will be extended to finance the establishment of Asian regional LNG supply as distinct from Japanese import supply.[13] There is one encouraging example of Japan's facilitation of credit for LNG exports to a third country, in the case of Taiwan. Pertamina expanded its Bontang LNG complex in Indonesia with Train E which began production in 1990. JEXIM extended financial support to Indonesia for 100 per cent of the project cost of expansion capacity for the export of LNG to Taiwan. The use of the proceeds of the loan was not tied to Japanese exports. Yet there was some fragile tie to Japanese interests as a portion of the gas supplied to the Bontang liquefaction facilities was produced by a Japanese production-sharing contractor.

6.5.2   The Multilateral Institutions

Everyone in the credit equation welcomes multilateral development bank support for project finance in order to increase coverage for risks that the private sector can be unwilling or unable to bear. The goal is to mobilise the AAA credit of the development banks to leverage the vast amounts of private capital required to finance worldwide infrastructure development. This is a topic high on the agendas of the World Bank Group, ADB, Inter-American Development Bank and EBRD.[14] Guarantee programmes have been newly invigorated by international institutions and are designed to provide targeted, and sometimes limited, support to reduce commercial

---

[13] 'How far the participation of Japanese financing can be counted upon in projects where the Japanese user is no more than one of the buyers and who in these cases will take the initiative in financing arrangements will be new issues.' (W. Aoki, *op. cit.*, note 9.)

[14] See Wright, 'Push for Development Bank Project Finance Support', *Project Finance International* (27 October 1994).

bank exposure to risks they are least able to manage. A guarantee programme can be effective in addressing two major problems. The first is
political risk arising from key roles played by host governments, both in
their sovereign capacity and as contracting parties. Guaranties can be
broadly stated as against political risks of nationalisation or expropriation
or revocation of approvals and licences, or focused upon performance of a
sovereign counter-guarantee in favour of the institution. The second
problem is the traditionally short maturities under which commercial
lenders will lend to these projects. The institutional guarantee can protect
against commercial risk in order to achieve lengthening of the loan tenor
to accommodate project cash flows by guaranteeing later maturities, by
rolling over its guaranty of a portion of the debt or by guaranteeing
foreign exchange liquidity.

6.5.2.1 *International Bank for Reconstruction and Development*

The World Bank traditionally engages in development lending to governments. But emerging roles have begun to transcend conventional development banking. The World Bank provides policy development assistance
aimed at achieving hospitable national environments for private investment. Technical advice and assistance, if effectively applied, can enable
host governments to unlock access to other financial markets, thereby
requiring commitment of less World Bank financial resources. New
financial programmes such as co-financing and new instruments such as
guarantees can expand credit facilitation while reducing the direct loan of
World Bank funds. In recent years the natural gas sector has seen
increased World Bank activities focused on privatisation, restructuring,
improving efficiency, establishing gas transmission and distribution networks, reducing flaring of gas and environmental degradation of air
quality and promoting gas trade. High start-up costs of gas projects often
create the necessity for sovereign investment and the need to attract
increasing private investment. The World Bank has signaled its willingness to play a role. Nearly half of the almost US$4 billion allocated by
the World Bank to oil and gas goes to pipeline projects for gas transmission and gas distribution. In addition, technical assistance funding will
directly benefit gas sector development, raising the total gas allocation to
US$2.4 billion. Although World Bank resources for natural gas infra-
structure are applied mostly in Eastern Europe and the independent
states of the former Soviet Union, emerging markets in India, Pakistan
and Bangladesh are expected to benefit from World Bank support.[15]

---

[15] *World Gas Intelligence,* 7 (28 March 1997).

A significant recent development (September 1994) is the expanded guarantee programme of the World Bank which can cover a wide variety of circumstances:

(1)   partial risk guarantees in power project financings for performance of host government contractual obligations, such as power purchase agreements entered into by state utilities;

(2)   partial credit guarantees to cover foreign exchange transfer risks;

(3)   partial credit guarantees to cover long-end maturities of commercial financings, guarantee structures to provide incentives for lenders to roll over medium-term loans at maturity, liquidity guarantees in the form of put options and take-out financings and rolling guarantees that cover a fixed number of scheduled payments.

Guarantees are intended to mitigate those risks which private lenders are not prepared to accept, in particular, project or country circumstances. When the bank extends a guarantee, it is required under its Articles to obtain a counter-guarantee from the host government. When the guarantee covers specific sovereign policy or contractual risks, the counter-guarantee demonstrates the commitment of the government to meet obligations entered into as part of the project. By covering risks that the market would not bear, or would price prohibitively high, the guarantee lowers the cost of financing. Guarantees can also extend the term of lending beyond the period for which the market would normally lend—an essential consideration for infrastructure projects which require long-term debt in order to match debt service with their typically long payback periods. For a government, a partial risk guarantee reduces its contingent liability to the minimum required to make a project feasible. This contrasts with the traditional pattern where a government takes full responsibility for financing and thus bears the entire risk in a project.

The international trading of natural gas is fraught with commercial and political perils that a multinational or regional financial institution can abate. The World Bank can play a catalytic role by engaging both the public and private sectors of the importer, exporter and transit states, drawing on established relationships with the necessary host governments. On a focused project level, institutional intervention can assist in establishing project viability, sourcing financing and mitigating risks through development loans to government, co-financing and guarantee programmes. World Bank participation to date in LNG projects has been extremely limited. As a policy principle, the World Bank recognises that development of gas infrastructure needs public sector support at least in its early stages. Its focus seems to be on infrastructure for importing LNG in order to encourage natural gas consumption, rather than on producing country LNG infrastructure. The relative profitability and foreign exchange generation of LNG projects is seen as permitting sufficient access to other credit markets so that the World Bank has seen little need for its assistance. In 1991, the World Bank granted a loan of US$100 million to Korea Gas Corporation, a state-owned entity which imports LNG. Much of the loan was devoted to expansion of the Pyong Tak LNG receiving terminal, with the balance applied to fund associated gas transmission lines.

6.5.2.2 *International Finance Corporation of World Bank Group*

The IFC pioneered institutional co-financing with commercial banks through a loan participation programme based on the 'A-B Loan structure', now also utilised by ADB, EBRD and most recently by the Inter-American Development Bank. The A loan is made by the institution to the private borrower and then syndicated in part by the institution to commercial banks as a non-recourse loan from the commercial banks to the institution pursuant to a loan participation agreement. As a result, the commercial banks are not the lenders of record to the ultimate borrower. This style of loan participation is seen as encouraging longer tenor of loan maturities, while expanding available funding sources for project finance. The commercial bank in turn obtains the benefit of the institution's 'preferred creditor' status for its B loan. As a preferred credit, the B loan can be exempted from the rules of the lender's national banking authorities for provisioning and special reserve requirements that apply to lesser developed country (LDC) loans, exempted from withholding taxes on interest payments (and consequent gross-up provisions for repayments net of taxes) and can protect against the sovereign borrower's debt rescheduling and currency inconvertibility.

IFC acts as a catalyst for private investment. Its participation in a project enhances investors' confidence and attracts other lenders and shareholders. IFC mobilises financing directly for projects in developing countries by syndicating loans with international commercial banks and underwriting investment funds and corporate securities issues; it also handles private placements of securities. The IFC sought to play innovative roles in supporting project finance of the Nigerian LNG project. Early in the financing process, IFC announced that it would act as arranging bank for a project finance. Moreover, IFC indicated its willingness to purchase a two per cent equity interest in the project and to make a loan to the project. The project company was reorganised to transform it from majority ownership of Nigeria National Oil Corp. to majority ownership by its private shareholders (Shell, Elf and Agip) and IFC. Discussions were initiated with ECAs, multilateral and bilateral institutions and commercial banks, relying upon an IFC appraisal study of the Nigerian LNG Project. In June 1995, the project company announced that in order to avoid further financing delays the shareholders decided to withdraw the project from the project finance market and proceed with shareholder-arranged loans. Later, the IFC announced that it would not participate as either an investor or lender to the project.

6.5.2.3 *European Bank for Reconstruction and Development*

The EBRD is the newest multilateral finance institution. EBRD is focused on financing private sector projects in designated countries of the former Soviet Union and Bloc. The EBRD is noteworthy for having incorporated and integrated all of the programmes of its predecessors, both multilateral institutionals and ECAs, and presents itself as a multifaceted mobiliser and facilitator of local and foreign capital, both public and private. This arsenal includes:

(1) standby (contingent) loans and subsequent tranche (later maturities) loans;
(2) co-financing loans and guarantees utilising the A/B loan structure;
(3) co-financing with ECAs in their direct loan and guarantee programmes;
(4) guarantees of project finance;
(5) repayment obligations upon occurrence of specified events of political risk;
(6) underwriter of debt securities issued by private sector enterprises to raise project finance;
(7) cooperation with MIGA, OPIC, etc. to catalyse other insurance against political risks; and
(8) financing technical assistance and project preparation, including development of project finance arrangements.

These programmes have not benefited LNG project development because of slack European demand for LNG and EBRD's limited regional focus. Nevertheless, its willingness to extend the limits of multinational support for energy projects can be exemplary for development banks in other regions.[16]

6.5.2.4 *Asian Development Bank*

Only four per cent of ADB's overall lending was in the natural gas sector. Yet development and utilisation of natural gas can be expected to receive increasing ADB attention due to its regional focus. It is an ADB priority to

---

[16] The European Bank for Reconstruction and Development established framework agreements (multi-project facilities) with industrial partners that enable a number of projects to be financed in accordance with principles jointly agreed at the outset (Larosiere, 'The Role of the MDB in the Changing Market Place', *Project Finance International* 51 (9 October 1996)).

support gas infrastructure projects, recognising that increased capacity to deliver greater gas volumes is now the key condition for the stimulation of new gas markets in Asia. Marine transportation of LNG to importing nations increasingly requires subregional and transcontinental pipeline systems to extend gas markets and gas transmission networks to serve domestic consumers. ADB's thrust is to promote country conditions receptive to international private sector investment and finance to construct these facilities. ADB has provided over US$2 billion in 25 loans for natural gas infrastructure development projects for Bangladesh, India, Indonesia, Korea, Burma, Pakistan, China and Thailand.[17] Infrastructure development in turn generates gas demand of a magnitude that can satisfy threshold volumes for LNG imports, so that ADB priorities indirectly support rising LNG imports. The first steps have been taken in the ADB-financed regional study on increased utilisation of natural gas, to be followed up by ADB-financed national studies where appropriate. Here ADB, alone or together with other multilateral institutions, has several key roles to play. First, its participation can allay security concerns that arise when gas projects involve multiple states in the region, for example natural gas pipelines carrying Middle Eastern gas supplies to Pakistan and India. Secondly, ADB carries its mission beyond development finance when it invests in creating a financially viable plan for an energy future based on regional or inter-regional cooperation.

6.5.3   Capital Markets

As LNG projects confront the substantial demand for non-recourse financing, it is natural that project sponsors are also searching for new sources of project finance. Capital markets offer a wider pool of funds and a broader range of lenders than commercial banks.

> To date, nearly US$4 billion of debt for power projects has been issued in the international debt capital markets, for power projects both in the United States and the United Kingdom as well as in such emerging markets as the Philippines and China. Similarly, non-power projects, such as toll roads in Mexico and telecommunication projects in Colombia, have successfully accessed debt in the international debt capital markets. As a result, it is fairly clear that generally, the international debt capital markets are in fact a viable alternative, and one that should certainly be considered as a financing alternative to the traditional sources of project debt for international projects. However, it must be recognised that the development of this market has only occurred over the last several years, first through United States projects and then branching out into international projects. As a new and developing funding resource, this market is currently somewhat more volatile in its pricing and size availability than the traditional commercial bank and multilateral/export credit agency forum.[18]

---

[17] Gray, 'ADB Makes a Dash for Gas', *Power in Asia*, 6–8 (July 1997).
[18] Hollihan, 'International Debt Capital Markets and Project Finance', Project Finance International Yearbook (1995), pp. 3–4.

The market for asset-based or revenue-based financing commenced in the United States in the mid-1980s with securitisation of credit card receivables and the issuance of sale and leaseback obligation bonds. This was followed in 1991 with the first capital market transaction for a large-scale power project, providing an alternative source of project finance to commercial banks. In December 1991, the first large-scale issuance of non-recourse securities (US$867 million) on behalf of the Midlands Corp. project took place in the US bond market. The issue was SEC registered and rated by four rating agencies. In 1993, another power project, sponsored by Sithe Energy, broke new ground in a US$700 million transaction that was the first public issuance of non-recourse project debt issued at the start of construction.[19]

In the United States, there are three distinct methods of accessing the long-term public debt market, namely Securities Exchange Commission (SEC) registration of publicly traded securities, rated issues exempt from registration with the SEC placed with institutional investors and subject to subsequent SEC registration (Rule 144A securities) and private placement of securities with institutional investors. The institutional investor market is composed of insurance companies, investment advisors, pension funds, mutual funds, banks and other institutions. A larger debt market, the possibility of longer maturities, and perhaps less cumbersome restrictive covenants than commercial bank lending are advantages for borrowers. But there are disadvantages as well. Disclosure requirements can be extensive. Widely disbursed debtholders can make it more difficult to adjust loan terms in case of unexpected difficulties in project performance. Underwriting costs can be added expense and interest rates can be volatile. For project finance of LNG projects, the major breakthrough was the issuance in December 1996 of US$370 million of rated bonds sold by Ras Laffan Natural Gas Co. Ltd, a Qatari corporation, in the United States to qualified institutional investors under SEC Rule 144A and outside the United States to non-US buyers in reliance on SEC Regulation S (Rules 903 and 904).[20] Repayment is the obligation solely of the project company. None of the project's shareholders (Qatar General Petroleum Corp.and Mobil QMGas, Inc.) or their parent companies (state of Qatar and Mobil Corp.) have any liability with respect to the project company's bonds, other than under completion guaranties and related startup obligations.

Ratings can be crucial to the broad marketing of project finance bonds because prospective bond purchasers do not have the resources to make a detailed study of whether the project's free cash flow is likely to be sufficient to service its debt. Rating implies that the project has been analysed and evaluated by competent third parties. The Ras Laffan bonds

---

[19] *The Competition for Capital in the International Oil & Gas Industry* (Petroleum Finance Co., 1993).
[20] 82% of the bonds were purchased by US investors. The effect of Rule 144a is that these bonds can be resold without SEC registration only to buyers that qualify as institutional investors.

carried maturities of 10 years (US$400 million) and 17.5 years (US$800 million) and were given investment grade ratings by Moody's (A3) and Standard and Poor's (BBB+). Had these agencies given a speculative rating to the bonds, institutional investors would have had considerably less enthusiasm. A later marketing change in the Ras Laffan project doubled the sales to Korea Gas Corporation, but eliminated the minimum LNG sales prices that assured payment of debt service. The factors relied upon by Standard and Poor's in re-evaluating the investment grade rating of Ras Laffan's bonds are instructive. In reaffirming its BBB + rating of the bonds Standard and Poor's weighed the following project risks and project strengths.

Risks:

(1)   since sponsor completion guarantees are several and not joint the credit support for completion is a blend of Mobil Corp.'s double-A rating for 26.5 per cent and Qatar General Petroleum Corp's treble-B rating for 66.5 per cent;

(2)   regional political risk could impair LNG delivery;

(3)   remedies provided in commercial and financing agreements may not be enforceable under the Qatari legal system.

Strengths:

(1)   Mobil added to the security package a US$200 million line of liquidity that supports a minimum price in case of debt-service shortfall;

(2)   all project revenues are paid in US dollars to an offshore New York trustee for application to operating expense, debt service and equity distributions;

(3)   use of commercially proven technology; KGC, owned by Republic of Korea and Korea Electric Power Corp., both rated double A minus credits, take-or-pay purchase contract for 4.8 million tonnes per annum (mtpa) of LNG at market prices giving the project increase scale of earnings;

(4)   natural gas production history of Qatar's giant North Field;

(5)   signed turnkey engineering, production and procurement contracts with qualified and experienced contractors;

(6)   Mobil's long experience and market share in LNG production;

(7)   minimum project debt service coverage ratio of 1.87 and loan life coverage ratio of 2.86.[21]

---

[21]   Press release, Standard and Poor's, New York (22 September 1997). In December 1997, Korea's financial crisis caused Moody's to downgrade the bonds to Baa$_2$ (20 *Middle East Executive Reports*, No. 11, p. 7 (1997)) and Standard and Poor's to place its BBB+ rating on 'Credit Watch with negative implications'. (Press Release, 12 December 1997).

The extension of debt maturities through access to capital markets in turn can improve project economics by apportioning repayment over perhaps 20 operating years in contrast to maturities of perhaps 10 operating years offered by commercial banks. Size of market, length of maturities, ease of execution and attractive pricing have established capital markets financing as a critical planning element for any LNG project finance.[22] Are bonds a good substitute for loans? The answer is subject to debate. Bonds provide fixed interest rates for longer-period maturities. In recent years bond terms may have become more favourable to borrowers than bank terms. A bond issue accesses non-bank pools of capital without bank-imposed country limits. But flexibility can be lost, particularly in times of distress when negotiating with a bank syndicate may be easier than dealing with the trustee for individual bondholders worldwide. Indispensable bond ratings mean widespread disclosure compared to the relative discretion of bank financing.[23] Nevertheless, the lure of capital markets project finance is great, particularly when bonds can be marketed at lower interest cost than ECA interest and premiums and floating bank interest rates.

6.5.4. Commercial Banks

In recent years, the role of commercial banks in providing limited recourse financing to projects has been challenged by the increasing role played by, and desired by borrowers to be played by, the multilateral development banks, ECAs and capital markets. Nevertheless, commercial banks have the experience to structure complex project finance, often at a lower price than ECAs or capital markets, and without the necessity of a bond rating by an external agency. Still, the role of commercial banks in LNG project finance is likely to be affected by developments in the international banking system itself. The rules drawn up by the Bank for International Settlements (BIS) impose strict lending criteria for loans to non-OECD countries. The BIS numerical rating system focuses on sovereign risk for each potential borrowing country. The higher the number, the higher the amount of money the lending bank has to keep in reserve. Also, the interest rate premium above OECD levels goes up in proportion to the assessed sovereign risk. In practice, it can mean that commercial banks will give to an LNG project a rating no better than that of the country in which it is located. Yet commercial banks continue to have an appetite for international lending as margins for domestic lending face increasing competition and premiums

---

[22] See Lief, 'Financing LNG Projects—The Role of the Capital Markets Going Forward', *Proceedings, Second Doha Conference on Natural Gas* (19 March 1997).

[23] O'Sullivan, 'Rasgas Leaps into the Bond Market', *Middle East Economic Digest* 7 (10 January 1997).

can be earned for accepting country risk. Country risk exposure for most commercial banks must be spread over a large number of countries. The commitment to international lending is an issue of allocation and reflects a portfolio approach. As a result loan amounts available from most banks are small and the syndication of project loans for major energy projects requires a large number of banks, each taking only a modest participation.

It is in the area of country risk that multilateral institutions and ECAs can be particularly supportive of commercial bank lending to LNG projects. For example, ECA guarantees of loans to a project can permit the banks to treat the guaranteed portion of the loan as sovereign debt of the ECA's country, thereby achieving a lower risk-weighting of this debt for the purposes of the commercial bank's capital adequacy. Lower risk-rating in turn can reduce loan costs to the project.[24] Although the commercial banks' portion of ECA project finance does not extend maturities beyond the term set by the ECAs, banks may be willing to increase average life somewhat by weighting principal payments more heavily in the later years. Commercial banks are likely to remain an indispensable source of funds in the financing plans of greenfield LNG projects, remaining the most flexible and competitive source of project finance.

6.6   THE PROJECT FINANCIAL PLAN

6.6.1   Estimating Capital Costs

Financial planning starts with capital cost estimates. The process of making capital costs estimates begins before the LNG project announces its debut. These early 'ballpark' estimates will undergo continual fine tuning throughout the period of project development and into the period of contracting firm prices and delivery dates for engineering, procurement and construction of project facilities. (See chapter 3.) In this planning stage the following categories of capital cost are likely to be addressed:

6.6.1.1   Natural Gas Production

The project chain begins with natural gas production, and the project capital cost estimate begins with initial costs of field development sufficient to produce gas supply for LNG plant production in the early years of project sales. (Periodic later investment to replenish gas production as new

[24] Parish, *op. cit.* note 11, p. 224.

wells or platforms replace depleted wells will likely be made from cash flows generated by earlier LNG sales). In an offshore field, this capital component will include in addition to drilling costs, the platforms and off-shore pipelines to a landing point near the LNG plant.

6.6.1.2 Onshore Facilities

Onshore, the gas will be received and undergo some processing to remove impurities. Gas cleaning facilities will be a component of onshore capital costs. Then pipelines to the LNG plant site must be built. The LNG plant site itself will include not only the LNG plant, but also housing, administrative and utilities facilities, LNG storage tanks and marine loading facilities, a package that can account for more than half of the total project capital cost.

6.6.1.3 Interest During Construction

To these facilities costs must be added interest cost during a construction period of three years or more which will be capitalised and added to project cost.

6.6.1.4 Development Costs

Project developers will also capitalise the costs incurred in developing the project over the substantial period from initial project studies until project startup.

6.6.1.5 Marine Transportation

If marine transportation to market is to be included within the capital framework of the project, then additional cost will be included not only for ship acquisition, but also for developing the shipping project itself until crewing and operation of the LNG ships. More likely, the capital costs of marine transportation will be incurred outside the LNG project capital cost and then charged to the project at a lease rate so that freight cost is an operating expense of the project. In this scenario, the capital cost of shipping becomes a separate financing supported by the project's acquisition of shipping services (or in the case of an FOB sale of LNG, by the LNG buyer's acquisition of shipping services).

6.6.2   Financial Analysis

It is perhaps not surprising that one of the initial decisions in the LNG project development process is the selection of financial advisers to counsel project sponsors on the calculation of the package of capital costs and operating expense, the likely sources of project finance and the approaches to be made to those sources by the project. It is likely that the project sponsors will seek to finance a large percentage of the project's capital costs on the basis of the project's own credit, rather than the credit of the sponsors. To achieve this result, a convincing case must be made that the project is creditworthy. A robust financial analysis is the foundation of the structure to support project credit. At the beginning of this process all calculations will rely solely on a variety of assumptions. Over time some numbers will become firm, but in the main the determinants of the extent of the project's credit capacity will continue to be based on assumptions and on sensitivity analysis which subjects the financial results to adjustment from the base case assumptions. The expense side of the equation calculates financing costs over the term of the indebtedness, calculations that are continually refined as capital costs and finance market data is incorporated into the analysis. Operating costs from the natural gas well-head to the LNG loading flange are estimated and refined, usually based on generalised historical data for each function in the LNG chain. Royalty and tax rates will become known as legislation, regulation, licensing or negotiation with the host state proceeds. In many projects the natural gas supply piped to the LNG plant is sold to the project by a separate entity, either an upstream producer or a sovereign owner. In such cases the transfer price for natural gas becomes a crucial operating expense. Working capital is estimated based on free cash flow assumptions, and this in turn depends upon calculation of the revenue side of the equation. Here there are few firm numbers, although estimates may be stated in ranges. Before making its entry into the financial markets, the project will have made some conditional contracts for the sale of LNG that fix annual contract quantity (often starting delivery at low rates and building up to a plateau rate within a few years). The sales contract may provide the LNG buyer with some limited offtake flexibility and this variable will be reflected in the offtake quantity range.

Volume is multiplied by sales price to calculate revenue, but contract sales price is a moving target. The initial unit price is subject to adjustment periodically by application of an algebraic formula that contains variables largely based on changing oil or oil product market prices, perhaps including annual inflation rate changes, electricity price changes, coal prices etc. The initial contract price in effect at time of making the SPA will vary from and after the first LNG delivery (still three years or more in the future) perhaps as often as monthly over a period of 20 years or more. Calculations provide an estimated revenue flow over these 20 years or more that must be based solely on assumptions. The project will present its projected revenue based on its assumptions of price and quantity; the lenders will make their own evaluation based on their own assumptions. But lenders also consider potential revenue upsides related to plant production capacities and operating rates that assure contracted quantities are produced and hold promise of producing additional quantities to be marketed after the financing is closed. The amalgam of these calculations will produce a 'base case' of financial conditions over the project life, and particularly for the shorter period when project finance is outstanding. A base case income statement, cash flow statement and balance sheet will be calculated in preparation for presentation of the project to financial markets. From these financial statements will be derived the ratio of debt-service coverage for each debt service period and a coverage ratio for the life of the loan sought from lenders. The base case, however, is only the first stage of financial analysis of the project.

A number of variable factors embedded in the base case must be subjected to sensitivity analysis in order to determine the effect of changes upon the base case assumptions. These are some of the variables:

(1) precompletion delay and its impact on the base case calculation of interest during construction;

(2) capital cost overruns and their impact on capital cost and the assumed debt:equity ratio;

(3) operating cost overruns that increase expense and reduce free cash flow;

(4) interest rate changes during the period before financial close, and rate changes thereafter on variable interest portions of the indebtedness;

(5) price changes in crude oil or oil products or index changes as they directly affect the factors comprising the contractual price adjustment formula contained in the LNG SPA.

Since there are a number of variables and a number of degrees of possible change in each variable, the sensitivity studies will be generated in the form of numerous computer printouts. Prospective lenders will receive a hefty package of financial reports establishing a range of financial performance of the project based on calculations made by the project sponsors.

6.7   APPROACHING FINANCE MARKETS

A description of the project that anticipates lenders' questions and seeks to provide assuring answers to these questions will be the project's prerequisite to approaching financial markets. The medium for this communication process is the financial information memorandum, a detailed project description and financial analysis provided by project sponsors on a confidential basis to selected lenders in various finance markets.

6.7.1   Financial Information Memorandum

The financial information memorandum tells a story, and the following subsections outline that story.

6.7.1.1   *The LNG Project*

The project is a chain of activities from the natural gas well to the point of delivery of LNG to the buyer. The description of this chain provides an introduction to the project.

6.7.1.2   *LNG Markets*

Historically, LNG has been sold into LNG import markets that have developed worldwide over the past 30 years. The location of the project is likely to restrict its market to a region of the world where LNG can most competitively be sold. This regional market as well as the market of the specific buyer(s) from the project will be described.

6.7.1.3   *Natural Gas Reserves and Supplies*

The LNG plant requires large quantities of natural gas feed on a regular basis over a period of 20 or more years in order to perform its sales contract obligations. The sales period will exceed the loan repayment period. Thus the reserves of natural gas for the project that remain beyond the debt repayment period provide added support for the loan. Usually, third party expertise of a reservoir engineering firm will be required by lenders in order to establish the reliability of the gas reserves estimate. The existence of the natural gas in the reservoir is thereby established as reliably as can be achieved before actual gas production occurs. Additional links must be added to the gas supply description. The initial and long-term plans for gas field development necessary to produce an adequate feed gas supply are described. Access to possession of the natural gas production pursuant to petroleum licence, production-sharing agreement or gas supply agreement with the resource owner will complete the narrative.

6.7.1.4   Facilities and Technology

By the time that the project approaches financial markets, capital cost estimates of physical facilities will be highly refined through EPC bids or contracts firmly in place, subject to availability of finance. The description of these arrangements underlies the evaluation of the physical system for producing and delivering LNG.

6.7.1.5   Storage, Loading and Shipping

The marine aspects of the project fill out the delivery chain to the buyer's receiving terminal. Even when marine transportation is the buyer's responsibility, it is necessary to provide assurance to lenders of reliable transportation and receiving terminal arrangements so that the LNG cargo is not left stranded at the project's loading terminal.

6.7.1.6   Environmental Impact

Within the realm of hydrocarbon projects, LNG projects tend to be environmentally benign. Nevertheless, environmental impact is a priority consideration of lenders, and particularly multinational institutions and national ECAs.

6.7.1.7   Insurance Coverage

Project property is subject to casualty risks and the project company is subject to liability risks that must be covered by insurance in order to assure project lenders of the project's long-term viability. Adequate insurance arrangements will usually be preceded by the insurer's own risk assessment and, if necessary, risk reduction practices developed between the insurer and the project. For the lender, the project's insurance programme provides not only replacement funds in the case of claims, but also another level of third-party assessment of the facilities and technology and of the project's operating practices.

6.7.1.8   The Host State

The multiple roles of the host state in the project as resource owner or licensor, as co-sponsor of the project and equity investor, as well as sovereign power, require description in order to assure lenders of the long-term support for the project from the host state.

6.7.1.9   Contractual Framework

Just as the project is a physical chain strong enough to ensure LNG production and delivery, so must it be a contractual chain strong enough for construction of reliable facilities, expert operation and maintenance, assured feed gas supply to the LNG plant and assured LNG offtake by the buyer. The comprehensiveness of the contractual chain, the terms of each contract, and the reputation of the contracting parties all lend credibility to the project.

6.7.1.10   Financial Presentation

The financial information memorandum for lenders will end with detailed numerical charts, tables, financial statements and sensitivity analysis to support the conclusion that all of the elements of the project have been combined to produce a viable LNG project and a creditworthy borrower.

6.8   THE LENDER'S ANALYSIS

The lender is asked to provide the majority of the capital required to complete the project and to share the risks of the project with its sponsors by relying upon project cash flow for repayment. Under these circumstances, the lender can be expected to examine the project in great depth. Inevitably this means longer lead times and higher front end and ongoing costs than charged by lenders for balance sheet loans of comparable size. The lender's analysis will be both qualitative and quantitative. Its aim will be to ensure that, as far as financial modelling will allow, cash flow will be sufficient to cover operating costs and debt service with a reasonable margin of safety.

The potential project finance lender has three major perspectives for evaluating the creditworthiness of the project, namely risk mitigation, financial coverage ratios and security.

6.8.1 Risk Mitigation

Risk is a concept that is equally significant for both the equity investor and the project lender. Both depend on the same economic performance in order to realise the benefits of their respective infusions of capital into the project. The sponsors will seek to present their project to the financial market in the most favourable posture as to risk. Here, again, the sponsor proposes and the lender disposes. These are the project risk factors that will be considered.

6.8.1.1 *Sponsors' Experience*

By the time the project approaches financial markets there will be a good deal of evidence that the sponsors can develop the project. Nevertheless, their overall corporate scope and experience in hydrocarbon production and processing will be considered. The lender must be assured that sponsors have the ability to field adequate human resources and technical resources to implement the proposed development and operation of the project. In this context it is understandable that many LNG projects include within their sponsor group an international oil major such as Shell, British Petroleum or Mobil. Moreover, experience in one successful LNG project is usually regarded as emblematic of a successful LNG project developer that will encourage lenders to support its next LNG project. For example, Phillips Petroleum and Marathon Oil joined in the successful Alaska (Kenai) LNG project 30 years ago, and currently seek new LNG ventures on the basis of their 30 years of LNG experience. But, 'lack of LNG experience' should not have the effect of limiting otherwise qualified new entrants into the LNG industry. A number of oil companies have announced their intention to pursue development of LNG projects, and it is likely that they will pass muster with lenders based on their international oil and gas experience in other ventures. Moreover, state oil and gas companies in Abu Dhabi, Indonesia and Malaysia are established LNG project sponsors that have succeeded in a number of LNG project expansions. New private energy companies that join in their future LNG project expansions or greenfield developments are likely to benefit from state company credibility.

6.8.1.2 *Proven Reserves*

The lender relies on the availability to the project of proven natural gas reserves which are economically recoverable. Full payment of indebtedness must be achieved at the latest by the time the depletion of the economically recoverable proven reserves has reached, for example, seventy per cent of certified proven reserves, thereby affording a 30 per cent cushion to lenders.

6.8.1.3   Proven Technology

The international LNG industry has improved and scaled-up its technology at a rapid rate over the 30 years of LNG trade. Technological performance has never been a problem. However, the increasing size and sophistication of liquefaction trains results in new applications of existing technology in every project presented to project finance lenders. Plainly, capacity to produce economic volumes, reliability of operation and reasonable operating costs are all crucial to the success of the financial modelling. This, and the large capital investments from project owners and lenders, as well as manufacturers of LNG equipment, encourages a conservative attitude toward LNG technology, making it difficult to introduce unproven technical concepts.

6.8.1.4   LNG Buyer Experience

The purchaser of LNG is as much a matter of concern to lenders as the producer of LNG. An established LNG buyer has an experience record to evaluate, experience both with the physical processes of receiving and vaporising LNG and with consuming or marketing the resulting natural gas. Over the past three decades the LNG industry has developed comfortably with buyers that are leading natural gas distribution companies and electrical power producers of Europe, Japan, Korea and Taiwan. Early LNG importers tended to become repeat customers for new projects or expansion projects, resulting in their construction and operation of additional LNG import terminals or enlargement of existing LNG import terminals. The expansion of the LNG industry was built on the strength of this experienced customer base. While these experienced LNG buyers will continue to be an important factor in expanding LNG trade, it is plain that project finance lenders will be increasingly confronted with first-time LNG buyers from less industrialised nations.

6.8.1.5   LNG Buyer Creditworthiness

The creditworthiness of LNG buyers has always been an important asset of LNG producers, but its role is increasingly significant as sponsors seek to raise funds for their LNG projects on the basis of project finance. When project lenders must look solely to the economic performance of the project for repayment of indebtedness, the revenue produced by the LNG buyers is the lifeblood of the project finance. The ability of an LNG buyer to sustain regular payment of extremely large sums for frequent tanker loads of LNG delivered during 20 years or more must always present an element of risk. If an LNG market is lost to the project, redeployment of LNG production to an alternative market may be difficult to arrange and will always be subject to lengthy delay. The take-or-pay sales and purchase agreement of a financially sound LNG buyer operates to mitigate this risk. The best risk mitigation strategy is to start the trade with a buyer in an extremely strong financial position and continued need for an LNG supply for decades to come. The experienced LNG buyers of the previous three decades projected this optimistic picture. The most serious constraint on future LNG project development lies in the creditworthiness of new LNG buyers and their evaluation by project lenders.

6.8.1.6   Marine Transporter Experience

Affiliates of one or more project sponsors transport LNG in trades from Algeria, Malaysia, Abu Dhabi, Australia and the United States. Also, transportation services have seen the growing role of shipping companies of nations that import LNG. Thus, experienced LNG buyers and experienced LNG transporters increasingly tend literally to speak the same language. Japanese shipping companies entered the LNG transportation business as transporters for Japanese LNG buyers in an Indonesian FOB trade that started in 1983–84. Japanese LNG transportation service for Qatar's export of LNG delivered ex-ship to Japan started in late 1996. Similarly, KGC purchased LNG from suppliers in Indonesia, Qatar and Oman on FOB terms to be transported by Korean shipping companies. Several shipping companies located in the United States and Europe also transport LNG. Altogether, LNG transportation experience is concentrated in a relatively small number of shipping companies. The Japanese and Korean shipping companies entry into LNG transportation did not cause ripples in the LNG finance market, as lenders relied upon experienced and creditworthy LNG buyers to make prudent arrangements for transportation of FOB cargoes. Nevertheless, it is difficult to perceive future new entrants into LNG transportation, other than established marine departments of international oil companies, that will not cause some extra due diligence investigation in project finance markets.

6.1.8.7   Host State Commitment

Project finance of infrastructure projects by private sponsors has required increasing focus on government support. Both equity investors and lenders look closely at the extent of commitment to LNG exports by the host government at the export site. A recent commentator offered these observations:

> Given the nature of such projects, the government is often the party best able to manage and control particular project risks, e.g., land acquisition, assured revenues through off-take agreements, subordinated loans if revenues fall below a certain minimum (as often used in toll-road projects) and change in law.
>
> Government support therefore fulfils a number of important objectives relating to the development and realisation of projects.
>
> (1) It establishes formally public sector support for and contribution to the particular project and the framework for such support during the development/financing, construction and operating periods of the project.
> (2) It demonstrates commitment and support to the project and gives more 'security' to the project in the positive sense which is an important consideration for lenders and sponsors.
> (3) It provides (or should provide) comfort to lenders and sponsors regarding the political and regulatory environment within which the project will be developed and will operate.
> (4) It completes the 'security' package for lenders by establishing direct contractual rights and obligations between the host government and the lenders/sponsors/project company.[25]

Invariably, the host state is an equity participant in LNG production, if not a sole owner such as Sonatrach in Algeria and Pertamina in Indonesia. State equity investment signifies at least the application of host state hard currency reserves to the project. But investors and lenders look for more than that. The host state in its sovereign capacity plays many roles critical to project success. Legal regimes must support the foreign investment and contracts (including aspects of the finance documentation) and fiscal regimes must support the positive financial analysis of the project. The host state is often the natural gas resource owner or shares in the natural gas production by another project sponsor. Positive economic terms for feed gas supply to the project are crucial to the project's economic viability. The state can also play a role in providing supportive facilities such as a deep water protected port for the LNG export trade, thereby freeing the project of capital cost for marine access to the LNG terminal. Finally, government roles can be played in project approvals, site development, environmental regulation, domestic content requirements or domestic labour constraints crucial to project construction and operation.

---

[25] Grambas, 'Role of Government in Project Finance: Host Government Support', *International Business Lawyer*, 23 (May 1995), pp. 196, 198.

6.8.1.8   Host State Stability

Initial host state commitment is one thing; long-term political stability is another. Plainly the latter presents some degree of long-term risk in even the most stable geopolitical areas. As a practical matter, the project's purchase of substantial plant, equipment and services is likely to attract finance from one or more national ECAs. Their finance terms will include political risk cover for commercial bank lenders that participate in the ECA finance. But the ECA finance is only a portion of the total commercial bank finance for the project, and therefore some portion of the bank finance will be 'uncovered' for political risk.

6.8.2   Financial Coverage Ratios

The project sponsors will have a debt:equity ratio goal based on their appraisal of the financial soundness of the project and their perception of the project finance market. Thus the project's estimated capital cost multiplied by a percentage to be subscribed as equity investment of the sponsors produces a target reciprocal percentage of debt financing, for example 30 per cent equity investment and 70 per cent project indebtedness. The lender's financial analysis of the LNG project seeks to establish the maximum indebtedness and annual repayment amounts that the project can comfortably sustain. The annual debt service cover ratio (DSCR) divides free cash flow after operating costs and taxes in each year of the project's life by an amount of debt service (principal and interest) due in that year, thereby providing a year-by-year evaluation of the project's capacity to repay debt. Free cash flow is itself subjected to various sensitivity tests for the effect of changes in one expense category or combination of expenses or in the revenue stream.

Cover ratios based on net present value (NPV) calculations relate the present value of future cashflow, both over the life of the loan and over the life of the project, to the debt outstanding at the point to which cashflow is discounted. As such these calculations provide an assessment of the future debt-servicing capacity of the project. The loan life cover ratio (LLCR) divides NPV of future cash flow during the remaining loan life by the debt outstanding at the beginning of the discounting period. The project life cover ratio (PLCR) is also calculated. The difference between the LLCR and the PLCR gives an indication of the debt-servicing capacity remaining in the project after the projected termination of the proposed loan. This additional capacity provides a buffer which can be drawn on if the project underperforms in cashflow and thereby extends the period during which a loan balance is outstanding.

These ratios determine the robustness of the project's financial analysis. When the lenders impose a minimum DSCR and LLCR on the project, the application of these ratios will determine the amount of debt that can be incurred. That in turn will determine the debt service schedule for the project finance and the debt:equity ratio of the project. The relationship between equity and debt as evidenced by these cover ratios is central to the project lender's evaluation of an LNG project.[26]

6.8.3   The Security Package

Let us assume that the essential risk elements of the project are within an acceptable range and that the lender's financial analysis of the project and imposition of acceptable coverage ratios produces an acceptable amount of project finance available to the project. Nevertheless, the assurance of loan repayment by the project can be enhanced by a number of techniques well known to project lenders, some or all of which will be included in the loan security package. The equity investment percentage is the complement of the loan percentage, the sum that adds up to 100 per cent of the capital costs of the project. Project sponsors seek to reduce their cost of equity funds by contributing the equity investment *pari passu* with borrowed money. The lender seeks to have all of the equity investment made in the project before borrowed funds are disbursed to the project.

Most of the project's capital cost will be incurred under contracts for constructing facilities. In order to preserve estimated capital costs, lenders favour turnkey contracts with fixed completion dates at fixed prices, performance warranties and liquidated damage provisions. Moreover, until the project is 'complete' and in an operable condition to begin earning revenue, project lenders seek guaranties from project sponsors both as to cost overruns and completion delays. 'Financial completion' differs from physical completion. Financial completion will require not only commissioning of facilities, but also sustained production with operating performance and LNG deliveries reaching agreed levels over a period of perhaps several months.

Once in operation, the project will require sufficient startup working capital to meet cash flow requirements until adequate revenues are earned. A satisfactory amount of startup working capital at project completion is likely to be another guarantee imposed on project sponsors.

Project lenders are likely to be situated in hard-currency capital markets while LNG projects are likely to be situated in developing countries. LNG

---

[26] Mills, 'Project Financing of Oil and Gas Field Developments', *Oil & Gas Law and Taxation Review*, 4 (1996), p. 151. See also the same author's article at *Oil & Gas Law and Taxation Review*, 11/12 (1993), p. 359.

is universally sold for US dollars and project finance of LNG projects is universally repayable in US dollars. Thus LNG project lenders do not face risks of foreign exchange availability or fluctuations in currency exchange rates. If these hard currencies are paid into the host state they will transit through its national foreign exchange accounts, thereby adding a dimension of risk to their onward transmission to lenders. This risk is abated by a trusteed revenue account established in a major capital market such as New York or London into which buyers make LNG payments, and out of which debt service is paid. An offshore trust account to collect Korean sales proceeds established in the project finance of Qatar's Ras Laffan project was reported to be a contributing factor to Standard and Poor's investment grade rating (BBB+) of the project's bonds because an offshore payment mechanism mitigates the political risk that revenue will be trapped in the host state.

Since the project's financial projections predict that revenue will always be in excess of debt service, there is a question as to how the balance in the offshore trusteed revenue account will be disbursed. The rules and priorities in disbursing revenues from the trusteed revenue account will be established in the loan documentation. There are a number of claimants to the revenue stream in addition to lenders:

(1) royalties and taxes must be paid to the host state in order to maintain the project's viability;

(2) operation and maintenance expense must be disbursed in order to maintain the project's viability;

(3) since revenue flows can vary from month to month, lenders are likely to insist on the project's establishment of two reserve funds after payment of current debt service. The first reserves for operation and maintenance expense; the second reserves for debt service in a future period;

(4) the project company's sponsors have made substantial investment on the premise that they will earn adequate returns. The balance in the account after meeting other obligations is paid to them. But the payment may not be automatic if financial tests imposed on the project company in the loan documentation must be met before the project company can make distributions to its shareholders.

Insurance proceeds are an additional source of security for the project lenders. In their hands the proceeds can either be transmitted to the project company for application to restoring the *status quo ante* or can be applied to outstanding indebtedness if project viability is in jeopardy. Similarly, liens and mortgages on project property are another source of security for project lenders. The project company will have several classes of property: facilities, contracts, licences and accounts. It is unlikely that facilities can be transformed into ready cash by lenders at anything near their capital cost in the case of project default on its indebtedness, but this package of property rights gives to lenders substantial control over work-out solutions in the event of project insolvency. This observation comes with a caveat. The enforcement of property rights by foreclosure of liens and mortgages in the host state will be subject to the operation of its legal system, a system which may not be as detailed as to substantive rights and procedures or as experienced in administration of claims as the legal system of the lender's country.

Finally, there is the issue of the 'uncovered' portion of lenders' political risk. This concern focuses upon the extent to which lenders are able to obtain host state assurances which reduce the possibility of future sover-eign interference with the project. Lenders hope to achieve the strongest and most binding commitments of the sovereign state in support of the project, but this goal can be elusive. Sponsor guaranty of project comple-tion has become common in project finance. After completion sovereigns are as intent as project sponsors (often including state-owned resources companies) to keep indebtedness 'off-balance sheet' by making the project solely responsible for repayment of project loans. Thus sovereign financial guaranties are usually unattainable in project finance. It should be noted, however, that not all sovereigns pursue project finance for LNG projects in which they participate. For example, Abu Dhabi and Malaysian govern-ments have established LNG projects on the credit of the project sponsors that include state-owned energy companies.

In the absence of sovereign obligation, lenders often seek some level of sovereign assurance, recognising that the earliest years of the project bear the highest debt burden and may face operational uncertainty and lower sales volumes until sales contracts call for delivery of full plateau volumes. Revocation of project licences, approvals and consents, expropriation or nationalisation, export restrictions, increased taxation, and discriminatory treatment are among the spectres of political risk that haunt project lenders. Three areas are often the focus of negotiations for sovereign assur-ances in the form of specific supports to be contained in:

(1) agreements, legislation or decrees;
(2) expressions of stabilisation of existing laws from future changes;
(3) non-binding expressions of state support, often-called 'comfort letters'.

Project economics are subject to the sovereign fiscal regime; lenders' security is dependent on the sovereign legal regime. These are examples of areas of state jurisdiction in which change could be detrimental to the project. States may give assurances against changes in laws impacting the project—that is that current legal and fiscal regimes will be stabilised and project property rights respected. A perhaps lesser level of assurance is found in comfort letters in which the sovereign expresses its national interest in the success of the project and its understanding of the reliance of project investors and lenders on non-interference by the state. The specifics of sovereign assurance will depend on negotiation. The only generalisation to be made is that lenders seek to mitigate political risk by drawing the sovereign into some direct relationship with the project finance.

6.9 NEW POLICIES FOR LNG PROJECT FINANCING

6.9.1 Gas Exports and Gas Imports for Economic Development

6.9.1.1 *Multilateral Development Institutions*

The multilateral institutions (World Bank Group, EBRD and ADB) have not in the main been a source of funds or credit support for LNG projects. There seem to be strong policy reasons for their taking a more substantial role. Natural gas is seen as a primary means of improving energy supplies and environmental conditions of developing countries. The increasing preference for efficient electricity generation from combined cycle gas turbine power plants is another factor which can focus developmental lending on sources of gas fuel supply. LNG importers of the first generation of LNG projects have been the United States, Japan and Western Europe, highly industrialised countries that are not beneficiaries of multilateral institutions. As we enter the second generation, it is China, India, Pakistan, Thailand or The Philippines that are increasingly identified as potential LNG importers. On the export side, developing nations such as Indonesia and Malaysia have successfully financed greenfield LNG projects and leased LNG ships without access to multilateral development loans, given the readiness of the private sector, commercial banks and ECAs to fund these projects in the past. As LNG projects become less easily financed through traditional means due to lower credit ratings of LNG buyers, a case can be made for multilateral institution loans or guarantees to support economic development through LNG exports. Also, it should be noted that in several instances (Western Australia, Indonesia, Malaysia) LNG exports have laid the foundation for development of domestic gas utilisation in the exporting country. The World Bank, particularly, can benefit first-time LNG exporters and first-time LNG importers by mobilizing the necessary finance. World Bank guarantees of contractual performance will reduce commercial risks and increase availability of limited recourse finance provided by other lenders. Its presence in any financing consortium will increase confidence in the long-term viability of the project.

Internationally assisted project finance is probably not the ideal least cost solution for financing LNG projects. Non-recourse or limited recourse finance of international energy projects tends to combine substantial leverage with expectations of substantial returns on both equity and debt to compensate for perceived risks. Traditional international development banking was seen as a transitional step to the development of capital markets that can fund infrastructure development with both local and external sources of private capital. Similarly, institutionally assisted project finance can be the essential transitional step to funding energy project development from both local and external sources of private capital. During this transitional stage, multilateral institutions and national export credit agencies can play the catalytic roles which enable an LNG project to obtain maximum access to private capital markets.

6.9.1.2   Regional Import Finance Initiatives

The Asia-Pacific region continues to be the largest potential market for expansion of LNG imports. Sections 6.4.1 and 6.5.1.2 describe in some detail the wide-ranging financial assistance developed by Japanese governmental institutions as 'import finance' for Japan's LNG supplies. Japan's financial strength, economic growth rates and policy of energy import diversification all contributed to this policy development. As Japan's appetite for increasing LNG imports levels off, there is no other visible source of national import finance to match the breadth of Japanese financial assistance. Yet, Korea and Taiwan, as expanding LNG importers, and China, India and Pakistan, Thailand, and The Philippines as potential LNG importers, have a common regional interest shared with Japan. Their goal is to maintain the adequate long-term supply of natural gas and diversity of natural gas exporters that are necessary to strengthen security of supply, increase domestic natural gas consumption and foster competitive energy prices. This shared regional interest can become the foundation for regional cooperation and financial support to attract LNG supplies. Greenfield LNG projects pursuing economies of scale require large markets. First-time importers at the early stages of domestic gas consumption often require small initial tranches of LNG. At present, the knitting together of diverse demand to support a large greenfield project's supply is seen simply as the marketing hurdle for LNG producers. When viewed as a strategic supply opportunity for LNG importers, the cooperative application of import finance techniques by multiple importers from a single supply source can provide an impetus to LNG project development for the Asia-Pacific region.

6.9.1.3 Government Support

A number of factors are contributing to make government support an increasing necessity for financing new LNG projects. These factors include market uncertainties in fast-growing economies of developing countries spawned by privatisation, and the introduction of deregulation and competition in markets previously dominated by franchised or state owned gas and electricity monopolies. Host government support for LNG producers has always been present. In all LNG projects, except Alaska (Kenai) and Australia North-West Shelf, government-owned oil and gas companies hold large equity stakes in export projects. Some of these projects have benefited from favourable tax rates and low threshold prices for feedgas purchased from state oil and gas companies. In some cases, government-to-government agreements or loans linked the markets of LNG seller and buyer. The challenge is to mobilise similar strong host government support for LNG importers. Generally, the less advanced an economy in terms of LNG import experience, the more likely that government support in some form will be required. A key factor is assuring availability, convertibility and transferability of foreign exchange to pay for US dollar imports, thereby moderating currency exchange risk incurred by LNG buyers that earn revenues in local currency. Governments can also play a role in supporting establishment of the gas infrastructure at the import site (e.g. port development and LNG receiving terminal) or the end-use of imported LNG (e.g. natural gas distribution pipelines or gas-fired electric power generating plants).

6.9.2 Shared Security

Documentation for a syndicated loan from commercial banks will include an intercreditor agreement, that is, an agreement which links all of the bank lenders in the syndicate into arrangements for loan oversight and for sharing of the benefits of security for the loan in the case of default. As LNG project sponsors seek project finance from multiple finance sources of export credit agencies, capital markets, commercial banks and multilateral institutions the issues involved in lenders' sharing of loan security become substantially more acute and complex. Intercreditor issues can raise concerns about loan acceleration rights, commencement of enforcement of rights in loan security, distribution of proceeds of liquidation or enforcement, and waivers of restrictive covenants, breaches and defaults. These issues are exacerbated when multiple finance sources provide project finance. The concept of a 'syndicated loan' from a group of ECAs utilising common loan documentation has been gaining momentum. Its advantages are clear. Common finance terms are likely to reduce costs and shorten negotiations. The project finance of Ras Laffan carried the step further by negotiating a single set of loan documentation accepted by ECAs, commercial banks and bondholders. The process for accommodating these lender interests should begin at the inception of financing efforts rather than developing through the pulls and tugs of lenders as commitments are being solicited.[27]

A related area, both for ECAs acting in concert and for multiple financial markets lending to a project, is the high degree of due diligence investigation practiced by project finance lenders to complex projects. The process of technical, economic and legal study undertaken to evaluate an LNG project is cumbersome, expensive and time-consuming, all the more so when engaged in respectively by separate lenders or finance sources. A common group of technical and legal advisers for a common group of lenders can streamline the process. As necessities of project finance draw together more lenders from different financial markets there is reason for constructing more efficient loan structures that will establish joint risk appraisal, unified loan terms and shared security in financing a successful greenfield LNG project.

[27] Bogaty, Financing Considerations in a Changing LNG Business', *Project Finance International* (30 March 1995).

Chapter 7

LNG: The Strategic Planning Issues

Kimball C. Chen

7.1 INTRODUCTION

For many thinkers, in the last century and this, the elements of strategic thinking have been most clearly expressed by Clausewitz in his famous book *On War*:

> Strategy is the theory of the use of combats for the object of the war.[1]

> War belongs ... to the province of social life. It is a conflict of great interests ... it would be better ... to liken it to business competition, which is also a conflict of human interests and activities; and it is still more like State policy which may be looked upon as a kind of business competition on a great scale.[2]

Conflicts of interest are the essence of war, politics and business. Clausewitz's vision of strategy focused on how to reach a goal, in competition with others, by planning and carrying out a series of actions. Underlying the planning and implementation there would have to be facts, experience, resources and viewpoints. The foregoing paradigm is a useful starting point for discussing strategic planning in the LNG industry, the subject of this chapter.

---

[1] Carl von Clausewitz, *On War* (1968), Book XI, Chapter I.
[2] *Ibid.*, Book VI, Chapter III.

In order to think properly about LNG, it is important to realise that, for most parties, LNG is an area of interest whose importance must be weighed against that of other areas of interest and activity. An energy company, for example, might be trying to plan activity in oil, pipeline gas, LNG, coal, electric power generation and renewable energy. LNG is one of several 'wars' that might be engaging its attention. Therefore strategy for LNG might really be one of many strategies which would have to be harmonised in the context of a party's multiple goals. The planning and carrying out of LNG business takes place over much longer periods of time than other businesses. It rewards good execution and persistence; it rewards accretion of advantage. It is not what an economist would consider an efficient market: domestic politics and geopolitics are important, sellers and buyers cooperate and compete simultaneously and transactions are few.

This chapter will discuss the following topics:

(1) the structure of the LNG industry and the motivations of the key players;
(2) the nature of value;
(3) important externalities;
(4) competition and comparative advantage;
(5) possibilities for creating change;
(6) case studies.

The progression of topics is designed first to create a conceptual framework based on what history and the present tell us, and then to anticipate the future as best we can. The chapter closes with a series of brief case studies that show the utility of these concepts in understanding and learning from actual circumstances.

7.2 THE STRUCTURE OF THE INDUSTRY AND THE MOTIVATIONS OF THE KEY PLAYERS

Described simply, the LNG industry consists of entities which sell LNG (each called a 'seller') to entities which buy LNG (each called a 'buyer'), supported by service providers, vendors and financing sources. The bulk of the commercial activity takes place through long-term contracts. A seller is often a consortium of several sponsors ('sponsor' or 'sponsors') and is often majority-owned by the nation where the gas reserves are located ('host country'). On the sell side of the trade, there is always heavy host country government involvement, as is typical in oil and gas production and sales in general outside North America, the United Kingdom and Australia.

There are three defining economic characteristics of LNG:

(1) *Project structures.*
Commercial and physical activities are organised around 'projects'. In an LNG project, seller and buyer are closely linked by long-term contracts. Spot market and short-term relationships are not a major factor.

(2) *Very large front end investment.*
There must be significant front end infrastructure investment for each tonne of LNG delivery capacity. The critical mass of infrastructure and, therefore, required financing, for an LNG project must be very large in order to achieve production quantities adequate for realisation of economies of scale.

(3) *Long-term contracts based on large, proven gas reserves.*
The long term of contracts is necessary in order to achieve a price acceptable to buyers, acceptable financing to build the project and adequate returns on investment to sponsors. The proven reserves must be adequate for many years of production of LNG at an annual rate large enough and at a cost low enough to attract the interest of both seller and buyer. The physical factors which govern the market value of any hydrocarbon deposits are of great importance in consideration of the gas reserves proposed for a potential LNG project. Any physical disadvantages of the gas in quantity of reserves, quality of reserves and location can doom a proposed project.

(a) *Quantity.* Obviously, enough proven gas must be physically accessible and contractually dedicated to the LNG contract. An extra margin of gas must be committed to allay any fear of banker or buyer that contract quantities will not be delivered or that original reserve estimates were in error.

(b) *Quality.* If the composition of the gas is high in CO_2, the additional processing cost to separate the CO_2 and reinject it into the field or into separate reservoirs can render the production cost uneconomical. This is the famous 'Achilles' heel' of the huge Natuna field offshore Indonesia. The need to extract water and other impurities drives up the production cost of gas in similar fashion. On the other hand, the presence of saleable heavier gas fractions such as ethane and propane, and heavier, adds net value.

(c) *Location.* If the location of the gas is remote from markets, the cost of transportation can be as much as one-third of the delivered cost of LNG. Profit to a long-distance LNG supply project may be thin if it is forced to engage in pricing competition with LNG produced closer to market. The strategic aspect of transportation cost was illustrated clearly in the early 1990s when the Nigerian export project bought inexpensive, used LNG ships to lower transportation cost dramatically. This was the only way the project could bring the project rate of return to an acceptable level.

The physical steps in the production and use of LNG are:

(1)   gas gathering and production;
(2)   gas treatment and processing;
(3)   liquefaction;
(4)   export terminalling;
(5)   LNG shipping;
(6)   import terminalling and regasification;
(7)   gas transmission and distribution; and
(8)   gas end-use.

All these activities must take place simultaneously in order for revenue to flow to all parties as planned. These steps are often called the 'LNG chain', because the activities are linked.

Commercial tasks must also be accomplished in order for a project to start: project organisation and implementation; gas marketing (the seller); gas purchasing (the buyer); and financing. Not least of the jobs is solving organisational issues, as Figure 7.1 summarises.

Given the necessity of the tasks outlined above, who are the groups that will have to work together to create the business? What are their interests?

7.2.1   Sellers

The seller is usually a national company or a consortium in which the national company plays an influential role.

The host country in some cases takes an operating lead if it is experienced in hydrocarbon exploitation and LNG. In other cases, it is a passive partner. The host country tries to optimise its long-term economic take from the resource. In some cases, this means exporting more now; in other cases it may involve banking the resource and not producing gas. In still other cases, it means choosing how much gas to use domestically. In addition, the host country has foreign policy goals which may impact on how it commercialises gas.

Arduous negotiating takes place among the sponsors. The foreign corporations who participate in LNG consortia must reach compromises with each other and with the host country in order to achieve a project go-ahead decision and funding. These foreign corporations generally are

Figure 7.1 Organisational Issues

Strategic planning must encompass organisational issues in order to be useful. The limit of possibility is the limit of the organisational resources and process focused on realising the possibility. There are many ways for an organisation to respond to a business challenge. Below are listed some concepts which would have to be considered in any strategic plan to participate in the LNG industry:

1. Strategic commitment
   i. If buyer, commit to LNG import infrastructure and gas distribution infrastructure and to seller risks.
   ii. If seller, commit to LNG export infrastructure and to buyer risks.
   iii. If vendor, commit to product line and marketing.
   iv. If government, commit to policies.
   v. If capital market, commit to risks.

2. Commitment to a long-term economic structure
   i. Long-term cost of gas for buyer.
   ii. Long-term revenue for seller.
   iii. Long-term overhead structure.
   iv. Risk-sharing.

3. Decision-making process
   i. Careful data gathering and analysis.
   ii. Making judgements about the future.
   iii. The need for a plan.
   iv. The need to follow the plan for years.
   v. Long lead times.
   vi. Choosing the form of corporate organisation to do the job. Activity configuration must be aligned with activity co-ordination.

4. Corporate attention and focus
   i. Operating management.
   ii. Senior management.
   iii. Board of directors.
   iv. Shareholders.

5. Resources
   i. Money.
   ii. People.
   iii. Credibility/credentials.

integrated oil companies, Asian trading companies and gas utilities who wish to develop long-term revenue and gas market positions.

Oil company majors used to have a pure seller interest. However, now they are linking their LNG seller activities to power plant projects in gas-consuming countries. These oil companies, as potential buyers of LNG or of pipeline gas as fuel for their electric power projects, have inherent conflicts with their seller partners in the pricing of LNG. This is in addition to the classic historical competition between the various oil company marketing units which produce and sell different fuels. The LPG traders, the naphtha and diesel salespeople, the fuel oil department and the refinery manager responding to the marketing department do not all necessarily care about LNG marketing success or allocation of resources to LNG. These intramural conflicts must be arbitrated by oil company senior management; more importantly, settling these conflicts requires taking a longer-term strategic view on the role of each fuel product in the oil company's opportunity portfolio.

The trading companies, especially the Japanese majors such as Mitsubishi, Mitsui and Nissho Iwai, have delicate balancing acts in their roles both as sellers and as facilitators to buyers. The focus on LNG sales profit must be harmonised with regard to their long-term relationships with utility clients. The supplemental income for them lies in the profit made by their heavy industry affiliates in building and operating LNG ships, in building storage tanks and liquefaction plants and in arranging finance.

Increasingly, buyers are considering becoming members of seller consortia. The inherent conflict of interest with other seller sponsors is obvious. Yet buyer participation can also be viewed as a strong support and a plus to a project. The other sponsors, however, may circumscribe the role of the buyer-sponsor, feeling that the buyer should actively act only as a buyer and should not have any power as a member of the seller joint venture.

7.2.2 Buyers

If a buyer is a state utility corporation such as Gaz de France or Korea Gas Corporation (KGC), its strategy will directly reflect its country's energy policies and strategy. Decisions about primary energy mix, security of supply, foreign policy, national security and long-term cost of economic factors will be reflected in its actions. Its credit will be stronger because it represents the whole energy sector in the country as well as the sovereign credit, even if the sovereign guarantee is not formally given.

If a strong private utility is the buyer, its interest is long-term and economic, though inevitably at least indirectly reflecting national energy policy. To the extent that it is not the sole buyer from an LNG project, its negotiating power will be diluted by the terms being negotiated with other buyers, unless all the buyers negotiating with a given seller act in concert. Often the buyer's national government 'guides' the buyer's negotiations with the seller. Utilities may become involved in LNG not only to serve their traditional markets, but to broaden their ability to sell into other markets in their country or abroad where they have not formerly been active.

7.2.3   Energy Majors and Trading Companies

An oil (or energy) major or trading company has many other interests to worry about besides its activities as a sponsor in an LNG export project. It may have many interests in the buyer country as well as with other energy suppliers. It must be conscious of priorities and relationships. In regard to LNG, the energy major or trading company must come to a settled judgement on the long-term profitability that will result from committing capital and manpower to the multi-year LNG business development and implementation process.

Many companies feel that an LNG project, if successfully developed, will deliver long-term revenue, contractually assured, with a high probability of a profit. The rapid rise of gas in the priorities of major companies reflects the fact that market positions in gas can be extraordinarily stable and large sources of profit. However, these companies recognise that success comes from transactions which are few and far between, unlike oil marketing. Today, gas marketing, control of gas transmission and distribution infrastructure and control of power generation opportunities are prerequisites to being able to make a success of gas production opportunities. Downstream dictates to upstream. In contrast, for oil, the presence of a large, liquid, fungible market worldwide means that cost-competitive upstream supply can achieve sales and profit without dependence on simultaneous development of a creditworthy, long-term market.

7.2.4   Governments of Buyers

Policymakers must face many inter-related issues presented by LNG imports. Below is a partial list of major policy areas that LNG involves:

(1)   foreign policy;
(2)   energy security policy;
(3)   environmental policy;
(4)   electric power policy;
(5)   energy tariff policy;

   (6)   infrastructure policy;
   (7)   infrastructure ownership and investment policy;
   (8)   maritime policy;
   (9)   use of long-term sovereign credit;
 (10)   balance of trade.

The development of knowledgeable and competent civil servants to create and implement adequate policies is important. If state companies are the instruments of policy then the link between state company action and national policy must be firmly established. Also of great importance are stability and consistency of policies, in order to attract financial market confidence.

7.2.5 Vendors and Engineering Service Providers

Large contracts are at stake in LNG projects. The motivations of the vendors and engineering service providers range from pure corporate profit and line-of-business focus to linkage with national industrial policy.

Countries that have heavy industry aspirations and also buy large quantities of LNG can use their buyer power to promote LNG infrastructure contract awards to their companies. Japanese and Korean industrial groups in particular have received contracts to build LNG ships, storage tanks and liquefaction plants with support from their national LNG buyers. Such success results from strong cooperation between public and private sectors in those countries.

Vendors and engineering service providers must understand that participation in the LNG markets takes significant monetary and technical resources and political power. There are not many market participants. Those who are not possessors of proprietary technology valued by the market or are not part of a national bloc must obviously develop strategic relationships with parties who can affect procurement decisions.

7.2.6 Financing Sources

The growth in LNG project activity has occurred simultaneously with globalisation of financial markets. The increase in cross-border trade of money has resulted from the need of commercial banks, life insurance companies and pension funds to lend or invest money; they seek projects meeting minimum criteria of creditworthiness and transparency. The financial markets have recognised that LNG projects cannot depend only on support by sponsors. Consequently, there has been a great focus on use of non-recourse or limited-recourse finance for LNG projects. Energy projects are particularly popular with the project finance community due to the essential role of energy in all national economies and therefore the high assurance that energy buyers will honour their purchase contracts. There has been a tremendous broadening of interest in LNG among the leading commercial and investment banks. The multilateral development institutions, including the World Bank, Asian Development Bank (ADB) and International Finance Corporation (IFC), have developed expertise and interest in LNG.

Once financing sources have placed money in a project, their instinct and reason lead them to take all measures to protect their loan or investment. They, in a sense, become partisan, willing to oppose threats to the project. Thus there can be a long-term political dimension to allowing a project to achieve financing. As an example, the United States spent years attempting to prevent Iranian gas projects from reaching fruition because those projects would integrate Iran into the world economy.

Huge capital investment is required to produce LNG, as well as to receive and regasify it, and transmit and distribute it to end-users. Since the foundation of LNG financing is the credit support deriving from large, long-term contracts, institutions financing LNG infrastructure want to see long-term credit capacity in a buyer. Financial markets must be convinced that the buyer has a significant mass of financial capability up-front and for the long period of time an LNG contract may run.

If an independent power producer (IPP) is the buyer, the credit challenge is very large because the sources of LNG export project finance face an additional layer of risk between them and the electricity market which is ultimately paying for the electrical generating activity and the concurrent supply of the LNG fuel. The IPP itself is dependent on a complex power purchase agreement (PPA) with what is hopefully a creditworthy off-taker. An LNG seller arguing with an IPP buyer is really arguing with the IPP's banks for a share of the revenue represented by the PPA.

7.2.7 Who Does What

The starting point of natural gas commercialisation is a decision by the host country to have its gas reserves developed. That decision usually results after feasibility studies by experts. Obviously, for an LNG project to move forward, a preliminary judgement must be reached that selling LNG may be a viable means of accomplishing the country's economic and other goals. In many gas-owning countries, major oil companies and trading companies join together with the host country to assess feasibility, either directly, through the Ministries and state oil companies, or indirectly, through unilaterally developed reports, with data, or access to data, supplied by the host country government. The development of technical credibility in the LNG market is a key concern of LNG project developers.

If an LNG project seems possible, the inevitable question becomes one of how to develop it. Usually those foreign companies that have participated in a preliminary feasibility study are the front runners to be considered for partnership in an LNG export venture. The scope of an LNG project can be designed broadly or narrowly, depending on the specific situation and the preferences of the host country. The gas production can be integrated with the liquefaction, shipping and trading or it can be separated. The economic sharing can adopt many contractual forms. There can be different partners with different percentages of sharing at different levels of a project. In Indonesia, for instance, natural gas exploration and production are differentiated from ownership and operation of the liquefaction plants and from ownership and operation of the LNG ships. In the Qatargas project in Qatar, the gas production ownership percentages of participants are different from the LNG plant ownership percentages of the same participants.

Who fulfils which operating functions is partly related to who gets what rewards. Most, if not all, oil companies involved in LNG projects seek to maximise their operating responsibilities. In order for them to increase their presence in the LNG industry they must develop internal reservoirs of operating experience to be able to present their capabilities favourably to other projects and partners, as well as to sources of capital and insurance. The provision of technical services to a project is a common way for a sponsor to make money from the other sponsors and thereby mitigate some of the risk undertaken by making an equity investment in the project. Operating responsibility and knowledge are also ways of exerting control.

7.2.8   Who Gets What—Host Government and Foreign Partners

It is a difficult negotiation to set how much revenue the host government will receive from an LNG export project (especially in fiscal take, such as excise taxes and income taxes) as well as what operating roles it will be accorded. Most hydrocarbon-exporting countries have a conscious strategy of accelerating the development of competent citizens to carry out key LNG project functions. This policy goal can be at odds with their foreign partners' desires to develop staff and to control operations and commercial activity. Banker preferences and insurance markets can also influence who is allocated operating roles in a project.

7.2.9   What Technical Choices?

Choices of technology are important in project planning. Choice of technology is also intimately connected with choice of vendor; choice of vendor involves not only political and economic considerations, but also a desire to maintain competition in the market. For example, the selection of the Phillips liquefaction process for the Trinidad project signalled that price competition in liquefaction plants would become vigorous because the Phillips process and perhaps other plate and fin liquefaction processes were technically acceptable, and because Phillips liquefaction plant operation capabilities were also acceptable. This challenged the market dominance and pricing margins of Air Products and Chemicals, whose liquefaction technology had been the only choice made by LNG projects for 20 years.

7.2.10   Commercial Strategies

The choice of project commercial strategies often highlights differences in viewpoints and incentives among the project partners. For example, the sponsors may not agree which markets to focus on or what contract terms to offer. An oil company sponsor may have to choose which project to emphasise, if it is participating simultaneously in several projects which are all pursuing the same buyer. In most projects the sponsors have complicated webs of other interests which affect the positions they take in internal project negotiations. The choice of what compromises to reach in initial contract negotiations can have great and long-term consequences, affecting the course of contract extension negotiations as well as project expansions.

Financing approaches can diverge greatly. All-equity is one extreme. Total non-recourse project finance is the other extreme. An all-equity project can start more quickly as there may be no need to spend time arranging bank loans or going to capital markets. The project can then leverage itself after it is in operation, attracting better terms because risks are lower. On the other side, non-recourse financing with 20–40 per cent sponsor equity obviously makes smaller capital demands on the sponsors. However, organising the finance may take some time.

Pricing policy is another potential subject for contention: should a project seek a floor price, or not? For years, it has been generally accepted that sponsors and lenders must have assurance of minimum cash flow. Therefore a floor price and minimum contract quantities were thought of, by those outside the industry, as necessities. In reality, floor prices have not been as prevalent in contracts as has been assumed, although contract quantity obligations on take-or-pay terms have. LNG price theory and practice bear re-examination. Linkage to oil prices is not obviously applicable. Gas reserves have their own production and marketing costs not similar in pattern or magnitude to those of oil or coal. Oil products are not necessarily fungible for gas. A premium for low-emission fuels should emerge once the market prices emission cost, as it may with pollution trading rights sanctioned under global treaties on the environment and greenhouse gas. Opportunity cost—i.e. rise in oil price leading to rise in gas price—is an opportunity to the seller, but counter to the interest of the buyer who may want to arbitrage fuel cost by switching to other fuel supplies or by not using LNG-fuelled plants as base-load power generation. Sharing of opportunity and allocation of risk as price moves down or up do not need to be symmetrical. All parties benefit from project robustness because project disruption equally harms each side.

The fear of new price formulas is an inherited bias, deriving from inertia and custom. In Europe, the relative unimportance of LNG due to the large and diverse pipeline gas supply makes LNG pricing reactive to gas-on-gas market moves. In the Far East, there is relative inelasticity of supply and transmission, especially in Japan where there is no national grid to make gas sourcing a tradeable risk. Thus price is more the result of a more focused negotiation and less the result of reaction to other fuel prices and availability.

An interesting negotiating subject in all projects is who will own and operate the LNG ships. Because ships represent 20–40 per cent of a project's infrastructure cost and are strategic points of control, LNG sellers and LNG buyers negotiate for control of the shipping. Often trading companies with ties to LNG buyers are part of LNG selling consortia. In recent years, project LNG shipping has been awarded to shipping companies controlled by the national companies of the buying country. In those cases, the commercial rewards of shipping and incremental strategic power in the deal are being conceded to the buyer.

7.2.11 Monopoly, Monopsony, Oligopoly

In the LNG world, there is a tendency towards 'mono' concepts: monopoly in the host country (sole seller) and monopsony in the buyer's country (sole buyer). Due to the large size and long term of LNG contracts, government authorities tend to get involved in the business on both the seller and buyer sides. In Japan, the actions of buyers tend to be harmonised and orchestrated (oligopoly behaviour).

As a planning matter, sellers of LNG look at national markets, although in the case of Japan there are certainly differences between the individual utility buyers. However, the contract terms agreed with one buyer are likely to be the terms reached with other buyers by that project. In negotiation of terms one must bear in mind historical precedent as well as the standard industry mantra of the need for 'mutually beneficial cooperation'.

In most countries other than Japan, there is only one LNG buyer and that entity will have control of the necessary LNG import and gas distribution infrastructure. In Japan, government-sanctioned monopoly gas markets based on major city areas are large enough to make the local utility a viable LNG buyer by itself, having terminal capacity and a pipeline distribution network. In recent years, the risk characteristics and economic terms of LNG contracts have not been uniform among Japanese buyers, despite emergency sharing agreements in case supply interruption occurs. In other countries, the principal buyer diversity has arisen from the conflict of interest between the fuel sector and the electric power sector. In Korea and Taiwan the state electricity companies have struggled to break the state oil company monopoly on LNG importing. Italy has also seen a struggle between the state oil and electric companies over LNG import rights. However, the nature of the seller negotiations with a national market will still be determined by a buyer national commercial strategy, even if there are several entities buying LNG. Having outlined the types of concerns that occupy companies participating in the LNG market, it is now useful to consider how they seek economic benefit.

7.3   THE NATURE OF VALUE

The activities which take gas from underground and finally deliver it as LNG, to be regasified and used in a variety of end-uses, are a chain of discrete tasks, each of which creates value, confers control and requires expertise. There is a contractual relationship between each of these activities which allocates risk and value. There are political, economic and operating risks associated with each activity; there are also mutual dependencies, subjecting each activity to partial or complete project risk.

The chain begins in time and space with agreements governing exploration for gas. These agreements then mature in a subsequent set of gas production contracts, typically in the terms of a production-sharing contract (PSC). Exploration and production taken together create a set of economic and physical conditions leading to a cost of gas and quantity of gas available to an LNG project. If the LNG project developers are not the same as the gas explorers and producers, there is naturally an opposition of profit incentive which must be settled by the negotiation for the terms on which gas is provided to an LNG project.

The traditional dividing line between buyer and seller occurred at the water's edge. In the early days of the industry, buyers purchased LNG on a delivered ex-ship (DES) basis and the seller controlled the transportation function and all other value creation upstream from the buyer's LNG import terminal all the way back to the gas reserves. The buyer controlled all the value creation downstream from the discharge of the cargo. Today, the interests of the parties are becoming blurred as buyers reach upstream and sellers reach downstream. Buyers have been investing in the LNG export projects from which they buy, as well as investing in and controlling the LNG transportation. Sellers have been seeking to reach downstream into development of LNG import terminals and power plants which use the regasified LNG. In the jargon of the trade, companies extol integration along the 'value chain'.

Knowledge can create value. Relatively few companies have expertise in gas liquefaction, LNG shipping and LNG terminal operations. Therefore, those qualifications are used as credentials to gain entry into new projects and trades, as well as to extract operating revenue from partners and customers through technical service agreements.

Control of the assets used in the chain also provides access to several sources of value which were ignored in the early days of the industry: the residual value of assets, as well as their excess capacity. Most LNG ships and LNG liquefaction plants are now recognised to have useful lives far in excess of the original 20 to 25-year LNG sales contracts which they were built to service. By the 1990s, it had become clear from various reputable studies that first and second generation LNG ships, when properly operated and maintained, would be serviceable through a ship age of as much as 40 years. The LNG liquefaction plants that have serviced the industry even from the beginning are capable of continuing for many more years than their originally planned service and indeed some are beginning to serve long-term extensions of their original sales contracts. The excess capacity of the liquefaction plants and the ships are also hidden values to their owners. All LNG plants have been designed conservatively with 10–20 per cent more capacity than 'nameplate capacity' (the original design capacity). All LNG projects maintain 8–15 per cent excess ship fleet capacity in order to be able to maintain delivery obligations even if one ship goes out of service. The incremental revenue that the extra capacity of the liquefaction and shipping can generate is of enormous value since the operating and capital costs of the assets are for the most part fixed.

Value is inherent in control of gateways. LNG export and import terminals are expensive and import terminals especially are hard to get permitted. However, if a terminal is expandable, it will have an obvious competitive advantage when demand growth requires more capacity.

An existing LNG terminal with expansion capacity has an inherent economic advantage over any proposed greenfield terminal to be built in the same area.

Value exists in the end-use activity, particularly power generation. The allocation of economic rent between fuel end-user and the fuel supplier is an ongoing battle of interests. Option valuation under conditions of uncertainty must be considered. What is the value of an option to buy more quantities? What is the value of flexible quantities? What is the value of control over extra ship capacity? What is the value of extra liquefaction capacity? What is the value of probable gas finds that will extend sales contract life and the value of particular LNG infrastructure? The struggle to apportion value will be examined again later in this chapter when we consider the foundation of competition and comparative advantage.

7.4 IMPORTANT EXTERNALITIES AND THEIR TRENDS

The nature of LNG and its long-term contract and financing commitments demands careful consideration of those factors which can affect those contracts and financing over many years. A strategist must assess LNG within a broader general context of:

(1) macro-economics;
(2) industrial policy;
(3) geopolitics;
(4) financial markets.

7.4.1 Macro-economic Issues

The main focus of macro-economic analysis must be the energy market, a market far broader than natural gas or LNG. The starting point is energy consumption, actual as well as projected.

The time span considered must be at least 25 years because project development of LNG projects takes at least five to seven years and a major project requires construction periods and follow-on long-term contracts aggregating at least 20–25 years. From a financial point of view the most important period of time is the first 15 years after investment is made. The financing structures which historically and presently are used to support the development of an LNG project require loans used to finance the bulk of the project capital cost to be repaid to lenders within the first 10–15 years of project operation.

World energy consumption and world energy supply, of course, do not provide detailed enough guidance to a planner. The real question is projected regional and national energy consumption and supply, in relation to defined LNG buyers. Those projections have components ranging from highly certain base-load consumption of regional utilities to optimistic forecasts of growing consumption based on variable demand from IPPs whose output of power (and thus demand for fuel) depends on discretionary demand from the electric utility buyer of the IPP output. Energy demand projections depend on projections about economic activity and the amount of energy intensity required by that economic activity. Inefficient, obsolete heavy industry capacity can consume two or three times more energy per unit of output than state of the art energy-efficient industrial plant.

The rate of gross domestic product (GDP) growth in emerging markets with a mix of old and new industrial plant (particularly China, India, Turkey, Brazil, The Philippines and Indonesia) poses a forecasting challenge. One must focus on their rate of renewal of industrial plant, as well as the types of new plant being installed, in order to predict energy growth, fuel mix and import requirements. Energy providers and utilities in countries such as those just mentioned must simultaneously answer present energy needs, predict and plan to satisfy future energy needs and plan and implement policies that enhance the success of the economy and attract long-term support from the financial markets. To the extent that policy reform is slow to get started, capital market interest in the country will be slow to develop and new energy projects will take a longer time to be financed. When policy blockages are relieved, a huge amount of activity can be generated in a short time. The March 1994 reform of Pakistani power policy attracted 20,000 megawatts of power plant development offers within a few months.

An additional factor in judging the prospects for LNG is the nature of interfuel competition. To assess the future pattern of relative costs of different forms of energy requires prediction of both the fuel cost and the relative and absolute cost of infrastructure required to utilise each fuel. The long-term competitive relationship between fuels is also affected by environmental concerns, commitment to existing infrastructure, development lead time, national security considerations and user preference. In addition, the willingness of capital markets and banking markets to support energy projects will determine the rate of change possible in a country's energy mix. The possibility of technical revolution changing the nature and economics of interfuel competition must also be taken into account. Long-term supplier pricing policies must also be projected, particularly the profit margins a fuel supplier is willing to settle for. In the case of LNG, the principal pricing benchmark is oil to which LNG pricing is indexed in major contracts. A view on LNG price trends, with or without price floors and ceilings, is therefore highly linked to a viewpoint on oil price trends. Whether contractual habits will change and LNG pricing will be linked to non-oil benchmarks is yet to be determined. All the foregoing macroeconomic issues are affected by industrial policy, which is discussed next.

7.4.2 Industrial Policy

National policy, as well as pure economic forces, helps determine the share of primary energy mix that natural gas will be allowed to provide. For instance, Japan has consistently attempted to keep LNG at an 11–12 per cent level in overall Japanese energy consumption and has announced that as a 'goal'. LNG sellers and LNG buyers alike worry about 'economic colonialism'. They need capital, technology and knowledge. Yet they do not wish to turn over key infrastructure to large foreign companies for long periods of time. Both seller and buyer must contemplate the economic and political commitment represented by a long-term LNG project. Countries tied into a multinational gas grid can negotiate gas contracts varying in both quantity and term. Countries dependent on LNG must basically contract in large, long-term contract 'lumps'. Each lump represents a bilateral relationship and set of obligations.

An exporting country's willingness to sell gas now (as opposed to slowing down development and selling gas in the future) may depend on the country's projected domestic gas consumption. In addition, the exporting country will surely consider the strategic value of maintaining hydrocarbon reserves as a buffer against variability in its domestic needs or as a speculation on the prospect of much higher prices in the future. Generally speaking, the interest of a host country with uncommitted gas reserves is to maximise the realisable economic and strategic value of its reserves through development and implementation of a long-term energy plan.

The concept of value, of course, has many dimensions. The most common criterion of value is net present value (NPV). However, many of the assumptions that underlie the making of an NPV calculation involve highly subjective judgements about the world as it is today and the world as it may be tomorrow. For example, NPV depends on choosing discount rates to evaluate cash flows over time. The choice of discount rates over time is a subjective decision relating to political stability and economic strength. If a country's main exports are oil and gas, the country's credit capacity is vulnerable to changes in the market price for oil and gas and the discount rate attached to cash flows dependent on the country's credit must be considered carefully. Decisions reached today might need to be altered 10 years from now because relevant numerical assumptions have changed radically. For instance, a major downward trend in a country's credit rating may suddenly cause projects to be postponed, not expanded or not extended.

The role of gas in transformation of a consuming economy must be studied. Rate of conversion of inefficient coal-fuelled power plants is of great importance, coupled with the policy choice of what fuel should be used by new power generation capacity. Investment in gas-handling infrastructure is a question of particular concern to developing nations which have an opportunity to leapfrog the consequences of the type of fuel choices made in earlier times by developed countries. In order to determine what gas infrastructure should be built and at what speed, many policy questions must be understood, answered and linked:

(1)   what industrial energy needs will be;
(2)   energy pricing and subsidies;
(3)   import tariffs;
(4)   energy transmission tariffs;
(5)   ownership (especially regarding foreign ownership);
(6)   privatisation;
(7)   perceived need for national monopolies;
(8)   external pressures to open markets;
(9)   multilateral pressures;
(10) capital market demands; and
(11) consumer preferences.

National industrial policy approaches of two LNG importers are presented in Figures 7.4.2A and 7.4.2B.

7.4.3   Geopolitical Considerations

An increase in cross-border flow of gas in large quantities is necessary for the growth of the LNG market. Gas can move either in pipelines or, transformed into liquid, in ships. Both exporters and importers of natural gas must consider the nature of dependencies, and the long-term nature of dependencies, that will be created as a pipeline project or an LNG project is carried forward. The three dependencies which are important are:

(1)   contract dependence;
(2)   transit risk; and
(3)   form dependence.

Figure 7.4.2A   The Strategy of Japan

---

1. Natural gas imports (all in the form of LNG) are handled by well-established, creditworthy, large regional utilities.
    a. Electric utilities.
    b. Gas utilities.

2. The Japanese government encourages tariff stability and indirect support. No use of sovereign guarantees is necessary. The support consists of:
    a. Government lending to LNG export projects delivering LNG to Japan.
    b. Support of Japanese consortia for risk-sharing.
    c. Support for Japanese control of more LNG shipping.

3. There is no foreign participation in strategic gas infrastructure such as LNG terminals or gas transmission pipelines.

4. Risk reduction tactics by Japanese companies:
    a. Control transportation of LNG to Japan.
    b. Investment in upstream gas production for LNG export projects.
    c. Creation of consortia to share and spread risk.
    d. Purchase of LNG from multiple sources:
        i.   Indonesia
        ii.   Malaysia
        iii. Alaska
        iv.   Qatar
        v.   Abu Dhabi
        vi.   Brunei
        vii. Australia.
    e. Negotiation for access to expansion potential of sources with large gas reserves, sources with low production costs and sources with low political risk:
        i.   Indonesia
        ii.   Malaysia
        iii. Brunei
        iv.   Australia
        v.   Qatar
        vi.   Abu Dhabi.
    f. Pooling and sharing of LNG supply among buyers in event of supply interruption.

Figure 7.4.2B   The Strategy of France

---

1. Natural gas import (both LNG and pipeline gas) and gas transmission
    are consolidated in a state company: Gaz de France (GdF).
    a. GdF controls the LNG import terminals.
    b. GdF, as LNG buyer, controls some LNG shipping. The LNG
        sellers, Algeria and Nigeria, control some LNG shipping.
    c. GdF sells the gas to users internally in France.
    d. GdF is able to finance LNG investment in its own name in
        international markets.

2. The French government provides tariff stability to support GdF. There
    is no foreign participation in LNG terminals. The state controls
    supply strategy. No sovereign guarantee is used.

3. France has contracted multiple sources of gas, with multiple transit
    options.
    a. Pipeline:
        i.   Norway
        ii.   Netherlands
        iii. United Kingdom
        iv.   Russia
        v.   Algeria.
    b. LNG by ship:
        i.   Algeria
        ii.   Nigeria.

4. French companies control liquefaction technology, and have
    capability of building liquefaction plants, LNG terminals and LNG
    ships. French state oil companies participate in LNG export projects
    and development of gas reserves in exporting countries.

5. The French government supported Algerian LNG price stability
    (in the mid-1970s).

7.4.3.1   Contract Dependence

Contract dependence occurs, particularly in the case of LNG, because
there is not an active spot market of dependable size. LNG trade is based
on a long-term contract relationship between buyer and seller. If supply is
not available by accident or by intent, there will be an unsatisfied need in
the buyer which can only be met by switching fuels, if technically possible,
or by spot LNG purchases (perhaps). If cargo is refused or not paid for, the

seller has a cash flow interruption and an immediate need to sell the commodity but no assurance of a ready market.

7.4.3.2 Transit Risk

Transit risk exists for trade by both pipeline and LNG. It is more pronounced in the case of pipeline because the pipeline has a fixed route and an increase in the capacity of the pipeline is still dominated by the same route risk. Furthermore, the route risk is an additive risk because interruptions can occur at any point in a pipeline. Therefore, each political jurisdiction (or zone of physical control or risk) on the route contributes a quantum of risk. A pipeline gas seller is dependent on his gas buyer and shares the same concern about pipeline transit risk. In that sense, the concern is symmetrical. If the seller has other buyers or if the buyer can switch to other fuels or other sources of gas, the reliances on each other may not be symmetrical. Although LNG ships generally go through international waters, many of the key trades involve transit of choke points controlled by one or two countries. For example, Middle East gas must transit the Malacca Straits to reach Far East markets economically. Middle East gas must transit the Suez Canal to reach Mediterranean and northern Europe markets because the passage around the Cape of Good Hope is grossly uncompetitive. The transit risk for LNG shipping is also different in that it is modular. If any part of a pipeline is cut, the buyers downstream from the cut surely are without gas. In the case of LNG, the loss of one ship does not mean the loss of other ships. Gas trade can continue, especially because most LNG projects maintain some reserve shipping capacity.

Aside from the parties directly involved in a proposed LNG trade, others may take an interest in the long-term economic and political commitments. For example, throughout mid-1997, the United States sought to delay the economic integration of Iran into world markets and tried to prevent contracting and financing of Iranian LNG and gas pipeline deals. As another example, multilateral lending institutions supporting use of clean fuels have created pressure on their borrowers to buy and use gas. These are examples of unilaterally and multilaterally imposed policy which can affect the prospects of a particular LNG trade.

7.4.3.3 Form Dependence

Form dependence refers to the inability of infrastructure to adjust instantaneously to fuels whose utility requires different infrastructure. For example, Romania depends on piped natural gas for over 40 per cent of its primary energy. It cannot switch overnight to fuel oil utilisation. The delivery means and storage do not exist. A switch to liquid fuels results in less use of gas infrastructure and requires development of adequate liquid fuel infrastructure. If the power sector uses much LNG, the infrastructure required for liquid fuels to be a credible back-up will need to be substantial.

Reduction of political risk and economic risk go hand-in-hand with reduction of physical supply risk. Creation of supply options obviously diversifies risk and is an integral strategy of all LNG buyers. The future participation of multilateral development institutions in LNG infrastructure finance, especially in emerging markets such as India and China, will also be a discipline on government contract performance, whether on the seller or the buyer side. The co-ordination of LNG strategy with fundamental national policy is inevitable when the LNG represents a significant portion of a buyer's base-load energy requirements. Thus Japan and Korea have announced that LNG shipping will be reserved for themselves. India has wavered in its attempt to act similarly, as various Indian commercial and political groups struggle over whether domestic policies should favour opening or closing markets. France, Italy and Taiwan each face their own policy struggles. France and Taiwan have also not opened key LNG infrastructure to foreign ownership and participation; Italy is considering it. Whether these policies can be sustained in the face of pressure to open markets remains to be seen.

7.4.4   Financial Market Capacity

Each LNG project represents a variety of risks, all of which must be considered by the project's sources of finance. The willingness of each source of finance to support the construction and operation of the project depends on analysis of economic and political factors as well as that capital source's own strategic directions. Today's LNG export project calls for the following types of capital:

(1)   non-cash support in terms of natural gas supply contracts and access to existing infrastructure such as pipelines, harbours and terminals;

(2)   cash, for construction of the project, for required debt and operating reserves and for working capital;

(3)   insurance capacity, on standby to cover cash needs created by events; and

(4)   performance guarantees by both vendors and operators.

The capital can come from:

(1)   international oil and utility companies as developers;

(2)   the host country;

(3)   trading companies as developers;
(4)   buyers who are willing to integrate upstream into supply investment;
(5)   commercial banks;
(6)   capital markets (US Rule 144a bond issues, for example);
(7)   export credit agencies;
(8)   national development banks;
(9)   national strategic import funds;
(10) vendor guarantees;
(11) insurance markets; and
(12) multilateral institutions.

Each of these financing sources has a strategic plan which will govern the amount of investment in the LNG industry. Each is likely to have country risk limits, industry risk limits, limits to the term of lending risk, required rates of return, objectives in relationship development and maintenance and objectives in terms of increasing the number of parties with whom they do business. There is a manpower constraint. Sources of finance must develop enough expertise not only in general LNG industry issues, but also on a specific LNG project. Advancing into serious project evaluation requires allocation of scarce time and money. The speed with which an LNG project can be evaluated will vary from institution to institution.

Insurance coverage is a little-understood, but important, aspect of international project development. Construction risk, political risk, property risk, liability risk and business interruption risk; all of these can be handled by insurance markets. Often, insurance is better than direct finance as a way to solve a problem. If one were to define the concept of insurance in the broadest sense, performance guarantees by vendors could be regarded as a form of insurance.

The enormous financial turmoil and credit problems in Asia, particularly during 1997, may affect the LNG market for many years, creating the perception that certain seller and buyer credit risks are higher. This may increase LNG project cost of capital, thus affecting the economic competitiveness of LNG as well as the ability of a project to complete financing at all.

7.5   COMPETITION, COOPERATION AND COMPARATIVE ADVANTAGE

Competition and comparative advantage are complementary concepts. In order to win (however defined) in competition, an advantage usually has to be created and converted into a successful outcome. Competitors must be identified, studied and assessed. Needs of other parties, near- and long-term, must be understood.

The criteria for success in LNG depend on one's viewpoint. Normal financial measures include profit, cash flow, NPV and cost per million British thermal units. However, there are additional non-financial criteria which are also important:

(1) beneficial relationships;
(2) contract renewal potential;
(3) portfolio balance of risks.

To put together an LNG project is to achieve alignment of multiple interests on the seller side and buyer side at one point in time. However, this alignment of interests must be accomplished in a dynamic environment in which other LNG projects are trying to accomplish the same goal with participants from the same small universe. Most existing LNG projects have overlaps of consortium members. In the Pacific LNG market, for example, most of the sellers have Shell as a partner. Where Shell goes, often Mitsubishi goes. On the buyer side, Japan and Korea are the bulk of the market; inevitably LNG sellers have to deal with the same Japanese utility buyers or KGC (as purchaser for all Korean demand). On the other hand, established buyers can choose to deal with existing sellers or to bless new sellers—the market is not symmetrical in negotiation or business power. Whether this will be changed by growth in demand and the appearance of more buyers remains to be seen.

The complete unhooking of LNG pricing from oil pricing is far away. In terms of the logic of what fuels should be competing with LNG, the only market competitors are liquid hydrocarbons derived from oil or gas. Due to the nature of energy consumption, infrastructure inflexibility and fuel contracts, efficient and quick fuel switching between high-quality liquid fuels and gas cannot take place in all uses. Therefore, a market may not have the structural ability instantly to take advantage of changes in relative prices of liquid or gas fuels.

7.5.1 Complementing Other Fuels

LNG competes with other forms of energy. Yet LNG in the product inventory of a multifuel energy user may have contract characteristics that round out a fuel cost portfolio. LNG must be bought on a basis of long-term relatively fixed quantities, with pricing volatility inherent in the pricing formula according to negotiated terms. Oil is typically not purchased in large base-load quantities on such a basis. Petroleum products such as naphtha, LPG and diesel have varying rates of correlation with the pricing of crude oil. Coal, due to its relatively low energy density and solid nature, presents logistical problems for rapid fuel switching.

7.5.2   Competition with Energy Conservation

Although energy conservation is considered generally a most effective form of energy investment, it does not necessarily hurt prospects for LNG. The real question is whether LNG has a role in the energy mix of a user or nation. Should gas substitute for coal or for oil? Is gas a peak demand fuel (which is not attractive for LNG) or a fuel whose use is more suited to level utilisation as base load?

7.5.3   Choosing Not to Compete

Choosing not to be involved with LNG is itself a strategic decision.

For a potential sponsor, choosing to avoid LNG would generally be decided on critical mass issues: the company does not have enough money, international skills or markets; the front end effort is too large; and the outcome is uncertain. At the end of the 1990s, it appears that many oil companies and trading companies want to be participants in the LNG market, even if they are not involved in active LNG projects now. It seems the contractually assured long-term cash flow, revenue and profit of LNG sales are very attractive components of a long-term business plan. For a potential buyer, rejecting LNG is often a pure cost issue if the intended use is electric power generation. Most markets do permit a variety of fuels for power generation; the use of clean fuels to save the environment, even if more expensive, has not yet taken hold in full force, due simply to the lack of economic incentives on a broad scale internationally.

For vendors, the issue is simple: if no significant cost or safety advantage can be proven for the vendor's products, the only way to win business is through politics. If contract awards are not profitable, then the cost of staying in the business is not worth it. Special cases may exist where a government wants the vendor to remain in business. Then the economic analysis is really that of pricing opportunity cost; does the government wish to subsidise the maintenance of the industrial capability? For lenders and lawyers, having LNG clients is simply another line of business. Not having an LNG practice probably does not hurt the ability to win other energy business; having an LNG practice probably does not attract customers who are active in other energy businesses.

7.5.4 Comparative Advantage

Inherent advantage should be differentiated from *created advantage*, and the sustainability of advantage should be considered.

Inherent advantage can include:

(1) location of gas reserves;
(2) quality of gas reserves;
(3) size of gas reserves;
(4) political relations;
(5) form of government/business cooperation;
(6) credit rating/lower cost of capital;
(7) control of proven technology;
(8) historic cost position; and
(9) physical infrastructure in seller or buyer favouring natural gas

Created advantage can include:

(1) new technology;
(2) new political factors;
(3) windfall cost reduction;
(4) new gas reserves;
(5) new alliances; and
(6) new business combinations.

7.5.5 Horizontal Integration

The horizontal integration practised by oil company sellers does not create advantage except by increasing numbers of trained, experienced managers and by deepening relations with buyers. Being a sponsor in several projects that compete with each other for markets can even be detrimental if it raises issues of conflict of interest between allegiance to each host country and its project.

Horizontal integration by a buyer would probably be most likely in the form of taking shares in power generation projects or gas distribution systems outside the home market. This form of reducing aggregate business risk is much too recent for its consequences to be apparent. The revenue and risk diversification implications are obvious; however, the argument that spreading expertise and capital offers highest risk-adjusted return on investment has yet to be justified in substantial long-term results.

7.5.6 Vertical Integration

Some LNG export projects have integrated contract structures in which the project partners share all the way from the well-head to the receiving terminal of the buyer. Other LNG export projects break up the contractual operation into production, liquefaction and transportation. A strategic planner must look at the contracting strategies of the host country and of the existing LNG consortium to understand what might be possible and what the consequences would be of participation or even of negotiation.

The new form of vertical integration is the link between electric power generation by an IPP and LNG as a fuel. The argument for such linkage is the economic analysis which suggests that electricity produced by an efficient gas-fuelled combined cycle gas turbine can be competitive to electricity produced by other fuels in that country, at the same time improving air quality. The principal argument against such linkage is that incremental power generation capacity should be based on taking advantage of the cheapest fuel at a given moment in time. In that respect, LNG, purchased on long-term take-or-pay contracts, may be more expensive than the spot price of liquid fuels at certain periods in market cycles.

To emphasise upstream or downstream investment (or both) is a perennial strategic question for the gas division of the oil company or for a proactive buyer. Participation at each point in the activity and value chains has implications in terms of economic benefit, economic risk and volatility, access to strategic information, building of management capability, access to options on future participation and creation of partnerships which offer expanded opportunities.

7.5.7 Technology

Technology is not usually included in the concept of vertical integration, but one should link technology to the role of project operator in order to understand the control potential. An example would be the struggle between Shell, designated as liquefaction plant operator, and Exxon over Exxon access to Shell liquefaction plant technology in the planned, but unrealised, Venezuelan Cristobal Colon LNG export project of the early 1990s.

Whenever an LNG project partner is designated as developer of upstream gas supply, as operator of the LNG plant or as operator of the LNG ships, valuable control and economic rights have been awarded. Oil companies profit from the operating contracts they get in their LNG projects. That is why the position of project leader is very important.

From the viewpoint of the national government of the buyer, benefit can be achieved by buyer participation as a sponsor in the seller consortium. In this way, the buyer will be extending its experience beyond its borders, expanding markets and creating the possibility of directing procurement to buyer-country vendors.

7.5.8   Financial Integration

When a buyer integrates vertically into LNG supply, the buyer is hedging its cost of energy. The share of profit made on the LNG sale mitigates the expense of an LNG price increase paid by that buyer. In addition, the buyer gains valuable knowledge because there is a great deal of economic transparency in LNG seller–buyer relationships when the buyer is able to participate in both the purchase and sale of the LNG.

7.5.9   Cooperation (Even Between Competitors)

The history of the LNG industry is a history of cooperation, as is often required for major energy projects worldwide. The form of cooperation and its extent have varied, but the fundamental characteristics of cooperation remain constant.

The critical mass of capital required to plan, develop and implement an LNG export project is of such large size, compared to the balance sheets of companies and countries, that risk-sharing has been absolutely necessary. The aggregation of technical, marketing and political critical mass has historically also required joining the capabilities of several companies to the capability of the host government.

On the seller side, all existing LNG export projects with the exception of Algeria are consortia of the host country as resource owner plus international oil companies and trading companies as project development partners. Risk-sharing occurs on the buyer side also. The buyer is either a national utility representing all demand in a country or an actual or quasi-consortium of major utility companies. For example, KGC shares risk by having Korea Electric as its principal gas customer. For vendors, the political, technical and economic challenges of responding credibly to large, complex LNG tender requirements typically engender vendor consortia of tried and tested partnerships.

In order for cooperation to take place, prospective consortium members must be credible to their prospective partners. The LNG world in the 1970s and 1980s encompassed a small number of interested participants with experience. In the 1990s the fast growth of the world gas industry and the rapid expansion of cross-border trade in natural gas, particularly in LNG, have attracted new participants to the industry. Every major oil company has studied LNG and most have proposed development of LNG projects. Major electric and gas utilities worldwide, especially those in the United States, have also joined the game in an effort to link fuel supply to their IPP and gas distribution projects abroad. The potential for emerging economies to become viable long-term importers of natural gas has materialised. China and India are seriously assessing the development of LNG imports. Inevitably, they will turn their attention upstream and become participants in the export projects from which they intend to source LNG.

Cooperation, therefore, is necessary even though it requires parties with incompletely aligned interests to live together with each other for many years.

7.5.10 Cooperation and Competition within an LNG Export Project

The balancing of interests among participants in an LNG export project is a delicate act which may not necessarily be stable forever. Project shares can be readjusted or can be nationalised by the host government. The first question is who should be partnering with the host country. The nature of the partnership also has to be determined—it may be segmented into separate consortia for each function (upstream gas field development, liquefaction, trading and transport) or it may be an integrated project, with one consortium participating in all functions. LNG development strategy will depend first on the host government's long-term resource exploitation policies and its long-term view on appropriate strategic partners. If gas relationships already exist, the choice of LNG partner may be more limited and not wholly subject to the host government's sole decision. The strategic dilemma is mirrored in the oil company's need to choose host countries carefully, as platforms for long-term market positions, with one major exception. Only Shell has succeeded in being almost everywhere that supplies LNG to Japan.

Vigorous competition and intrigue can take place. The growing sophistication of host countries has been demonstrated in the trend towards opening up the prospect of LNG partnership to newcomers, not only to original LNG partners. For instance, in Qatar, the Ras Laffan project was Mobil's reward for coming in, after British Petroleum's withdrawal, to make the Qatargas project achievable. However, the government of Qatar created further LNG competition and interest by negotiating with Enron to establish LNG production before Ras Laffan project volumes were fully developed and marketed.

A host country with gas reserves wants access to markets, adequate supply of capital at the most competitive rate and partners with capital and technical capacity adequate to serve the long-term needs of export projects both in the development stage and in the operating stage. The political relationships brought by partners are often of critical importance. Gas-exporting countries, particularly in the Middle East, depend explicitly or implicitly on the military protection of the United States and on the economic demand of a few energy consuming countries, particularly Japan.

7.6 POSSIBILITIES FOR CREATING CHANGE

7.6.1 The Importance of Time and Timing

In many businesses a preemptive announcement can prevent a competitor from initiating a project. The same thing is true in the LNG world. The announcement that an LNG project is under development can slow down the marketing and financing of another LNG project. This is particularly true if a large amount of natural gas, easy to produce and cheap to bring to market, is announced as ready for development. Such a statement will slow down buyer willingness to deal with other projects which are more expensive. Project timing is also vulnerable to the pace of pricing negotiations. There is a natural ceiling on the price a seller can expect; that ceiling is the most recent contract concluded by the market to which it is selling. An LNG major such as Shell or Mobil may be involved in several export projects with several different host governments. The oil company must worry that its proposed selling price and terms in one project may be undercut by the pricing and timing it proposes in another project.

The timing of an LNG project is very important. The ability of a project to commence deliveries at a certain time can be crucial to its marketability. The in-service date depends, of course, on lead time issues being solved. On the seller's side, major lead time issues include:

(1) development of host country policy for exploitation of hydro-carbon resources;
(2) host country negotiation and execution of development and partnership agreements with foreign partners;
(3) project organisation, including the sequential activities of feasibility study, project formation, project financing and project construction;
(4) satisfaction of capital market needs in order to ensure availability of financing.

On the buyer side, lead time issues include:

(1)   reaching a decision on long-term LNG import needs;
(2)   planning and construction of any necessary additions to LNG receiving and storage infrastructure, pipelines and electric power generation plants;
(3)   development of legal, accounting and financial sector policies that, in conjunction with appropriate energy sector policies, can persuade the international financial markets to provide funds to build an LNG chain;
(4)   reaching agreement with national authorities and other utilities on various matters of risk-sharing and informal or formal financial support;
(5)   assessment of the various LNG sellers and development of a negotiation strategy for each one.

The greatest source of change, favourable or unfavourable, in cost is still cost of capital, which can be greatly influenced by timing. The shape of the yield curve and the magnitude of fixed rates have a permanent effect on a project's cost and competitiveness. Often market timing of sales will not be at the best point during interest rate cycles. Yet if a gas sales and purchase contract has been signed, the project may have to seek financing from financial markets at that time, even if interest rates are high.

7.6.2   The Creation of Markets

The creation of an LNG market depends on cooperation between seller and buyer. In many countries the true bearer of LNG cost is the consumer on whom ultimate energy prices are imposed. To a certain extent the electric or gas utility which is the nominal buyer of the LNG is relieved of fuel price risk because it can often be passed through to the consumer. The utility is more concerned with stability, security and timeliness of fuel supply. Therefore, its interests may be complementary to those of the LNG seller.

Creation of LNG markets takes place in various ways. The historical record, especially in England, France, Italy, Japan and Korea, highlights the necessity of a strong central government policy. To undertake the initial economic and political risk of receiving LNG and using natural gas requires governmental support and political will. This will was manifested in low-key fashion by state gas monopolies: British Gas (which at the time was not yet privatised); Gaz de France; SNAM in Italy; the major Japanese utilities guided by the Ministry of Trade and Industry (MITI) in Japan; and KGC in Korea. The import of LNG requires policy on permits, fuel pricing, electricity generation technology, land use, consumer subsidies, industrial policy and financing policy. Sellers of LNG can stimulate markets to import LNG with technological and commercial proposals.

The natural desire of sellers to control key infrastructure can be a point of dissension with the prospective buyer. In certain developing markets, foreign and private sector ownership of liquefied petroleum gas (LPG) distribution systems is permitted. However, the idea of foreign ownership of natural gas distribution infrastructure and LNG receiving infrastructure strikes a far different chord. Local distribution companies in most countries outside the United States and certain countries in Eastern Europe are under government control. Clearly, if a country is on a steep growth curve, whoever has control of the gas distribution system has some influence on the economic growth of the country, as well as an option on the economic rents to be gained from satisfying any increase in energy demand. From a national patrimony point of view, one is selling one's market too easily if local distribution company monopolies are privatised too soon. A long-term appetite for gas cannot be created if the economics run counter to the long-term development policies of the country. The long-term utility policies and energy policies of the country must signal that LNG is an economically, politically and managerially viable choice.

Some international energy companies have tried to create LNG markets by creating independent power producer markets. The linkage of IPPs to LNG has been proposed, but not yet achieved. The famous Dabhol project of Enron in India did not plan to use LNG in its startup phase; LNG is the fuel option to be provided later, if feasible.

Oligopolistic behaviour has been inherent in the structure of the seller side of the LNG industry at the end of the 1990s. The prevalence of the same few foreign oil companies and trading companies in the proven LNG export projects tends to homogenise their behaviour. Trading companies do not want to undercut their good relationships with oil companies by taking extreme positions in new projects. On the other hand, the host country inclination to achieve project success forces foreign participants to consider what must be done to make a new project succeed. All this is against the backdrop of the increasing sophistication and experience of the host country partners who are unconcerned about the relationships that an oil company partner may have in another country.

7.6.3 The Effect of New Entrants

As more buyers and sellers exist in the market simultaneously looking for transactions, oligopoly, monopoly and monopsony will become harder to sustain. There will be greater variety of contractual relationships and terms. There may be less back-to-back matching of risks along the contract chain. Those already in the market and committed to contracts will contend with the advantages and disadvantages of embedded economics and relationships. New entrants will face credibility hurdles. Financial markets and sponsors will choose to bear more risk in more varied forms. One paradox of the seller search for new business is that the emerging markets such as China, India, Pakistan, Turkey and Brazil, whose credit ratings are not prime, may ask for, and receive, contract concessions that traditional slow growth prime credits such as Japan may not have obtained. The sponsor equity at risk is, of course, betting that the growth potential of the new markets will reward them in the long term.

7.6.4 The Economic Impact of Technology

The possibility of inventions and increased manufacturing efficiency is high, but the cost reduction implications are small. Basic laws of thermodynamics cannot be changed; liquefaction cannot get much more efficient. Ships can get bigger and can be propelled more efficiently, but the order of magnitude of savings possible is small (after netting out shore infrastructure investment needed to accommodate larger ships). The possibility of a revolution in relative fuel economics remains a possibility: efficient gas-to-liquids technologies could create a large supply of clean fuel able to threaten sales of LNG and pipeline gas, if buyer form dependence can be dealt with.

7.7 CASE STUDIES

The following case studies are not meant to provide a history of LNG project development. They are not complete descriptions of projects or situations. They are expositions of concepts that are illustrated by actual circumstances. In coming years these concepts will continue to be important although actual circumstances of application will change.

7.7.1 Policy Formation as Condition Precedent: China

The future and timing of LNG project activity in China is inextricably tied to many policy decisions that would have to be made concurrently. As of late 1997 the policy development in all sectors looked as though it would mature by late 1998 and it seemed that an LNG development policy might then be recommended and approved.

In 1996, the People's Republic of China officially began serious study of LNG and what it would mean to China to import and use LNG. On the one hand, it could draw from an abundance of experience that other countries and many companies had in developing the LNG industry. On the other hand China at that time, and for at least the next decade, would be undergoing rapid changes in its political, social, economic, legal and financial structures and in its scale of transactions with the outside world. An essential element of LNG as it has been known to date is the requirement for viable long-term operating and contractual relationships and economic flows. Therefore, the question for China, as well as for those who sought to do business with it, was what Chinese policy development and implementation were necessary so that LNG trade could develop.

One fundamental issue was the extent of China's long-term commitment to the use of natural gas. To answer that question, a complex set of inter-related issues had to be considered:

— What would be the highest and best use of gas by the Chinese economy?
— How much gas would be used by China at a given price level?
— Where would the gas come from?
— For how many years could a given source supply gas?
— How much gas should come from a given source?
— What kind of infrastructure would be needed to import LNG and use gas and how much would it cost?
— Over what period of time would the development of a gas market and gas infrastructure have to take place?
— What contingency plans were required to handle natural gas supply interruption?

The creation of the demand side of a gas market was only part of the problem. The supply policy faced much uncertainty also due to the proliferation of supply possibilities for China. Substantial gas deposits were being proven in inconvenient inland areas of China. Smaller gas deposits were being proven offshore in Chinese waters. Large quantities of gas in East Russia were seeking markets. Gas in Central Asian republics such as Kazakhstan and Turkmenistan was also searching for customers. The possibility existed that gas controlled by nearby countries Malaysia and Indonesia could be supplied to China either as LNG or via long-distance pipeline. Long-distance LNG suppliers such as Qatar were interested in developing long-term sales to China. All of these gas supply options had to compete with the changing economics of Chinese energy supply as distribution bottlenecks and pricing to world norms were starting to make their effects felt. The rapid rate of economic reform in China and the gradual privatisation of state companies created an environment of uncertainty as to the nature of gas purchasers in China. The creditworthiness, focus of business and stability of offtakers are important to LNG financing. Restructured state electricity generation and transmission companies could be considered creditworthy buyers of LNG, except that major issues relating to structure of ownership and tariff policy had yet to be decided.

The nature of foreign participation in the Chinese economy was undergoing tremendous scrutiny in the mid-1990s. Most nations have policies aimed at retaining control of key or strategic infrastructure. In China, participation in energy distribution activities had been prohibited to foreigners. In any case, build/own/transfer (BOT) transaction policies and law were being revised by the Chinese government. At the same time, China was under pressure to open up its economy to foreigners if it wanted membership in the World Trade Organization (WTO). A policy decision about what rate of return to permit foreigners for specific infrastructure investments was also under study. In order to maintain and increase the flow of foreign investment and participation in development of China, banking and investment laws were being changed. Chinese internal securities markets were being regulated in order to mobilise domestic and foreign capital on behalf of investment needs of Chinese companies. Laws and regulations relating to secured and unsecured lending, leasing and other types of financing would have to be put in place.

In order to discipline the decision-making about natural gas, the State Planning Commission (SPC) requested China National Offshore Oil Corporation (CNOOC) to study the import of LNG and how to do it. The results of that study and its recommendations would be incorporated into the SPC master plan for Chinese energy supply. The principal policy issue, of course, was where to aim Chinese medium- and long-term energy demand and energy supply. Should coal continue to be emphasised? Should a shift to less polluting natural gas and clean liquid petroleum products be encouraged? How much increase in the unit cost of energy should China plan to pay to reap the benefits of a cleaner economy? How much could China pay for imported energy over time? China was becoming a net importer of oil for the first time; in other words, China's energy self-sufficiency was now ending. In the future, China would be a major buyer of oil and gas in international markets. Preliminary studies had indicated that as much as 80 per cent of natural gas imports, whether by pipeline or as LNG, should be allocated to electricity generation. Of course, electric power generation policy required further consideration, especially since a national electricity grid was under development. The pricing of electricity and of the underlying fuel needed to generate the electricity were fundamental concerns.

One important issue in national economic strategy was how to maximise Chinese buying power in international energy markets. In order for China to consolidate LNG buying power, one designated entity would have to handle China's LNG purchases and LNG development strategy. This raised the issue of central government authority versus authority devolved to provincial governments and economic entities. For instance, the Guangdong provincial government wanted to proceed with a Shell-led integrated LNG import and electricity generation scheme. The central government did not approve the project, pending review and development of national LNG policy. The leadership of China has been faced with the task of promoting rapid development while maintaining economic progress and political order. Of paramount importance is to understand the consequences of decisions. In the economic arena a decision to import and use LNG depends on other major policy decisions both prior to, and simultaneous with, the decision itself to import LNG. Developed countries with established legal and economic structures that interact with world markets have an easier and quicker route to establishing LNG imports. China had to create context; it would have a chance to avoid mistakes, but it also would have a chance to make big mistakes.

For China to make a decision, it had to feel that it had enough knowledge to do so. Thus the bureaucracy had to gather knowledge and educate its members. The process of gathering data and ideas itself is fraught with perceived risk, as the sources of information have biases which must be understood in order to understand the true worth of the idea or datum. Even among major oil companies, significant variation in LNG business approaches could be seen. China also wanted to maximise the value of its commercial leverage. Thus learning how to use political muscle in LNG matters and in overall trade and external relations policies would be a key concern. This learning would take time. Testing the market would take time. However, China knew that it, along with India, would be the future of LNG market growth, and that the market would come to it. China had also been patient and long-term-oriented and careful in its actions. Only time would tell.

7.7.2   Finance Strategy: Mobil Corporation and the Financing of the Ras Laffan Project in Qatar

Mobil Corp.'s long-term strategic objectives have been made clear in a succession of annual reports and other business statements since the mid-1990s. Among the key long-term efforts is development and expansion of the company's position in natural gas, particularly LNG. It is well known that during flat periods in the world oil market in the 1980s a major portion of Mobil's worldwide net profit derived from its participation in the Arun LNG project in Indonesia. Mobil felt that its LNG expertise and credentials could anchor a long-term leading role in the LNG industry and could provide decades of stable revenue and profit flows from LNG sales made on long-term contracts. Another long-term Mobil Corp. policy is to maintain its high credit rating and to maintain ample financing flexibility and capacity. The company has recognised that many important oil and gas industry projects require both large equity investments and use of the corporate balance sheet for varying periods of time. However, minimisation of balance sheet use and of contingent liabilities are normal goals for all corporations. Mobil had to choose the proper countries on which to base a long-term gas strategy. Choices were necessary on the sell side as well as the buy side. With which gas-owning countries should Mobil develop a deep relationship and with which countries on the buy side should Mobil cultivate offtake? Of course, the governments and state companies in those countries also would have to be interested in Mobil and Mobil's business objectives.

In execution of its long-term gas strategy, Mobil made the decision to become the lead foreign partner in the Qatari government's development of LNG export projects. This meant that Mobil became the largest foreign shareholder in the Qatargas project and the largest foreign shareholder in the Ras Laffan project. Because of the multi-partner project organisation and Japanese companies being the sole buyers , the Qatargas project decision-making and project development were complex and lengthy. In contrast, the initial development of the Ras Laffan project had Mobil as the only foreign partner of Qatar and thus project development was faster. The Ras Laffan project faced different market conditions and different tactical risks than the Qatargas project. The only viable markets near-term for the project were what at that time were regarded as the usual first class Far East buyers: Japan, Korea and Taiwan. However, Japan's interests were focused on the Qatargas project and Taiwan had purchased enough LNG for the moment. The Ras Laffan project was faced with Korea as the only viable and interested buyer at the time, a difficult position for a seller. On the other hand, Korea was an active buyer which had to satisfy a mushrooming natural gas demand, a need to diversify supply sources and a need to develop a position in major Middle East LNG project possibilities. In addition, the Korean establishment wanted in the near term to find a well-advanced LNG project into which Korean investment could be made to build Korean experience inside LNG export projects.

Therefore, the Ras Laffan project focused on closing an LNG sale and purchase agreement (SPA) with KGC for a quantity and term adequate to support finance of the project. Collateral goals were to lower the average cost of finance, lengthen the term of finance and maximise the amount of non-recourse finance, all the while aiming to meet project schedules. Mobil's management focused very early on how to access capital markets for a bond issue rather than rely solely on bank lending. The process issues involved in pursuing that strategy included:

(1) how to prepare to tap capital markets;
(2) obtaining sufficient lending commitments from banks so that if a bond issue failed, there would be adequate bank debt available;

(3)   persuading the Qatari government that the capital markets finance strategy was feasible, should be supported and justifying the substantial disclosure required by bond rating agencies; and

(4)   appointing a competent financial adviser and arranger early in the development of the project(something which did not happen in Qatargas and probably slowed down that project's financing).

The competitive situation for Ras Laffan marketing continued to put pressure on the project schedule. The Oman LNG project was also courting the Koreans. The original SPA between Ras Laffan and KGC for 2.4 million tonnes per annum (mtpa) contained a floor price, upon which Mobil and the Qatar government were able to raise both bank debt and a successful placement of project finance bonds in capital markets because revenue flow was highly assured. When KGC indicated to Ras Laffan that it would be willing to double the quantity in the original contract, it insisted on elimination of the floor price provision. Oman's willingness to offer an SPA without a floor price compelled Ras Laffan to offer the same concession to Korea. Mobil and Qatar were faced with a quandary: how to maintain the credit rating of the project and its finances? Standard and Poor's threatened to reduce the bond rating below investment grade.

The Ras Laffan project, advised by Goldman Sachs in New York and London, eventually arrived at a solution which satisfied lenders in the capital markets while imposing a relatively small additional commitment on Mobil and none on Qatar. Mobil undertook to supply up to US$200 million to the project in case the price of oil, to which the LNG purchase price was indexed, declined to a low level (not realistically to be expected) such that the decline in project LNG revenue impeded debt service. In other words, Mobil took on a low-probability, capped contingent liability in order to preserve the credit rating and the availability of non-recourse capital markets funding. As a result:

(1)   Ras Laffan expanded its sales and preserved its financing;

(2)   Mobil and Qatar succeeded in opening up capital markets for long-term, lower-cost, non-recourse finance;

(3)   Mobil took a major step to deepen its long-term relationship and presence in Qatar, a major seller of LNG in coming years;

(4)   Mobil preserved its own credit rating and financed the Ras Laffan project with a total exposure of only its direct equity investment in the project and up to US$200 million contingent liability (which is likely to be considered a small risk by its auditors);

(5)   Mobil strengthened its LNG market presence and successfully diversified its long-term LNG portfolio.

7.7.3 Geopolitics of Gas: Turkey

Turkey faces the most complex geopolitical challenges that any sovereign state must resolve in regard to natural gas strategy. It is a significant importer and user of natural gas and it is geographically placed to be an important transit state. Political relationships with two major powers which are neighbouring states, Russia and Iran, are heavily influenced by energy politics. Turkish economic and political development depends on the prospect of admission to the European Union as well as on its bilateral relationship with the United States. Turkey must keep in mind that many western European countries differ from the United States in their approach to foreign policy towards Russia and Iran as well as towards Turkey. So what should Turkey do? It needs gas. It needs satisfactory relationships with Russia and Iran. It needs satisfactory relations with Europe and the United States, which it can't maintain if its foreign policy displeases them. It needs to develop economically.

As a major importer, Turkey faces the typical macro-economic challenge of growing energy imports and the need to determine energy mix and ensure energy security as much as possible. The Turkish commitment to import natural gas by pipeline and as LNG has produced the greatest rate of gas market growth in the world. It has also highlighted issues of energy security since most of its natural gas is imported from Russia by one pipeline which passes through the Ukraine, Romania and Bulgaria on its way to Turkey. Turkish dependence on Russian gas markets makes the government uncomfortable. The ability of consumers to switch to other fuels is limited. Therefore, maximum security of supply must be attained for the portion of gas demand which must not be left unsatisfied (so-called non-interruptible demand). In the past, Turkey thought that LNG ought to provide as much as 50 per cent of its gas supply as a counterbalance to dependence on Russian pipeline gas. The current growth in gas demand has exceeded forecasts. LNG, presently only from Algeria, represented only 20 per cent of supply in 1997. Turkey therefore has continued to pursue additional LNG imports as well as the development of two additional LNG import terminals to complement the existing terminal in service at Marmara Ereglisi.

The growth of the power generation sector also requires making fuel supply choices. The lack of electricity has frustrated export manufacturers which can earn hard currency revenue to pay for production costs such as electricity. Much of the additional power generation being proposed is based on gas as a fuel, and any necessary gas imports would usually require hard currency. Gas supply and gas import infrastructure have to be developed in parallel in order to achieve gas-fired power generation capacity.

Another revenue earner could be gas pipeline transit fees. Such a role as a transit state is obvious, given the location of gas and oil compared to where they could be marketed. Turkey represents a geographic transition between Europe and Asia and the Middle East. It was a front line for US containment of Russia and it is the south-east bulwark of the North Atlantic Treaty Organization (NATO). Pipelines across Turkey would link Asian and Middle Eastern supply to western Europe consumption, but would also give long-term prominence and inclusion in world markets to Iran and other countries. Central Asian Republics such as Turkmenistan need non-Russian access to markets for their gas. Russia knows that despite the terms of the 1936 Montreux Convention regarding right of free passage through the Bosphorus, Turkey controls the maritime traffic. Increased exports of oil and other hydrocarbon products out of the eastern Black Sea area would depend on transit through the Bosphorus, even if the projected Bulgaria–Greece harbour and pipeline system (to bypass the Bosphorus) were ever completed. The linkage of Iran and central Asia to the West via pipelines represents a major decision for the countries and financing institutions involved. Iranian access to markets, particularly, is a contentious issue between the United States and its European allies. Iranian gas supply is also a political problem for Turkey. The monopoly gas company of Russia, Gazprom, has been trying to achieve a significant role in the utilisation of gas in markets which depend heavily on supply of Russian gas. In fact, Gazprom signed various joint ventures with Botas, the state gas company of Turkey, in order to develop, in Turkey, Russian participation in gas-burning power plants fuelled by Russian gas, as well as to promote various trans-Black Sea and trans-Mediterranean pipeline projects.

In this context, Botas and the Turkish government Ministries were in detailed LNG purchase discussions with LNG project sponsors in Nigeria, Qatar, Yemen, Egypt and Norway. The credit foundation for all this import activity would naturally be the Turkish economy which had had great volatility in the late 1990s. Despite the below- investment grade rating of Turkish sovereign debt, most banks and governments still believe Turkey is a worthwhile long-term investment. Obviously, the availability of export credit from the United States and Europe would depend partly on political factors.

7.7.4 Emerging Markets: Pakistan

Pakistan is an example of an emerging market whose long-term promise may be enough to offset near-term economic problems. The market fundamentals are good if viewed in the most general terms. The population is large (133 million); there are large urban concentrations; substantial new electric generation capacity is required; substantial gas transmission infrastructure is already in place; there is gas industry expertise in the country. Furthermore, Pakistan is well located in relation to many sources of gas. In addition, economies of scale could be realised by joining its market demand with that of a neighbouring market: India.

The rosy view expressed in the foregoing paragraph must be tempered by certain realities. Pakistan is a poor country as measured by GDP *per capita*. Its fundamental trade position and balance of payments are weak and it depends heavily on imported energy and technology. Political unrest, corruption and consumer avoidance of payment represent significant cultural obstacles to the viability of businesses. The country has very little access to credit internationally and is heavily dependent on the International Monetary Fund (IMF), the World Bank and the ADB. The abilities of major electric utilities, particularly Karachi Electric Supply Corporation (KESC), to pay for fuel and electric power are questionable. The possibility of pipeline gas from Turkmenistan via Afghanistan clouds the market prospects for Pakistani import of LNG from Qatar or any other Middle East supplier. In addition, offshore pipeline supply from Qatar, Iran and Oman have also been proposed.

Government policy is not sufficiently developed to give comfort to LNG financiers and project developers. The economic underpinning for increase of gas sales would be electric power generation. The generally accepted view is that KESC cannot pay for electricity on time because consumers of electricity do not pay KESC on time. There is a technical problem of big line losses and there continues to be tremendous theft from electric lines.

At the end of 1997, the commitment of the government to pipeline gas purchases limited its strategic options. Reliance on substantial quantities of gas from Turkmenistan flowing through Afghanistan to Pakistan was chosen over the LNG option. From a transit security point of view, LNG is less risky for Pakistan but on paper the Turkmeni pipeline gas is cheaper, although the cost and availability of capital have not yet been confirmed by bank commitments. Whether banks will finance such a pipeline project remains to be seen. The uneasy political situation in Afghanistan has not made the pipeline any easier to consider. The fact that there are no substantial Pakistani gas purchasers who are highly rated by the credit rating agencies makes the finance problem even worse. However, for the time being, the Pakistani government's interest in the pipeline diminishes the credibility and, therefore, the likelihood of development of an LNG import project.

Whether a combination of Pakistani and Indian demand could create the purchase volume necessary to justify a pipeline project is not in doubt. The difficulty is finding the political will to cooperate on something that is clearly beneficial to both countries. In consequence, India has embarked on what appears to be a massive programme of LNG imports, trusting that the short distance to Gulf suppliers will reduce the delivered cost and make it competitive with that of politically difficult to achieve, long-distance pipeline gas. Thus Pakistan is forced to seek gas supply and finance on its own.

7.7.5   Growth in a Developed Market: Italy

When fundamental structural change occurs in the economy of a developed nation, what might be considered a mature gas market can show dynamic activity. Up to 1998, Italy has been a country of large state companies, state utility monopolies, undeveloped domestic capital markets and managed pricing. Italy in the future will have private utilities, competition in electric power generation and competition via the privatisation of fuel supply and logistics. More money will be raised in international capital markets; major foreign companies will team with newly unleashed Italian companies. The flexibility of the European gas grid and the developed status of Italian gas transmission and local distribution systems offer many opportunities for creation of natural gas competition through properly planned privatisation and reforms. The major areas of activity are all open: supply (whether by pipeline or as LNG), transmission and distribution; independent power plant development; and strategic alliances of all sorts.

The prospects for LNG in the Italian scene depend on progressing in one or both of two directions: establishment of additional Italian LNG terminals from which LNG can enter the Italian market or negotiation of LNG throughput at existing European LNG terminals, with swapping of LNG landed there for pipeline gas delivered at the Italian border. The last 10 years have seen bureaucratic tangles in Italy as the state electric utility, ENEL, tried to purchase Nigerian LNG directly, to be landed at a proposed ENEL import terminal which was unable to obtain construction permits. In the past, SNAM, the state natural gas subsidiary of ENI, the state hydrocarbon company, had previously monopolised all gas purchases and gas transmission for Italy. SNAM, seeking to be the import terminus for ENEL's Nigerian LNG, also failed to obtain import terminal construction permits. In order for an LNG import terminal to be built in Italy, either ENEL or SNAM would have to succeed in simultaneously overcoming local opposition to creation of terminal capacity and achieving a firm and credible LNG supply agreement. Non-Italian LNG import terminal options such as the proposed terminal on the Croatian island of Krk proved difficult to bring to reality. In addition, Gazprom's desire to access markets and cooperate with gas purchasers, together with Norwegian aggressiveness at marketing gas to Mediterranean consumers, added to the diversity of supply available through Italy's existing pipeline connections to the European gas grid. The privatisation of the power market affects the natural gas market. Long-term power purchase contracts are bankable only if the long-term purchasers represent viable sources of revenue. To ensure the strength of each link in an infrastructure chain is a well-known problem. Nonetheless, the Italian economy is bankable and a properly negotiated long-term power purchase agreement can give comfort to sellers of gas under long-term contracts. All aspects of the gas chain are likely to benefit from the market openings and activities in Italy.

7.7.6 Creation of Markets: Enron and the Dabhol Project in India

The Dabhol project, in the Indian state of Maharashtra, is one of the most famous, and notorious, infrastructure projects in recent history. As India opened up its economy in the early 1990s, major energy companies realised that new power and fuel supply projects could be profitable. Several immediate and major obstacles stood in the way of realizing the pot of gold at the end of the electricity rainbow. The often contradictory web of laws and rules governing development of business and infrastructure projects would have to be tamed. Indian tendencies towards protectionism would have to be moderated. The relationship of the central government to the individual states would have to be clarified and harmonised. Projects would have to survive the rough waters of Indian politics and the declining power of the Congress Party which had dominated Indian political life since independence. The questionable creditworthiness of the state electricity boards would need to be shored up by Indian sovereign guarantees. Yet India wished to develop. In order to do so, it needed to attract foreign capital.

In its worldwide marketing, Enron Corporation had publicly avowed its intent to become the first natural gas major, participating in every aspect of the natural gas industry everywhere, whether gas exploration and production, LNG, gas-fired power plants or pipeline distribution systems. Enron had ambitious market share goals in many countries. In the case of India, Enron wanted to be the first to establish a major gas–power position in India and to gain a preemptive position in gas markets. In proposing the Dabhol power plant, Enron sought to link an LNG project to it. Its theory was that the long-term steady LNG fuel demand of the Dabhol power plant would anchor long-term sales of LNG from an Enron LNG project in Qatar. In other words, two birds would be killed with one set of linked stones: Enron would enter both the LNG industry and Indian power generation and fuel supply in a big way. Even more than that, the LNG project would also allow Enron to penetrate other gas markets besides India. LNG demand from Israel and Jordan would be used as additional political and financial anchors for the Qatar LNG project. United States government support could be expected for an Arab–Israeli long-term energy supply project that would be characterisable as an economic foundation stone of the Middle East peace process. Enron's Indian gas ambitions would also be furthered by the Dabhol project because the LNG terminal would sell its excess capacity into the surrounding market. In other words, the Dabhol base-load demand would justify development of a gas import terminal which would then have a strategic advantage supplying regional natural gas demand.

Enron originally took no local partner. The shareholders of the project at conception were all US companies: Enron (80 per cent), accompanied by General Electric (of the United States) (10 per cent) and Bechtel (10 per cent). Political relationships were not cultivated effectively with all parties. After the Maharashtra state government changed from the Congress Party to the Hindu nationalists, the latter repudiated the Dabhol contracts which had been executed with its predecessors, contending that Enron had obtained unacceptably large economic benefits from those contracts. This caused a major conflict between the state government and the Indian central government which had counter-guaranteed the Maharashtra state electricity board purchase of the Dabhol power output. Enron had started physical development of the project and was understandably upset. The fact that it had valid contracts which would have given it damages in a litigation taken to completion was not satisfactory recompense. If the project did not go forward, Enron's LNG ambitions would be delayed, its beachhead in India would be delayed and its relationships in a country representing 20 per cent of the world's population would be negatively affected for many years to come. In addition, Enron had to contend with the issue of how much profitability would be permitted and politically viable.

As of the end of 1997, compromises had occurred. Enron had taken Indian partners in both the power project and the LNG receiving terminal. Project economics had been renegotiated effectively to lower the price of electricity to be delivered. The litigation had ended and the project had resumed construction. The establishment of an Enron LNG project in Qatar is still 'in progress'.

There are some lessons to be learned from the Enron experience in Dabhol. To create markets requires local acceptance. Maintenance of political support of a multi-year development project is crucial, even if ministers or governments change. Timing issues must be solved in order to link several pieces such as an LNG project and a power plant. In a developing country, substantial legal and financial reform is often necessary. The control of infrastructure by multinationals is a long-term political and economic policy issue. The desire of India to develop strong indigenous companies will conflict with the demand of the multinationals to develop and maintain major market positions.

7.7.7   LNG Project Feasibility: Alaska North Slope

The commercialisation and export of Alaskan North Slope natural gas as LNG present a fascinating set of challenges. The State and several oil companies must reach agreement on a fiscal regime which will determine the State of Alaska's take of project revenue. The State of Alaska wants the project to go forward so that, through monetisation of royalty gas and collection of taxes, it can raise incremental long-term revenue and see the creation of more jobs. The oil companies themselves must reach agreement on their commercialisation strategy and then deal with Yukon Pacific which controls the permits necessary to begin LNG project development.

The project represents potential Pacific Rim supply of LNG with the lowest political risk. At the macro level, the United States in general is the lowest risk politically for international business. However, even the US government can change policy radically; the deregulation of the natural gas industry and the resulting impact on long-term take-or-pay gas sales contracts are examples of United States political risk events.

On the negative side, Alaskan North Slope LNG will not be price-competitive compared with the LNG from other Pacific projects which are being proposed. In addition, the North Slope producer group must resolve potential internal conflicts of interest. For example, ARCO may be more tempted in the near term to develop its large gas reserves in Indonesian Irian Jaya as the Tangguh LNG project, rather than to co-operate on an LNG project with the other North Slope producers. Alaskan LNG, because it is costly LNG to bring to market, may offer less profitability for the project participants than that offered by other available uses of capital. A serious problem is the large project size; critical mass of LNG sales to bring the LNG delivered cost to a manageable level is 14 mtpa, more than twice the amount of LNG ever required to be sold to give birth to a project.

There are interesting international political aspects to this project. First of all, Asian energy security concerns can be helped by supply of US hydrocarbons. The export of oil from Alaska has paved the way. Now the export of LNG could also contribute. The balance of payments relationships between the United States and Asia could enhance the political probability that Alaskan LNG, although more expensive than other LNG that might be offered, would be purchased by Japan, China, Taiwan and Korea. Major technical and financial challenges must be overcome. A slow ramp up of sales from initial quantities to the contract plateau of 14 mtpa would greatly reduce the project rate of return. Co-ordinating sales contract signings to reach a contemporaneous financial close will be a difficult task. The support of the US government must be given with the right timing and in the right measure. If one of the North Slope producers does not participate, the question remains whether the project can still go forward—this raises the issue of the relative ability of any single party to pressure the other participants. The North Slope producers have avoided negotiation with Yukon Pacific over control of the critical mass of issued State and Federal permits and findings; eventually, the issue of control must be faced.

7.7.8   Equipment Vendors and Industrial Policy: The Example of Shipbuilding and Ship Operations

Shipbuilding is a commodity industry, for the most part. It is a heavy industry whose capital investment and technical demands are large and whose financial returns are ever-smaller. The leading shipbuilding countries not only wish to maintain their share of commodity shipbuilding but also want to dominate high-value-added speciality shipbuilding. That is why LNG ships are of great interest to the world's shipyards.

A typical large-size LNG ship takes three years to build, sells for two to three times the cost of an equivalent size oil tanker and can significantly enhance yard capacity utilisation. There are now 14 shipyards around the world which are considered capable by most LNG project developers of building LNG ships competently. These yards have the technology licences, the technical experience and staff and the pricing and delivery capability required by the market. One would think that the competition would be severe due to the presence of so many competitors. In reality, this is not true. One informed 1997 estimate (French shipbroker Barry Rogliano Salles) forecast a range of 104–130 large-size LNG ships to be built by the year 2010, representing, at today's prices, US$25–33 billion of business. For such expensive vessels, a key component of sales success is the availability of export financing supplied by the shipyard's home government. Ship finance has been a fertile area of international disagreement for many years. There is an Organization for Economic Cooperation and Development (OECD) consensus on ship finance terms, covering interest rate, percentage of asset financed by debt and term of loan; all these are areas where creative violation of international accords occurs.

It is against this background that Japan and Korea have chosen to seek synergy between their purchases of LNG and the sales needs of their shipbuilding industries. Based on the reality that LNG is a demand-driven buyer's market, in the last 20 years Japan and Korea have systematically linked sales of heavy industry products to incremental purchases of LNG by Japanese and Korean utilities. The Japan, Inc. approach is to insist that LNG purchased by Japanese utilities be transported mainly in Japanese-built ships owned and operated by Japanese shipping companies. In recent years, because the LNG market has strongly favoured buyers, Japanese companies have been able to win many shipbuilding and ship operating contracts.

When Korea began LNG imports it also decided to follow a national strategy. All buying was to be done by the state company, KGC, on FOB terms. All LNG ships to transport KGC purchases from the load port were to be built by Korean industrial groups and all LNG ship operations were to be performed by Korean shipping companies. The explicit long-term goal was to use satisfaction of Korean LNG demand as a base of business to give Korean shipyards and shipping companies sufficient experience and economic strength eventually to enter third party markets. Against objections from European shipyards that they were not allowed to compete for Korean LNG ship orders, the Korean government pushed forward its strategy, systematically spreading shipyard and ship operations awards to the major Korean companies and making sure that Korean shipyards gained experience in building all types of LNG cargo containment systems.

In parallel, Japanese and Korean trading companies sought and obtained admission to joint ventures sponsoring LNG export projects. Having a presence on export project operating committees gave them insight into LNG project economics and an opportunity to influence award of contracts for goods and services. Inside knowledge was used to great effect in the Qatargas Phase I tender for seven 135,000-cubic metre LNG vessels in the early 1990s. Originally the Japanese project partners urged the project to do a negotiated procurement of ship construction and ship operations. The non-Japanese partners in the Qatargas project insisted on a competitive tender for dollar-denominated time charter offers. In the interim, the Japanese parliament approved a change to the charter of the Japan Development Bank (JDB) so that the JDB could lend dollars on a long-term basis to Japanese shipping companies, eliminating the yen–dollar exchange risk and improving the financing which supported their response to the tender. Normally, Japanese ship orders would have been financed by the Japanese Exim Bank on less favourable terms. The unprecedented JDB financing attracted protests from the governments of several non-Japanese bidders, to no avail. In any event, the tender was awarded to Japanese shipping companies.

7.7.9 Comparative Advantage and Comparative Disadvantage: The Natuna Project in Indonesia

The Natuna field offshore Indonesia is blessed with huge reserves and proximity to markets. It is cursed with a huge carbon dioxide content. The necessity to separate this CO_2 for reinjection in a reservoir that will not leak CO_2 to the atmosphere makes Natuna LNG high-priced to produce. The large critical mass of infrastructure necessary to achieve economies of scale so that LNG pricing could be low enough to achieve sales necessarily led to a projected US$20 billion plus project cost. Any plausible financing would have required a large equity commitment by the project sponsors and the necessity to bring in additional members to the development consortium. In the hierarchy of LNG project attractiveness based upon pure economics, Natuna is inferior to other Indonesian reserves, as well as reserves in other countries. In fact, Qatari LNG, though much further from market, can be delivered to Japan more cheaply than the projected delivery price of Indonesian Natuna LNG. So how did this project stay alive well into 1997? First, the Indonesian government put its weight behind the project to maintain market share in its gas export markets during the 21st century and to replace depleting gas reserves of existing LNG export projects. Secondly, Exxon and then Mobil joined to put their weight, money and technology behind the project.

In any event, external circumstances turned against Natuna from 1995 on, as additional and cheaper-to-produce Australian, Malaysian and land-based Indonesian reserves were proven. In addition, Natuna pipeline sales to Thailand, discussed as an alternative to LNG, became unfeasible after the Thailand economic recession and market collapse in mid-1997. The inability of LNG sellers in Oman and Qatar to obtain floor price commitments from LNG buyers increased prospective financial risk to the Natuna project sponsors in both relative and absolute terms. Alternative markets for the gas, including pipeline ashore to Indonesian markets, became more difficult as Indonesia suffered its share of trouble in financial markets at the end of 1997. Perhaps dollar exports to a creditworthy buyer could be financed, but domestic consumption paid in rupiah would be much more difficult to finance. The economics of gas-to-liquid conversion on a massive scale using Exxon proprietary technology were at an early stage of assessment. The bottom line is that the vast Natuna gas reserves represent troubled potential. Although backed by a veteran LNG-exporting government and huge oil majors, the risks and lack of market combine with inherent technical and economic disadvantages to render project prospects problematic.

Index

International Energy and Resources Law and Policy Series

Other titles in this series:

(Please order by ISBN or title)